Pictures on the Piano

A Family Chronicle of World War II

Pictures on the Piano

A Family Chronicle of World War II

by Alex Stewart

Sunflower University Press®
1531 Yuma • P. O. Box 1009 • Manhattan, Kansas 66505-1009 USA

Printed in the United States of America on acid-free paper.

Cover by Nona Hengen, Spangle, Washington

Edited by Carol Williams

Layout by Lori L. Daniel

ISBN 0-89745-239-9

Sunflower University Press is a wholly-owned subsidiary
of the non-profit 501(c)3 Journal of the West, Inc.

For our children:
Nancy Claire Stewart McCracken
David Alexander Stewart

And to our grandchildren:
Joshua David McCracken
Megan LeeAnne McCracken

Contents

In Memoriam

RUTH AND I ARE THE lone survivors of our respective families, those wonderful people who created, raised, nurtured, and loved us. They are those invisible stalwarts of this story who, with the exception of Ray and David, fought World War II on the home front and, unhappily, did not know of this book or see it become a reality. Our intent here is to honor all of them.

Ruth Anna Wasson Stewart was the youngest child in her family and was born in 1918.

Father:	William Wasson	1883-1943
Mother:	Clara Grace Gear Wasson	1885-1970
Sister:	Viola Pearl Wasson Carlson	1903-1992
Brother:	William Walter "Bud" Wasson	1906-1992
Brother:	Robert John Wasson	1909-1930
Sister:	Alice Grace Wasson Sweetman	1913-1996

Alexander Conrad Stewart was next to the youngest child in his family and was born in 1920.

Father:	Alexander Cameron Stewart	1872-1950
Mother:	Margaret Eloise Baird Stewart	1883-1967
Sister:	Margaret Florence Stewart	1907-1992
Sister:	Jean Ellen Stewart	1908-1984
Brother:	Cameron Barton Stewart	1910-1983
Brother:	Raymond Robert Stewart	1915-1980
Brother:	David Barton Stewart	1923-1945

Acknowledgments

*N*ONA HENGEN ASKED ME when I was going to write *my* book. The question jumped off the page of her letter to me in the fall of 1994. I had sent a letter of praise and gratitude to her for *Palouse Pilot*, that banner World War II story about my fellow pilot and friend, Scotty Rohwer. Strange, I thought, that an author of Nona's stature would have any interest in me or what I would have to say. I had never written a book and only recently had become editor of the *57th Bomb Wing Newsletter*. She had read one of my war stories and liked what I had written. Nona declared that my "wordsmithing talent should be shared with the reading public."

You don't ignore such an appraisal from one who has authored more than 14 books and dozens of published articles, is in demand for lectures on a variety of subjects just as she was during her university professorships, and now was extending to me her friendship and her generous offer of assistance.

You, dear reader, are holding the product of Nona Hengen's early scrutiny — the inherent elements of her knowledge and intellect penciled in margin notations that can be characterized with one huge word — ENCOURAGEMENT.

Pictures on the Piano is my first book. My second could be a compilation of our many lengthy letters exchanged since 1994. Nona's are true literary treasures.

And so to Nona Hengen, Ruth and I acknowledge our gratitude and highest esteem for your subtle contribution to this story, crafted during the past three and one-half years.

Jim Harton of Richardson, Texas, is one of those rare individuals who seems to know something about everything. Though his degrees are in mechanical engineering, he is a master of extending the life, use, and repair of otherwise obsolete computers. He decided several years ago that Ruth and I needed to be brought up to baby-boomer speed, and literally transferred a chunk of his inventory to our permanent care. Instruction in its use and sufficient knowledge of its software to avoid undue confusion was part of the package, plus his quick response to our calls for help of every kind. *Pictures on the Piano* became a reality, thanks to Jim.

I have asked Jim on many occasions how much I owed him. His answer has always been the same. "It's all a labor of love, Alex." And so, Ruth and I chorus our reply with like enthusiasm, Jim. We love you and your family for loving us and for the luster, computerized and otherwise, that you have brought to our lives.

In many of my troop-train travels during the war I often wondered whose railroad we were riding on, and thought I would try to identify them in *Pictures on the Piano*. I knew of only one authority on the subject, Robert C. "Bob" Caldwell of Dallas, Texas, and a native of Harvey, Illinois. Bob is a walking encyclopedia of railroad history, and in almost every instance he could identify the rails on which we traveled. Bob's long career was in the field of transportation. Well, almost. He and Celia parented six children who have produced thirteen grandchildren and three great grandchildren. Thanks, Bob!

Occasionally, illness stalked the Stewart household and the word processor was idled for days, sometimes weeks. I was stricken with pneumonia in 1997 and was rushed to the Baylor Hospital emergency room in Dallas. Our neighbor, Steve Wade, an off-duty policeman instantly responded to our need and drove us through darkness, rain, and rush-hour traffic the 25 miles to Baylor. But that wasn't enough for Steve. He remained at the hospital for an hour or two to be sure that I was being properly cared for and that we would need no further assistance. That kind of love and caring has no purchase price. Our thanks to you, Steve.

Warren Robbins and his wife, Barbara, are also special people. When Warren got word that I was hospitalized, he soon showed up at my bedside, sized up our situation, and became Ruth's driver for her every need. There were round-trips to our home, some special shopping, two or three visits with Barbara to check on my healing, and finally the trip home when I was discharged from Baylor. A day or two later he appeared at our door with a beautiful flower display. All this, with pre-Christmas nipping at our heels. I asked Warren why he had done this for us. With a big grin he replied, "Hey, Alex, we have to get you back to work on the book. We're sick of hearing about it. We want to read it!"

These acknowledgments would lack their intended flavor without the inclusion of our friends of almost 50 years, Eugene and Charlotte Cuny. More than just a taste, it was the feast of their indomitable spirit as it shone through months of uncertainty leading to the loss of their beloved son, Fred, a world-renowned disaster-relief expert. Their steadfastness reinforced in us the inspiration needed to master our own difficulties.

Accolades for solving special pre-publication printing problems go to our daughter and her husband, Nancy and J. B. McCracken, owners of J. B.'s Printing in Graham, Texas. It seems there is nothing these two can't do in the graphic arts field. See that letter written to Ruth by Major General Cannon in December 1945, reproduced herein. Thanks a lot, kids.

Because our son David made his home in Kansas City, carving out an exemplary career in fine woodworking, he was not handy for consultation during my years at the keyboard. But David chose to keep me supplied with gifts of books, some on the art of writing, which taught me as much what not to write as to write. Thanks, Dave.

And then, Ruthie, a superb proofreader with an amazing memory for wartime details. She vetoed some anecdotes and passages that were better left unsaid. Memory sparkles when I recall her special salad lunches and the tantalizing aroma of supper simmering all day in the crock-pot, the underwear and sock drawers fresh and full, and CD music setting the mood for creative effort. Our 55-year flame glows. Let's do it all again!

And, finally, to our many friends who have championed my efforts and showered me with encouragement, I acknowledge and extend to each of them our warmest and deepest gratitude. To all my friends and cohorts in the United States Army and Air Force in all venues, living and dead, I salute you in humble gratitude for your noble care and service at my side.

Alex Stewart

Introduction

PICTURES ON THE PIANO is a story of brothers who went to war and of the family at home whose lives were disrupted by that war. It has been written so that succeeding generations might look through a window to the past at the values by which post-Depression-era America lived, to understand and appreciate deeply felt convictions that translated into commitment to serve one's country.

Step with me, onto the beach of a remote Pacific Island. In your mind's eye, visualize the 4th Marine Division's large Landing Ships disgorging dozens of amphtracs and smaller amphibious craft, laden with platoons of Marines moving swiftly up on the beach. It is nine in the morning and suddenly before you, the #2 amphtrac of the 23rd Marine Regiment is spilling its platoon of infantrymen out onto that stretch of black sand. It is a light surf, a dry landing, and nobody has wet feet. The air explodes in a cacophony of shellfire — a din of Japanese mortar and machine guns raking the beach and terraces. The Marines dive onto the sand, flatten out on their bellies, and begin using their elbows to furiously propel their bodies forward in crab-like motion over the fine volcanic sand toward their goal, that of somehow establishing a foothold on this worthless-turned-valuable spit of real estate called Iwo Jima.

Suddenly you notice quick movement, a soldier pulling himself up off the sand. Crouching low, he races toward a buddy writhing in pain with a shattered leg. The medical corpsman takes a hit in the shoulder, but he rushes to reach his fallen comrade to do the job he was trained to do.

The terrible scene dissolves and the corpsman's framed picture appears on the screen of your imagination. It has been lovingly placed on a crisply starched scarf spread atop a polished piano in the Alexander Cameron Stewart home in a middle-class Chicago neighborhood. A diffused morning light streaming through lace curtains illuminates a vase of fresh flowers on the piano and the image of a handsome youth — David — the youngest Stewart son, resplendent in his uniform, handsome in his youthfulness.

But, wait. There are other pictures, two more sons in uniform. This one, Ray, whose picture has been set next to David's . . . who is he? Again the scene changes and the curtain of imagination is drawn back. The 321st Medical Battalion is in the thick of shelling on Okinawa. In this nightmarish scene of nearly exploding artillery and bursts of machine-gun fire you recognize the youth in the second picture on the piano. He is desperately trying to insert a blood-transfusion needle into the vein of a crumpled 96th Division rifleman, and his trembling but determined fingers can't seem to make the needle penetrate.

"Why can't I get the needle into the vein, Doctor?" his features are contorted as he turns toward an Army physician who has come alongside. The doctor bends down and feels for a pulse.

"You can't transfuse the vein of a dead man! Move on."

"But I tried to save him!" Ray's anguished reply is drowned out by the roar of artillery as the doctor motions him to leave this one and to hurry to another.

Again the scene fades. This time the stage is set and the curtain of the past reopens halfway around the world. Five bombers have made it back to an airstrip after a dangerous mission and landed. A sixth one is missing. The rest have cut their motors to a fast idle and are taxiing down the rough strip to the turn-off path leading to their revetments, clearing the runway for the next arrivals. Apart from the activity that surrounds their homecoming, it is an otherwise ordinary setting for November. The wind is strong and steady out of the Northwest, with occasional gusts. High cirrus clouds block the sun, depriving the sea of its azure hue and robbing this remote outpost on the Mediterranean island of Corsica of more pleasant memories. Alesan is a launching site for air raids by the 489th Squadron that will, if successful, interrupt critical supply lines of the Axis, thereby foiling Hitler's desperate legions in Italy and France.

There is much activity on the strip, readying it for the arrival of the next incoming formation. Suddenly a lone plane appears. Here and there groundcrew members stop in their tracks. All heads turn to stare. There is something eerie, ghostly, about this low-flying bomber. There is no sound! Both engines of the B-25 are dead. It is the missing bomber, riddled by enemy flak. What is holding it up there, and on course? If pilot and copilot are alive — that is, if the plane is not flying itself — will they try to bring it in on a downwind landing? Incredulity freezes the expressions of those on the ground who watch in gapemouthed astonishment. The outlook for getting the completely disabled plane safely onto the ground is as grim and rationally unlikely as the bizarre fact that unless one's senses are deceiving, it seems to be flying without power.

A dead-stick landing! The odds of a safe landing in such circumstances defy calculation or estimation. But suddenly, miraculously, the bomber is down on the ground right side up, brought to a screeching but tenuous stop at the end of the strip. Fire crews rush to meet it, but there is no fire. Though overcome by shock, like an automaton the pilot turns to see that his crew has scrambled to safety before he makes a wobbly-legged exit from the cockpit, succumbing to the violent tremors that follow his spent surges of adrenaline. You catch a glimpse of his ashen features as ground personnel rush up and he is quickly assisted into a waiting vehicle. In that moment of bewilderment and relief you recognize his likeness — he is the one looking out of the third picture on the piano in the quiet neighborhood in Chicago. The captain of this ill-fated flight is Alex Stewart, signing off on his 60th mission.

It is his odyssey that awaits you in *Pictures on the Piano*.

Pictures is an epic tale of war and peace and ordinary lives dislocated by extraordinary circumstances. The Chicago Stewarts are a closely knit family who live by faith rather than fear in the most troubling times, meeting crises with uncommon courage, facing evil tidings with unshakeable serenity, and unspeakable tragedy with quiet dignity. The primeval, voiceless dread that haunted parents with sons in the military was expressed eons earlier in the brooding premonition of Job (Job 3:25) when he cried, "That which I greatly feared has come to pass; that which I dreaded most has happened." That same prophecy-fulfilling foreboding will find its mark in the Stewart household when the telegram arrives with the shattering news: the lifeblood of their youngest son David has spilled out on the sandy beaches of Iwo Jima.

The Stewarts' outcry of grief and profound sense of loss mingles and flows with tears in pain-laced letters exchanged among bereaved family members at home and the sons yet fighting on opposite sides of the earth.

And now they are just like other American families with the stars in the front windows of their homes. Where there once were three blue stars on a banner in the Stewarts' window, there are now two, and a gold star. The picture of David has been placed between that of Ray and Alex, at the center, and the bouquet on the piano has been replaced by a single, beautiful red rose in a crystal stem vase.

Alex Stewart has written an heroic war story and a tender love story. What will make it linger in memory and reserve its place among the many excellent accounts of combat and tales of valor told by veterans of World War II is Stewart's unusual ability to not only describe these events in all their sound and fury and authenticity as he experienced them, but his gift of articulating the range and depth of the powerful emotions the events engendered in expressions to and among members of his family and to his beloved as the war progresses. From the network of support among members of the Stewart clan there emerges a rich tapestry of affection, tenderness, passion, and sensibility. But interwoven into a fabric of encouragement, faith, and love are dark threads that find their way into the tapestry, as death stalks its prey on the fields of battle and in the air corridors over enemy territories.

Pictures on the Piano brims with fascinating tales about combat, about crisis situations met and braved, about victories and defeats. At the heart of the story one will also be gratified to discover a blueprint for meeting life's challenges regardless of circumstance, and a challenge to balance the scale of rights and privileges on the one hand with the obligations of responsibility and duty on the other, to discover, in the end, meaning to one's existence.

In an era when much is written and spoken about the dysfunctional family, this extraordinary account might well serve counselor and clergyman, teacher and historian, with its truth and wisdom.

Nona Hengen

Chapter 1

Heath, Texas
February 17, 1986

HE SECOND DAY OF my drive to Chicago would soon see the end of the tiresome 1,000 miles since I left our home in Heath, Rockwall County, Texas. Ruth was still snug in our king-sized bed, grateful for the luxury of an extended sleep, delaying for a few hours her assumed role of lone caregiver to my 80-year-old sister, Margaret. "Don't get up," I told her. "I'll stop for breakfast in Greenville. I have your cinnamon rolls and a Thermos of coffee, and the cooler with my lunch. I'll do fine. I'll call you from the Blytheville motel tonight. Oh . . . be sure to call Viola and tell her I'm on my way and will be happy to stay at her place while I'm in Chicago."

She smiled, invitingly, her silver-gray hair, tousled on the pillow, her outstretched arms encircled my neck. "Be careful, and . . . I love you!" Her prolonged kiss was as sweet as the one we shared on our wedding day many years ago. I closed the bedroom door and paused at Margaret's door, heard her soft steady snore, and was satisfied that Ruth's extra hours of sleep were secure.

Margaret had been with us for several months, recuperating from injuries incurred in a bad fall in Chicago. Leaving the hospital, she convalesced for five weeks in the Walkerton, Indiana, farm home of our niece, Susan Awald, before

I brought her to Texas. She endured the first airplane ride of her life without incident. But her future place of residence had been in question for some time as we evaluated the level of her ability to function.

Margaret came to Texas under protest. She sometimes resentfully reminded me that a brother, 13 years younger, whom she tended as a baby and assisted in his birth, and who was now calling the shots, rankled her.

She had been the chief breadwinner in the reduced family of Dad, Mother, and sister Jean, had staked a claim of independence in the household, and held fast to it for many years. Then, with the others gone, she held full reign over her domain and dug in both heels of resistance when the move was proposed. It was one of those "tough love" situations for Ruth and me, for we could foresee problems that she refused to acknowledge. But reason finally prevailed and Margaret became reconciled when she saw the cozy, small apartment she would occupy and the assisted-living services she would enjoy. Ruth, with her firm but loving ways, worked overtime to secure Margaret's needs and ensure her comfort and as much independence as she could handle.

Driving a U-Haul truck to close out the old homestead was not my idea of joyous adventure, but necessary. Furniture was needed for the apartment, and the large collection of family treasures and memorabilia awaited disposition. Unoccupied, the old house would fall victim to deterioration and vandalism. It must be cleaned out and sold.

I closed and locked the front door and climbed into the cab of the 18-foot bob-tail truck parked in our driveway. I started the engine, checked the gauges and windshield wipers, tuned the radio to WRR-FM, the only classical music station in the Dallas area, secured the seat belt, and backed into the street. The February day was chilly and damp; the overcast sky was black, with a faint hint of first light barely touching the horizon. I drove east, past the Heath City Hall and fire and police stations, waved to two officers parked in their idling cruisers, and headed out onto the Farm to Market road leading north to Rockwall, seat of Rockwall County, the smallest in Texas. Five miles ahead, I entered the eastbound ramp of Interstate 30, accelerated to 60, set the cruise control, and settled back for the long drive. At 6:10 a.m. there was little traffic.

My route took me through East Texas, stopping in Greenville for bacon and eggs, then to Texarkana and a rest stop for coffee and Ruth's cinnamon rolls. I-30 veers to the north there and on to Little Rock, where I took a late lunch break at a roadside picnic area. Sliced roast beef on my home-baked bread hit the spot and fortified me until I stopped for the night. Supper would be a light snack, an apple and a few crackers. Estimating that I would make Blytheville before dark, I crossed Arkansas to West Memphis, then north again for the final 75 miles. This put me past the halfway point of my journey.

A short, brisk walk before breakfast loosened the stiffness in my legs and shoulders, reducing the dread of another day behind the wheel. I was ready for an early start from the Blytheville motel. I had phoned Ruth of my progress and whereabouts, and she reported the call from the Chicago real estate firm that would handle the sale of the house. They would also assist in changing over utilities to a new owner when the time came. I had previously arranged with our Chicago attorney to handle the closing when a sale had been made, relieving me of the need for a return trip later on. And best of all, Ruth's sister Viola was ready for my visit and happy that I wanted to stay with them.

I made good time, crossed the mighty Mississippi, then up through central Illinois and into Kankakee. Significantly, Kankakee was not only the hometown of Mr. and Mrs. Hasker, from whom Dad had bought the old house, but also the origin of former Dallas neighbors Jim and Betty Campbell. Betty had died recently and Jim had brought her cremains for dispersal on the Kankakee River. I thought of Betty now as I crossed that river where she and Jim had spent many happy hours together in their younger days. Another hour and I would pull into the side drive of our family home on the southeast side of Chicago, the site of my youth from age 18 months to 21 years, when I left for military service on September 26th, 1941.

Mile after mile, now accustomed to the rhythm and hum of rubber on pavement and the whine of the engine, thoughts of that refuge we had grown up in crowded out the rigors and unpleasantries of cross-country travel. Even the orange-colored plastic highway barricade barrels, channeling traffic into and out of tight squeezes to accommodate road repairs, became a less-than-annoying infringement on my solitude. With Ruth by my side, the journey would have been adventuresome, not laborious.

It was in the old house, which we commonly referred to by its street numbers — 1414 — that we had experienced the practicalities of living, where we had learned and shared family and moral values endowed by parental witness and example rather than precept. It was home in all the true meaning of the word and was often affectionately referred to by sister Jean as "Headquarters." I wondered what to expect, what had become of the old neighborhood and the neighbors, many of whom had been a part of my nurturing. Surely they were all gone, but to where? I contemplated the turn of events in Margaret's life that had invaded our lives and had brought Ruth and me to this juncture.

Our wonderful family of eight, reduced now by illness, age, and war to two, had its start in 1906. It was in 1904 that a dashing emigre from Liverpool, England, arrived in Omaha, Nebraska, to join his brother Henry, a seminary student. Landing a job as director of the Knox Street Presbyterian Church choir, he was quick to notice the "most beautiful woman he had ever seen" singing in the soprano section. A courtship ensued and their marriage was consummated in July 1906.

The beauty of Alexander Cameron Stewart's bride, Margaret Eloise Baird, was ethereal-heavenly, celestial — queenly, as Dad often described her. Deep, dark-brown eyes and her naturally arched brow guarded a rose-petal complexion. The dark-brown hair piled in a neatly waved and crafted coiffure crowned her slightly high cheekboned, classic countenance. Her steady eye and totally honest face, supported by the high, lace-necked collar of her gown, exemplified the essence of innocence. Slender of form, erect in stature, about 5 feet, 6 inches tall, she rejected any artificiality, needed no cosmetic enhancements. A touch of face powder to remove any shine and a hint of cheek rouge were her only concessions to the makeup industry. She was the epitome of understatement.

Their wedding picture was a compliment to the photographic art. Dad was attired in a black cutaway coat, black trousers, high-wing collar, and ascot. His hair and eyes were

also brown, his 5'7" stature erect and of slender build. Pince-nez glasses were his distin-
guishing label. His refined English accent was captivating, his grammar impeccable. A
fine-tuned, well-modulated speaking voice matched his superb singing talent, placing him
in demand at many and various functions. He was truly a romantic and chose to sing love
songs to his bride at their wedding reception. "I Love You Truly," "Come Into the Garden,
Maude," "The Rose of Tralee," and a lively Scots favorite, "She's a Bonnie Wee Lassie."
Professionalism was his beacon; he was a classic showman but never a showoff.

Following their marriage, Dad and Mother migrated from Omaha to Chicago, the great
music center west of New York, where he launched his career as a voice teacher, a coach
to local and visiting operatic tenors, and a choral director and tenor soloist in some of the
great Protestant churches and in the Catholic Holy Name Cathedral.

Home for Mother and Dad had been in rented apartments on the near North Side, the
far West Side, and finally the Southeast Side, where I was born on March 15, 1920. It was
there, in a large apartment above a machine shop where gaskets for the automotive industry were manufactured, that I saw the first light of day with Margaret's assistance. Then in
September 1921, they bought the Victorian styled, turn-of-the-century house that was now
my destination.

The roles of trustee and caregiver were self-imposed assignments that Ruth and I had
never anticipated. Some friends were amazed, others generous with their praise, that we
would take on such a task for a sister or sister-in-law. But no question entered our minds
when the distress call came. All I heard was what would be Mother's declaration, rushing
up from my subconscious, "Why of course, you will take care of your sister!" It came
through as loudly and positively as it would have if she had been there in person. Childhood training taught "Honor thy father and thy mother," and I presumed this also to mean,
honoring the products, the extensions of their love. We were family.

Never married, Margaret had lived in the old house most of her life and was there when
the others passed on or left the nest. She had been sickly as a child, had scoliosis and a defective heart valve that I was never apprised of until she faced major surgery for a broken
hip in her 85th year. She had a slightly stooped posture and hunched-over way of walking.
However, in her best years, before the onset of osteoporosis, she overcame the poor posture, either out of the sheer force of will or the occasional use of concealed shoulder
braces, adopted fashionable dress, and thrived socially on opera and concert attendance.
She taught kindergarten and first grade in the Chicago school system for 30 years, retiring
at 55 to pursue part-time work as a substitute teacher and to enjoy extensive foreign travel. Her education for teaching started in the Chicago Normal College, later named the
Chicago Teachers College. Margaret also took summer courses at Northwestern University where she was eventually awarded her Bachelor's degree. She was a consummate
teacher almost till her death and would never pass an opportunity to engage me in discussion of a subject. In our home, by her insistence, we would explore the dictionary or encyclopedia for answers. Her failing eyesight reduced the reading of her extensive library
of poetry and the classics, requiring the use of a magnifying glass. This was awkward and
tiring and I was soon enlisted to read to her. She loved my voice and the drama and feel-

ing that I tried to impart. Edgar Allen Poe was a real favorite, and my treatment of "The Raven" put her on Cloud Nine.

From Kankakee, in the heart of Illinois, fields and farms feather-edged into towns and small rural industrial complexes, then on into the urban sprawl. Freeway piers, supporting winding concrete roads like long-legged caterpillars, straddled feeder roads, sometimes creating blight before its time. I exited I-94 and was soon tooling on and off streets with familiar names but unfamiliar landscapes. Many old buildings had been razed in urban renewal projects — with little of the promised renewal — some replaced with modern apartments and stores, others overgrown with weeds. Change in structure seems to change perception. I was in the old neighborhood before I knew it. But once familiar landmark buildings had disappeared.

What had happened to the elegant hotel where the Big Bands played for dancing on Saturday night, with diners seen through gleaming windows, their silhouettes framed by swagged draperies? They sat at candle-lit tables covered with white cloths, partook of gourmet fare with sparkling silver, and drank from shimmering crystal. We had yearned for but never could afford to join them. And where was the drug store, run by Sam Cohen, who went to prison for selling "bootleg booze" during Prohibition? He was always nice to us, and we were all shocked at his fate. Gone, too, was the grocery store where I had my first job as a stock boy and where Herb Channel, the manager with an over-active imagination, rented an "organ grinder monkey" to provide a tropical atmosphere for use in a front window banana sales promotion? The monkey ate too many bananas and got sick and died, and its owner, irate at losing his means of making a living, insisted on a sizable remuneration, which Herb gladly paid out of his own pocket. Some of us wondered how the health department never got word of the incident and decided there was a payoff somewhere.

Gone, too, was the short half-block of stores that we passed on our walk to grade school. The drug store and soda fountain where Harold Olsen, about two years older than me, dispensed better and larger sodas and shakes than the owner; and the barber shop with one chair, manned by Nick Earl — he of "two first names" — where I got my first professional haircut at age 13, and then only because my mother was sick and I had to look good for my part in the upcoming church pageant. All the family decided that Mother could do as good a job, and hers didn't cost a quarter.

Next came the delicatessen and adjoining candy store where we each squandered our two pennies on a licorice whip, jaw breakers, green leaves, or Mary Janes on our way back to school after lunch at home. Sometimes Connie, Mr. Wild's pretty blond daughter, waited on us. How unfortunate that she had lost her sense of taste due to an injury in an auto accident and could not enjoy all the free candy available to her!

Then came the bakery where we pressed our noses against the window for the best view of the displayed delicacies, but seldom bought other than sweet rolls for we were convinced that Mother was a better baker than Mr. and Mrs. Swenson.

And old Jake Posner had his shoe repair next to the bakery, creating an odd combination of odors — polished leather and fresh bread. Since Dad half-soled our shoes with sharp, headless shoe nails and replaced rubber heels, we seldom had the luxury of sewed-on soles and were often plagued with the prick of a nail or two biting into our feet. Dad's work was good, but not free of occasional trouble that required some adjustments.

And finally, the grocery store and meat market where Harry Gold sprayed uncontrolled saliva through his missing teeth spaces when he talked and repeated my mother's name after delivering to the counter each item on her list. Leave it to a kid to keep track! One day I heard him say Mrs. Stewart 32 times! And when his wife Bessy served Mother, she would always say, "Alrighty, and what else, Mrs. Stewart?" Then the price of each item was listed on a large paper sack and totaled up by hand. They didn't use an adding machine, and the big brass cash register, operated with a hand crank, only recorded and displayed the total. But Mother had a quick eye and could read and add up the prices in their inverted state on the sack and would, on rare occasion, catch an unintentional error.

There were times during the Depression when Harry was short of cash to make purchases at the wholesale market and would come calling on my Dad for a short-term loan — as much as $100. And Dad always came through, even walking eight blocks to the bank to make the withdrawal, as he never had a checking account. Harry once told Dad that no matter how hard times got and as long as he had food on his shelves, the Stewarts would eat.

I passed my old yellow-bricked high school with its tall, white columns where the pigeons still roosted on the capitals. A poem came to mind that had appeared in the school newspaper in 1938, and which we had committed to memory — a ditty we loved to recite: "Ashes to ashes, dust to dust, I winked at a pigeon and boy did I cuss." The school was now called a Career Center.

A few blocks farther on was our grade school, old and severely vandalized, vacated and waiting for the wrecking ball. Here we had formed columns of fours and marched into the building to our classrooms while martial music was played on old upright pianos stationed on each floor. My younger brother David was often at one of the pianos. We six Stewarts were all graduates of both the grade school and high school.

I was surprised to see that the city park nearby had only trees now, no shrubs or bushes or flower beds. I was later told they were all too costly to maintain or too protective of predators, crouching unseen to prey on pedestrians. The park had been part of the site of the World Columbian Exposition in 1893 and contained sports fields, two golf courses, a lagoon for canoeing and ice skating, and a yacht harbor section, connected by a channel to Lake Michigan. It was here that brother David had saved the life of a crippled man one Sunday afternoon. Boating with his girlfriend, David saw the man fall from his boat into deep water; he removed his shoes, dove in, overcame the struggling man who was going down for the third time, and brought him to shore and revived him with artificial respiration. Proclaimed a hero in the newspapers, David never realized that saving lives would be his ultimate destiny.

A bridge over the channel was the sight where the infamous kidnap-murderers, Leopold and Loeb, had tossed the typewriter upon which their ransom note was written in 1924. Strangely, while cleaning out the house, I found a letter secreted high on a closet shelf written by Nathan Leopold to my sister Jean. It seemed that Jean had a fascination and perhaps compassion for celebrities, especially those downtrodden or in trouble. She had written to Leopold when he was in prison at Stateville and some years later, after he had been paroled and was living in Puerto Rico, he answered her letter. A condition of his parole required that he shun all forms of publicity and he insisted that the letter was for her eyes only. The letter was dated November 19, 1958. Jean died in July 1984, never having violated that trust. Richard Loeb had been killed in a knife fight in prison in 1936.

I finally arrived at our street. Turning left, I was surprised that it had not changed very much. The old six-story "high rise" was gone, where my oldest brother, Cameron, and his fearless friend, Benny Ogle, made "bathtub gin." That Prohibition era enterprise came to an abrupt end one Saturday night when the boys were caught peddling their product to dancing couples at a local night spot. The bouncer literally threw them down a long flight of stairs, broken gin flasks rattling in their pockets and the powerful odor of cheap booze establishing their identity. When Cam told brother Ray and me, he swore us to secrecy. He would be known today as a juvenile delinquent, and this would only add to his unsavory record. If Dad were informed of the incident he would be terribly angered but not surprised, as he was accustomed to Cam's misdemeanors. More than once, Dad successfully pleaded with the police to release Cam to his custody and kept him out of jail.

Across the street from the high rise was Robert Coffey's house, whose brother Bert became a priest and left the area at an early age. Robert was my age but attended the Catholic school. Next door on the third floor lived the Everett's, Jack and Ralph and sister Dorothy. They were Seventh-Day Adventists and could never play out on Saturdays. Years later, when my father was dying, Jack came and prayed with him. Jack was a fine, fun-loving friend whose many childhood injuries exempted him from military service. Once he responded to a dare, ran from the sidewalk with his sled, and belly-flopped to slide under a milk-wagon horse parked at the curb. He didn't make it to the crown of the street, and the sled came sliding back under the horse and stopped against the curb. The startled horse raised a front hoof and brought it crashing down on Jack's leg, causing a multiple fracture. Jack's leg was permanently deformed. He became a minister in his denomination.

Then came Myron, who lived on the first floor, a rather chubby kid who always had candy but never would share it with us. Kept in the house for some infraction, he would moon us before the open window when we came calling. His father owned a clothing store and always drove a fancy Packard convertible sedan. His mother wore all the latest fashions. She was a slender woman and walked with short, rapid steps, mostly due to the tightness of her skirts. Mother said she wasn't a "flapper" but looked like one.

Across from our house lived Jack Reed, my age, and his older brother Tom, about Cameron's age. Their father was a plastering contractor and went duck hunting every season. The dead ducks, their feathers caked with frozen blood, looked rather grotesque lying there in a heap on the back porch, and we wondered how anyone could eat them.

Down past our house in the corner building next to the alley, alongside the Illinois Central Railroad stone-reinforced embankment, lived Sonny and Jimmy Brown and their sister Mary Anna. Sonny died at 16 from a ruptured appendix, being stricken with the emergency as he delivered his paper route early one Sunday morning. Sonny was my best friend, a year older than me, and we took his death very hard. I remember Jimmy coming over and sitting next to me at the funeral parlor. He showed me a sympathy card he had received. "See, Alex; it says, 'He Is Not Dead, He Is Just Away'," and then we cried in each other's arms.

Above them on the third floor lived a large Irish family — Jimmy, my age; Jackie, a year or two older; Tommy, the youngest; and three or four girls. Their father was a streetcar motorman. My only memory of him was the Saturday afternoon when he came staggering up the street, blind drunk. We heard his wife scream at him and vent her considerable displeasure. The tirade hit a fevered pitch, and we heard him cry out as she struck him with what we learned later to be a vacuum cleaner. He retreated to the steps leading down from their back porch and we could hear him wailing and bawling. We ran through the alley to their back yard and saw him sitting on the steps holding his head, blood running down his face and dripping from his hands. He was blubbering and crying like a baby. We kids were impressed and horrified. And I can still hear his cry.

In the same building lived Leona Anderagen and her older brother Al, whose face and ears were deeply wrinkled, said to be the result of frostbite. He became a professional golfer, of sorts, without the expensive clothes and trappings that usually went with that sport. We kids would watch Al in the public links tournaments held in the city park, where he wore ordinary pants and sometimes a blue work shirt, while his competitors were decked out in fine tan knickers, knit sport shirts, fashionable white sleeveless sweaters, argyle stockings, and brown and white golf shoes. Al proved that it took more than fancy clothes to win at golf and took home his share of trophies and cash.

Across the street lived Winifred Kaufman, whose nickname was "Weeny Fry" and next door to her was Elizabeth Smith, who we thought had large feet and gave the title "Gun Boat Lizzie." They were both in my younger brother David's age group. Answering Mother's reprimand, we assured her we never called them by those names to their faces. It was all just boy talk.

Next door to our house was the six-flat, three-story building with a limestone facade and high, narrow windows where Zella lived with her tall, heavy-set mother. We nicknamed the building the "White Onion," and our amusement was mixed with mild disdain when Zella's mother, referred to as the "Old Lady," washed a viewing panel — much like the stroke of a windshield wiper — in the upper sash for herself and one in the lower sash for Zella, leaving the rest of the window untouched. The dirty part got dirtier till spring, when someone cleaned all the windows.

In Frankie Friedman's flat upstairs, I had my first taste of alcohol, in the form of "home brew." God, it was terrible. And the O'Leary family on the first floor, across the hall from Zella, having burned all their firewood in the central, pot-bellied stove, in cold desperation broke out and burned the bottoms of dresser drawers. The Great Depression bred unreasonable solutions.

This was my growing-up neighborhood and I could spend hours telling unbelievable stories of our lives here in big, dirty, fascinating Chicago. But time was running out. The sun was low over the railroad tracks where we had watched citified sunsets for years, and electric commuter train trolley wires and steam engines, pulling freight and passenger cars to Florida and New York, belching black smoke from their stacks, silhouetted against the hazy orange glow. I had arrived, I was "home." I turned into the side drive of our house, shut off the engine, and took a deep sigh of relief that more long hours behind this wheel would be set aside for several days.

Ours was a middle-class region, a mix of blue- and white-collar workers, located within walking distance of our public schools and Catholic grade school, and boys' and girls' high schools, in the midst of public transportation. I suppose my Dad was more "professional" than anyone else.

The "white collars" rode the Illinois Central Electric or the Elevated train to downtown, the blues rode these and the streetcars to distant factory and service jobs. Cars were used more for pleasure in the evenings and on weekends. The only horse-drawn vehicles were wagons carrying ice, milk, farm produce, or junk up and down the alleys. Dad knew most of the drivers. His work as a voice teacher and opera coach, and related activities, required his presence at his studio in The Auditorium Building in the afternoons, leaving his mornings free for home-bound activities, principally repairs of every nature. He enjoyed the variation afforded by this schedule and used it to full advantage.

Dad greeted all the alley vendors by the common name of Jack and would engage them in conversation, especially those collecting and selling junk. I don't think he ever bought a new paintbrush, but would pay a dime for a bucket of hardened paint supporting a half-dozen hardened brushes, proceed to soak them in a quarter's worth of paint remover till they were soft, then clean them up like brand new. We had some of the finest, most expensive brushes available.

Dad had fun, too. An elderly Jewish tailor would tour the alleys, seeking to buy old clothes. He would repair his purchases of men's clothing and sell them from his tiny shop on the famous Maxwell Street near downtown. Carrying a large cloth sack, he would ply the alleys, calling out in a gravely but penetrating voice, "An-ny-y ole cloze sah sell." One day, working in the garage, Dad decided to be his competitor. After the man had passed by and was about 200 feet away, without being seen, Dad opened up with his great tenor voice and sang out, "Any old clothes for sale?" The old tailor retraced his steps, looking in every yard and area-way for his interloper. As he passed the garage, Dad said in his most innocent and unsuspecting manner, "Hello, Jack, how are you today?" The man quizzed Dad, who played dumb and was never suspected of being the culprit.

I left the U-Haul truck, climbed the seven wood steps to the porch, then turned and looked up the street. Visions of my Dad loomed before me, when at mid-day he would kiss his "Lassie" goodbye, tuck the thin sheet music case under his arm, and with his rolling stride, walk toward the Illinois Central Station. He would reach the corner then turn and wave to Mother before disappearing past Roger's house. Standing at the side window in the living room, Mother would answer his wave with a kiss thrown from her fingertips. It was their never-failing daily ritual.

I inserted the key in the heavy Yale lock, opened the oak door, and entered the front hall. Latching the door behind me, I flipped on some lights and took a quick walk through the first floor and turned the thermostat up to a livable level. I checked the upstairs rooms and decided all was in order, undisturbed.

It was time to call it a day. I was tired from the long hours at the wheel and looked forward to one of Viola's fine meals. Fifteen years older than Ruth, Viola had been widowed on V-J Day 1945, when the Japanese signed the peace treaty ending World War II. Now 84, she lived with her son Wayne, a truck driver for Amoco Oil Company. Their apartment was in Calumet City, Indiana, across the street from Hammond, about a 30-minute drive.

She would be waiting to hear about her "baby" sister, listening for the beep of the horn on the truck announcing my arrival. I closed and locked the heavy front door and headed the truck in the direction of sustenance and lively fellowship.

The next morning, fortified with a breakfast fit for a stevedore, I returned to that door and the adventures it concealed. The February air was dull and cold, with a fresh two-inch layer of snow covering the previous day's slush and grime. I swept the new powder from porch and steps and the narrow path leading to the sidewalk, then beat the clinging flakes from the broom, against the stair rail, and returned it to the front hall.

My starting place on the wearisome task would be in the attic. Ascending the long flight of stairs to the second floor and then the dark, narrow, curving climb to the third floor to that uninviting sanctum, I was soon seated on an overturned, medium-sized, rough-sawn crate with faded shipping instructions stenciled on four sides. It had been the container for a three-piece mantel decoration purchased at nominal cost in Liverpool, England, by my father in 1929. The elegant Marli, black-painted, cast-metal horses, rearing on their hind legs in protest to their haltered restriction by crouching, loin-clothed African handlers, guarded a classic eight-day chiming clock.

The complex French movement, with its white porcelain dial and gold Roman numerals, was housed in a Greek Parthenon-like structure with black marble base and fluted metal columns supporting a marble roof and carved gable figures, presumably Roman soldiers in battle dress on horseback. The entire ensemble formed a focal point in our home for more than 50 years.

On the marble mantel above the cast-iron reinforced fireplace, the horses and clock formed the backdrop for a highly polished ebony grand piano. They were perhaps the only artworks in our home, save the sepia-toned print of the very beautiful "Gibson Girls," a product of American illustrator Charles Dana Gibson and made famous during the World Columbian Exposition in Chicago in 1893. The piece was admired more for its four-inch-wide polished oval wood frame made in four curved sections with opposing grain forming a "V" at the joints, than for the picture itself, and hung in the stair hall near a set of four brass chimes, a wedding gift to Mother and Dad in 1906. Those chimes were always on the list of polishing chores when company was expected.

Significantly, the majesty of the horses and clock became a subliminal symbol of solidarity and permanence in our home as they provided background interest to photos taken of family members during their musical performances. And the broad plateau of the piano served as the revered choice to display the favorite photos of we three brothers in the service, its shining surface reflecting our gold-framed images. Fresh flowers alternated with a vase of beautiful soft pink and blue, feather-like silk flowers to honor the scene.

I sat on the crate in the attic of the old house knee deep in nostalgia, the horses in repose on the dusty floor. The clock was gone, I know not where. A large, bare light bulb, suspended by a braided cloth-covered wire from the roof rafters, cast an eerie glow over the scene. With no light-reflecting surfaces, the bulb's output was absorbed by the time-darkened wood, leaving a rather cave-like atmosphere.

Everywhere, material evidence of our lives loomed, and the encounter with so many memories tugged at my gut. I picked up an old shoe box that was set apart from other items and read the crayoned inscription on the cover: "David." I undid the neatly tied twine, opened the box, and there on top was the Western Union Telegram from the U.S. Navy to

Mother and Dad, informing them, *"with deepest regret,"* of David's death on Iwo Jima on February 19th, 1945.

February 19th — that was today's date! I glanced at my watch — 9:15. This was the very day, and in a strange, ironic twist of fate, the exact moment David had caught the full burst of Japanese machine-gun fire that ended his life 42 years earlier.

The resurfacing of long dormant grief flooded over me — the deep catch in my throat, the involuntary sob, super-heated tears burning my eyes, running down my face onto my neck under my open-shirt collar. I heaved a deep sigh and heard myself cry out in the deep recess of that winter-darkened attic, "Oh, God, does grieving never cease; when can I ever accept your grace?"

I arose from my pine-board seat, leaving the remainder of the shoe-box contents undisturbed, made my way down the dark stairway to the kitchen, and prepared a mug of strong coffee.

As I sat at the kitchen window sipping the pungent brew, I watched cardinals and sparrows flitting about in their search for seeds in the new-fallen snow. I opened the window and tossed them small chunks from the plain hard roll I had bought at the bakery and watched them scramble. The sparrows were outranked by the cardinals but managed to get their share. Was God watching all this? . . . I wondered. His word guarantees that even a fallen sparrow does not escape his notice.

I closed the window and turned my attention back to the shoe box — piano recital programs; report cards from grade school showing all "E's" and "S's," *Excellent* and *Superior*, and those from high school showing "A's" and "A+'s"; Sunday School and high school assembly programs where David was the featured performer or master of ceremonies; the folded sheet music of the piano duet, "Dizzy Fingers," that David and I had played for a Sunday School talent show. He had played the lead with all the finger action while I played the simpler rhythm base. We were a hit.

Finally, the last item in the box was the original draft of his commencement address as president of his 1941 high school senior class. My job as night service dispatcher for a major appliance firm had prevented my attendance at the ceremonies, and though I had heard about the speech, I had failed for some reason to read it. I decided to set that treat aside for a more relaxed time, when I could let my thoughts and emotions have free reign.

I faced the almost formidable task of evaluating a lifetime accumulation of old furniture, clothing, books, Christmas ornaments, luggage, childhood toys, an array of Army, Navy (and Marine), and Air Forces uniforms, and a considerable collection of wartime letters, photos, and memorabilia. The basement matched the attic with similar clutter; a teenage visit to the Stewarts' basement always had been an adventure. My economy-minded father saw value in most everything, reminding us that some time we may need this or that. To this day, an old friend loves to recall my resourcefulness in using an old, but worthy, ironing board to replace the rotted running board on my 1929 DeSoto. The seasoned wood responded to old well-honed tools and, covered with rubber matting, served as long as I had the car.

I found much to keep and take to Texas, more to dispose of locally, and limited time in which to do so. But a "flea-market" dealer named Steve, from Hammond, Indiana, answered my call responding to his ad in a local business paper and agreed to take anything

I didn't want, as well as, in exchange, help me load my truck with the goods I would be taking to Heath. We completed the job in three days, and Steve made a haul of considerable worth.

We shook hands and I wished him luck with his sales. His usually somber expression changed to a broad grin. "I didn't tell you this before, Alex, but when you called me I had already decided to quit this business and go back to working in a garage. You've been a life saver and I appreciate it."

"One hand washes the other, Steve." The feeling was mutual and as he revved the engine on the overloaded pickup, I told him I hoped he would be well paid. Returning my thumbs-up salute, he pulled away from the curb. I stared at the receding vehicle with its homemade high-board sides and wondered if he would make it to Hammond. He disappeared from view behind Roger's house and was gone, and so was the last of the family's more modern acquisitions that had no future in our Texas home and little claim on our sentiments.

Back in the house I had a gnawing urging inside, something I had yet to do. The front hall and its straight passage back to the dining room, then a left turn into the parlor, were all stark like an empty warehouse. I opened the opposing double sliding doors separating the back parlor from the living room. My eyes drifted to the piano, bleak in the dreary setting of the cold and lifeless room. I walked over and raised the lid of the keyboard. I hit a few keys, then fingered and struck the starting first three chords of my last recital piece at age 17, Rachmaninoff's *C-Sharp Minor Prelude*. The result was a cacaphony of dull, flat tones, some sticking keys, and only a hint of the composer's intent. I closed the lid, distressed by its unsatisfying performance.

What was to be its fate, I wondered? Had its time come for total retirement? And what *is* total retirement? The piano could serve no one in its degenerate condition. Was it worth restoration? Who could restore it?

That precious Conover grand piano had been in our home for over 50 years. But some of the ivory keys were worn down to their wood base; the beautiful polished ebony surface had become dull and badly crazed. It had had no mechanical attention since David left for service in 1943.

I consulted the Yellow Pages and selected three of the most likely dealers to call. The first two proposed doing the work and paying me when and if a sale was made — both unacceptable. The third dealer showed some interest and offered to come out and look over the family treasure.

Mr. Baker arrived in the afternoon and first referred to a book of serial numbers to determine the piano's age. It had been made in 1920, the year of my birth. He checked everything, using tools to test this and that and measure the next thing. I asked if he had a stethoscope, and much to my surprise he produced one from his brief case. He probed between some strings, found the sounding board, and had me strike some keys while he listened. He gave a reassuring nod, then explained that this was his own best method of checking the instrument's heart. The examination complete, he detailed everything needed to restore the Conover to brand-new condition.

I explained that I was as much interested in the piano's destiny as I was in the price he would pay me for it. And he explained that its next owner would probably be a young, talented student on his or her way up, graduating from a spinet or an upright and this would be the last step before advancing to a Steinway. He named a price and waited for my response.

Actually, he had described David's situation when Dad and Mother had made this purchase. Convinced that the piano could not be placed in more capable or caring hands, I contemplated his offer: "Was this his best price?" I suggested a higher number, knowing instinctively that he would not raise his bid; and he did not.

"Well, Mr. Baker," I said, "you just bought yourself a piano." We shook hands on it, then he pulled out his wallet and gave me half the purchase price in $100 bills. "My men will pay you the other half when they come for the piano tomorrow," he said.

The movers came on schedule. They were not the big husky fellows I had in visioned, but young, rather short and strong. There was no hesitancy as they brought an odd-looking device into the living room, a piano "sled" they called it. While they returned to their truck for a four-wheel dolly and some heavy pads, I turned to the piano and touched some of the worn, bare keys. The ivory had been martyred to the tens of thousands of times the keys had been struck by those strong, powerful fingers sounding the fury of a Rachmaninoff *Prelude* or a Hungarian *Rhapsody* or caressed through the lyrical passages of a Brahms *Lullaby*. What glorious tones those keys had sounded; what artistry they had collaborated in producing to thrill the hearer! And what love had been defined by the display of family portraits arrayed on the cover of this instrument, watched over by Mother's ever-present vase of specially selected flowers.

I squinted and envisioned our photos under the arch of those lovely blossoms. There was Ray, his wavy hair glistening in the Hawaiian sunlight, open khaki shirt collar contrasting with the South Pacific tan of his lean, strong countenance. Then David in his Navy blues, strong, deep-dimpled chin, heavy eyebrows, and dark, piercing eyes. And, finally, the first portrait-type photo of myself, taken the day I transferred from the Coast Artillery to Army Air Corps flight training — now called Army Air Forces — in 1942. These were the elements that were daily arranged and rearranged by the home-front family, moved for dusting and then replaced for best viewing. They had been a comfort, a consolation to Mother and Dad, Jean and Margaret, and had appeared many times in their letters to us in far-off lands. They were that indescribable link that held us together as family. I sometimes felt that we were, in our inanimate frames, sharing in their conversations. When I wrote to them, I visualized myself speaking from my exalted place on the piano, Ray and David tuning in.

I watched as the haulers did their work. Apparently in a time-honored sequence, they maneuvered the piano onto the sled, resting on its side, removed the three legs, and padded and strapped it to the sled's super-structure. Rolling on the wheeled dolly and sliding down the steps on the sled's runners, then rolling again on the dolly, they were soon raising it on the hydraulic tailgate to the floor of the truck. Leaving it on the sled, they secured the piano with ropes to the truck's stanchions. Then, jumping to the ground, they closed the truck's sliding overhead door, shutting off my final view of that great cargo. The entire process took about ten minutes. I was gratified that they had exercised such great care, and I continued to watch as the truck disappeared from view. I felt a piece of something precious leave my life, then thought about the piano's next owner and hoped it would be another young, aspiring artist anticipating a more secure future. Certainly David would want that. I was satisfied.

The old house, no longer a home, was completely stripped of furniture and decorations. A hired clean-up crew had washed and scrubbed and swept all evidence of habitation. And Steve, from Indiana, had done his job well. My truck, with its cargo of antiques and family treasures stood at attention in the driveway, silently begging to be underway, the wartime letters written to one another and those from friends and sweethearts, sent home for safe keeping, carefully tucked inside.

Those from my father to we three brothers in service carried a more philosophical message, holding before us the vision and source of our origin and the love and values imparted through profound parental witness. He often expressed his intense love for America, his adopted homeland, and though obviously concerned for our safety was nonetheless proud of his contribution in manpower to the war effort. "America must be saved," he once wrote. "Your mother and I will do our duty, as we see our duty, as long as we have breath." Their patriotism defied description.

I was about ready to leave. I placed my coffee mug and jar of coffee in a shopping bag and set it on the floor near the front door. This moment of final departure warranted one last look around. I made that twisting climb to the attic and paused at the railing surrounding the stairs. Visions of my youth came into focus. Here was the storage area where the beautiful American Flyer Electric Train, a gift to David and me in 1929 by family friend Henry Marcy, had set during those periods between holidays and bad weather, inside play days. Next to it, in its triangular-shaped wooden carrying case had been Dad's nickel-plated cornet that he had acquired as a youth in England and played, at our insistence, on New Year's Eve, at the stroke of midnight. Awakened by Mother in time for the event, David and I would sit on the front porch swing bundled in blankets while Dad played "Auld Lang Syne," the "Star Spangled Banner," and a few other favorites, concluding with "The Lord's Prayer." We shivered, not from the cold, but from the thrill of the moment and the sensation that we were making neighborhood history. Who among our friends could bring in the New Year as we did? All this, while neighbors rang "call-home-to-dinner" bells and Roger, down at the corner by the Illinois Central Railroad tracks, fired his pistol. I have celebrated many New Years, but these are the ones most remembered.

In this area was the space below the half-circle window where oldest brother Cameron had slept, before leaving to marry Rita, and where he had had a nightmare fight and split a large gash in his knuckles from hitting the iron bedstead. Behind the chimney was the larger room where David, Ray, and I had slept in two three-quarter-sized beds, pulled together to provide a larger expanse for fast-growing youth. The time I was sick and vomited on Ray's side, then rolled back to drier territory flashed through my mind. Boy, was he angry as he grabbed a blanket and descended to the living-room couch, leaving me to clean up or sleep in my own mess.

Down on the second floor, I moseyed one last time through the five bedrooms. Mother and Dad had the larger front room where David had been born. My earliest memory dated to May 1923 when at age three I beckoned family members to come to the crib where David lay. "See," I said proudly and possessively, "He's my little brown brother." Like all of us, he had our mother's coloring — deep, dark-brown eyes, dark-toned complexion, and hair that would change from light to dark brown. Here, too, was where I had visited Dad as he sat in an armchair at midnight on June 30, 1950, dying of stomach cancer. Sister Jean handed him two pills and said, "Here Dad, take these, they will ease your pain." Wry humor surfaced as he replied, "If they'll kill this pain, they're worth their weight in diamonds." Soon after, I said goodnight and drove the three miles to our apartment where Ruth was waiting. At 6:00 a.m., Mother called to say that Dad had died at about 4:00.

Next to the master bedroom was what had been an alcove, converted to a small bedroom. Sisters Margaret and Jean had slept together there for as long as I can remember.

The other three bedrooms had been rented out to roomers. Dad's frugality and need for income to meet mortgage payments required it. Four garages at the rear rented at $10 per month each; our cars were housed in a side yard shed. The east two rooms had once been occupied by a Mr. Curtley and his teenage son, George, a year or two older than me. George had a fine musical talent and his harmonica playing approached virtuosity. I could listen for hours as he brought forth old and new tunes. I was drawn to his room one hot summer afternoon when I heard the strains of "Yankee Doodle Dandy." He paused to remind me that it was an old song popular during World War I. The conversation led to talk of war, whereupon he brought from the closet a badly stained American flag. "See these stains?" he said. "Those are from blood. When my Dad was in the war in France he dipped the flag in the blood of his dead buddies on the battlefield." I was impressed — and sickened. Later, I determined that this was a grim souvenir among the troops of that time. At age 12, I was thus remotely introduced to the horrors of war, and the sight of that flag was forever engraved in my memory. I visualized Mr. Curtley making the rounds, bending over each body, finding the wounds, dipping the flag, wiping his tears on the sleeve of his muddy jacket, then looking around to locate the next victim. The scene haunted me then, and haunts me still.

I went down the creaking staircase to the front hall. The stair noise reminded me of our habit as older teenagers to wait for an Illinois Central train to pass before entering the house, thus shielding our late homecoming from parental earshot. It was on these same stairs that one late night Ruth found the sure cure for hiccups, as she and I returned from a party during a visit to Chicago. Three or four steps up she paused, turned to me, and whispered, "I think I'm pregnant." My hiccups vanished instantly. The next day we talked of the incident and I remarked that, true or not, it was certainly an odd time and place for so important an announcement. "Yes," she said, "but it sure cured your hiccups."

In the hall I noticed the slight smudge mark left by the Gibson Girls and the spot on the opposite wall where a long, narrow mirror had hung, used by the whole family for last-minute checks on appearance before leaving the house. At one time, the telephone rested on a small, half-round end table under the mirror. Next to it was the black coin box attached to the wall. I always liked watching the phone company collector select a key from a large ring, open the box, remove and very rapidly count the nickels, roll them in colored paper, and charge Mother for the slugs that had been used in place of real coins. We knew where she hid them and used them for our calls when we were short. And she used them too.

Next to the phone was a large sliding door that opened into the living room. Many times, when talking to our girlfriends, we would slide open the door and hold up the phone so that they could hear David's great piano playing. Sometimes the girls would make a request, and David was always glad to oblige. The living room was the scene of those many Christmases — the tree set in front of the bay window trimmed with old ornaments, lights that would all go out when one bulb failed, tinsel and colored garlands, and red and green mesh sacks filled with popcorn and candy prepared, filled, and hung on Christmas Eve.

In lean years, the tree was sometimes an assemblage of a quite bare center trunk, with hand-drilled holes made to receive loose branches, all gathered from discards behind local grocery stores after closing time. Dad, David, and I teamed for the search-and-build effort, never once alluding to any imperfections but sighting our creativity as matching the skills of Mother Nature. It was Christmas, it was a beautiful tree, and we were all happy.

The back parlor, behind the living room, housed a collection of books and sheet music, a long mahogany library table, and an old fashioned pump organ that Dad had bought in St. Joseph, Michigan. He had it shipped across Lake Michigan to Navy Pier, several blocks east of downtown Chicago, and trucked to our house. In time, he completely dismantled and rebuilt the instrument to its original perfection. David did an outstanding job of urging music from this prized relic and enjoyed leading the family in hymn sings and Christmas carols.

The dining room next to the back parlor had a large walnut table where we all gathered for the evening meal. Dad's voice-teaching schedule kept him downtown on weekday evenings and Saturdays, but he was always home for Sunday dinner. This was the only time we had prayer together, led by Dad, who managed to keep it fairly short. It was also the scene for Saturday lunch when several of us gathered from our various chores to partake of Mother's fare. There was always a place set for Corinne, the Negro lady who came every Saturday to do the ironing. She had been preceded by Andy, a heavy-set, short black woman with very bad feet. One morning Andy had arrived before most of us were out of bed, and called up to whoever could hear her, "Waas donin bowed?" Sister Margaret answered, "Oh, he's still in bed." Margaret thought she had asked, "Where's the darling boy?" Of course, Andy was looking for the ironing board. Margaret never lived down that translation.

The large pantry and kitchen were behind the dining room and that was where, as far as young boys were concerned, the greatest artistry was performed. Mother was an outstanding cook and could make a feast from scraps, or so it seemed. She made 15 loaves of bread every Saturday, plus cinnamon rolls, pies, and — in season — the finest fruit cakes I have ever eaten. It was the habit of several of our friends to gather around the two enamel-topped kitchen tables late on Saturday afternoon to share in the first large loaf of Mother's bread, still oven warm. Large slices, slathered with fresh tub butter were devoured with ample dressings of her homemade currant jelly. In summer, our friends congregated on the large back porch. Ray's friend, Phil Clark, once remarked that Mother's bread was better than any cake he had ever eaten.

There wasn't much to look at in the basement of the old house, though it had been the place of many projects over the years. The coal stoker I had installed after the war had been replaced with a gas conversion burner. The washtubs in the laundry section had not been used for some years since the purchase of a modern clothes washer. The do-it-yourself shower head with curtain ring were still suspended from the ceiling where I had placed them long before the war, but had seen no use since.

I secured the laundry-room door leading to the back yard, went up the worn wooden stairs to the front hall, took one last look around, stepped onto the front porch, and locked the door. The old porch swing had been replaced with a new model some years back but still reminded me of those New Year's Eve celebrations back in the '20s. It was the same porch where the family had gathered on September 26th, 1941, when I left for the Army, and the scene my mind's eye had focused on so many times since.

I descended the seven stairs, walked to the waiting truck, then stopped. Something told me to return to the living room.

I retraced my steps, again unlocked that door, and entered the living room. Had I failed to pay due homage to that almost sacred quarter, had my final goodbye been too casual, was there something more that the room had to tell me? Opposite the bay window, near the fireplace that was located on the inside wall in the corner, had been that revered place for the piano. Its keyboard was on the fireplace side, the graceful curve of its cabinet open to the view of all who entered. The Marli horses on the mantel stood in mystic union, the old clock chiming the quarter hour, once a faded memory, now stood in sparkling imagination.

Again, the piano, long years deprived of its Master's touch, devoid of the medley of loved and loving images borne on its elegant plane, starved for the gentle caress of those charged with its care — did I now hear it echo the poetry of Bach, of Beethoven and Brahms, the raw power of Tchaikovsky, Rachmaninoff, of Liszt and Grieg, the serenity, then the glory of Handel?

Had the spirit of its Master returned for a final concert?

The room seemed to be floating. I turned and saw the family — Dad, Mother, Margaret, Jean, Cameron, and Ray — gathered at the sliding door.

"Come in," my words echoed. "See, he's my little brown brother . . ."

Chapter 2

Ellis Island, New York
1904

EEP IN THE HOLD OF White Star Lines' RMS *Cedric*, where the steering mechanism noisily responded to the demands of the helmsman, several hundred immigrants endured the poorly ventilated — at times almost breathless — atmosphere common to Steerage Class passage. The ten-day voyage from the Liverpool docks on the River Mersey to New York harbor would soon be over and their dreams of a new life in America would sparkle with reality. September 2, 1904, was a clear, warm day and all the passengers were on deck, their weariness forgotten.

The immigrants let out a great cheer as they passed the Statue of Liberty, knowing that it had been a gift to the United States from France, dedicated on October 28, 1886, just eight years earlier. The vocal greeting matched in fervor if not in volume the ship's huge steam horn as its blasts echoed among the towering buildings of Manhattan. All the passengers rushed to the side of the ship. "*Look at her!*" they shouted in all kinds of tongues. "*There she is!*" It was like someone was greeting them. They would be counted among the 15 million immigrants who would enter America between 1880 and 1924. And none of them was more enthusiastic or excited than my father.

Concealed in a handmade, moisture-proof, oil-skin money belt strapped to his bare waist beneath long underwear, he carried his life's savings in British currency valued at $5,000. Though able to afford better accommodations, he opted for the money-saving Steerage fare, dismissing it as "a few days of discomfort." This thriftiness characterized a frugality born of a hardscrabble existence from beginnings as a printer's devil at age 14 to printing plant superintendent at 32. Having set the goal at an early age of saving 50 percent of his earnings (a goal more often desired than achieved), he was perhaps one of the wealthier of his shipmates.

With his handmade sailcloth sea bag slung over his shoulder, he filed down the long gangplank to the solid soil of Ellis Island where he processed through Customs without incident, while some 20 percent of the others were turned back due to illness and disease or lack of the $25 subsistence funds required for entry. Dad carried a straight razor, shaving mug, brush and leather strop, soap, towel, and wash rag in another oil-skin pouch. These, plus extra underwear, stockings, shirt, trousers, and jacket were rolled up seaman's style in the sea bag. Having lived near and played on the great Liverpool docks as a youth, he was familiar with the ways of the seafarer.

He made his way to the Baggage Room where he claimed his only other piece of luggage, a hand-crafted wooden box in the shape and size of a suitcase. From his sea bag he extracted a box harness equipped with a heavily padded shoulder strap and attached it to the box. So equipped, he was prepared for his two-day venture into New York before boarding the train for Omaha, Nebraska, and a reunion with his older brother, Henry, a seminary student, who had emigrated in 1895.

Dad's pulse quickened as he rode the Ellis Island Ferry to its landing at the Battery at the lower end of Manhattan. The moment he set foot on American soil, he knew his dream of becoming an American would soon be a reality. There was an eagerness, an enthusiasm in his step, and a sense of pride and accomplishment when, making his first stop after leaving the ferry, he entered a bank near Battery Park and converted some of his British pounds to American dollars. The exchange rate there was better than that available at Ellis Island.

Tradesmen of every sort solicited business from the immigrants. "Rooming-house runners" were in abundance, striving to fill their vacancies with short-term occupants. Dad bargained for a facility with a private bath and which provided horse-drawn transportation to the train station the day after next. He was soon established in a small hotel, savoring his first bath since leaving England. After splurging on a sirloin steak dinner, he secured train schedules and planned for his departure to Omaha.

The only clothing he brought from England was in the sea bag, for he had decided to adapt to American ways and style as soon after arrival as possible. But the wooden box contained items that tied him to his roots and would be an ever-present reminder of his life as a Briton and the source of the values bred into his character. As his mother lay near death in 1900, Dad promised her that he would not emigrate as long as his father was living. In the spring of 1903, my grandfather succumbed to pneumonia and was buried next to my grandmother in the cemetery adjoining the Liverpool Cathedral. Soon after, Dad made emigration plans and prepared for the great adventure.

Secure in the box, its cover fastened with screws, were treasures, the value of which accrued only to him. In it he carried his nickel-plated cornet in its triangular-shaped wooden, red felt-lined carrying case; the *Prendergast Method of Speaking French*, a book from which he taught himself and perfected his fluency; his well-worn Bible, with its many penciled notations and underlined passages; favorite pieces of music, which included his own compositions; an assortment of letters; his birth certificate dated May 23, 1872; his parents' marriage and death certificates; and some photographs. Also included was a piece of ivory shaped like a crude letter opener with a piece of leather secured on one end with twine, and a small black snuff box with a hinged lid. His mother had earned mere pennies with the ivory, creasing mailings for a Liverpool merchant. The snuff box held a cache of small coins from which she would retrieve a "tuppence" or two to buy a piece of meat for the evening meal. All these were precious keepsakes that connected Dad to his heritage and would inspire him as he carved out a career in the New World.

But perhaps the most significant items in the box were two large, heavy medals, about one and three-quarter inches in diameter and one-quarter-inch thick. One of pewter-like metal bore the image of a man walking behind a hand plow drawn by two oxen with a Bible verse inscription on its perimeter: "Let us not be weary in well doing for in due season we shall reap if we faint not." On the reverse the inscription read: LIVERPOOL COUNCIL OF EDUCATION — PUBLIC ELEMENTARY SCHOOLS — AWARDED TO Alexander Stewart, St.Andrews, FOR REGULARITY OF ATTENDANCE & GENERAL GOOD CONDUCT DURING TWO SCHOOL YEARS — 1880.

The other medal, in bronze and more handsome than the first, bore the images of a boy and a girl, students standing before a bearded educator who was seated and holding a large tome and obviously listening to the boy's recitation. The perimeter Biblical inscription read: "The fear of the Lord is the beginning of wisdom." On the reverse the inscription read: LIVERPOOL COUNCIL OF EDUCATION — PUBLIC ELEMENTARY SCHOOLS — AWARDED TO Alexander Stewart, St.Andrews, FOR MARKED REGULARITY OF ATTENDANCE AND GENERAL GOOD CONDUCT DURING THREE YEARS — 1881.

The dates indicate that Dad was eight and nine years of age and had probably completed the second and third "standards," or the equivalent of second and third grade in American schools. But even more striking were the Bible verses quoted on public school objects. I remember Dad saying that they stood and repeated the Lord's Prayer every morning before commencing with their studies.Of course, the Church of England was a government entity of Episcopal origin, and religion was taught in the classrooms. The separation of church and state was peculiarly an American ideology.

The medals proved to be symbolic of Dad's quest for learning and served him as a constant reminder of a pledge he had made to himself to study and commit to memory a new fact or word daily. He practiced this discipline most of his life. The one great distraction he remembered from his school days was the liberal use of the "cane," a hard, ruler-type stick applied to the palm of the hand as punishment for some infraction of rules or failure to accurately recite a lesson.

Dad only knew one schoolmaster, Charles Roberts, who had been in control for Dad's entire school experience. He was known to all the students as "Cockie" Roberts and to the more impoverished as a mean, totally unfair tyrant. He catered to the "rich" kids, the saloon-keepers' boys who were never sent to the "line," but he applied the cane generously to the poor. This observation created in Dad a dislike for school and certainly a dislike for Cockie Roberts. "A caning was painful," Dad often remarked, "but what hurt more was the indignity of it. It was so unnecessary and supplied nothing to the learning process."

The Church of England tolerated non-Episcopal backgrounds in the schools. There were Catholics, a few Jews, and some Protestant faiths. My grandmother, Jane Fidler Stewart, was born into a devout Presbyterian family in Aberdeen, Scotland. My grandfather, Alexander Stewart, was born in Glasgow. He was a lithographer in the printing trade, as was his father, Henry Stewart (my great-grandfather) before him. Following my grandparents' marriage, they moved to Liverpool where their three sons were born: Henry in 1870, Alexander in 1872, and John in 1875. The three boys were all primed to enter the printing trade upon completion of elementary school.

That "dashing emigre" from England was not very dashing, however, before he met Margaret Baird in Omaha in 1904. Life in the "old country" had been hard, and monetary progress was measured in farthings (one-quarter of a penny) and pennies or a twopence. A shilling's value was about 25 cents, while a pound sterling was about the same as the American five-dollar bill. Extreme thrift and the adherence to very simple tastes was required in order to accumulate means of wealth. Adding to the challenge was the lack of money to seek advanced educational opportunities. Almost every waking hour was spent in the pursuit of the basic necessities of food, shelter, and clothing.

When Dad had completed elementary school at age 14, he was accepted as an apprentice at Ratliff Brothers, a large printing establishment. An apprentice was known as a "printer's devil," and the nature of the work measured up to its designation. The "devil" did all of the dirty, menial tasks: washing type, plates, and rollers, oiling machinery, sweeping floors, and disposing of trash. Oddly, waste paper was at a minimum due to careful use, handling, and reusing of scrap. A sheet of paper was used on both sides before it was discarded. Rarely did Dad write a letter using just one side of the page. And if only half a page was used, he would neatly cut off the bottom half with his very sharp pocket knife and save it for another letter. I found much evidence of this economy among his accumulation of papers and his business affairs after his death.

In the course of his seven-year apprenticeship, Dad arrived at the journeyman designation with a considerable knowledge of the trade and its technical components. His father was a lithographer. Dad's brother Henry became an engraver, and his brother John became a typesetter, whereas Dad was a general printer and performed the final function of producing the finished product. All the specialties were critical to total quality, and the acceptance of the work by management and the customer rested on Dad's shoulders. A stellar performance earned him the job of general superintendent, forever branding him as a perfectionist.

Dad's boss was a Mr. Beresford, a man who in the eyes of his employees was never satisfied. He was mean-spirited and never gave anyone any peace. Dad said that in his 17 years with Ratliff Brothers, Beresford never paid him a compliment or congratulated him on his work. But superintendents' jobs were scarce and of necessity, Dad learned to tolerate Beresford's volatility, ascribing it to his sense of how underlings should be treated. Historically, this was the way of boss-employee relations in that era. Nonetheless, it had a negative effect on Dad. Years later he often remarked that the happiness he had known in America virtually eliminated from memory the heartache and drudgery he had experienced in his earlier life in England.

The sorrow and tension a drunken father introduced into family life was a constant strain and a burden that Dad's saintly mother bore in noble fashion. Jane Fidler Stewart was the daughter of Alexander Fidler, a successful coal broker. Soon after her marriage to Alexander Stewart, the couple migrated to Liverpool where Stewart found employment in a large printing shop. A letter of recommendation by his Glasgow employer, found among Dad's papers, indicated that my grandfather was a very capable and trustworthy worker. Dad said he never drank during the week and never missed a day's work until shortly before his death. But on Saturdays he went to the pub, staggered home late in the day, exercised his wrath and meanness on the family, and then spent all day Sunday recovering for work on Monday.

All three brothers loved and respected their mother, a woman of strong character and devout convictions. She came from an active background in the Presbyterian Church of Scotland and encouraged her sons in the faith. As teenagers they were drawn into the Colesium Presbyterian Church of Liverpool and became involved in Sunday School under the guidance and leadership of two great men, Charles Quayle and W. B. Hambley. Several other young men — friends from school — also participated in the Colesium work.

As church superintendent, Mr. Quayle had a keen eye for talent and saw great potential in his charges. Their near-poverty status was never a deterrent, and he succeeded in elevating their sights to grander purpose. They were poor, but hungry to learn and responded well to Biblical teaching. An organization within the church was formed, "The King's Heralds" — with no reference intended to the King of England but to Jesus Christ the King.

The seeds of Christian service were planted. The Heralds prospered in their knowledge of scripture and conviction and became ambassadors for Christ in the inner city. Preaching forays were commonplace, and crowds large and small gathered on street corners and in public squares to hear itinerate missionaries present their messages. Although Dad was a very fluent and articulate preacher, he leaned heavily toward music. An additional leader, a Mr. Pierce, was brought into the Colesium organization. He quickly recognized Dad's musical gifts and gave Dad a cornet, which he taught himself to play. Other instrumentalists in their number joined Dad in producing some very acceptable music, which helped to draw a crowd for the preaching service. They played, while the "preachers" sang. Dad was also a gifted singer and added his solo numbers, enhancing these student productions.

Mr. Quayle and Mr. Hambley were impressed with Dad's voice and arranged for him to take lessons from the choir director at no cost. He progressed beyond the director's ability, and sought instruction from a leading teacher in Liverpool. Eventually he acquired a part-time, low-paying job as choir director for a small church and offered private voice lessons to some of the choir members.

Although Dad's formal schooling stopped at age 14, his thirst for knowledge was insatiable. He read and studied books on English grammar, sentence structure, vocabulary, and spelling. He became a reader of classical literature, the operas, and musicology, learning the science, history, forms, and methods of music. His intricate study of the physical structure and function of the components of the human voice was a unique contribution that placed him in the forefront of the ranks of voice teachers. It was one thing to effect a certain tonal quality, but another to know how and why it happened, and what to do to produce it.

Armed with unusual insights and techniques he had developed and refined, Dad worked out exercises for his own and his students' benefit in the application of these techniques. In a promotional folder he once likened his teaching methods to those of "the great teachers of Europe," the suggestion being that he had studied under them. When I asked him who these teachers were, he replied with a broad smile that "there was really only one," referring to himself. His teaching approach formed the hallmark of his career and prevailed throughout his life. It was only when I began to understand the origin of his techniques and methods, which he had enumerated in a folder that I found some time later on his desk, that I discovered the secret of his success.

As a youth, he had worked after school as an errand boy for a watchmaker and clock repairman. Time in the shop was devoted to observing the owner, a kind and generous man working as he answered Dad's questions. Dad learned about clocks and watches and applied this knowledge to his own timepiece acquisitions all his life. I was often amazed to see him disassemble the works of a tiny watch, then clean, repair, and restore it to accurate time-keeping operation. Striking or chiming clocks became his hobby, and at one time there were ten or twelve of them in our house announcing the hour simultaneously, sometimes to Mother's distraction.

On September 4th, 1904, when Dad boarded a New York Central train for Chicago, his habit of frugality again was not compromised by traveling in style or comfort. He rode in a coach rather than a Pullman sleeping car, which would have required an extra fare. From the Dearborn Street Station in Chicago, Dad made his way to the Northwestern Railroad Station, where he embarked for Omaha. He sat upright on non-reclining cane upholstered seats, as he had done on the trip from New York. Sleep finally overtook him, as he yielded to exhaustion.

When he arrived in Omaha, Dad rode a horse-drawn tram to the Presbyterian Seminary dormitory where his brother Henry lived. Henry was to have been on hand to greet him, but was nowhere to be found. Securing Henry's room number from the desk clerk, Dad made his way to the designated room and found his brother sound asleep. In later years, in true brotherly fashion, Dad was critical of Henry's apparent irresponsibility. Nonetheless, their reunion was a joyous occasion, their first meeting in more than eight years. They talked hours on end, and filled in the pages of the passing time.

Dad stayed at the Seminary that night and located a room the following day in a well-appointed rooming house, chosen for the duration of his visit. The first matter of business to attend to was the renewing of his wardrobe. And Henry introduced Dad to Omaha, where he became familiar with the ways of the city; Dad soon was able to make his way around town without assistance.

Dad was anxious to launch his career in music, and Omaha looked like a good place to start. He learned through Henry and the Seminary that the Knox Street Presbyterian Church had an opening for a Director of Music. He landed the job, with a starting salary of $8 per week — $5 for directing the choir and singing solos for Sunday morning and evening services and $3 for Wednesday evening choir rehearsal. It wasn't much for one of his ability, he thought, but it was a start. Included in the benefits was free use of the sanctuary for teaching voice to private students, and soon after he had announced his availability, he attracted a small "class" of vocal aspirants. Though he gave only private lessons, he always referred to the aggregate of individuals as a class.

It was mid-September when he was introduced to the choir by the pastor. He had met the organist a few days before and had discussed with him the music to be used at the first rehearsal. He had received a roster of the choir members and asked each one to state his or her name and voice range — soprano, alto, tenor, or bass. Halfway through the roster, the sweetest speaking voice he had ever heard announced, "My name is Margaret Baird. I sing soprano." Then with a slight blush and ever so faint smile, her head turned just a little and her deep brown eyes glanced to one side, breaking eye contact. In the Biblical "twinkling of an eye," Dad was captivated, and romance had its inception. For many years, Dad told and retold the circumstances and impressions of that first meeting and described how Mother literally stole his heart. "Not only did her voice produce the sweetest music I had ever heard, but she was the most beautiful woman I had ever seen," he declared. His opinion never wavered. She was his "Lassie," his "Queen."

"Oh, that I could have known that Lassie in childhood," he once said, "and witnessed firsthand her transition from a feisty five-year-old in a long gingham dress to the lady of beauty and grace and dignity upon whom I gazed for the first time on that fateful day in an Omaha choir loft."

Chapter 3

Kansas City — Omaha

*I*T WAS, IN FACT, that bare-footed five-year-old in her long gingham dress that stood on the rotting door stoop of the two-room clapboard shack, hands on hips, brows knitted above deep brown, piercing eyes, as she demanded of the approaching Indians to "go on, get along out of here, go on!" The beggars altered their course and sought bounty elsewhere down along the Missouri River bottoms in Kansas City. Mother's three-year-old brother, George Washington Baird, was asleep. Seven-year-old brother, Paul Revere Baird, was off trudging along the Missouri-Pacific railroad track, gathering coal that had fallen from the steam-engine tenders and would not return until the two bushel baskets balanced on his homemade wagon were filled.

Their father, Thomas Jefferson Baird (son of Benjamin Franklin Baird), had deserted the family sometime after the birth of George, leading to the divorce from Harriet (Hattie) Matheny Baird. Hattie was off fending for her family as a domestic in some fine homes in Kansas City while five-year-old Margaret fulfilled her responsibility as self-appointed protector of tiny George.

Whatever the source of the spunk she employed to dispatch begging Indians, it was not a casual characteristic, for it would be called upon many times in her life as a mother of six and wife to the dashing young Scotsman who called her

"Lassie." But her true nature more readily fit the mold of the soprano in the church choir.

Margaret Eloise Baird was born in that Kansas City shack on June 9th, 1883. How she had escaped a family tradition of being named for a great person of history was never explained. Perhaps the names Martha Washington and Betsy Ross were the only prominent females of the time. My mother's family had known little more than poverty, and the year 1888 held no promise for improvement. My grandmother Hattie bowed to the task of providing for her children, scratching out sustenance from a small garden patch next to the house. Her meager earnings supplied other dietary essentials and ingredients for bread, which was baked in a sheet-iron oven atop the wood- and coal-burning stove. Water was carried from a community well 100 yards away, and heated in a lard pail for laundry. Bathing was accomplished in the same sheet-iron washtub. A privy at the rear of the small yard served their sanitary needs.

Uncle Andrew Matheny, Hattie's brother, wrote that she could do better in Nebraska, for there he would be able to help her. He had located a three-acre tract with a small house and barn and a deep well for rent outside Omaha, in the community of Florence. There she could keep a cow or two for milk and butter, and raise chickens. These animals could produce enough revenue, he suggested, to pay the rent. A horse to transport the children to the one-room school four miles distant was also a possibility.

Hattie packed their meager belongings in flour sacks and their hardware in the large washtub and two wooden boxes, and she and the children boarded the train for Omaha. She won an argument with the ticket agent over the proposed seating arrangements, insisting that all four occupy two seats; thus she and the children rode for one and one-half fares. The children were delighted with the train ride. They busied themselves making the acquaintance of the other passengers, and soon each one had his own seat. They ate from a bag of provisions Hattie had prepared.

It was late evening when the train pulled into Omaha. Uncle Andrew met them with his wagon and two-horse team, and they were soon off to the country. They looked forward to settling in on the little farm he had written about and commencing a new life.

The horse did become a reality, and most days was ridden to the rural school by the three children. With the completion of grade school, Paul became an apprentice brick layer and stone mason, like his Uncle Andrew. Later, George worked at several jobs before landing a permanent position with the Santa Fe Railroad. His employment by the railroad was somewhat akin to that of their grandfather, Benjamin Franklin Baird, who had been featured on the front page of the Sunday rotogravure section of either the Omaha *World Herald* or the Omaha *Bee* in 1900 as being the first United States Railway Postal Clerk. Mother once reported this to me, but the lack of an actual date made it impossible for me to get microfilm confirmation from either paper.

With the completion of grade school, it was time for Margaret to find a high school sponsor in Omaha. As was customary with many rural children, she exchanged housework and cooking chores for room and board in a private home. She was engaged by a Mr. and Mrs. Roy Brown where she sharpened her cooking skills and developed social graces under the benevolent eye of Mrs. Brown, all the while excelling in her studies. After the prescribed four years of high school, she enrolled in an "Elective" course, a two-year postgraduate study culminating with teacher certification. She was awarded her diploma from the Omaha High School on June 19, 1903. However, she did not pursue a teaching career.

An opportunity presented itself to work for Thompson-Belden's Department and Dry Goods Store, and she decided to take it. She worked first as a sales clerk, then assistant cashier, and finally as head cashier.

Margaret had long since left the Brown home to take up residence in a highly respectable boarding house for ladies. She was an outstanding asset to Thompson-Belden's, with the unique ability of being everyone's friend, disarmingly pleasant and helpful to both customers and fellow employees. Most all who came to the store wanted her to serve them and were willing to wait until she was available. She was diligent in the performance of her duties and carried every task to a successful conclusion.

One day, a shipment of diamonds came to the store and the jewelry manager reported the shortage of one stone. Several employees were called upon to help search for the missing jewel. When all had given up on finding it, Margaret conducted her own search. She gathered up all the wrappings. On hands and knees she scanned every inch of flooring, every crack and crevice in the area where the unpacking had occurred. She felt certain that the tiny diamond had to be there somewhere. Using the light of a candle, she searched the dark corners around display cases. Finally a sparkle flashed in her eyes! She carefully wrapped the missing diamond in tissue paper and presented it to Mr. Thompson the next morning.

He was ecstatic. He praised her for her persistence and resourcefulness. Whether or not she received any monetary reward was not told us, but she earned a treasured place in the company's esteem. It was no surprise that in her three years with Thompson-Belden's she advanced to head cashier, the highest position attainable by a woman at that time. She occupied an office on the mezzanine, where she received sales tickets and cash in small, spring-driven baskets that arrived from the sales floor on trolley wires. She would register the transaction and return the customer's change and receipt by gravity on the same trolley.

Thompson-Belden's was a quality establishment and its reputation in Omaha was legendary; it enjoyed the favor of the city's most discriminating clientele, many of whom considered her a personal friend. She was often invited to Omaha civic and social affairs, and frequently attended Saturday luncheons and teas in their homes, and she was an oft-invited guest at musical performances and theatrical presentations.

With Dad's spiraling reputation as "that great new tenor," Margaret became one of his most ardent fans. Some time after they met at that first choir rehearsal, Dad made his move. He initiated a courtship and soon they were enjoying each other's company on a regular basis.

Meanwhile, Dad's brother Henry had completed his Theological Seminary schooling, was ordained into the ministry, and accepted a call as pastor of the Presbyterian church in Bancroft, Nebraska. From the time of his arrival in America in late 1895, Henry had completed four years of college and three years at the Seminary. Whether he returned to Liverpool to marry Hannah Jones or had her come to America to be married here is not clear. Scanty evidence indicates that she was not in America when Dad located Henry at the Seminary upon his arrival in September 1904. However, the notation on the back of a snapshot identifies Henry and Hannah on the steps of their cottage in Bancroft. I don't think Henry ever formally pursued the ministry after his stint at doing so in Bancroft, Nebraska.

Hannah Jones had lived with her brother Henry Jones, his wife Alice, and their children in the old Jones family country home near Liverpool. Henry Jones had three children, Kathleen, Harold, and Reginald Watson Jones. Knighted by King George VI, Sir Reginald Watson Jones was cited for his genius and service as an orthopedic surgeon to the Royal Family and his heroic work in mending the broken bodies of British military men in World War II.

The Joneses were quite well-to-do and, as described by my mother, "quite aristocratic." Both Hannah and her brother had been active in the Christian youth work at the Colesium Sunday School where they associated with Dad and his brother Henry, which led to Henry Stewart and Hannah meeting and their subsequent romance.

In late spring of 1906 Hannah and Henry Stewart were expecting their first child. About the time that my Father and Mother, Alex and Margaret, were discussing their future plans, Hannah's baby was due. The birth was severely complicated by a disabling stroke, which hit Hannah at the time of delivery. The baby was healthy and robust and was named Kathleen, after her Liverpool cousin. It appeared, however, that Hannah would not soon, if ever, recover from the effects of the stroke. The doctors told Henry his wife was going to need continuing professional medical help.

Hannah was paralyzed on her right side, causing her arm and leg to become limp and her mouth and tongue to be distorted. Her speech was severely affected, and the effort to decipher her words seemed almost as difficult as it was for her to produce them. Fortunately, her mind was unaffected by the stroke. She remained in the hospital for an extended period and was cared for by the Catholic sisters (nurses). It would be to visitation and Hannah's needs that Margaret would soon be devoted.

Dad enjoyed the work at the church and the teaching and social opportunities, but saw their limitations when viewed in the light of his long-term objectives. His infatuation with Margaret had quickly escalated into something deeper. Alexander Stewart was a man profoundly in love.

Meanwhile, Margaret's fellow workers at Thompson-Belden's were becoming very curious about the possibility of a romance in the making, but her quiet, noncommittal way was disarming and kept them at bay. She would smile while slightly knitting her brows, turn her head a little to one side, and quietly say, "Oh, my goodness!" then turn her attention back to her work.

About this time, Dad saw an opportunity to advance professionally in the Chautauqua movement. He had learned of the acute need for singers and realized his own need to advance his reputation. Chautauqua, a successor to the Lyceum Association, which became popular after the Civil War, engaged in adult education and was a development of the Methodist Episcopal Summer Sunday School Institute. Its courses included programs and lectures in the arts, science, humanities, and religion.

Following considerable discussion with Margaret, Dad terminated his work at the church and registered with the Chautauqua. He made appearances in Nebraska, Kansas, Colorado, Wyoming, Iowa, Illinois, Indiana, and Michigan and was rewarded with thunderous applause wherever he sang. And the separation due to his travels only made his homecomings to Margaret that much sweeter.

At that time, travel by train was tiring. It was also dirty, due to the engine's coal smoke drifting through the open windows. Any glamour there may have been to "show business" quickly paled. Association with fellow performers with crude ways and vile language thwarted the development of meaningful relationships. But Dad's chief objection to life on the road was being separated from Margaret Baird.

In early 1906, Dad proposed marriage, which was accepted. He continued traveling, however, all the while gaining experience and learning the ways of America. During these travels he kept Margaret informed of his whereabouts and his singing successes through his letters. And he looked forward to her letters awaiting his arrival at a particular hotel or posted to General Delivery at his destination. On May 28th, 1906, he wrote:

The Palace Hotel
Pender, Nebraska

My dear Margaret,

This is the first letter I have written to you on this trip and I trust it will be a happy surprise. To give you happiness has for some time past been my greatest joy, and the many hours we have spent together have been among the happiest I have ever passed.

The journey to Pender was very interesting. I met and conversed with a gentleman named Hoag who made himself known, having heard me sing at Unity Church. He is a friend of your Mr. Thompson, and spoke very highly of him. When he left, I found myself alone, so peeled an orange, wishing heartily that you were there to share it. Half an orange would have meant double pleasure.

I arrived at Pender about 4:45, and was met at the train by Mr. Rice, the gentleman who engaged me for the concert. He conducted me to the Palace Hotel. Later I was introduced to the accompanist, with whom I practiced about an hour.

The concert commenced at 8:30, and the church was well filled. My voice was in excellent condition, and I never sang as well before. The audience seemed enthralled and Mr. Rice said it was a very successful performance.

I am about to retire, 11:00, weary but quite happy.

Good-bye, dear, and may we both rest in the Saviour's love.

Affectionately yours, Alex.

Alex and Margaret chose July 16th, 1906, for their wedding date, and much time and conversation centered on that coming event. After considerable thought, they decided to make Chicago their home. Dad went there on several occasions to both survey the city for possible housing and to explore business opportunities. His brother Henry was ready to leave Omaha and settle in Chicago as well, believing that Hannah would fare better there with opportunity for better medical care. After accompanying Henry on a trip to Chicago in early July, Alex wrote to Margaret:

80 Institute Place   Chicago. July 5, 1906

My dear Margaret,

My brother and I reached this city quite safely at eleven o'clock this morning. When you left us last night, Henry had a sick spell at the depot, which lasted about two hours. We took to our sleeper about eleven o'clock but did not sleep very well, so tonight we are rather tired. Henry is taking room and board, but I am only boarding, having found a room for myself on LaSalle Avenue, which is a better sounding address for professional purposes. Chicago is a large and wonderful city. I have wished for you many times, just to see your large eyes open wider at the great sights and busy traffic. It makes me feel that I have been sleeping for two years in Omaha. It has somewhat mystified or stupefied me for the time being. I took a mile walk this evening alone through Lincoln Park. The atmosphere here is very cold indeed, and I wish I had brought a coat with me. Lake Michigan is just like a great ocean. Large steamers and sailing vessels float about just as on the Atlantic. I have taken down some addresses, and located some people whom I shall visit tomorrow. Since our arrival today we have only been resting. Tomorrow I must go after business. I got a new Fedora hat, light colored which I think you will like. It looks well. I hope you do not feel too lonely tonight. Perhaps you have written me a letter to relieve the monotony. You will tell me all about the transactions for the dresses and hat. It would be lovely to have you near tonight, but we can be with each other in thought. I am looking for guidance in my movements tomorrow and know you will not forget me before the Throne. Henry has enclosed a note for Mrs. Stewart which you may take when you visit her.

Good-bye dearest, and with all kind thoughts, I am, most affectionately yours,

Alex.

In the modern vernacular, Dad would be termed a "people person," and although most of his working life in England was restricted to the confines of a printing plant, he obviously had gained an affability among his many friends away from the job and was served well by this trait in the great new adventure of becoming established in the vast Chicago metropolis. Margaret was his daily sounding board and shared in his excitement through the mails. His contacts with leaders in the musical professions came easily, and he once wrote that he was "in the swim of things." The next day he wrote to Margaret:

80 Institute Place
Chicago. July 6th, '06

My dear Margaret,

You will be anxious to know how I got along yesterday. Well, I did some hustling. I saw some gentlemen who gave me a little encouragement regarding prospects for work in Chicago. Later in the day I called on Dr. W. W. Hinshaw of the Chicago Conservatory who asked to hear me sing. He took me into his music room, where I sang "The Perfect Life." My voice was in splendid form, and I sang well. At the close of the song he said I had a most beautiful voice, and my articulation was perfect. He immediately offered me a church position for next Sunday. It is a large Congregational Ch. in the suburbs of Chicago. I am to take my place with the Quartette and sing a solo, for which I shall get $5.00. So you see I have begun to make money already.

Some gentlemen informed me that positions for singers in choirs were hard to get in Chicago, but Dr. Hinshaw said I would have no trouble. Still I find that there is plenty of competition, and things are not so easy as we thought.

One thing I have discovered is that churches do not pay much better than in Omaha. $10. is considered a good price. Some get $15. per Sunday, and only one or two above that. I have begun to wish for a look at Omaha already, with all its superior attractions. You would feel lost in Chicago at first. In fact it will take a long time to become familiar with this city. Everybody lives in flats here. I have not yet seen any small houses like we have in Omaha. The only thing to do at first is to go into furnished apartments either for light housekeeping or to board. Of course I would like a home of my own, but that seems impossible here. Flats of 3 rooms cost about $30. a month and upwards.

As no mail has yet come I am wondering how everything is going with you. I trust you are getting plenty of good rest and food, and are not worrying. Let me know everything when you write. Good-bye dearest, and with a heart full of love I am

    Yours lovingly,
                Alex

Meantime, back in Omaha, Margaret was perhaps busier than most prospective brides, with an added feature to take into account: a honeymoon in England. Preparing for the trip lent an urgency to the preparations by adding travel arrangements to their itinerary. She had much to report in her next letter to Alex and in her beautiful Palmer Method handwriting wrote eight pages on her employer's letterhead:

Thompson, Belden & Co.
Omaha, Neb.

July 7-1906

My Dear Alex:-

Do you think I am cruel not to have written you? I will explain: I was just too lonely to write, but when I got your letter this morning, it left me somewhat. "I look for thee in every flower," that explains.

Well, I will tell you what I have been doing. I sewed until 10:30 Thursday eve. Last night I went to Mrs. Johnson's for the mail and took the music to Mrs. Yeoman and Esther, and went to Mrs. Ochiltree's for some of my things.

When I called at Mrs. Yeoman's she had me sit down for a visit. She was lovely; invited me to come to dinner with you when you returned, and feels very sad that your brother is not so well. She noticed him when he left and thought he looked tired. But I cannot tell you all the praises she had for you, you would be vain, I fear. She thinks your brother is fine but that you are more devoted and very unselfish, and that any man who loved his mother as you did, has all the manliness desired.

I then went to Esther's. She is not with her mother now so I left the music there to be given to her. I think I should have inquired where she lived and given it to her myself. When I called at Mrs. Ochiltree's she was not at home, so did not see her. I played croquet next door for awhile and reached home at nine. I had a good rest and am very well today.

Concerning the dresses, I am waiting until the reduction comes on the silk one then I will have it fitted. I think I can fit everything else myself. I would like to make a gray silk waist for train wear. I can do it for less than $1.00 if I can get to the counter where the silk is to be on sale. That will save wearing the light ones. I think I can make two other waists also, if I leave here in time.

I am thinking a great deal about this trip. I try to imagine how large the ship is and how it is built, the St. Lawrence, Montreal, Chicago, Liverpool, and all the people. I wonder if they will like me. I suppose as well as they could an American girl.

I think I will like Chicago. There is life and bustle there and its size is immense too. I suppose the streets are so filled with vehicles and people one can hardly get across. The Chicago Auditorium is considered a fine building of its kind and you will visit there no doubt. I think you will find it easier comparing Chicago with Liverpool. In size they are more alike, and also in greatness in all business ways from what I have heard.

I don't suppose there are any big concerts now as the season is over. I wish there were so that you could enjoy them.

I was sorry to know your brother was sick again. It was not so serious as the last I hope. Perhaps the cool air will bring him out alright again. Give him my kindest regards.

No Alex dear, I never forget you in prayer nor at any time. I sometimes think if I could for a very short time it would be so lovely to turn my thoughts back to you again, but I can't forget you long enough (I guess I don't want to though).

I must close now, hoping that you will meet with the best success in all things you see and undertake. May the dear Savior guide you with His own tender hand.

> I am yours,
> with love and affection
> Margaret

Undaunted by the apparent magnitude of the undertakings her new life promised, Margaret forged ahead like the trooper she was. She had known little more than rural life on a very small farm, the limitations of her transportation in a close-knit, relatively small urban community, and an occasional summer vacation on her Uncle Beal's farm in Kansas. From the time she left the farm in Florence to enter high school in Omaha and work for room and board in the Roy Brown home, she had had no occasion for viewing new horizons nor for the testing of any possible opportunities. Her extended Elective education at Omaha High School had qualified her for teaching in the Omaha schools, which had been her goal upon graduation in 1903.

Now, at age 23, she would in one grand flurry marry the man of her dreams, visit places she had only heard of or read about, sail the Atlantic to England on a steamship, the size and construction of which she could only guess, and then settle down to a new life in the huge, strange environment of Chicago where she would encounter vast numbers of new people and wonder if they would like her.

I must say that in my total knowledge of Mother, I never knew or heard of anyone who did not like her.

Alex had boarded the train in Omaha bound for Chicago in the late evening of July 4th, 1906. He wrote letters to Margaret on the 5th and 6th and she answered them on the 7th. For a man in love, the elapsed time between their letters stretched to an eternity, a phenomenon he acknowledged in his next missive:

80 Institute Place   Chicago, July 9/06.

My dear Margaret,

> Your long expected letter came this morning. I could not account for the delay, and even your explanation does not clear you altogether. Because you were lonely you thought you must make me lonely too. Why, my dear Margaret you should have done as I did. As soon as I felt lonely I sat down and wrote to you and just felt that I was talking with you, and the sense of your presence made me feel as though you were near.
>
> Your letter is lovely, so full of news and good spirit. I have noted all you say about your visits to the various friends, and it is all very interesting. . . .
>
> Now I shall tell you of my experiences on Sunday. The church I sang

at is a very large Congregational Ch. The choir was composed of four voices only. The soprano and contralto were beautiful singers. The Basso only moderate, but far above any Omaha Basso. The music was very difficult but at the rehearsal I mastered it very well.

The organist was somewhat indifferent toward me at first on Saturday evening. I told him that Dr. Hinshaw said I might sing a solo but he said he had not arranged for any. My heart fell at once, because I knew it was only by my individual work that I could win out.

At about 8 o'clock the practice started. The soprano sang a solo: her voice was grand; full and rich. She sang well. Then Mr. Darling, the organist, asked if I had any music with me, and I gave him "Now the day is Over." He asked me to sing it. At the end of the solo he said, "Mr. Stewart, you have a most beautiful voice and sing fine." I kept quiet, so he went into the vestry, spoke to the minister, and on his return asked me if I would sing that solo at the Sunday evening service. His interest was aroused at once. The minister was then introduced to me and praised my work very highly, as also did the soprano Mrs. Cutler.

Sunday morning came and I arrived at the church in good time. I sang all the music alright and Mr. Darling (organist) said I did fine. Sunday evening the Basso sang "Rocked in the Cradle of the Deep" before the sermon. After the sermon I rose to sing my solo, and felt perfectly at ease. It had been announced in the morning that I would sing a solo at night, and great were the expectations of the people. Well, I started, softly and confidently, and won my audience from the first note. Fans ceased to wave and people turned from easy attitudes to face the platform straight. Not a soul in the church moved while I continued to sing. My voice was in grand form and never before have I realized my power. A dead silence filled the place and my softest notes were distinctly audible at the back of the church. I finished the solo in a whisper on the high G, with the words "In Thy Holy Eyes." The afterlude on the organ was fairly long but I stood motionless to the end of it, and nobody moved. The minister pronounced the Benediction and people moved softly away. The effect was wonderful. . . .

I enclose check for $75. to buy your dresses, etc. Do you think Mrs. Brown would like you to be married at her home? or have you any other suggestions to make along that line? I think however it ought to take place at the home of one of your friends instead of mine.

Do you think also that it ought to take place a day or two before we leave Omaha? Our last day in the city would be a very busy one with the baby Kathleen and Hannah, and looking after baggage. I don't think that my brother will return to Omaha. We shall join him here in Chicago. He is some better today. This climate agrees with him better than Nebraska. I also have felt better since the cold weather ceased, and now the air is lovely.

I have been making enquiries about the residential districts of Chicago and think we shall locate in Englewood, the suburb where I sang Sunday. Nearly everybody lives in flats. How would you like that? Wherever it is I trust we shall have a nice little home.

And now, adieu, Margaret; let me have a reply to this as soon as you can, please. With a heart full of love and longing to see you, I am,

Most affectionately yours,
Alex

Margaret reacted naturally to Alex's discouragement over his prospects for church work and sought to counter it with her words of praise for his performances and possibility for work in other aspects of the music business. In characteristic fashion, she saw the good and positive in those with whom she was close and sought to open their eyes to their own abilities and opportunities. Not one to dwell on the negative, she continued to expound on the plans for their marriage and the trip back to England. The dates of their correspondence indicated their letters were crossing in the mail. While Alex was writing to her on July 9th she was writing to him.

Thompson, Belden & Co.
Omaha, Neb.

Omaha, July 9-'06

Dearest Alex:-

Your letter received this morning. I was sorry to learn you had not received much encouragement regarding the churches but do not get discouraged, because when a man of the position that Mr. Hinshaw holds speaks so highly of your singing it will go much farther, that is, you will be talked about by people of influence. That is not all, as Chicago is one of a number of large cities. Certainly there must be demands for a tenor like you.

I am in excellent health, sleep well and have a fine appetite. Agnes and I took a walk through Kountz Park last evening. It reminded me of the time when you and I sat under the little pavillion and by the water, and I grew very lonely. Sunday was a very long day to me. My brother Paul came to see me in the morning. He wanted to see you and I was sorry you were away. I then went to see Mrs. Stewart. She is as well as usual, but says Sister Josephine is not agreeable. I did not go to see my mother. I had to go to the hospital first and then it was too hot to attempt the journey. . . .

So you can see it was a long day. The girls at the house kept reminding me that this was just a beginning. The weather has been cool and pleasant here until Sunday, and it is very warm today. I hope it will keep cool in Chicago for awhile. It is so much better for your health as well as your brother's. Tell him that everything goes well here and that Mrs. Stewart is waiting patiently for the journey to begin. I am sure I would feel lost in Chicago until I had become acquainted with the city. Bertha has been there and says there are no small houses until one reached the suburbs and I suppose they are very expensive. I think Dr. Hinshaw likes you very much. If you make as many friends there as here you will be a favorite. Perhaps there will be other things besides the churches for you, I mean additional to the churches.

It will not be long until I see you for a long talk, and then you can tell me of your experiences.

I hope you are in pleasant quarters for your rest means much to you. Hoping for success to you in every way, I will close.

With kindest thoughts and a heart full of love,

> Yours affectionately,
> Margaret

Two days later Margaret wrote another letter to him at the Institute Place address in Chicago, which was returned to his room at 2103 Locust Street in Omaha, as he had already vacated and left for Omaha and final preparations for their wedding on the 16th. With his absence, wedding arrangements were almost entirely left in her hands; she appears to have handled them all in good order.

> Thompson, Belden & Co.
> Omaha, Neb.

> July 11,'06
> Wednesday Morn.

My Dear Alex:-

Your letter arrived yesterday morning. I was so glad to know how well you sang on Sunday. I think the people felt the power of your voice as I have. They knew how to appreciate it better than the people here. Your description was very interesting. I could just see the fans stop waving, the attention turned to the platform and you standing there so lovely. It makes the tears come when I think of the way the organist treated you at first, but of course his treatment afterwards made things alright. And it seems that it would strengthen his praise afterwards; to have him in the spirit he was at first and then to make him change to the gratefulness and appreciation he showed.

. . . You certainly must have been very popular with them. I do think the organist was very enthusiastic over your singing. You have always thought the people here did not appreciate it and I think you will have reason to think so more than ever now.

The effect it had on the people at the close was grand and I would liked to have been there. You remember I have said that your singing should come after the sermon, for I think the effect is beautiful when produced as you did on Sunday.

Do you think I should get a trunk now? I had thought best to leave it till the last of the week, as Mrs. Smalley and the girls are very suspicious. They have told me that all that was missing was the steamer ticket. I would not deceive them in any way but just agree with them and treat it as a joke. The people at the store have told me that I was going to be married so all I can do is say, "It looks that way" and say no more. Harold Thompson thinks I act the part fine.

I think as you do it would be more proper, or rather customary for the marriage to take place at the home of one of my friends.

. . . I have thought of Mrs. Patton, that is the young Mrs. Patton, where I stayed. I think she would feel quite honored as she likes you, and speaks very highly of you. I am quite sure Mrs. Smalley would have no objections, if that would do. Lets ask the Ochiltrees?

The church makes it quite public or that would be open for consideration.

I think we ought not leave it till the last day. Perhaps the day before would be better. We leave here about the seventeenth do we not?

I was out to the hospital last night. Mrs. Stewart is fine but is anxious to have you come back. Sister Josephine talked with me and says she is much better when your brother is not where she is, and I think myself it is true but also better for him. I am glad he is feeling better and do not urge him to come back to Omaha but try and keep him there if possible until we reach Chicago. I am afraid he will have another bad spell if he helps with the starting and baggage.

I think the suburban part of Chicago would be lovely but of course it is whatever circumstances would allow. I could make a home for you any place, my dear. The house is not the home always.

The weather is very hot here yesterday and today, but we keep cool in the office. I am going to quit tonight, I think. I must go to the hospital again and have lots to do.

I will close now, dear one, hoping you may be successful, and that God grant you a safe return.

With best wishes and all the love that this heart of hearts can give.

Yours Affectionately
Margaret.

Alex had been away for almost two weeks, making this reunion the sweetest of them all. Arrangements for the wedding would be finalized as they sandwiched in packing for their honeymoon trip to England and the preparation of Hannah and baby Kathleen. Alex's brother Henry had arranged for Hannah and Kathleen to go back to England for

Alexander Cameron Stewart,
July 16, 1906.

Margaret Elouise Baird Stewart,
July 16, 1906.

an indefinite stay with Hannah's brother, Henry Jones and his wife Alice and their children, Harold, Kathleen, and Reginald. This would afford Henry Stewart time and opportunity to get more permanently situated in his work in Chicago.

Mr. and Mrs. Patton were very pleased to have the marriage take place in their fashionable Omaha home and expended every effort for its success. Margaret had worked diligently in the preparation of her clothing and the securing of travel gear for the greatest adventure of her life.

Dad was equally engaged in his personal preparation as his wedding picture would indicate. His attire was immaculate, every hair in its proper place and parted in the middle, which was quite fashionable for the time. He wore a black bow tie over a high stiff, straight collar, swallow-tail coat and gray-striped trousers. His pince-nez glasses added a touch of his professionalism to the ensemble. He no doubt had worn or would wear this attire at future singing appearances. Oddly, the pictures of Dad as a young person in England and family and business photos before my arrival on the scene never pictured him with a middle of the head part; but he did maintain the brushed back wave on the left side. I have never been too fond of the wedding picture. Though he was groomed and attired conventionally according to the formal dress of the day, to my generation's notion such apparel and hair styling made him look rather "pretty," a contradiction to masculinity. But he was definitely all man, a total gentleman.

The great wedding day arrived and was well described in the Tuesday, July 17th, 1906, edition of the Omaha *Morning World Herald* newspaper. Wedding photos of the bride and groom accompanied the announcement:

SOCIETY WEDDING

Baird - Stewart

The marriage of Miss Margaret Elouise Baird, daughter of Mrs. Harriet Baird of Florence and Mr. Alexander Cameron Stewart, was solemnized Monday evening at 8 o'clock at the residence of Mr. & Mrs. F. C. Patton, 2413 Bristol Street. The Rev. Mr. McBride, pastor of the Central Presbyterian church, assisted by Dr. Patton, performed the ceremony. Mrs. M. M. Loomis played Mendelssohn's wedding march and the bridal pair stood in the bay window of the drawing room, which had been converted into a bower of smilax, ferns, white carnations and plumosis asparagus. The groom was tended by his best man, Mr. David Sharp of Liverpool, England and the bride by her maid of honor, Miss Helen Eller. The bride wore a beautiful gown of deep cream taffeta trimmed with real valenciennes lace and carried a shower bouquet of bride's roses. Miss Eller wore a pale blue mull with valenciennes lace trimming. Her bouquet was a shower of sweet peas. The house was profusely decorated. The drawing room was in green and white carnations and feverfew; the library in pink and white carnations and roses and the dining room in sweet peas and asparagus fern. The table had a cover of lace and a center piece of sweet peas.

The bridal gifts were many and costly. Mr. Stewart, who is a distinguished tenor, late of Liverpool, England, is director of music in the Central United Presbyterian church and the Knox Street Presbyterian church. The bridal pair left immediately for the east and are booked to sail from Montreal July 21 on the Manitoba. On their arrival in Liverpool they will be tendered a large reception at the home of the groom, later going to London. After touring Great Britain Mr. & Mrs. Stewart will travel extensively through France, Switzerland and Italy. In Italy Mr. Stewart will remain for some time to make a special study of voice culture. October 1 Mr. & Mrs. Stewart sail for America from Naples.

Whoever was the author of this announcement must have seized on some casual conversation or some expressed hope voiced by Margaret or Alex. There was no mention of the fact that brother Henry's invalid wife Hannah and infant daughter Kathleen would be accompanying them to Liverpool from Omaha, that they would take the Chicago & Northwestern Railroad to Chicago for a brief visit with Henry before boarding the Grand Trunk and Western for Montreal, and that Dad did not have a home in Liverpool. And I don't remember Mother ever saying anything about having been to Switzerland or Italy, though she might have visited Paris on this trip. Of course these details would not enhance the announcement so, if known, were left unsaid. Nor did they sail for America from Naples.

With Dad's great voice and flare for showmanship, he was most always appointed as entertainment chairman for the passengers in his travel class, or at least a performer on one or more programs. These gatherings were often in the form of concerts, and on their return trip on the SS *Parisian*, a Grand Concert was held at sea on Friday evening, September 21, 1906, at 8:15 p.m. The all-passenger performance included five or six singers, a cornet solo, banjo and violin solos, and two recitations. In "Part One," Dad was number two on the program and sang "M'Gregor's Gathering." In "Part Two" Dad was the first on the program and sang "Lady Moon." Of 15 performers, Dad was the only one who appeared twice. The program was concluded with the entire company singing "God Save Our Gracious King" and "America, My Country, 'Tis of Thee."

This was a benefit concert for "The Sailors' Orphan Society of Scotland" with a collection taken for the society's benefit.

Dad's return to England was perhaps nothing short of heroic, at least in the eyes of his many friends and relatives. There were receptions in Liverpool and its environs, and the best in fare and service were generously offered. All who knew him were eager to see him again and learn firsthand of his life and successes in his new world across the Atlantic, but they could hardly contain themselves at the prospect of meeting the beautiful American girl who had captured his heart. His old friend Charles Quayle immediately characterized her as "queenly" and so addressed her and for the rest of his life, referred to her as "Queen Margaret."

There were aunts, uncles, and cousins in Scotland to be visited, and their receptions easily matched the outpouring of welcome to the newlyweds. They journeyed to Glasgow to meet those on his father's side, then to his mother's people in Aberdeen. All the while, Margaret maintained her sweet composure, showed her genuine interest in their lives, their homes, and families. Her sincerity was as captivating as her gentle laughter and brilliant smile. As Dad once wrote of her, "Margaret publishes her beautiful nature and bountiful goodness in her face, irresistible to all."

The newlyweds had deposited Hannah and Kathleen with Hannah's brother Henry Jones at his fine home in Liverpool, not knowing that it would be three years before Henry would be financially able and physically equipped to come from Chicago for them. Nonetheless, mother and daughter fared well in the Joneses' home.

Almost two months elapsed from their sailing date from Montreal until they boarded the SS *Parisian* for the return trip to America. It had been a great time for them and Margaret was overwhelmed by Alex's vast roster of friends and their open expressions of love and interest in his new life and the adventures he was experiencing. And likewise they embraced Margaret and drew her into their exclusive fellowship. There were some 50 relatives and friends at dockside to say goodbye and wish them a *bon voyage*.

The return trip retraced their journey to England and they docked at Montreal. From there, the Grand Trunk and Western took them to Chicago, where they stopped for a few days to select and confirm the renting of a partially furnished flat in the 300 block of North LaSalle Avenue south of Maple Avenue. Again, the Chicago & Northwestern took them to Omaha, where they packed their belongings for the return to Chicago.

In Omaha, the Thompsons and Beldens staged a generous going-away party, which was attended by their many friends and Margaret's few relatives. A collection of cards and letters attests to their love for Margaret and their admiration for Alex.

The next morning the couple boarded the train for Chicago. Standing on the rear platform of the observation car, they waved goodbye to the assembled crowd of well wishers. In his characteristic style, Alex burst into song. With his arm around Margaret's slender waist and looking into her moist eyes he sang, "She's a Bonnie Wee Lassie." He kissed her, then turned to the crowd and sang "Auld Lang Syne." Then before the crowd could react, he sang, "Till We Meet Again." Now the people released their emotions, cheering and crying, a response Margaret never forgot.

The train whistle gave out with two mighty blasts signaling its readiness for departure. The conductors retrieved their step-stools, waved the all-clear to the engineer, climbed aboard, and closed the doors. The train began to move, but Alex and Margaret remained on the observation deck waving their last farewells until the train was lost from view.

It was an emotional time for Margaret, as tears welled up in those sparkling brown eyes. Omaha, and before that the small close-by community of Florence, had been her home for 17 of her 23 years. So much had taken place since that day in 1889 when she left the Missouri River bottoms where she had dispatched the begging Indians. She had grown from a feisty five-year-old to a beautiful, charming bride with no room in her heart for regret, no remorse. Dabbing at her tears with the delicate lace kerchief that she carried tucked into the sleeve of her gray silk traveling dress, she turned to Dad and with a broad smile said, "Well, here we go Dearie, what's next?"

Chapter 4

Omaha — Chicago

ROTHER HENRY MET THE TRAIN in Chicago and helped make arrangements for delivery of Alex's and Margaret's belongings to the La Salle Avenue flat. In a few days they were settled in their home, the first of several rental units they would occupy before buying the old Victorian-styled house on the South Side in the Woodlawn area near Jackson Park. They bought some additional furniture — a mahogany table, a used upright piano and swivel-seat stool, and a large, mahogany rocking chair.

When Margaret asked Alex, "What's next, Dearie?" she was not yet aware that she would soon answer her own question. It was early October 1906 and a doctor confirmed her suspicion that she was pregnant. They decided the rocking chair purchase was a wise investment, and indeed it was. Not only did Margaret nurture her six babies in it over the next 18 years, but it would survive to lull to sleep her first two visiting grandchildren, Susan and Sharron. It would serve in like capacity in Susan's Walkerton, Indiana, farm home for her six children and her several grandchildren. At last report, the rocker still squeaks, as always.

Dad had launched into his profession as a voice teacher, renting time in a shared studio in the downtown Auditorium Building, which also housed a theater and a hotel. He eventually rented his own suite, #706, when his volume of business warranted. Some of his clientele were visiting opera stars who sought him for coaching in operas to be performed in the Auditorium theater.

These were the days before electronic amplifiers, and the Auditorium was famous for its outstanding acoustics, which made it so desirable for operatic performances. Dad's coaching work attracted the attention of some opera companies, and he was chosen as lead tenor in two or three productions, though he declined to accept the offer of traveling with one company, as it would take him away from home and his developing family.

Dad's most commanding interest was in teaching, and it was in this area that he concentrated his greater efforts. His Liverpool experience in printing and its adjunct of advertising came into play as he appealed to prospective singers through small ads in the Musical Instruction sections of the evening newspapers, the Chicago *Daily News* and the Chicago *Herald and Examiner*. Over time he developed an advertising plan that would survive for most of his career, contracting for three months of daily inserts twice each year. The three- or four-line ads were effective in their simplicity, and productive. He discovered the value of consistent exposure as compared to the larger Sunday splash insertions practiced by his competitors. His were always "blind" ads, never revealing his name, but showing only a newspaper box number. Other teachers would often complain about how newspaper ads were a waste of money, sometimes quizzing Dad; he would simply smile, nod his head, but give no reply. He was not about to reveal his method for obtaining a regular flow of new students.

Coupled with teaching were the opportunities for community concert and recital performances and singing engagements in some of the larger churches. It seems he had, for many years, a church choir or music director's job, most of the time being the featured tenor soloist.

On June 4th, 1907, Margaret Alexandra Stewart was born at home. (Reviewing her personal papers after her death in 1992, I found that in her twenties she had her middle name legally changed to Florence. No reason was shown. I suppose she disliked the name Alexandra.) With the advent of a second Margaret into the family, it was now time for the "Omaha Margaret" to be known to the family as Mother. Baby Margaret was the joy of their lives, and Dad was as devoted as any father could be.

It soon was evident that a larger flat away from the noise and confusion of near-downtown Chicago would be desirable. They chose a first-floor apartment at 233 South Waller Avenue, on the west side of Chicago in the Austin area, and made the move in October 1907. Being out in a neighborhood also made it more convenient for access to Dad's church work.

Though his teaching schedule was growing, Dad had time for occasional out-of-town performances and responded to Chautauqua invitations for special evangelistic programs in Illinois and Michigan. Included was a series of services in November 1907. As usual, he wrote to Mother on a regular basis, always with the clearest evidence of his love and devotion.

THE PHOENIX HOTEL

Pontiac, Illinois   November 14th, 1907

My dear Margaret,

It is just 10 o'clock, the meeting is over, I have left Gray and am now settling down to have a chat with you my dearie. I guess baby is sleeping. God bless her little heart, and keep her well that she may smile sunshine into our hearts for many years to come.

I wonder why we have so many blessings together. Even when clouds do come we seem to see sunshine through them and neither of us are ever unhappy. Contentment is the source of all happiness and we strive day by day to be satisfied, and not to expect too great things.

Well Margaret God has given me a wonderful gift of song and my heart is too full tonight to tell you how I sang. All I can say is that my voice & health & spirits were better than I ever knew them to be before.

. . . I called for Gray, and we walked to the M. E. Church, a fine large auditorium like the First M. E. Omaha. Was introduced to the organist & Mr. North the conductor.

The former played the pipe organ splendidly & I had nothing to fear. North is the best conductor I have ever seen. He is not at all musical, but he gets the people to sing like to split their throats. The choir is splendid, & the church was almost full — about 500. In the song service I sang "I have Read of a Beautiful City" & the effect was just what you can imagine. The soft notes just thrilled (as one lady remarked to me) and my big voice was perfectly easy. After the reading I sang "Face to Face," never sang it better. Gray preached a good & telling sermon. . . . His manner is light, but effective.

In the after meeting I sang "O Where is My Boy Tonight" which accorded with the sentiment of his sermon.

The meeting was a good one, and many nice things were said about the new singer.

I am going now to mail this, and then go upstairs to eat the lunch you put up for me. I wasn't hungry on the train. Good-bye, dearie; a thousand kisses to our darling & may the Father bless us all. Good-night,

Affectionately
Alex

The services at Pontiac were perhaps similar in scope to a Baptist Revival, though it was held in the fall and for a three-day weekend. As was customary, Dad wrote again on the 15th and 16th.

November 15th, 1907

My dear Margaret,

I have been thinking and talking about you and baby all day. Interest in my work and self is completely aroused, and when I speak to some people whom I have not spoken to before, they ask about my baby, showing that they have been making inquiry. How I wish they could see my two babies, & how I wish you and baby were here. Everything and everybody is so pleasant. I never spent a happier time, and you could easily have been here too, as the accommodation at the hotel is fine & the meals elegant. This morning I rose at 7:30 & took a good breakfast at eight. Nice bacon & eggs, toast, coffee & grapes for dessert. I felt so selfish that you were not with me enjoying the good things.

After breakfast I took a walk with Gray & the Y.M.C.A. secretary. Took a splendid dinner at the home of one of the pastors, and at 3 o'clock conducted a meeting for women; at 4 o'clock I conducted a meeting for children and did well.

Had a fine supper at the Hotel at 6:30 — oyster stew, sirloin steak, baked potato, toast, tea and cake.

At 7:30 the song service began conducted by Mr. North. Church was crowded long before the service started. I sang "Dream of Paradise" with wonderful effect, and was in better form than last night, if possible. Just before the service I sang "Ninety & Nine," which created a deep impression. Gray preached a strong sermon with good results. At the after meeting I sang "O Don't You Hear Him Knocking:" and a few words from Gray brought a wonderful meeting to a close.

Gray and I got on very well together. At the afternoon meeting a gentleman came to me and spoke about my singing. He turned out to be the manager for the great evangelist Billy Sunday. He wants me to join the forces of this man, as he is always on the lookout for men of distinctly exceptional gifts. I may go with him to Bloomington, Illinois in December, and would like to take you and baby along too. I don't know now what to think of free tuition.

Your welcome letter came this A.M. You say you miss me very much: I miss you equally my sweetheart. Glad to hear that baby is so well. I trust you posted the letters. I got the mail & also the black tie. It was fortunate you sent it as the one I had came to pieces last night & I had to pin it. I hope you get along safely at Ulrichs.

I may mention a recital here, or perhaps write in a month or so, and I'm sure it would take well. I have not caught cold in this strange bed. In fact, I never slept in a softer bed in my life. But I miss my dearie. Tomorrow is our day off, but Sunday will be very busy.

They are calling for mail.

Good-bye, kisses for both.
Affectionately, Alex

Dad was certainly flattered to be invited to join the famous Billy Sunday organization, which would be akin to the modern-day Billy Graham Crusade organization. He discussed it further in his next letter on the 16th.

November 16th, 1907

My dear Margaret,

These are surely the happiest days of my life and I'm so glad you are with me to enjoy them. The building up of business is very fine when our Father is the Guide, and grateful I am that I ever said — "Jesus, Saviour Pilot Me." I look back on the past and see very few blunders. True I have not risked much, but guidance has been given in all matters, leaving nothing to regret. God's best gift to me was your dear self, to sweeten my life and fill it with love, to teach me gentleness and kindness and unselfishness, in fact to make me more of a man in every way. You are an artist in these things, for true art is to conceal art, and you do this naturally. You have a lot to teach me yet, so don't give up.

Well I got your letter this forenoon which you wrote on Friday morning. I would have felt more comfortable if you had sent one at night, as I wanted to know if you got home safely from Ulrichs, but I guess you were too tired to write after the long day's visit. Although I am writing this Saturday night you will not receive it until Monday morning, but you will be glad to have it, as I leave here at 10:30, and will not be home till afternoon. I may go to the dentist upon arrival in Chicago to have the plate fitted.

This has been an easy day. Just resting & walking around the town. It is a pretty little place. Gray is very agreeable, but my work has taken his breath away. Everybody is talking Stewart. One pastor told him that he was held up many times during the day in the street, and showered with questions about the singer.

The fact is Gray had a successful time before I came, but the effect now is simply overwhelming. He had good meetings on the two Sundays, but audiences fell off during the week. When I came on Thursday there was a fair number, but Friday, usually the poorest meeting of the week, the church was simply packed out & crowds turned away.

Two society ladies called at the hotel today & asked to hear me sing. I sang "I'm Wear'in Awa," "Just a Wearing," "Still Unexprest" etc. One of them takes lessons in Chicago every week. She sang for me & sang well too. A great swell & real pretty, about 20 years of age. I could easily get a class here if I wanted it, but I'm afraid if Sunday wants me to go with him, I'll have to go & give up teaching.

He could pay well & that would enable me to take you and baby & Beauty [the dog] along & still have money to send to Henry and also to save. I would expect at least $400.00 a month plus all expenses. I don't know what Gray will pay me but he expects between $200.00 & $300.00

for the two weeks. If he realizes this amount I will look for $50.00. I think I can get a recital here in a few weeks.

Now good-bye dearie, kiss our angel a thousand times for Papa. My heart is just bursting to embrace you and hug my baby. Tomorrow I sing all day. Monday morning I travel, Monday afternoon I shall be in your arms.

Your affectionate - Alex

Thus ended all conversation and recorded information of Dad's involvement with the Billy Sunday organization. Certainly his love of family, the powerful call he possessed for teaching, and his need to establish a more secure and enduring source of income influenced his decision to decline the offer. And though he would not so classify the Billy Sunday people as such, he knew he could not avoid being cast into unsavory relationships with theatrical performers of questionable habit and character.

Was Dad Puritanical? Perhaps, but I never thought so. He had his moral and ethical standards. In my years before leaving home for the Army, I never knew him to lie, steal, cheat, swear, tell dirty stories, gamble, drink alcohol, make suggestive remarks or gestures, or commit any other offense that would discredit his name or character. Caught in a profane encounter, he would quickly excuse himself. He had no time for non-beneficial discourse. Nor did I ever know him to preach to or in anyway chastise offenders. And he was almost painfully honest, going to considerable lengths to correct a wrong, especially if the error was in his favor.

Asked by friends and acquaintances if any of his children were inclined toward music, he would reply that he had never encouraged them to pursue such a career, not wanting them to endure or have to deal with the associations that such involvement would demand. Of course, he could only speak from his limited experiences and was aware that these elements were present in all walks of life.

During the ensuing years, Dad maintained his contacts with the Chautauqua and periodically accepted singing engagements in distant cities. His reputation grew and requests were fulfilled when he could blend them in with his Chicago church work and his teaching schedule. This proved a worthy source of extra income and often provided opportunity for putting on recitals and other appearances in the towns where he served.

In the early years in Chicago he served in Presbyterian, Baptist, Episcopal, Congregational, and Methodist churches on short-term invitations. He also served the St. James Episcopal Congregation for several years and was Choir Master at the Catholic Holy Name Cathedral for many years. There is no record that he ever served as a cantor in a Jewish congregation, but he certainly had the musical wherewithal to do so. His direct involvement in church work virtually ended in 1927, though he continued to instruct and guide his students in their respective church music endeavors.

The addresses on a large accumulation of old letters indicate that Alex and Margaret made several moves on the west side of Chicago. From Waller Avenue the family moved to North Austin Boulevard, to 52nd Avenue, and finally to 5322 West Madison Street. Seventeen months after baby Margaret was born, a second daughter, Jean Cameron Stewart, put in an appearance on November 14th, 1908. Jean's middle name of Cameron, however, never became a reality. At the time of her infant baptism it was given as Ellen and was without a family precedent.

Dad's teaching business prospered and an old savings bank passbook showed weekly entries that totaled over $7,700 during a 14-month period. Though he had had a checking account before they were married, there was no evidence that he ever used one afterward. Most of the time he was paid in cash by his voice students, and he found it convenient to pay his bills in like manner. The balance in excess of projected needs was, per his habit, faithfully deposited in the savings account.

Whatever the motivation for doing so, he and Mother and the two girls took a trip to England. They sailed from Montreal on Friday, July 30th, 1909, aboard the Allan Line's SS *Corsican* to Liverpool. The Second Cabin passenger list included: Mr. Cameron Stewart (Dad used his middle name professionally), Mrs. Stewart and Infant, Miss Margaret Stewart, and Mr. Henry Stewart. Dad's brother Henry chose this time to visit England and bring wife Hannah and child Kathleen back to America.

In spite of Hannah's disability, Henry rented a third-floor flat at 1039 East Marquette Road. Hannah's old wicker-style wheelchair was kept parked under the first-floor stairway in the street-level entry. Taking her out was quite a chore. Henry finally had landed a fine position with the Chicago Association of Commerce, heading up its membership and fund-raising activity. His title was quite lengthy, and Dad often commented that he should have had a double glass door, adequate to handle the cumbersome wording lettered in gold leaf.

Finally, on July 10th, 1910, Alex and Margaret's first boy was born and was named Cameron Stewart, without a middle name. He was born at the Madison Street address. No doubt the rapidly growing family required more space, which probably accounted for the frequent moves.

Like most doting young parents, Dad applied fond nicknames to his children. Margaret became Margie, and the name stuck with Dad for the rest of his life. Jean was referred to as Sitter, slang for Sister, which did not stick; and Cameron became Boy, sometimes enlarged to Boydie. For years, if Dad was calling Cameron to get up for school or work he would stand at the foot of the stairs in the old house and sing out, "Ah, Boy." Cameron hated it. At all other times Dad called him Cameron.

With Dad's teaching business and his family growing, more mobility was required than public transportation could provide. He had become quite Americanized and decided to buy his first automobile, a 1912 Cadillac. The car agency had shown him how to drive it in forward mode, and he proudly brought it home to the Madison Street flat. The building had been constructed before the advent of the automobile and was equipped with a horse-and-carriage barn at its side, which would now serve as a garage. Dad parked the car in the barn and was delighted to show it off to all the neighbors. The next day he started the engine and put the car in gear. He was shocked when it leaped forward and mildly crashed into the wall of the barn. He was very upset, called the car agency, and had them come and take the car back. They had failed to show him how to drive it in reverse. He didn't drive for a whole year.

About this time, the physical strain of having three children in three years had exacted a price on Mother's health and she was apparently in need of a rest and a change of scenery. Her mother also was ailing and she had invited Mother and the children to visit her in Florence. After six years of marriage, the love Mother and Dad shared for each other was as vibrant as ever. On October 21th, 1912, Dad wrote:

> I know you're way off yonder
> But still you seem with me,
> And in the evening shadows
> Your form I almost see.
> I almost hear you whisper,
> These words - "I love but you,"
> And soon we'll be united,
> Sweetheart, be brave, be true.

Yes Dear Margaret, although you're a long way off, I have not felt real lonely, because I have felt all along that your thoughts were with me. This is all that is worth anything in life: I remember, the first song I was taught at school, when a very little child, began with these words —
"One true heart to know and love me,"
"Is the only gem I crave."
and you my sweetest are the one who was given to me as the most precious of all gems. The longing of my heart you were sent to fill, and you have been a good wife, and a lovely mother. And we are only at the beginning of things yet: we are only realizing what true love means, and I suppose we shall never sound the depths or reach the heights until we see the Author of love. But dearie, haven't we had a lovely six years together, your first thought has been for me and mine has been for you. The years fly because they are filled with joy, and these beautiful children have come to complete our happiness, and we lose ourselves in them, thinking of them, dreaming and planning for them, and yet all the while we are deepening our own affection for each other. When I am alone, either day or evening, it is so nice to feel that you are with me in spirit, and Oh! how I am looking forward to the time when I shall clasp my dearie in my arms, and look upon a beautiful, healthy, strong, happy woman. Don't be impatient about returning, but be very diligent about getting all the good possible out of your trip. I want to see the modest, blushing Margaret Baird of old; the sweet, simple, honest lassie that fairly broke my stubborn heart without knowing it. Get well and strong again like you used to be, don't be afraid to spend a little on extras that you would fancy, because this is the chance of your life to regain your old vim. We'll have lots of time for courting when you get well, and it will be so nice to hear you say that you are as well as ever you were in your life. But it will not be done all at once:

I am only expecting that you will lay in a good foundation during the weeks at Florence, and do some up-building when you return. We'll all try and be good to you, because you are our most valuable treasure.

Now about Margie: perhaps you should see someone while you are at Omaha, or leave it until you return and we'll go direct to Dr. Shafer.

The money you have accounted for has been well spent, and I don't want your mother to suffer in pocket at all by your presence with the children.

I am sending another check for $10.00 to Bertha.

It is just time to leave the studio now, and as I want to mail this downtown I'll have to stop right here. Uncle Henry sends love to all.

Love to my dear little Margie, and my sweet little Jean and my Boydie. Tell them Daddy is always thinking of them, and likes to get their kisses.

Good-bye all: remember me very kindly to Grandma.

Lovingly,
Poppie

One year later, Dad had recovered from the wall-banging incident and bought a new 1913 Ford. The original invoice shows he paid $615 plus an extra $35 for a self-starter package. It was equipped with carbide gas-burning headlights and parking and taillights, all powered from a central carbide gas-generating unit mounted on the running board. He later bought an electric lighting system. The old carbide lights became souvenirs and hung in their storage place from the basement rafters in the old house for many years.

The Ford provided great mobility for the family and was used extensively for recreation ventures to various city parks and vacation trips to Wisconsin and Michigan. Lake Geneva, Wisconsin, became Mother's and Dad's favorite destination and remained so for most of their lives before World War II.

Making trips to the southeast side of Chicago to visit Henry and Hannah revealed new territory to them, and they became enamored with the Jackson Park area. Their next move was to 6320 Blackstone Avenue, just one block from the park.

Although Dad's business was doing quite well, he responded to invitations by the Chautauqua organization to participate in the 1914 Summertime series. Mother was now expecting again, after a four-year reprieve from having babies. The extra money would be helpful in their plans to buy a home. As usual, they kept in touch with one another by mail. Dad wrote:

Parke Hotel
Rockville, Indiana   Sunday August 16, 1914

My dear Margaret,

I have been with you all today, and as I have had nothing do this morning, have had plenty of time to think of you.

There is a little boy just like Boydie here and I have been hugging him and playing with him a good deal. But he isn't like our Boydie. Have been thinking about Margie's cough. If Dr. Shafer does not come home soon, like her examined before she returns to school, just plan accordingly.

Jean I guess is alright, and Daddy would just like to have them all here, scrambling over my neck and shoulders.

I hope you are going to rest up a bit. Don't do too much sewing, it is hard on your back. You can get to bed early now, and you don't have to get up at eleven oclock for my supper.

But Lassie, its nice to see you at the end of the day, even if you are sleepy, and how I wish you were here with me, to get your advice and opinion on my singing.

I sent you a card from Terre Haute. After lunch we came on to Rockville, a neat little town, something like Crown Point, but smaller.

Had supper at this hotel and enjoyed a very good meal. Then we got ready for the evening concert, where I made my first appearance in Chautauqua.

The Auditorium was very large, seating about 3,000 people. The choruses went very well, but the solo voices sounded quite small. The singing was beautiful, but far above the heads of the audience.

The receptions were very poor, and the applause meager. My turn came just before the last chorus, but many people had left the hall. They had had ten hours of it that day so I guess they were sick of it.

I sang "M'Appari" from the opera Martha, and the "Dearest, Sweetest Story Ever Told."

My voice was grand, I never sang better. My high notes easy and flexible. The high A and B flat were brilliant and quite easy. I had no sign of being nervous or afraid. I don't think I'll sing in Italian again in this kind of work.

Tonight I am down to sing the "Holy City," and believe it will be the best selection.

We leave here tonight for Ludington, Michigan. You can write to me there — C. Stewart, Cathedral Choir, General Delivery, Ludington, Michigan.

I believe we have to come through Chicago Monday morning to get to Lud. and if so I shall call you up. I may be able to come from Lud. to Chicago, and stay home one or two days, before going to Pana, Illinois. I hope I can, and we will have a good time together. We sing at Ludington on Monday night.

The life is very easy, strolling around all day waiting for the evening concert. The small town is pleasant and peaceful, and the people nice and agreeable.

The meals at this place are fine home cooking. John B. Miller and Arthur Middleton were here this week, and the bass made a great hit. The tenor seems to be considered the weak end of the quartet. Leanora Allen and Rose Gannon were with them; so I'm in the swim.

I must add something humorous to my repertoire. I guess you will get this Monday.

Good-bye for the present — kisses for all my babies — and daddy's love.

I hope you will see Henry, Hannah and Kathleen.

Good bye,
Daddy

Dad arrived in Ludington and his first letter to Mother revealed that he was tiring of the grind of travel, of meeting the demands and the associations of the stage.

The Stearns   August 18, 1914
Ludington, Michigan

My dear Margaret,

This is the first morning I wakened homesick. You don't know how I long for your dear self; and to have no noisy babies jumping on my bed seemed so strange.

Your face would be so welcome now and your soft voice so grateful. As I think of it, you have the softest speaking voice I have ever heard, and I just love it. And you have a way with you that is all your own, and I hope I shall never get so used to it that I will miss its sweetness.

You must take the greatest care of yourself, 'cos you are very valuable and indispensable to us.

I was down on the shore this morning watching the youngsters and adults bathing. Boydie would have been in his glory. The water was lovely and warm, the air fresh, and very few people. It would do you good to be here, and Margie would take on new life and color. But I don't worry much about the children, I just want you to get strong, and if possible to get more rest, even if we pay more for help, because you don't seem to have much leisure except when we go in the car.

The concert last night was a great success and while the audience and auditorium was much smaller than at Rockville, the reception was much more cordial. We were all very tired however, as we were on the train from 10:20 on Sunday night, until 6:00 PM Monday night. We just had time to eat, clean up and get away to the show.

Although I was tired, I sang well. "I Hear You Calling Me," and "Jean," were my two numbers and I could have given an encore. My soft tones in the first number were fine.

I got a good rest last night, slept fine, and ate a sumptuous breakfast.

The meals here are great. I have to go now, hurriedly, as a call has come for me.

Lovingly to Margie, Jean, Boy and You,
Pap

Dad had about a week at home before leaving for another series of concerts. He wrote a short note to Mother.

Commercial Hotel   August 27, 1914
King City, Mo.

My dear Margaret,

I have just a minute to write you before catching a train. We leave King City now for Macomb, Illinois and expect to put in a long journey on the train.

I don't like the long jumps, and I just hate the company I am in. I shall be so glad to get home to my dear ones, and hear some good clean language. I enjoyed your letter and got your postal this morning. Hope Jean is better. Shall write you from Macomb, or Camp Point, Illinois.

Love to all
Daddy

The grind of "show business" was taking its toll on Dad, and it became obvious that being away from home and his loved ones was too great a price to pay for whatever compensation he received. The last letter he wrote bore this out and also indicated his disenchantment with local church music jobs. In spite of his considerable talent and the sacred musical ministry aspect of his work, there always seemed to be a low limit that churches would pay. But it was, and still is, traditional that church musicians came from the ranks of music teachers and other professions, and that the church jobs were always considered to be supplemental sources of income. He wrote:

Hotel Pace   August 27, 1914
Macomb, Illinois

My dear Margaret,

You never looked so good to me as you will when I get back next Monday.

Margaret Baird fills a larger place in my heart than either of us realized, and I am looking eagerly to the hour when I shall hold you again in my arms.

This tour has been so full of disappointment that life would not be worth living except for the prospect of coming to a real home, with a real wife and real babies all my very own. I am so proud of you all, and yet nobody wants to hear about you.

However I must not spoil my letter by reciting all the miseries of this trip, we shall have lots of time to talk it over.

We got into Macomb at 3:30 this morning, after traveling all night on the train. I did not sleep much at the hotel, but got up before eight and had breakfast. All the others slept late.

It is now 3:00 PM and the rain has poured down incessantly. They have all gone to the afternoon concert, but I thought I would stay here and write, as I did not have to appear.

I guess I'll have to sing at the evening show tonight, but I have lost interest in the whole business.

Now about plans for next week. I have not notified any scholars that I will be at the studio next week. I think the children should have a little change before going back to school, and as I may get in sometime Monday, we may be able to take a trip somewhere starting on Tuesday or Wednesday morning.

I'll have a pretty good class to go to the week after so if there is no reason to the contrary, I guess you might make preparation for a few days vacation, even if we stay over night at hotels.

I hav'nt written to the church to say whether I'd be there next week or not. I'm not anxious to hold the place anyway. I think I'll get around the choir bureaus and see if I cannot get something that pays better.

It seems such a long time since I left home, and I'm so anxious to see you all.

I enjoyed the letter and postal you sent to King City and was glad to read the first letter Margie sent me. We must keep it for a souvenir.

I am thinking so much of you all today, for I am all alone here, and it will be so nice next week to have you all with me.

Love to Margie, Jean and the Boy, and your dear self,

with kisses from
Daddy

Child number four was born on February 6th, 1915. Officially I believe he was named Howard, but because of his considerable size at birth and his rather mature, little mannish ways as a small child, Dad referred to him as his "little man." That was shortened to Mannie and the name stuck till he was about 14 or 15 years old. When he entered high school he decided it was time to get a real name and chose Raymond Robert. The entire family championed his choices and he became known to all as Ray.

Dad's fascination with cars became somewhat obsessive, and he spent most Saturday mornings in the alley behind their Blackstone Avenue flat, tinkering with the Ford and

The Stewart family's first car, a 1913 Ford. L to r: Dad, Margaret, Jean, Cameron, a friend, Ray, and Mother. (The photo was taken in 1916. The original was printed backwards, which is why the license plate is reversed. For years that was an old family joke.)

talking and comparing notes with neighboring car buffs. Someone had built a row of 18 garages across the alley, renting them out for $10 per month each. Imitating the name "Gasoline Alley" after the popular comic strip of the same name, the area became known by that name by all the garage renters.

Back to back with these was a fairly new two-story building facing east on Stoney Island Avenue. The ground floor was occupied by a machine shop where gaskets were manufactured for the automotive industry. On the second floor above the shop was a large flat, adequate to house the entire family. The address was 6330 Stoney Island. On March 15th, 1920, son number three was born.

My birth certificate showed my name to be Alexander Stewart. No nicknames were ever awarded to me except the shortening of Alexander to Alex. For no particular reason, my baptism was delayed until I was eight years old. A middle name was discussed, and I was asked what I would like. Because Cameron had Dad's middle name, I declined to choose that as my middle name but I did prefer having the middle initial "C" — to be like Dad's. At the time Conrad Nagle was a popular movie star and I liked the name. So I became Alexander Conrad Stewart. And it stuck.

World War I had come and gone before my birth. The Armistice was signed on November 11th, 1918. Dad was in his mid 40s, with a wife and four children, so was never subject to Army conscription. But his brother John, who had never emigrated to America, was subject to service in the British Army. He was 40 years old in 1915 and served in France, mostly in clerical work. A few letters to Dad spoke of the horrors of that conflict. In World War I, no encroachment on the British Isles was realized, though the loss of life and limb was heavy among the troops sent to the aid of France.

The American Expeditionary Force (AEF) — The American Army in France in the First World War— suffered severe casualties and much loss of life. While cannon and gunfire took a heavy toll, the German use of poisonous mustard gas was equally maiming and deadly. As youths encountering a disabled war veteran, we were often told that he was shell-shocked or gassed. Shell shock was likened to the psychoneurosis experienced in World War II, the psychological effect of prolonged combat. Both were nominally termed "combat fatigue." Gassing was the more deadly, and a victim seldom had an extended life. As a child in the '20s and '30s, I saw many veterans in our neighborhood so afflicted.

Ever since my parents married, it had been Dad's dream to have a home of their own. They liked the southeast side of Chicago and their proximity to Jackson Park and Lake Michigan. The Jackson Park elevated train station was a short walk, as was the steam-engine-driven Illinois Central commuter train. Dad and Mother located an old frame house on East 65th Place and at once saw its possibilities for their large and still-growing family. The Stony Island flat had been one block east of Blackstone Avenue; the house was about a block west. East 65th Place almost dead-ended at the Illinois Central elevated tracks but had unpaved alley-type outlets. Turn left and you headed south one-half block to Marquette Boulevard. Turn right and you were northbound to 65th Street. Both streets had passes under the railroad. The Illinois Central had a suburban commuter station at Marquette, and these tracks also served the Illinois Central and New York Central long-distance carriers, affording both passenger and freight service.

The house on East 65th had been built about the time of the World Columbian Exposition in 1893 and was located about six blocks from the grassland that had served as the Midway for the Fair. The University of Chicago is located at 59th Street, on the north side of the Midway, and some large residences and flat buildings are on 60th Street, on the south side. The Midway extends from Stony Island Avenue on the east to Cottage Grove Avenue, one mile to the west. A divided boulevard runs through the center from east to west. On the east end, the boulevard crosses Stony Island Avenue and enters Jackson Park near the main site of the Fair.

To Dad, the house had the potential for producing income. Car theft was rampant, due mainly to the non-existence of ownership titles. These did not become law until the early 1940s, as did the licensing of drivers. Those who could afford it kept their cars garaged or in fenced yards with locked gates. Those who parked on the street often removed the distributor rotor at night. Others disconnected a battery cable or removed the power cable from the ignition coil. But perhaps the most compelling reason for keeping the car in a garage was to protect its finish, make it easier to start in winter, and have a place to make repairs and perform maintenance.

The four garages at the rear of the house would bring $10 per month each, and two or three of the five bedrooms could be rented out. And there were two large open areas in the attic that could be converted to sleeping areas for the boys. It apparently didn't bother Dad and Mother that there was only one bathroom in the entire place.

The owner, a Mr. and Mrs. Hasker of Kankakee, Illinois, offered the house for $6,000, with $1,500 down and $40 per month at 6 percent interest. We moved in that fall of 1921. I was 1½ years old. Mother was expecting her sixth child, but suffered a miscarriage. She became pregnant again in the fall of 1922, and on May 15th, 1923, gave birth to her fourth son, David Barton Stewart. With the long string of six children progressing through the Walter Scott Elementary School, it became evident that the teachers were heaving a feigned sigh of relief when David announced upon his entrance into the kindergarten that he was the last of the Stewarts. His teacher, Martha Raymouth, had become a good friend of our family and delighted in telling us of David's proclamation. Indeed, we were perhaps typical of most large families, each with varied talents, interests, and desires.

David's birth, in fact, had been a very difficult one for Mother and a special, newly designed support device had been employed to prevent a premature delivery. Sometime in the years before David started school, Mother went to the hospital, then convalesced at home. I remember asking her why she had been to the hospital and her simple answer was that after having had several children, it was sometimes necessary for a Mother to "have her insides straightened out." The word hysterectomy was never used, and her answer satisfied me. I don't remember Mother ever saying that she could not have more children, and later this caused me to wonder how David knew he was the last of the Stewarts.

My earliest memory dates to a time five years before David's first day of school when I was three years old. As the newborn David lay asleep in his crib in Mother's and Dad's room, I proudly invited family and visitors to come and see him. With finger pressed to my lips, I hushed them to silence and softly announced, "See him, he's my little brown brother."

Chapter 5

Chicago

HE BIG HOUSE PROVED TO BE everything Dad and Mother had hoped for and became the headquarters for our large family and the varied activities for each of its members. The four garages at the rear were served by a crude dirt alley that became a muddy mess in the rainy season, and sometimes impassable with heavy snowstorms. The citizens petitioned the city to pave it with concrete, as had been done in nearby areas, and surprisingly paving came to pass when one of the politically knowledgeable neighbors appealed to an alderman who was seeking reelection. This was my first exposure to the power of politics. None of the four garages was vacant for very long after that. The rent revenues covered the monthly house payments for many years.

In their spare time the folks finished off the attic areas, making them suitable for sleeping by the older boys. As David and I grew, we became eligible for attic sleeping, thus releasing one more room for rental. Of the five bedrooms, three were rented out to roomers for many years. Mother and Dad occupied the large master bedroom and Jean and Margaret shared the small adjoining bedroom. The three rented rooms produced a total of $50 to $60 per month when all were occupied. Board was never offered, which made the rooms less attractive to

A Stewart family portrait, 1929. Front: Margaret (22), David (6), Mother (46), and Alex (9). Rear: Jean (21), Ray (14), Cameron (19), and Dad (57).

renters seeking both room and meals. But Mother had more than enough to do to prepare meals for her big family without the added burden and varied time demands this would impose.

When the Depression hit, following the stock market crash in 1929, the rooms were quite often vacant or their rates were reduced to keep them occupied. On rare occasion, a roomer was asked to leave, due for the most part to non-payment of rent or undesirable habits.

During the era of the "flapper" in the "Roaring Twenties," one young lady created enough disturbance to cause her eviction. Her short, tight-fitting, fringed-bottom dresses, close-fitting hats over short-bobbed hair, high-heeled shoes, and heavy cosmetics were bad enough, but her loud, hoarse voice and mocking way of laughing while she waved her cigarette in a long, slender holder fell below Dad's and Mother's standards of ladylike habit. A final straw was seeing her riding on the folded-down roof of her man friend's convertible for all the neighbors and we children to witness. David and I were present when Dad issued the verbal notice to her, and as expected, she was quite indignant. Though not saying so, we kids were a little disappointed, as she was always very nice to us, calling us "cute" or "handsome," and letting us select our favorite chocolate from a box of Fannie Mae's. We often wondered what happened to Velma.

A tenant couple was Mr. and Mrs. Jack Winters. Jack managed a tire repair business on 67th Street, and we men folk made it our business to stop in and see him in action. We marveled at how quickly he could remove the split rim, or in some cases a clincher ring and its tire and tube from the wheel, patch the tube, locate and remove the puncturing culprit, and remount the entire repaired assembly, inflated and ready to go. All this was done with hand tools. The air-powered machines would come several years after the end of World War II. Dad said that Jack never made a false move, and this proved to be a small part of our practical training in mechanics.

During Chicago's 1933-1934 World's Fair — "A Century of Progress Exposition" — we rented rooms to a Mr. and Mrs. Adams and son Elwood. The parents were large people, quite "broad in the beam" as Cameron described them, whereas Elwood was a slim 22-year-old. All three had packed themselves, into a Model A Ford coupe with Elwood at the wheel and, at his insistence, drove non-stop from Oklahoma City to the windy city of Chicago. They arrived very hot and tired and heavily coated with grime from the Oklahoma Dust Bowl and other accumulations from Kansas, Missouri, and Illinois. It took several hours for our 30-gallon hot-water storage tank with its Berkay "side arm" gas heater to supply enough water for their baths. With no work to return to in Oklahoma, the Adamses stayed for about two weeks, saw every inch of the World's Fair, and dreaded the return trip home, as Elwood would again insist on driving straight through. The Adamses became quite friendly with our family and enjoyed long evenings of conversation about politics and the state of the nation and the world. We exchanged Christmas cards with them for many years.

Another roomer that comes to mind was a middle-aged man who was unable to find work during the Depression and occupied the two adjoining rooms. The back room contained a sink and the man had a one-burner electric hot plate on which to cook. He earned enough money to live on by finding lost golf balls on the two courses in Jackson Park. He would bring home a sack of balls, wash them, and then repaint them by dipping them in a pure white lead enamel. He had constructed a drying rack by driving small nails in groups of three on a large board. Each group would support a painted ball. When the balls were dry, he would carefully touch up the nail marks with a small artist's brush.

He carried the painted balls to the first hole of each course early in the morning and sold them for perhaps 10 to 15 cents each. He then spent several hours looking for more lost balls. He spent his evenings refurbishing his restocked inventory. My guess is that new balls probably cost 25 to 35 cents each.

This account about the golf ball painter reminds me of an incident that occurred one Saturday morning, unrelated to room rentals or roomers, but underlining the plight and resourcefulness of some citizens during the Depression. Dad answered the doorbell ring of a middle-aged man selling drop-lights. They were the first we had seen, with a molded rubber handle and socket, rubber-covered wire, and a steel shade with hinged protective guard. For years we had used an all-wire guard with no shade, attached to a plain brass socket and a cloth-covered, green-and-tan twisted wire in one of the two electrical outlets in the basement. It was frequently requiring repair.

The drop-light man had three or four lights draped over his arm, offering them at $1 each. David and I witnessed the transaction and were surprised when Dad said, "Yes, I'll take one." Dad paid the man, then engaged him in conversation, asking about his enterprise. We had noted that he had a child's coaster wagon equipped with a rather large cardboard carton parked on the sidewalk in front of our gate. The man said he paid 70 cents

The Stewart family "Headquarters" at 1414 E. 65th Place on Chicago's South Side.

for each light, started out with 50 sets each morning, and didn't quit for the day till all were sold. He worked everyday except Sunday and was making close to $90 per week, his only restriction being bad weather. We were all impressed, even as we considered the tiring, tedious effort the man put forth. At 12 years old, I observed that hard work could pay dividends.

Of course, the roomers most significant in my memory are George Curtley, the harmonica player, and his father, the house painter and World War I veteran who kept his American flag containing the blood stains of his fallen battlefield buddies.

About the time I entered high school, the mortgage had been paid off and the renting of rooms was gradually discontinued. However, Cameron slept in the attic until he left home to be married in 1938. Ray, David, and I each acquired our own rooms on the second floor, a move that we had long envisioned. Cam often griped about still having to sleep in the attic, but in reality he preferred it. He liked his privacy and did not want to share space with Ray. Besides, he smoked cigarettes, though never in the house or in the presence of any family members. He could do so in the attic with impunity.

One bathroom in the house was quite troublesome for us attic sleepers, as the stairway down to the second floor was curved, narrow, and unlighted and an urgent bladder call demanded a simpler route to relief. A portable receptacle requiring emptying each morning was provided to take care of this inconvenience. The argument about whose turn it was to empty the jar wore thin, and we found other things to pick on.

The Depression took a tremendous toll on the economy, and it showed up in the garage rental rates. Down from the $10 per month, they bottomed out at $4. Our long-time tenant Mr. M. D. Sweeney kept his maroon-colored Oldsmobile in the first unit. A sudden change in jobs caused him to vacate without giving notice before leaving for Atlanta. He wrote to Dad:

Dear Mr. Stewart:

I am enclosing herein the key to the garage. Before Mrs. Sweeney left Chicago she tried to see you but no one was at home.

I will be here in Atlanta for one month before going to New York. If you will let me know what I owe you I will gladly send your check, also the other key as soon as I see Mrs. Sweeney. I expect to be gone about one year.

Kindest regards,
M. D. Sweeney
650 Boulevard N.E. Atlanta, Ga.

Mr. Sweeney and Dad had become quite friendly and Dad chose to send him a humorous reply. Dad too was touched by Mr. Sweeney's honesty and faithfulness, even over a small bill.

Dear Mr. Sweeney,

When your letter containing the key arrived, I felt it and felt it, and concluded that some new kind of chain letter was circulating.

The post mark — Atlanta scared me by raising fears that the prison authorities of that noted city had mistaken me for a counterfeiter and were trying to cover me.

Wasn't it a grand and glorious feeling to discover a friendly communication from a quiet and peaceful old friend, who had won the lasting regard and esteem of a critical but unimportant community in notorious Chicago.

Still you must confess that you ran away, leaving your wife and children behind. Mr. Sweitzer stood his ground, and refused to leave his office, despite threats of government: and he only in default $500,000.00. [Mr. Sweitzer was a much publicized tycoon caught up in a scandal raging in the Chicago business community at that time.]

Our books show that you are $4.00 in the red, April 14 to May 14th. The few days following are forgiven and forgotten, with a prayer that we may secure another tenant one tenth as good as Sweeney.

Eight of us wish you and yours the best of luck and I, take pride in signing myself, your friend.

A. C. Stewart

Eventually Mr. Sweeney returned to Chicago and relocated in our neighborhood and again became one of our garage tenants.

Although the house seemed to be the fulfillment of my parents' dreams, there were times when a grander place in a newer, more refined, neighborhood captured their imaginations. Scanning the classified ads in the Sunday *Tribune* would sometimes motivate an afternoon's drive to the South Shore area, the Jackson Park Highlands, or Longwood Drive in the Morgan Park region. In retrospect, I would look upon these adventures as entertainment rather than as a serious investigation. Dad and Mother were realists and understood the economics of rearing a large family. Though Dad's income from teaching peaked in the years following World War I and preceding the so-called Great Depression (at the time it was never referred to nor was it considered to be "great"), he realized its limitations and seemed content to let the house do its job of providing a comfortable, though somewhat quaint, shelter for his diverse brood. He subscribed to the premise that a "man's home is his castle" and that a home was not a specific place but rather a state of mind. And he made every effort to establish ours as a haven from the adverse forces of a mean society. Here you could find love and understanding, happiness and health and counsel, rest and sustenance. Here, too, were the elements of art and culture and, most of all, a deep and abiding Christian faith. These were not stitched into a "Whitman Sampler" wall hanging, popular during these days, but were integral components of daily habit and behavior.

The house itself became a workshop for every phase of repair and construction. Seldom was a professional craftsman employed. The need would be outlined and a plan of action would be mapped. We had a basement full of tools, devices, and materials with which to attack every job, and we each learned their proper use and application.

The same was true of our automobiles, which were housed in a shed in the side yard. One of the garages was used for a major repair if a vacancy existed, but was never allowed to deter a rental. Dad's training and experience with printing machinery carried over into our "do-it-yourself" activities, as preparation for each job included an old dish pan, a gallon of kerosene, and an old paint brush, all to be used for washing parts and keeping them in a safe place for reinstallation. When the job was finished, we knew we had performed to Dad's satisfaction if there were no parts or nuts and bolts left over in the bottom of the pan. Cotter pins were the exception, as Dad insisted that a cotter pin should never be reused, but replaced with a new one. And, of course, to substitute with a nail was grounds for a lecture.

Auto repairs ranged from simple tune-ups to total engine overhaul, and on two occasions, total engine replacement. Brakes, clutches, and manual transmission work became quite routine. Body and fender work and painting were an unhappy requirement but were handled in somewhat routine fashion since most of our cars were black. Torn upholstery required special handling, and I became quite adept in the use of a large curved needle for sewing tears in seat cushions and head liners. Mother had shown me how to do a blind stitch, and often my sewing was undetectable.

Dad and Mother enjoyed telling stories of our early motoring days in the old Ford and how they took the hardships in stride. Because many country roads were unpaved — as were suburban and some urban streets — they wore "dusters," smock-like coverall coats to protect their clothing, and loose-fitting head covers similar to today's shower cap. Goggles were used for eye protection, and the children's faces were often covered with muslin scarves or lightweight towels.

A tool box mounted on the running board contained a jack, a monkey wrench (probably the forerunner of today's crescent wrench), hammer, screwdrivers, pliers, and a multipurpose wrench with square and hexagonal openings for use on hubcaps and other screwed-on devices. But the most important and most frequently used items were the tire-patching kits and hand pump.

Flat tires were an accepted hazard, and the rate of success of any trip seemed to be measured by the number of flats encountered. Early tire construction was little more than a black or red natural rubber inner tube inserted in a heavy canvas casing. Two or three spare tires were the usual back-up on a trip of reasonable distance. On a round trip of 150 to 200 miles, 10 to 20 flats were not unusual.

Gasoline in those early days was of poor quality, causing frequent removal of sparkplugs for cleaning. Most gas stations consisted of one pump at a roadside grocery or general store, or even near a vegetable stand. Radiator water was dispensed from a bucket with a handle and large pouring spout. Air for tire inflation was a rare commodity and the better garages and gas stations had signs posted: "Free Air." Road maps were almost non-existent, and road signs were crude and confusing and their posted distances inaccurate.

Over-the-road sleeping accommodations were rare. Hotel rooms were infrequent, inadequate, and rather costly. Tourist rooms in private homes became an accepted mode and prevailed till the advent of tourist cabins. These "cabin camps" sprang up across the country and became quite popular. They usually consisted of a complex of identical one-room cottages on a roadside acreage near the owner's house. One room of the house would serve as an office, and a prominent sign would tell if a vacancy existed. Sometimes a small store would be on hand to sell fresh garden produce, bread and milk, soda pop, candy, and fishing tackle — and the ever-present locally made souvenirs.

The cabin camps varied in size from 3 or 4 to possibly 12 or 15 units. Many bore unusual or fetching names such as "Paradise Lodge," "Traveler's Hideaway," or, one of my favorites, "Do Drop Inn." Many prospered, though others fell into disrepair, became seedy, and attractive only to the "short-term" trade.

Cost was always of prime consideration, and even the cabin camps could play havoc with a limited budget. Dad truly loved the roughing aspect of camping out in a tent, and there was something akin to the pioneering spirit that captured the imaginations of we boys: the pitching of the tent; the pounding of stakes into hard ground with a large, wooden mallet; fetching water from a squeaking hand pump at a community well; and eating Mother's tasty fare from tin plates at makeshift log tables and benches. The meal was cooked on a gasoline-powered camp stove, and wood was gathered for the after-dark campfire, the ashes from which were used for cleaning the iron skillet. The campfire had woven its magic. Yawns preceded eyelids falling to half-mast in company with the graying embers.

With the family bedded down on straw-stuffed pallets, Dad could usually find subject matter that would have us all in stitches, our sides aching from laughter. Our first tent was an Army surplus, white canvas sidewall left over from World War I. He and Mother slept on folding canvas cots, while the rest of us stretched our young, strong bodies on our blanket-wrapped straw beds on the ground. The fact that a huge bundle of this barnyard straw had been secured from a local farmer for 25 cents and often carried the "distinctive" identification with the barnyard added to our source of revelry.

I believe Dad and Mother were at their happiest when we were all in that state of exhilaration, hunkered down in a tent in a strange piece of country, laughing ourselves silly over nothing. With the kerosene lantern extinguished, the odor of burned fuel and wick lingering, and the sounds of a distant train whistle, a barking dog or a croaking frog or chirping locusts imposed their tranquilizing balm on the rigors of the day and our consciousness, and we drifted, one by one, into that blissful sleep of childhood. Dad and Mother joined in the chorus of true contentment. In spite of the travel hardships, discomforts, inconveniences, and individual hurts and disappointments of the day, all seemed to evaporate in the darkness where our comic imaginations had soared and were now laid to rest. We were family, we were happy, and all was right with the world.

Travel with a large family and its belongings in the old Ford, and its "caravan" of successors, was certainly awkward and cumbersome. Most of the camping gear and luggage had to be carried on the outside of the vehicle, in a luggage carrier mounted on the running board or strapped to the front fenders. Dad was on the lookout for an under-carriage assembly that could serve as a base for a luggage-type trailer. But if there had been such a contraption on the market at the time, it would have been unaffordable. And since we still lived in the flat over the machine shop on Stony Island at this time, there would have been no available storage space for a trailer, but Dad harbored the unique idea.

On a trip to Lake Geneva, Wisconsin, he spotted an abandoned buggy spring chassis in the ditch at the side of the road, complete with wheel spindles. He decided then and there that it would be the start of his trailer and brought it home, tied to the back of the car. He designed the trailer so that the wheels, end boards, and folding top could be removed, and the side boards could be hinged flat against the floor. The remaining assembly could then be stood on end and strapped against the back wall of the garage, leaving room for the car and passage around it. A rack suspended from the ceiling provided storage for the portable parts.

Working only with hand tools, Dad did a superb job of construction. Everything fit perfectly and was waterproof. All the components were secured with carriage bolts, lock washers, and square nuts, requiring only a hammer, pliers, and the monkey wrench for assembly. The only hired work was the strong steel tongue and hitch braces that were fashioned by a blacksmith and the bumper-mounted hitch anchored to the car's frame. Dad was able to use Model T Ford wheels and tires, size 30x3½. The peaked top was covered with an artificial rubber-like material impregnated into canvas, called Pantasote. Over time it would dry out and crack, but it could be sealed with roofing compound and a waterproofing paint — an annual pre-vacation requirement.

The trailer was unique, with nothing on the road to match it, and it served our needs for many years. Once during a strike by the Teamster's Union, coal deliveries came to a sudden halt. We boys assembled the trailer, drove to the coal yard where both car and trailer were weighed on the huge scale, purchased 600 pounds of coal (the trailer's capacity) in large canvas bags, then hauled it home and carried those heavy bags from the alley to our coal bin. It was hard work and the project took all day Saturday and about seven round trips to the coal yard to secure two tons. We were the envy of a neighbor in need of coal, and we supplied them with one load. They paid for the coal, but Dad would not accept any payment for our labor or trailer use. He subscribed to the motto, "A friend in need is a friend indeed." Fortunately, the strike ended before we had to repeat the coal-hauling performance.

Devil's Lake at Baraboo, Wisconsin, Niagara Falls, and Washington, D.C., were other destinations on our vacation itineraries. The trailer served us well. Our contingent usually included at least six of us — Mother and Dad, Margaret, Jean, David, and me — there was no space inside the car for luggage. Seven of us went to Niagara Falls and Devil's Lake (Cam was working and could not, nor would he want to go). Ray did not make the trip to Washington as he, too, was working that summer of 1933.

Our family car was a 1927 Chrysler and though it ran well, it was underpowered and unable to get over the mountains east of Clarksburg, West Virginia. Halfway up the long eastern incline, Dad decided to turn around and go back to Clarksburg. Discussion ensued and it was decided that Dad, Jean, and Margaret would take a Greyhound bus to Washington while Mother, David, and I remained in the tourist home we had vacated that morning. The next day we received a telegram from Dad: "WASHINGTON IS GREAT STOP TAKE GREYHOUND TOMORROW STOP WILL MEET BUS STOP FORGET THE COST-LOVE DAD."

Mother, David, and I were delighted. We parked the car and trailer in a public garage. Though only 13, I had learned to drive at 12 and, in fact, had driven at least half the trip from Chicago to Clarksburg. I remember Dad telling me to hold our speed at 40 mph as it was a comfortable, steady rate. Most roads were two-lane and traffic was rather light due to reduced travel caused by the money shortage of the Depression.

We were thrilled with Washington and all its famous, historic attractions. We stayed in tourist rooms and made our way around the city on buses and streetcars. Most meals were eaten in a chain of cafeterias where they served a wonderful blueberry pie, and I am sure David and I had that for dessert every day. Several rolls of photos were taken and included scenes snapped on the lawn of the White House. One of them featured David feeding a squirrel, while others were group shots of the family taken near the west side entrance.

There were no locked or guarded gates to the grounds, and I don't believe we encountered anyone during our informal visit.

Dad felt that we had not done justice to Washington and proposed a return trip in 1934. With the shortage of money during the Depression and with the quest by many to learn to sing and get into live radio work, Dad found what seemed to be an untapped source for income. In lieu of money, he offered to exchange lessons for items of value such as diamond rings, watches, and even automobiles. The plan worked quite well and at one time he had items worth a few thousand dollars. His knowledge of such valuables enabled him to secure a straight-commission sales position with a diamond and jewelry firm. He used his free mornings to call on small local merchants. When unable to make a sale on new merchandise, he would offer his used items at considerable savings, thus acquiring needed cash and disposing of his personal inventory. I remember seeing four or five wristwatches strapped to his left arm for convenient display.

Dad had traded lessons for a few cars, which were not difficult to sell. Their value was easy to establish, and he would discount them for a quick sale. However, in the spring of 1934 he acquired a 1932 Graham. It was a jet-black, eight-cylinder, seven-passenger beauty that ran like a Rolls-Royce. He could not part with it and decided this would be our transportation to Washington that summer. The car had a large, pull-down luggage carrier mounted on the rear. Two spare tires with wheels were mounted in front fender wells. Dad designed and we boys helped him build a large wooden box to fit on the luggage carrier. The front panel of the box hinged down to receive four large suitcases standing on end. Waterproofed with sheet Pantasote, it served our needs perfectly. The car's large interior easily handled our other belongings without crowding seating space. Since we were not camping out on this trip, the trailer was not needed.

A few hours before completing the final leg of our journey to Washington, the car developed a rather loud clackety-clack noise. I determined that the problem was in one or both of the universal joints connected to the drive shaft and felt our best bet was to drive on into Washington for service. Pedestrians were attracted to our noise-making and stared at us as we cruised along the boulevard. I was at the wheel, David was in the middle, and Dad was next to the passenger door. Never one to be embarrassed, Dad, in his best celebrity mode wore a grin from ear to ear and waved to the sidewalk gawkers. "If Roosevelt can do it, why can't I?" he mused.

The next morning we located a Graham car agency and garage where their chief mechanic confirmed my diagnosis and replaced the faulty universal joint. Packed with grease, our noise-maker was silenced at a total cost of $17.56.

Our return route to Chicago was by way of Pennsylvania, with a stop at a large tourist home at Uniontown. The lady owner was very accommodating and immediately took a liking to us. "Would you boys like to take a shower?" she asked. "We have one out back in the shed near the garage." Rain water was collected in a large cistern and piped to the shower. The water was heated by the sun.

David and I put on our swimming trunks and made a bee-line for the backyard. Standing under the shower head, I tugged on the chain that opened the water valve, and we were at once flooded with water that would be too cold even for Eskimos. I yanked on the other chain that stopped the water flow. We briskly dried off with the lady's large towels and dashed back to our rooms. With teeth chattering as we dressed, it took several minutes for us to warm up and return to normal. Later that evening the lady asked us how we liked the shower. I looked at David and he looked at me. Then with his most beguiling smile, he replied, "Very invigorating." I agreed, "It was very invigorating." Under no circumstance would we express any criticism.

The "Uniontown Shower" became a part of our vocabulary and was used to describe frigid conditions for years afterward. "It was colder today than a Uniontown Shower" became our most graphic description of winter conditions in Chicago.

In our younger days, we all looked forward to an annual trip to downtown Chicago at Christmas time to meet Dad and see the sights — especially the toys and sporting goods sections of large department stores like Marshall Field, Carson Pirie Scott, and The Fair Store. We liked The Fair better than the others. It had a good Santa's Workshop display and allowed the children to pick up and try out the toys. Then, too, its prices were generally lower, and we felt the folks would be more generous in their expenditures.

We walked the three blocks to the "El" — the Elevated train — then climbed the long stairway to the overhead station where Mother paid the adult ten-cent fare each for her and Ray when he became a teenager and the "under twelve" five-cent fare for David and me. We hurried along the platform to enter the waiting train, found two pair of seats facing each other, and argued for a place near the window. The warmth of the car felt good after the chilly walk, and we soon shed our mittens and our wool stocking caps, and unbuttoned our plaid mackinaws. As the train lurched forward to start its run, the conductor came through the car to collect our tickets and invalidate them with a hand punch.

The train tracks were about 20 feet above street level on square steel-fabricated columns supporting horizontal steel I-beams. Power was transmitted through an outside "third" rail located a little higher than the other rails. A "shoe" or "boot" attached to each car contacted the third rail and carried electricity to the powerful driving motors while supplying heat and light to the cars. Sometimes on a fast straight run, or while making a turn, the train would sway, causing the boot to lift away from the rail and lights momentarily would go out.

The elevated track structure wound through strange neighborhoods, sometimes above a wide street where auto and truck traffic traveled and sometimes above alleys behind old tenement buildings and stores. We saw children playing in back yards strewn with broken glass, old junk cars, and trash. In freezing weather they were sometimes ice skating in yards that had been flooded with water for that purpose. Washed clothes could be seen drying on pulley-operated clotheslines stretched between buildings. In winter, the clothing was sometimes frozen, and men's union-suit long underwear swinging stiffly in the wind lent comedy to the scene.

Nearer downtown, the train would often pass very close to the buildings and the reflection of the lighted cars could be seen in the windows of the flats where families were gathered for their evening meals. We could see the children eating plain bread without butter, and a box or two of cereal and a bottle of milk open on a scarred wooden table top. A single bare light bulb cast a stark glow over the scene. There was seldom evidence of a cooked, sit-down meal at a cloth-covered table. Mother was quick to observe that "these people didn't have much, but somehow or other they seemed to get along." For us, it was a lesson in gratitude and thankfulness.

In due time the conductor would call out "Congress" and we buttoned up, ready to get off. The train came to a jerky stop and we followed other passengers onto the Congress Street platform. We descended the long flight of stairs to the street level and walked the short block to the Auditorium Building. The elderly uniformed operator took us to the seventh floor in the iron-caged elevator. Most of the tenants were teachers of singing, violin, piano, and the other instruments associated with classical music. With the open stairwell and elevator shaft, the sounds of myriad instruments echoed throughout the building and I wondered who these less-than-famous artists were and if they would ever achieve notoriety. Stopping at the door to Suite 706, Dad's domain, we could hear him demonstrating a vocal exercise to his final pupil of the day.

Quietly entering the reception room, I scrambled to beat Ray and David to the swivel chair in front of the old roll-top desk. The others sat on straight armchairs backed against the walls where large posters picturing famous opera singers kept company with photos of other vocal artists bearing handwritten messages and autographs. Most of these were opera singers who had received coaching from Dad.

The desk and its "pigeon holes" contained a variety of letters, cards, printed matter, and other paraphernalia pertinent to Dad's profession. To one side, near the front, was the familiar leather pocket folder containing Dad's appointment schedule, his address book, and his large, orange-colored Waterman fountain pen. He was a creature of order and habit and these items could always be found in one of three places: here on the desk, in his coat pocket, or at his place at home on the dining room table.

Scanning the contents of the desk, I found a buff-colored, pocket-sized folder bearing a fine likeness of Dad in younger days. It was an invitation to prospective voice students on which Dad had enumerated an almost formidable array of techniques and qualities available under his instruction. These were not found in any textbook or instruction manual but were products of his own research and development. He taught:

BREATH PRINCIPLE — LEGATO FINISH — VOLUME
EXPANSION
DRAMATIC EFFECTS — VOWEL UNIFORMITY — RANGE
WITHOUT TENSION
VOLUME WITHOUT EFFORT — TONE ENRICHMENT —
FEARLESS PERSONALITY
DIAPHRAGMATIC ENERGY — ABDOMINAL SUPPORT —
MAGNETIC EXPRESSION
ARTISTIC DICTION — EAR CORRECTION — LARYNGEAL
ADJUSTMENT

Dad branded the three basic components of a good singing voice to be TONAL QUALITY, RANGE, AND VOLUME. His ability to communicate and develop these assets in his students was at the heart of his teaching success. When he emerged from his studio and said goodbye to the lady student, I asked if I could keep the folder. With a knowing twinkle in his eye he granted my request and asked, "What is it you like — my picture, or all those fancy words?" "Both," I answered. I pocketed the folder and added it to my collection of souvenirs in a small cedar chest that I kept on top of my dresser. It would be in later years that I came to understand and appreciate the content of that folder and the vast knowledge and ability of its author. Where, I wondered, had Dad acquired these techniques? Eventually I would have answers to this and many other questions about this outstanding personality.

His day's work completed, Dad turned his attention to us. He donned his heavy overcoat and large felt hat, placed his leather appointment folder, address book, and fountain pen in his suit-coat pocket, and followed us through the door and to the elevator. He said, "Hello, Mr. Livingston" to the operator as we boarded and "Goodnight, Mr. Livingston" as we passed through the heavy doors to the street. I don't remember a time when Dad was ever less than courteous to all those with whom he came in contact. We walked the one block to State Street, then north to The Fair Store. Dad was as fascinated with the new toys and devices as we were, and for the record, posed with us beside Santa's sleigh for a traditional Christmas photograph. I don't think we ever made it to Field's or Carson's that night.

Chapter 6

Chicago
Spring and Summer 1941

UR FAMILY OF SIX CHILDREN, born during a span of 16 years, was always in transition, starting or finishing one school or another or locating in a new or different type of work. The Depression years with their scant opportunities and dearth of funds often forced us into endeavors for which we had little interest or aptitude. But a job was a job, regardless of pay or promise, and the aggregate of our limited contributions sustained our household and our dignity.

I entered Hyde Park High School in the fall of 1934 and registered, with Mother advising, for a general-language course of study. With the emphasis on languages, particularly Latin, rather than the sciences, Mother reasoned that I would garner an excellent background. The fact that it would also short-change my exposure to more advanced mathematics and science was never considered. If there was such a practice as aptitude testing at that time, it never was revealed to us, and selection of courses seemed to be a rather random process.

I was an average student and did fairly well in most subjects but was not too adept at Latin, though I did complete three years and was able to recite verbatim Caesar's *Gaelic War* — for the first and last time. Several of my friends were in similar situations, though they were not stuck with Latin.

At the height of the Depression, the national unemployment rate topped 25 percent of the work force, dropping to about 15 percent by 1940. The economic condition of our family was sufficient to maintain a nominal living but provided no room for extended education and certainly no luxuries. Besides, the advanced educational facilities — state colleges and universities or specialized institutions such as engineering — were located in distant cities and required living away from home. I was never encouraged to consider or prepare for college and, aside from Margaret who completed teachers college just before the stock market crash of 1929, followed the others in seeking work.

Dad had completed elementary school in Liverpool, England, at age 14 in 1886 and immediately entered the printing trade. From that time on, his additional education would be self-acquired and he would advance to an unofficial reference of "professor." His emphasis was in the languages and in music, where he excelled in orchestral and ensemble direction and especially in choral leadership. The mastering of his singing talent matched his affinity for learning to play a dozen different musical instruments. Because he had succeeded this way in pursuit of a career, I believe he felt some of us boys could do likewise, and he chided us for not staying home and "thinking about our futures" instead of wasting time hanging around with our friends. However, if we had expressed a desire and wish to go to college, I believe he would have exerted every effort to make it possible. But the economic reality of the times were so pervasive he felt that whatever we did we would have to do it on our own.

During the early school years I had continued to deliver the *Downtown Shopping News*, which provided me with lunch money and some school expense funds. But when I reached 16, Cameron helped me get work in an A & P grocery store on Thursday afternoons and all day Saturday. I was paid 35 cents per hour for 14 hours, pocketing less than $5 per week. When I got into this big money, I was able to turn the *Shopping News* job over to David.

But the big money didn't last long. One Saturday evening the manager told me he would have to let me go, as he couldn't afford the 35-cent rate. I pleaded with him that I really needed the job, whereupon he offered to let me work all day Saturday for $3.50. I accepted and was told to report the following Saturday at 7:00 a.m. We finished the restocking of shelves and clean-up of the store at midnight. For 17 hours of work, I averaged about 21 cents per hour. I continued in the job until graduation, knowing there were dozens of boys in the neighborhood ready to take my place.

In the summer of 1938 I joined the annual horde of high school graduates in search of employment, willing to take the first job opportunity that reared its meager head. Most of my friends, a compatible bunch from similar economic roots, charged the employment agencies and other work sources and were soon set up in jobs at beginners' salaries.

Larry McBrearty, son of an accountant, found a clerical job with a large paper company.

Robert Saxton, whose father worked on the open hearth of a steel company, got work with an oil company.

Richard Gentzler — his dad an executive with a wallpaper manufacturer — did refrigerator service dispatching.

Hale Huddleston, orphaned at age 12 and reared by his grandfather, went with a heavy truck manufacturer in its parts department.

John R. (Jack) Diehl, whose Dad was a sales manager for a large meat packer, was the only one who left us behind and went off to Drake University at Des Moines, Iowa.

And, finally, a job for me, a stock-room shipping clerk, in the basement of a downtown skyscraper, with a national finance company, supplying the branch offices with business forms and office supplies. Salary: $65 per month. It wasn't much of a job and offered no opportunities for worthwhile advancement, but it did fill my immediate needs.

I expressed my displeasure with the position to Dick Gentzler, and he suggested I apply at his firm, R. Cooper, Jr. Inc. I landed a job there as service department trainee at the same salary I was receiving at the finance company. The work was much more to my liking, but nothing one could look to for the long term. I advanced from trainee to assistant dispatcher and was finally appointed to manage the night service desk, a responsible and demanding assignment.

I worked at Coopers for about two years and was earning $22.50 a week when my military Draft number came up. I had registered on July 1st, 1941, and was classified 1A in what was termed the second Draft, following my 21st birthday on March 15th. Conscription at that time called for one year of military training. About September 1st, I was ordered to appear for induction on September 26th at Draft Board 89 located on 63rd Street.

Life from high school graduation to Army induction leveled out, and I enjoyed a lot of good times, but limited job and personal growth. The specter of Army service constantly hovered over those of us destined for induction. Older men who had become 21 before the first Draft in the fall of 1940 were snatched up by the Services and were populating both old and new training camps all across the country. It was easy for me to see what lay ahead, making futile any ambitious plans.

Younger brother David had entered Hyde Park High School in the spring of 1937 and had done exceptionally well. He was an "A" student, a leader in many activities, and an outstanding pianist. He and I had first taken lessons from Margaret and later from a fine teacher, Betty Rutherford. At 17, I had advanced about as far as I could go without additional study, playing Rachmaninoff's *C-Sharp Minor Prelude* at my last recital, and was allowed to quit lessons. In the meantime, David had enjoyed the fruits of a partial scholarship from the renowned Chicago Musical College and studied under Lillian Powers. She later left the college to open her own studio on Michigan Avenue and brought David along as her leading student.

David was very popular at Hyde Park and was elected president of the senior class, due to graduate in February 1941. The second 1941 class would graduate in June. Since I was working from 4:00 p.m. till 10:00 p.m., I was unable to attend the ceremony, which was held in the school auditorium. Dad, Mother, Margaret, and Jean were there, however, and later gave me a detailed account of the proceedings. Most impressive was David's commencement address which the family fortunately saved and which later became a special remembrance of David:

> Sang Robbie Burns, "A man's a man, for a' that." Yes, and he always has been; but how recent is his recognition. Unfortunately, the boundaries of race and class and even belief have too often the

limitations of regard for person or opinion. The accident of power
has proved superior to liberty!

To you, Mr. Gonnelly, we — the graduating class — pay tribute, and we extend our sincere congratulations on the growth and
ever increasing influence of this institution to whose prosperity
you have so vigorously devoted your energies. And not for her
sake alone, but for ours as individuals, shall our recollections of
you hold both honor and esteem. For we have reveled in your keen
discernment and fine fairness, and have felt its impulse; and we
depart with clearer conceptions and loftier ideals.

Dear teachers, as the realization strikes us that we are to sit as
learners at your feet no longer, the fuller appreciation of that daily
intercourse begins to foment. We have learned to honor you, not
vaguely because of your authority, but heartily, because having
met you face to face, we have perceived your learning capacity.
We have weighed you in the balance and found you to be sterling
men and women. The wisdom and consideration with which you
have met a class of men so hard to please is witnessed by the rare
degree of harmony prevailing between the faculty and student
body of our Hyde Park.

Fellow classmates, how large these four years of privilege seem
as we look back upon them! Much we have lost, which is now
vain to regret. Much we have won, and henceforth we must render account of stewardship. In these four years, we have learned
to know the value of one another, we have formed unrivaled
friendships of high school, we have shared our pleasures beneath
this roof and together have read through long chapter opportunities.

Now we leave all these, and step forth into a world seething
with turmoil, with hatred and with evil. The road branches, and
each must select a way. "To every man there openeth, a high road
and a low, and the choice is up to each — the way that he will go."
And here I pause, and I warn you to take caution against EVIL —
the disguised forces — so powerful in their deception. They slip
into our lives under appearance of desirable qualities!

1) Falsehood enters under the guise of politeness or diplomacy.
2) Race prejudice comes to us under the appearance of protect-
    ing the superiority of our race.
3) Hatred comes to be harbored by calling itself loyalty.

4) Violence slinks in robed as patriotism.
5) Alcohol comes to play a part in our career masked as good fellowship.
6) Dishonesty creeps upon us calling itself expediency.
7) Pride comes in the robe of self respect.
8) Injustice finds us a partner, because it claims to be custom.
9) The exaltation of property above personality takes us captive under the caption of preserving the Constitution.

It is just as though evil were a giant octopus, reaching out with its tentacles of wrong, striving relentlessly to envelope us. But do not forget that there is in every personality a bar of decision which crystallizes the integrity of the soul. This is not an abstract assumption, it is sound scientific theory, which has stood the test of twenty centuries.

Here and now, let it be our expressed desire and the entente of our hearts to choose — not the low road — but the lofty road and add our names to the ever growing list of men and women who can boast this invulnerable moral power. Now there remain but the last brief words of farewell, the words we may have heard so often here before. Commonplace? Yes; but always with a new sadness. We are drawn together now as we have never been before, and the last handshake has a new thrill in it.

But the last hour has struck. With changeless devotion to our Alma Mater, with steadfast loyalty to one another, with a heart bent on higher things — and broad enough for all — so go we forth, and Godspeed! And now let us ever remember that in this land of liberty and home of heroism, our concern lies in concord, not in conflict and that our true loftiness rests not in the conquests of war but in the victories of peace.

Let it be our earnest prayer that God will mercifully vouchsafe, sustenance, contentment and tranquility to all our neighbors, and like endowments to all the peoples and powers of this earth.

FINIS

The most significant observation of David's commencement address was made by the baccalaureate speaker of the evening, Dean Smith of the University of Chicago. In his very humble and forthright way he openly thanked David and regretted that he was unable to compose and deliver a speech to equal that of David's — a high compliment from a nationally respected official of one of our nation's most prestigious universities.

David was awarded a partial scholarship to the University of Chicago for the study of pre-medicine, enrolling in the fall of 1941. Still in an economic bind, Mother and Dad had difficulty making up the additional costs not covered by the scholarship and encouraged David to seek part-time work. With his great interest in the study of medicine, David found employment as an orderly at Billings Hospital on the University campus.

It was quite some time after I started work at Coopers, in the spring of 1941, that my wandering eye caught sight of a beautiful blond walking toward the water cooler. I had seen her on several occasions and decided it was now time to engineer an encounter. I timed my approach to arrive at the cooler and press the button for her. This led to an exchange of smiles, and the handing of my handkerchief to her on which to dry her lips.

"Now look what you made me do. I got lipstick on your hanky. I'll take it home and wash it."

"Oh no you won't. I'll just add it to my collection."

We introduced ourselves and the meeting proved to be a real icebreaker; our future encounters were casual and friendly.

Like the employee groups of many other companies, the Cooper male employees had bowling teams that competed with one another throughout the fall, winter, and spring months. Because of vacations and other diverse warm-weather activities, they did not bowl in the summer months and celebrated the season's end with what was headlined as a banquet.

The teams invited non-team members to share in their evening of revelry, which was to be held in a rented hall above a respected Northside tavern. After shutting down my service dispatch desk at 10:00 and directing later night callers to an answering service, I drove out and joined the crowd of bowlers.

The dim lighting of the room was enhanced with bright shaded lights over several poker tables where co-workers were exchanging portions of their hard-earned salaries. Tobacco smoke was heavy, and I wondered what there was about gambling and card playing that induced cigarette smokers to switch for an evening to big, fat, cheap Al Capone-type cigars. The deep blue haze surrounding the tables seemed to intensify as the betting surged with expectation and the pile of poker chips multiplied.

Nearby was a long table, well stocked with all the makings of most any type sandwich one could wish for, plus a variety of cheeses, sardines, smoked kippers, and pickled herring in wine sauce. Coffee, carbonated beverages, a choice of several hard liquors, and a keg of beer added to the fare.

A jukebox was churning out many of the Big Band era numbers, and I turned to see who had made these favorite selections. On the far side of a small dance floor I spotted several girls from the office, sitting in a row like a bunch of birds on a wire, talking up a storm while they gestured toward the card players. I had thought this was strictly an affair for men and wondered how they happened to be there. At the end of the row I recognized Ruth and at once felt the evening was not going to be a total loss. I left the sandwich table and went over to where she was sitting.

"Why aren't you dancing?" I quizzed.

"Who wants to dance with girls?" she quizzed back.

"I do," I replied as I took her hand and led her to the dancing surface. The turntable was spinning out Glenn Miller's "Moonlight Serenade," the selection I would have made and one of few with which I was comfortable. Ruth was a good dancer, and we had the floor to ourselves. I asked how she and the others wound up at this shindig.

It turned out that 60-year-old Harry Perry said he would take them all out there in his car, but Harry had already gone home.

"I don't know how I'm going to get home," Ruth worried.

When I found out she lived at 69th and Dorchester, just four blocks from my home at 65th and Dorchester, I offered to take her.

We said our goodbyes to the startled line of "birds," but ignored the poker players, intent on their games and eyeing the growing bets. I don't think they were even aware of our presence. I maneuvered the unfamiliar Northside streets and found my way to Lake Shore Drive and its connection south of downtown to the Outer Drive. We emerged at the north end of Jackson Park at 57th Street and Stony Island Avenue. Spotting the Hitching Post, an all-night eatery, I suggested we stop for one of their special hot-fudge sundaes. Between spoonfuls of the tasty concoction, we talked about our jobs at Cooper's and the unlikely prospects of long-term employment.

"What will they do if America goes to war and there are no refrigerators or electric stoves to sell? The service department couldn't carry the load and generate enough revenue to support their operation." Ruth's question was a reasonable one to which I had no real answer other than to hope they would get some sort of defense contracts to replace the lost revenue.

I wasn't much interested in pursuing that line of conversation at the moment. We were sitting opposite one another in a booth, which afforded me a well-lighted view of this charming and beautiful girl, and I was anxious to learn more about her. But it was past 11:00, and we agreed it was time to end the evening.

We drove to her apartment on 69th Street where she lived on the third floor with her mother, father, and older sister Alice. I asked her for a date and suggested Saturday night, two days hence. She was scheduled to attend the afternoon wedding of a girlfriend, but agreed we could meet after the reception, about 6:00 p.m. I suggested we go to Hottinger's Gardens, a well-known and respected place for dining and dancing to a live band. We had both heard of the beautiful beer garden, but neither of us had ever been there. I said goodnight at her door as we confirmed the time and place of our Saturday meeting. I drove home the four blocks to my house, and although it was midnight, I lay awake for quite awhile thinking about that lovely and intriguing blue-eyed blond.

I saw Ruth for a fleeting moment when I arrived for work just before 4:00 the next day and again verified the time and place of our meeting on Saturday, in front of the Shorewood Hotel near 53rd and Hyde Park Boulevard at 6:00 p.m. The incoming service calls were unusually light for a Friday evening and I found myself whiling away the time with a pencil on the scratch pad, writing, printing, and doodling over and over again the name of Ruth Wasson.

A good part of Saturday was consumed in preparation for our 6:00 meeting. I washed and serviced the Plymouth and covered the front seat with an out-of-service white bedsheet that Mother had given me, pressed my ice-cream-colored flannel slacks, checked my camel-hair jacket, and cleaned and polished the brown-and-white shoes that went well with the outfit. The dark brown plain tie on the white shirt would complete my uniform. Mother stopped me at the door and tucked a fresh, white handkerchief into the breast pocket of my jacket, gave me a once-over inspection, and rendered her approval with a kiss on my cheek.

Ruth emerged from the hotel where the wedding reception had been held, and I spotted her looking up and down the boulevard. I started the engine and slowly drove the short distance to where she stood in the shadow of the entrance awning.

The passenger-side window was open and I called to her, "Taxi, lady?"

I was out of the driver's door before she could answer. I circled the car and held the door for her to enter, noting her attire, her spectator shoes and especially the straight seams of her stockings as she stepped onto the high running board of my old car. Her dark-green linen suit with the white, bold lapel and collar stitching was ideal for the balmy June evening.

Hottinger's Gardens was on the far southwest side of Chicago near 115th Street and Harlem Avenue, a rather sparsely populated area with several eateries and "road houses." These were usually identified with colorful neon tubing running clear around the buildings at eave level and usually catering only to the drinking trade.

Hottinger's was set apart from them with its outdoor dining and dancing facility. Twinkling lights and Japanese lanterns outlined a series of narrow concrete spoke-like walks fanning out from a large central bandstand gazebo, joining several round intersections before terminating at the perimeter in one-table cul-de-sacs. Well-trimmed lawns and shrubs were planted between the walks. I decided a cul-de-sac some distance from the bandstand would allow us a quieter, more intimate setting.

A waiter appeared and took our order for chicken sandwiches, complete with potato chips, lettuce and tomato slice, and pickle, the most expensive menu item at 85 cents each. The cokes were 15 cents. I was mentally calculating the total and hoped she would not accept my offer of additional food. The $2 for our cokes and sandwiches plus the $1 per person Hottinger's cover-charge already had me sweating the capacity of the $6 in my wallet, plus some loose change — at least enough to leave a 50-cent tip for the waiter. But it seemed like Ruth preferred dancing to eating, which left me secure with the $2 surplus languishing in my hip pocket.

We knew the words to most of the songs and sang them softly as we danced. Occasionally, the band would play a fast number and I would use it as my reason to sit one out and just talk. Conversation came easy, and we learned much about one another's likes and dislikes and about our respective families, both of which were quite large. As it was June 1941, I had the Army breathing down my neck and although I had not yet registered for the military Draft, I knew I would have to do so on or about July 1st. So we talked briefly about that prospect.

Dancing to Glenn Miller's "Moonlight Serenade" for the fourth time and the clock on the bandstand reading 10:30, we decided it was time to leave. I drove to a moonlit lookout point near the Jackson Park yacht harbor known as the "crow's nest," a little-known spot where our family used to come for a Sunday evening picnic supper when we were children.

Benches faced Lake Michigan along a narrow walk, and I was surprised to find that we were alone. We sat down and watched the moon play tricks on the rippling wakes of slowly cruising boats putting into and out of the harbor. Sounds of laughter from happy people and music from portable radios drifted into the night. It was a magic moment. I drew Ruth to me and kissed her. She did not resist, so I kissed her again. I said something about her being experienced at this sort of thing, and she said she came from a big family of kissers. We laughed.

We drove to her building where I said goodnight and collected a final kiss at her third-floor apartment. We had had a good time, and I decided before falling asleep that I would be seeing more of this lovely creature.

The summer wore on and we had many more dates, several of which were combined with my friends and their girlfriends. Occasionally, we would plan what we referred to as a mass date — all six of us guys would get dates and go together in three or four cars to a favorite haunt. O'Henry Ballroom in Western Springs, a far western suburb, was our number-one preference. In 1941, Chuck Foster was the featured orchestra and we had many memorable evenings dancing to his music.

Some of our friends were able to hold the Army at arm's length due to physical inadequacies such as poor eyesight, while others were waiting for their birthdays to declare them eligible for the Draft. Larry McBrearty, 19 days older than I, was the first to be called. I followed him two weeks later. Dick Gentzler and Jack Diehl were deferred due to poor eyesight, but would later be called to service. Swede Huddleston soon enlisted in Army Air Forces communications, and Bob Saxton, youngest of our aggregation, entered Army Air Forces pilot training in mid-1942.

It wasn't "those wedding bells breaking up that old gang of mine," but rather a call to arms to battle a vicious war.

Chapter 7

Camp Grant, Illinois

I FUMBLED FOR THE ALARM BUTTON on the Baby Ben clock on the dresser next to my bed. Squinting through the darkness of the room, I saw the green radium-coated numbers on the black dial with the glow-in-the-dark hands signaling 6:25. In five minutes I would have heard its ring but for years my mental alarm had beaten the urgency of the twin bells. I stretched full length, laced fingers behind my head, and wondered where I next would awaken. It was Friday, September 26th, 1941, the day of my induction into the United States Army, and I was due at Draft Board 89, on 63rd Street, at 9:00 a.m.

Mother's call — never a shout — from the kitchen below, "Alex," echoed up the back stairwell to the short hall leading to David's room. I scrambled out of my ¾-size bed to deliver the accurate answer: "I'm up." Between the alarm clock, my mental alarm, and Mother's call, there was never a reason for over-sleeping. I heard her rattle of breakfast preparation and sensed that today's fare would be a little special. I quickly bathed in our ancient tub, the iron clawed feet stating its vintage, shaved with a new blade in my razor, dressed in brown slacks and yellow sport shirt, new brown-and-yellow argyle socks and my best brown oxfords. Per custom, I'd wear my brown felt fedora-type hat.

The two-handled, black leather Gladstone bag that I had borrowed from Dad (and would be returned to him when the Army had supplied me with GI-type luggage) received my toilet articles, a small Kodak Bullseye box camera, extra film, a letter-sized ruled tablet of paper and some envelopes, a booklet of three-cent stamps, my mechanical pencil and fountain pen, a bottle of Sheaffer's Scrip Blue Ink, cigarettes, some hard candy and chewing gum, a change of underwear, handkerchiefs, extra socks, a lightweight jacket, a sleeveless sweater, a few family photos, and — last but by no means least — a beautiful 8x10 tinted photo of Ruth Wasson, mounted in a gilded frame. My last evening as a civilian was spent with Ruth, when she gave me two pictures. I had asked her for one that I could carry in my wallet, never expecting her to supply me with both. She laughed and said, "You're silly," when I inserted the small one in my wallet and returned it to my hip pocket, patting it while promising to carry it there, "next to my heart."

Mother's breakfast was sumptuous: slab bacon fried slightly limp, fried eggs basted with the hot bacon grease, buckwheat pancakes enhanced with sweet tub butter and real maple syrup from Vermont, fresh blueberries trying to float in a shallow portion of half-and-half cream, and percolated coffee with egg mixed in to settle the grounds. It was a hero's breakfast and, at 21, I had gained a hearty appetite while learning from a family with six kids that one did not linger in claiming a reasonable share of the provisions. Ray, David, and Dad had joined Mother and me at the dining room table. Jean and Margaret would have to fend for themselves, which was customary. Girls were just slower. Mother's offering was soon devoured, with high praise from all, and while sipping a second cup of coffee, conversation centered on my impending departure.

Ray and David detailed those possessions of mine that each would appropriate in my absence, mostly my limited but worthy wardrobe and my considerable collection of tools. (I was the more serious mechanic in the family.) David relished the idea of having two rooms, his present one for sleeping and my room converted to a study, which he had already named "Dave's Brain Factory." The hand-printed sign on his desk included the order, "Knock Before Entering," where he prudently kept it, awaiting my departure. Ray had his own car, but David made much sport of finally acquiring his own set of wheels — mine. Mother and Dad enjoyed the repartee and laughed heartily at our bantering. The intimacy of those moments spent together would be remembered and recalled many times over.

Then that dreaded lull loomed, and one by one each voiced his regret that I was leaving and told me I would be missed. Dad observed that I was only the second one to leave the fireside, Cameron having been the first when he and Rita were married in 1938. "We hope and pray that your one year of service will go quickly and that you will return in good order and good health, Alex. Remember that when you are thinking of us, we are thinking of you. And may you draw happiness and strength from those moments of reflection." I responded in kind and asked them to write often and keep me current with all the family "goings on."

The ultimate moment had arrived. It was time to go.

Jean and Margaret had come downstairs and now joined with all of us on the front porch. No one had asked me how I was fixed for money, perhaps assuming that the Army would supply all my needs. Nonetheless, Jean and Margaret each gave me $5 while Mother and Dad each handed me $10. Ray shelled out $5 and David gave me a promise that he would "take care of me at Christmas." He had recently enrolled as a pre-med student at the University of Chicago and was woefully short of cash at the moment. I had not expected or really wanted money from any of them.

Though my own cash situation was rather slim, I did have the remnants of my final pay-check. My job as night service manager had been more title than remuneration and paid the healthy sum of $22.50 per week. From that, Social Security was deducted and I paid $1 per week into a Christmas savings club at the bank. Withholding tax had not yet been invented, but filing and paying of tax annually was required. Ever since we had begun earning, an iron-clad family rule required the payment for board and room into the ongoing household expense. I paid Dad $6 or $7 per week. The remainder covered lunches, gasoline and car expense, dry cleaning, clothing, incidental expenses, and entertainment — mostly dates. In spite of all the outgo, I still managed to save a dollar or two amid the nagging presence of the Depression.

With the family gifts my wallet bulged under the rare strain of about $60. Money in abundance was a dreamed-of condition in our household, and I knew these were gifts of love, wrought by hard work and careful accounting. I dared not refuse them. (My first month's Army pay of $21, less of $6.60 deducts for insurance, and $3 for laundry, would happen at the end of October). The family gifts would prove to be an emergency back-up for me for a long time, and as my fortunes improved, any withdrawals were always repaid.

Ray and David waited for me on the walk at the foot of the stairs. I hugged and kissed Jean and Margaret and asked them write to me. I knew Jean would, as she was the correspondent of the family. Margaret, as a public school teacher and a major provider to the household, always seemed to be preoccupied with her work. In my four years in the Army I would receive perhaps two or three postcards, a few Christmas cards, and one or two letters from her.

I turned to Dad and Mother, instinctively saving my final goodbyes for them. Crippling arthritis had taken its toll on Dad's outstretched hands, reaching to enfold the measured physical strength of mine. The years had begun to tell on him, and although he was only 69, he suddenly looked much older. Those superbly gifted, once nimble fingers that had helped earn our livelihood at the piano and in the studio were relentlessly tormented. Now when music flowed from the piano in the living room, it was David at the keyboard. When David was away, silence reigned where the lilting strains of a romantic aria or love song used to sound through the rooms of our house. As our hands met in a firm clasp, my grip was consciously light in touch in deference to his painful hands.

Then perhaps for the first time since I was about 12, my father put his arms around me. "God be with you, laddie," he said, his British-accented words accompanied by a slight catch in his voice. We drew back from the embrace and when our eyes met I saw in his a hint of melancholy. Impulsively I kissed him, an expression of filial love we boys had abandoned in our pre-teen years when we decided that men did not kiss.

Dad's eyes brightened and he smiled. Then he returned the gesture, without comment. A dormant bond had been rekindled, a remembered familiar chord struck again. I knew I loved and was loved.

Mother stood, tentatively, hands half raised, anticipating her inclusion in these parting moments. Where there was perhaps an occasional frown of disapproval or a look of anxious concern, there was now only an expression of supreme confidence and pride. I took her in my arms and held her tight for several moments. She reached up and took my face in her work-roughened gentle hands and kissed me. "Do be careful, dear boy. Be sure and let me know if there is anything you need. We'll be praying for you and you pray for us." A vision of childhood bedtime prayers at her knee flashed before me. Her traditional role of chief provisioner would not cease but would be increased, and her life's commitment to the welfare of her family would not be abridged. If the effects of absence or separation could ever be measured, I knew in an instant that I would miss all of them, but I would miss her most. Her love knew no bounds.

Ray sat waiting in the car, engine running. I picked up my bag, went down the stairs, and handed it to David.

"Here, take my luggage to the car, and don't drop it," I said, feigning authority in my best commanding voice. He grabbed the bag with one hand and wrapped his other strong arm tight around my neck and almost dragged me to the car. We shook hands. I wished him well in his school work and expressed hope that he would be able to go on and fulfill his goal of being a doctor. He was already working as an operating room orderly at Billings Hospital in the service of one of America's top brain surgeons.

"See you later, Alzo," he said.

"Take it easy, Dazo," I responded.

These were pet names we dug up that moment from our childhood days as inseparable siblings. Ray gunned the engine, put my old Plymouth in gear, and with an exchange of waves and blowing of kisses to those watching from the porch, we pulled away. I looked back to see the waving continue until we passed from view. My tears hovered on the brink.

We turned left at the Illinois Central embankment, then right on Marquette Road heading west. We had passed Vasalow's Pharmacy, where Mr. Vasalow once had advised me to eat lettuce for roughage; Lenzen's Ice Cream Parlor, where they still hand-packed a quart of the best vanilla in town; Mrs. Tripp's Delicatessen, where Mother sent us for a whole pound of thinly sliced peppered beef, homemade rye bread, potato salad, and tiny sweet gherkin pickles to tantalize the pallets of unexpected Sunday evening guests; and the Chinese Laundry, where Dad had his detachable collars laundered and our only communication with the oriental ironers was to announce the laundry mark and item, "CST Collars," and pay their "30 penny." Their workplace was very hot and steamy and always smelled of chicken noodle or rice soup, which they ate while working, shuffling in sandaled feet, and occasionally blowing water mist on the work piece from a can equipped with a mouth spout. We told Mother that was superior to her method of sprinkling and rolling.

Turning north on Cottage Grove Avenue, we passed the Tivoli Theater where we had attended movies and saw many great vaudeville acts. I remembered seeing Jackie Cooper with Wallace Beery in *The Champ* and on the same billing Jackie appeared in person on stage in his show. He was presented to the audience riding atop a small upright piano as it was wheeled out by two stagehands. Jackie sang a song or two as an accompanist played. While singing, he took a jackknife from his pocket and proceeded to carve on the back edge of the piano. The audience uttered a mild gasp at the apparent destruction, but it was obvious that a board painted to match the white piano had been attached for carving purposes. As we drove past, I recalled this incident to Ray and he, too, remembered that show.

We turned east on 63rd Street where the Jackson Park branch of the Elevated train rumbled overhead, drove two blocks, and stopped in front of the Draft Board building. I turned to Ray and said, "Well, this is it, Stinky. Sure hope you don't have to go. Take good care of the folks, write to me and . . . I'll see you in a year."

Ray replied, "Here is your chance to have a year's worth of fun. Good luck, Al."

We shook hands. I grabbed my bag from the back seat, then stood at the curb watching my old, reliable Plymouth disappear into the heavy traffic. "You have my car and now you tell me to have fun," I hollered to no one in particular, smiling.

Before I got that Plymouth, I was driving a 1929 DeSoto, really a family cast-off I had acquired during my senior year in high school. I had struggled with its temperamental ways for quite some time. One day, I spotted the 1932 Plymouth for sale at a Texaco gas station at 71st Street and South Shore Drive. The price tag, $60, was painted in white on the windshield. I asked the owner what he would allow me on the DeSoto, and we agreed on $40. With no car titles to be concerned about, the buying/selling process was simply and quickly handled with a bill of sale. I made the deal on the spot and drove off in the Plymouth. Knowing that it needed tires, I drove to Harold Wirth's Standard Oil Station at Marquette and Stony Island in search of a set of good used "skins." Harold had nothing used that was suitable, but offered me a set of four brand new Atlas tires and tubes mounted for $20.

"I'm a little low right now, Harold. Can you give me any terms?" I asked.

"How about $5 down and $1 per week for 15 weeks," he offered. An hour later, I drove out of the station on my first set of brand new tires and never had another flat. And I paid Harold off in nine weeks.

The Plymouth had one persistent fault, however, a leaky roof. (The first all-steel-roof on cars, which certain car makers dubbed a "turret top," didn't come until 1933). Ruth was puzzled one evening when she got into the car and I instructed her to sit closer to me and get under my umbrella. The rain water dripped down on the seat right between us, so I raised the umbrella to deflect the water. She complied, but teased me about doing most anything to get her to move closer to me. From then on, rain or shine, she never reclaimed the far right seat.

Draft Board 89 occupied the second floor space above several retail stores. I opened one of the heavy wood and glass doors, stepped into a small vestibule, and mounted the long stairway, two steps at a time. This was the product of youthful habit and energy and not a sign of eagerness to surrender my freedom to the "hup-two-three-four" of the Army's marching order. The stairs abruptly ended in front of a tall, obese soldier seated behind a too-small desk, his olive-drab shirtsleeves covered with sewed-on stripes and hash bars, designating his rank as a Staff Sergeant and each bar representing a three-year hitch in the Service. He had eight of them. I also learned that the few colored ribbons on his chest signified duty in Panama and the bright red one with oak leaf clusters was the Good Conduct medal. With the considerable girth of his waist, I concluded he had behaved himself while establishing strong, friendly relations with the mess Sergeants in the various commands in which he had served.

"Gimme your classification card," he ordered. I fished it out of my wallet and he impatiently took it from me. Reading, he said, "Stew-art, 1A. Right?"

"That's right," I answered, quickly deciding against correcting his pronunciation of my name. He consulted a loose-leaf notebook filled with pages whose holes were torn from the rings. He finally found my name and matched it against my card. He checked off my name with a heavy red pencil, then handed back the card along with a paperwork to fill out. I don't remember what information the form called for, but I went over and stood at a high counter that encircled three walls, along with 10 or 15 other guys, and completed the form as ordered. A younger soldier of lesser rank circulated among us to answer any questions, then collected the completed forms before directing us to an adjoining room to take a physical examination.

I stepped into the room and took my place at the end of a snake-like line of about 100 totally naked men of all sizes and shapes, each holding their clothing rolled in a bundle wrapped around their shoes. Still clinging to my bag, I quickly undressed and was able to jam my clothes into it. The line moved slowly and like all the others, I suffered all the indignities common to mass medical scrutiny. The only smidgen of privacy occurred when two or three inoculations against diseases I had never heard of were administered behind a three-sectioned screen. When it was my turn behind the screen I was surprised to see two men lying on cots who had apparently fainted at the sight of the syringes. The screen shielded them from view of the yet-to-be-stuck recruits, hopefully reducing the number of additional fainters. Meanwhile, some of the emerging immunized acted out exaggerated pain from the ordeal, holding their arms and gesturing that they had been stuck with a device the size of a large knitting needle, all for the benefit of the remaining uninitiated. Moments later, the actors were bunched together, laughing at their pretense and pointing to some who they thought they had traumatized.

Next, we were told to get dressed and be seated on the folding chairs in an assembly-type room. Presently the room was filled and it was obvious that most all who were scheduled for induction on the 26th were there. In every formation there are a few no-shows, and the roll call now confirmed this fact. Those who failed to pass the physical exam were identified and directed to another room. Some felt they had been wrongly classified as being fit for service and loudly protested, but to no avail. We were all told that we would receive another physical at the reception center at Camp Grant, Illinois, and could appeal at that time.

Soon the bulky Sergeant from the reception desk lumbered into the room and called for attention. He was followed by an officer, a Second Lieutenant with gold bars on his shoulders. He had no hash marks on his sleeves or ribbons on his chest. The Sergeant ordered everyone to stand. He introduced the Lieutenant, whose Polish name I could not pronounce and immediately forgot. The officer then told us to be seated, proceeded to drill us on the glories of serving our country, and to lecture us on how military service can be a great learning experience.

"Now everyone please stand and raise your right hand to be sworn in." He rattled off in a monotone something about supporting and defending the Constitution of the United States against all enemies foreign and domestic, then called on us to say, "I do." As far as I know, everyone complied. He then confirmed that we were now officially members of the Army and that our pay as Privates would be $21 per month, starting "today."

Four chartered buses were parked at the curb, their gas engines running at a fast idle (for no obvious reason) as they spewed annoying exhaust smoke and fumes over a wide area of 63rd Street. We emerged from the building in single file according to the alphabetical listing on the original manifest, were checked against the list by "Old Sarge," and climbed aboard "Old Smokey #4." I momentarily praised the Army for some semblance of efficiency, found a vacant seat near the middle of the bus, and sat down. I stowed my bag on the floor between my legs, then turned to greet my seat mate. To my surprise, he turned out to be George Bowman, a Hyde Park High School acquaintance that I had not seen since graduation in 1938; it was strange that I had not encountered him upstairs. "How, George," I asked, "did you of the 'Bs' wind up in here with we 'Ss'?"

"Don't ask me, Alex. This is the Army. I guess we can look forward to all sorts of surprises."

Each bus was filled to capacity, carrying about 40 men. Bus #1 was the vehicle of choice for the old Sergeant with the notebook. He would be our escort (chaperone) for the trip downtown to the Dearborn Street Station, where we would be turned over to his counterpart, who would accompany us on the train to Camp Grant at Rockford, Illinois, 88 miles west of the Windy City.

The four-bus caravan finally pulled out into traffic, drove to the first intersection, and turned left onto what I believe was Ellis Avenue. We turned left again on 62nd Street and proceeded to Cottage Grove Avenue. I took a brief look at the Trianon Ballroom, on the southeast corner, and noted on the marquee that the current attraction was Ted Weems and his orchestra and that the ballroom was still featuring singer Perry Como. George, too, remembered that we had the same entertainers at the Trianon for our Senior Prom.

The buses turned right on Cottage Grove, and I noted that the nightclub located on the northwest corner at 61st Street, the name of which I cannot remember, was still featuring "The Chicago Beef Trust Review." High on the exterior of this one-story building was a series of huge photographs of very large, obese women, each reportedly weighing over 500 pounds. The photos ran the full length and depth of the building and displayed these "dancers" in what were for those times, scanty costumes. I asked George if he had ever seen their show, and he had not, though he heard that it had a lot of jiggling going on and "uncontrolled movement" of flesh. I learned later that the Chicago Beef Trust review had been a feature of the famous Rialto, the leading Chicago burlesque theater, before it started touring the nightclub circuit. (When the Rialto yielded to the wrecking ball, the wrecking company made headlines with a sign it had posted in front of the theater claiming to be the "greatest stripper of them all.")

The bus ride continued north on Cottage Grove to the Midway, that stretch of terrain a mile long and a city block wide, planted to carefully tended grass, dividing 59th Street and 60th Street and extending one mile from Stony Island on the east to Cottage Grove on the west. The University of Chicago campus fronts on the 59th Street side and many stately old homes and flat buildings front on 60th Street. Two east-west boulevards and the north-south cross streets divide the area into large rectangles, the center ones of which are depressed about eight feet below street level. The Park Department erected portable warming houses in the winter and flooded a few of the rectangles for ice skating. This was the Midway holdover from the World's Fair of 1893, where Fair-goers rode the latest rides —

a huge roller coaster and the first Ferris Wheel. It held fond memories for me of fun times in my carefree youth.

We were now passing the entrance to Washington Park on our left. The famous sculpture by Lorado Taft (1860-1936), a huge panorama of people of many eras carved in stone, formed the backdrop for a reflecting pool and fountain. As kids we had often hiked the length of the Midway and ate a sack lunch of peanut butter on Mother's homemade bread while dangling our hot, tired feet in the water. When Mother asked where we had been we replied, "to Lorado Taff." Years later we learned the work was "The Fountain of Time" and that the sculptor's name was "Taft."

North of 59th Street we entered less-familiar territory, where the imposing National Guard Armory was the only known landmark I recognized. The bus rumbled on and George dozed off with his mouth hanging open, while the conversations of others swirled around us. Dad had alerted me to be aware of what he termed "barracks talk," profanity at its highest (or lowest) level. Such expressions had been sounded the moment I entered the Draft Board and had gained in intensity and vulgarity, especially during the physical examinations. I thought I had heard every perverse word and phrase in my 21 years of big-city schooling and work environments but what now accosted my ear drums was, well, un-believable . . . and I was to find later would get worse. It wasn't an occasional "hell" or "damn" but seemed to be a language all its own, a constant stream of vile expletives blended into an on-going sentence structure. These were normal-appearing young men of nearly every ethnic source, speaking a common language in a fluency I had never heard before.

It also became apparent that almost every recruit had been a huge success in civilian life. Though the country was still economically depressed and the unemployment rate hovered in the 15 to 20 percent range, down from a high of 25 percent, the stories being swapped back and forth would indicate they each had been snatched by the Army from a high-paying career. My guess was that at least 20 percent were unemployed and the rest of us earned less than $25 per week. I gradually concluded that my $22.50 salary was above average.

The buses finally arrived at the Dearborn Street Station and maneuvered around the rear to the freight-loading area. We filed out of the bus and immediately boarded the old train coaches for the trip to Rockford. Draft Boards in other areas of the city had been as busy as we had been, and their contingents of recruits added to the noise, profanity, and confusion. The total train of about 20 cars was soon filled and ready to depart.

Now well past noon, my wonderful breakfast had become history, and I was ready for refueling. The train began to move and an undertone of grumbling about lunch was adapted to the profane vocabulary. The *xzy*#@$* Army and its doctors became the *Yx*&* Army and its *ZX*Y%* food. Presently, our Sergeant escort came swaying through the cars and announced that we could line up and walk forward two or three cars to pick up a box lunch. The grumbling subsided and our line was soon meeting returning traffic, each man carrying a generous slice of Spam on heavy, thick-sliced Army bread, and two large oat-meal cookies, all wrapped together in waxed paper. The term "box lunch" was a misnomer. No drinks were provided, but we were reminded that there was a water tap at each end of the car with folded flat paper cups in a wall-mounted dispenser nearby.

In spite of the dryness of the sandwich and cookies and the struggle to get adequate liquid, the grumbling fell to a mere murmur. I noted then and several hundred times since that sated hunger has a soothing effect, even on the most belligerent malcontent. The accuracy of the statement "An army travels on its stomach" was confirmed. The Army provided the food, but the railroad took charge of the clean-up. A porter came through the car with a large paper sack in which we tossed our waste paper.

The train's progress was slow and was frequently diverted to sidings to allow the passage of scheduled passenger service. During the afternoon, candy butchers (the burlesque theater term for vendors) came on board and sold out their portable inventories before the train resumed its journey. Though it was late September, the weather was warm and pleasant and we rode with the windows open. Occasionally, smoke and cinders from our steam locomotive would find their way into the train, but no criticism was voiced. Air conditioning perhaps existed on the great cross-country, luxury trains that were pulled by huge diesel electric engines, but such comfort was non-existent on troop trains and was yet to be experienced by most of us.

The normal 1½-hour travel time stretched into 5 or 6 hours and a great cheer went up when we finally chugged onto the Camp Grant siding at 7:00 p.m. and came to a screeching stop at a long gravel-covered clearing. The porters and conductors opened the doors and lifted the hinged steel plates covering the stairs. A Camp Grant soldier entered each car and instructed us to "fall out" and line up beside the train . . . "And pick up all your stuff now 'cause there's no coming back for it. This train is heading back to Chicago for tomorrow's load of 'Dog Faces,'" he barked. (I learned later that GIs were known as Dog Faces because in their uniforms they all seemed to look alike and, according to some perverted mind, resembled dogs.)

Several hundred recruits piled out of the train and stood in some crude semblance of a line. An officer speaking into a microphone on a raised platform told us that we would proceed to the auditorium to be welcomed by the Base Commander, then to the mess hall for supper and finally to our barracks.

The welcome speech at the auditorium was short and its content was not much different than what we had heard that morning at the Draft Board. Next, we straggled to the mess hall and got in a double line to be served from two steam tables. We each picked up a compartmentalized stainless steel tray, steel knife, fork and spoon, paper napkins, and a large gray-white, handleless coffee mug. The recruits who arrived a few days before us were our servers on KP (kitchen police) duty and seemed to enjoy wielding their long-handled serving spoons. Quantities were generous and you took whatever was slapped onto your tray, whether you wanted it or not. A sign over the steam table cautioned, "*Take all you want but eat all you take.*" It was a good rule but difficult to obey. To my surprise, the food tasted pretty good. The meal finished, we took our trays to a kitchen window and scraped leftovers into one garbage can and paper products into another; flatware was put in a large bucket of soapy water. When leaving the mess hall I saw two men emptying the day's collection of garbage into a large truck. I asked one of the cooks what they did with it, and he told me they were farmers and took the garbage to feed their pigs. It was a while before I regained an appetite for ham or pork chops.

A number of barracks had been designated, and I found my way to one near the end of the complex that still had some vacant bunks. I noted that it was about 9:45 and lights would be turned out at 10:00. I selected a bunk not too close to the latrine, set my bag on the bed, and went to brush my teeth. I rinsed my face with cool water, dried off on my undershirt, and used the first vacant urinal before returning to my bunk. I had just removed the neatly folded blanket from atop the pillow when the lights went out. The light was left on in the latrine, and light from street lamps shone dimly through the windows.

I undressed and laid my clothes on the shelf above the hanging rod. There were no hangers. These would be issued the next day, along with towels and our uniforms. It seemed that the Army had some sort of quirk about hanging civilian clothes on GI hangers. I wondered what happened to those that the previous occupants had used. I would soon hear that they packed them with their stuff when they shipped out and that we would be doing the same.

Bone tired, I tried to crawl between the sheets. Something was wrong. Those sheets didn't work right. My feet met a blank wall about 36 inches south of the pillow. I struggled, kicked, and cursed, trying to get some stretch-out room in that bed. I was glad Dad wasn't around to hear my newly acquired vocabulary. But I wasn't alone. All of my 50 recruit buddies in the barracks were having similar problems, and the profane utterances became a chorus. After kicking down with my feet and tugging up with my hands for quite some time, exhausted, I assumed a fetal position and fell sound asleep. The next morning, after a fitful night of bedsheet torture, we learned that the previous occupants had had the same experience and had learned the hard way, as we had done, about short-sheeting a bed. When I shipped out about two weeks later, I perfected my short-sheeting technique and felt that quiet surge of exhilaration as I contemplated my victim's ire. Ray would be glad to know that I had my first Army fun.

The shrill blast of the Top Sergeant's whistle bore no resemblance to my mental alarm, or my Baby Ben, when it jarred me awake at 5:00 Saturday morning. But the whistle wasn't as bad as his screaming command to "fall out" of bed for "short-arm inspection." Only half awake and somewhat alarmed, I scrambled to the floor and stood at the foot of my bed, wondering what in the hell a short-arm inspection was. Suddenly, a medical officer and his staff barged through the front door of the barracks, tromped down the aisle between the rows of cots, and demanded that we drop our shorts. With flashlight in hand, the doctor visually examined our penises, looking for evidence of gonorrhea. To those who had not been circumcised, he ordered certain manipulation. Finding no evidence of the disease, they stomped out the back door to the next barracks. We heard the repeat of the Sergeant's whistle and commands next door as our guys made a bee-line for the latrine. It occurred to me that these inspections were held before the men had the opportunity to use the latrine and that the evidence of infection would be at its best with a full bladder. That was a "short-arm inspection," and many of us were not only surprised but appalled.

Soon a Corporal entered the barracks and told us to be ready to march to the mess hall for breakfast at 6:30. "Don't bother to shower 'cause you don't have towels yet. But be sure and shave, and dry your face with toilet paper. When you hear my whistle, fall out and line up according to height in front of the barracks."

I figured I could snatch another 30 to 45 minutes of sleep before shaving and dressing, and several of the others had the same idea. But I managed to be ready about 10 minutes before the whistle. When the Corporal's blast came ahead of schedule, there was a mad scramble by some to shave, swish water on their hair ahead of the comb, ignore socks, pull on pants and shirts, and clog out of the barracks in untied shoes while tucking in shirttails and zipping up flys.

Somehow they managed to line up according to height, and at 5 feet, 11 inches, I was about number 10 out of 50. The Corporal had every other man take one step forward, thus forming two lines. We closed ranks, did a right face, and on command started straggle-marching to the mess hall. Before entering, the Corporal told us to return to the barracks on our own after eating and to be ready to go to the warehouse for our GI Issue at 8:00.

The standard breakfast fare was greenish-looking, watery scrambled eggs, bacon that was either over- or under-fried, choice of dry cereal in individual boxes that could be opened on a perforation and using the box as a bowl, oatmeal, bread toasted on one side, stewed prunes, tough pancakes with very watery syrup, and very bitter coffee in those huge mugs. I was hungry, and so I ate; it really wasn't too bad. I was already becoming conditioned to Army food. I cleaned off my tray and ambled back to the barracks thinking about the pleasant conversation I had just had with the fellow sitting next to me in the mess hall, a Jim Gordon from Chicago. He had been an officer in his high school ROTC — Reserved Officer Training Corps — unit and knew a lot about the military routine. He said he would apply for Officers Candidate School at his first opportunity, and I believed he would succeed.

We loosely marched to the warehouse to receive our clothing and equipment. We had previously filled out a form showing our sizes and measurements and now faced long counters covered with huge stacks of various duty uniforms, boxes of socks and kerchiefs, neckties, piles of towels, and undershirts and shorts that were all white. Hand-stenciled signs fastened to the counters stated sizes and quantities to be issued.

The first sign said, "Barracks Bags — Take 2." These were large blue denim bags with heavy rope drawstrings that would forever identify us as enlisted men in the Army. Whatever mode of travel, GIs were seen struggling with those two barracks bags tied together, carrying their worldly possessions slung over stooped shoulders Now, as we passed down the line the supply people selected sizes and quantities to be received and told us to put them in the bags.

I received two blue denim uniforms, known as "fatigue suits," which consisted of pants and a shirt-type jacket and a matching floppy round-brimmed hat, two pair of scratchy wool olive-drab (OD) dress pants and matching shirts, an OD "blouse" (the Army term for jacket), an assortment of underwear and accessories, a so-called wide, brown garrison belt and peaked hat with brown strap and brass Army insignia, a pleated field cap, which had earned a suggestive name, and finally two pair of brown shoes, one ankle high and one oxford. Here, my first clothing trouble began.

My civilian shoe size was 10½D. The first day I wore the ankle-highs I got blisters on my feet from their being over-size. I was excused from duty away from the barracks for a day to allow my feet to heal and was confined to quarters. But the Sergeant wasn't going to let me just lie around all day, and promptly appointed me "Latrine Orderly." I had often cleaned the bathroom at home, but never before had I taken on ten toilets, urinals, wash basins, mirrors, a ten-head shower room, concrete floor, and a large, rectangular dish-pan-sized disinfectant foot bath for the control of athlete's foot located in front of the shower entrance. Now it was my duty to keep all this clean, all day. The next day I went to the warehouse for shoe changes and finally settled on Army size 9D, which fit perfectly. Until then, I had been wearing my civilian shoes, loosely tied.

Topping off the GI Issue was a water canteen encased in a heavy, quilted fabric case with belt hooks, a folding aluminum mess kit and steel utensils, and finally a huge slicker-type raincoat and a supply of wire coat hangers. As soon as we received our stuff, we returned to the barracks on our own and set to work trying on our new wardrobe. Everything fit me quite well, though I was determined to have some refining adjustments made at a tailor shop. Being Saturday afternoon, we were free for the weekend and learned that passes were available. It was too late to get ready for a trip to Chicago, and little time to do anything once there, for I would be due back in camp by 6:00 p.m. on Sunday. So instead, I went into Rockford to "see the sights."

I rode the bus with dozens of others and joined the throng of GIs wandering up and down the business streets, all of us looking for excitement but mostly patronizing the bars, cafes, and cheaper restaurants. There wasn't much excitement in Rockford unless you created it. There were a few inebriated fights, some unseemly remarks made to passing girls, and several mud-clogged shoes and pants where over-indulging guys wearing their new olive drab staggered into what had been rain-swollen gutters. I had two beers and a hamburger, talked with two barracks acquaintances for awhile, then caught the bus back to camp. I continued to organize my gear before going to bed. Sunday was a dull day around camp, and I was sorry then that I hadn't made the effort to go to Chicago, even for a few fleeting hours. I called Ruth long-distance and talked for six minutes, three past the usual three-minute limit, after depositing additional coins required by the interrupting operator. Ruth was glad I called as she was writing to me and needed my address. I capped off the weekend by writing to her and a general letter to the folks.

Up before dawn, a clear, bright Monday morning sunrise soon crept over the horizon on my fourth Army day and was punctuated with the second physical as promised by the Draft Board, a rather strenuous calisthenics period with exercises unfamiliar to me in previous regimens, a period of instruction and practice in close-order drill and all its various maneuvers, and a two-mile hike around the camp. Interspersed with these formations was time devoted to more work on uniforms and attendance at a movie and lecture on venereal disease. It was late in the day that my blistered feet became an important issue. A trip to the dispensary produced the treatment and medications for the disorder.

Tuesday was the day spent alone in the barracks, with initiation into the society of experienced Latrine Orderlies. A check of the bulletin board had me scheduled for KP duty on Wednesday. I secured a temporary delay, to get my shoes exchanged for the good-fitting 9Ds, then reported to the mess kitchen.

The mess Sergeant assigned me to operate the potato-peeling machine. It consisted of a large, tiltable steel barrel with a rough granite-like interior. It was powered by a strong electric motor, and the turning action of the barrel caused the peel to erode away from the potatoes while a water flush carried away the tiny scraps of peel. As instructed, I dumped in half of a 100-pound sack of Idahos and pushed the start button. It worked fine, and I soon pushed the OFF switch and tilted the barrel to dump the spuds into a large, stainless-steel tub. I noted that the abrasive interior surface removed everything but the eyes of the potatoes. Someone picked up the tub and hauled it over to the corner of the room where five GIs sat around several tubs, removing the eyes with hand peelers. I dumped the remaining half sack into the machine and repeated the process.

Someone came over and told me I was not leaving the potatoes in the machine long enough, and that the running time should be increased to reduce the number of eyes. I increased the timer setting and succeeded in reducing the number of eyes while wearing away quite a bit of good white pulp. I finished that load and reloaded, then left the machine running while I went to the latrine. When I returned, I discovered that this third batch came out with no eyes at all, and the spuds were now just a little larger than golf balls. Somebody had reset the timer. I was dumping the batch when the mess Sergeant walked up and observed what had happened. He checked the machine and concluded that I had intentionally increased the erosion time and was being compensated by the "eye removers."

"Not true," I pleaded. He remained unconvinced and reassigned me to Dining Room Orderly. I did discover that an eye picker had sabotaged my effort so that they would have less work to do.

The dining hall was about half the length of a football field and contained two rows of long picnic-style tables with bench seats attached on each side. Each of the 60 tables would accommodate about 20 men. My job was to secure a bucket of warm water containing some soap and a disinfectant and wash the varnished, Masonite-like top surface of each table. Then I was to fill salt, pepper, and sugar shakers and replenish bottles of catsup, pepper sauce, mustard, syrup, and one or two other items.

I accomplished all this in partnership with another KP and was about to go out on the back steps for a cigarette when the mess Sergeant walked in to inspect the job. Since the potato incident, he had me pegged as a goof-off and made a special effort to check me out. He could not find fault with the clean-up but climbed on me for not lining up the condiments in proper order. He described the way in which they were to be arranged, the tallest bottles in the center and the other items tapering down evenly on each side. He provided a large ball of twine to stretch from the first table to the last and align all table edges evenly with the twine. Then using the twine again, I was to locate the two sets of condiments on each table so that they were in perfect military, precise order from table to table. I became exasperated, but held my tongue and finished the job. I did this twice on Wednesday and three times each on Thursday and Friday, the last day of my KP stretch. By then, I was less than enthused with the military but knew my date with Ruth on Saturday night would iron out the wrinkles in my composure.

After a brief barracks inspection on Saturday morning, we were turned loose for the weekend. I had arranged for Ray to drive over to Camp Grant and pick me up. He was glad to do so and wanted to hear all about the Army. I carried my toilet kit and clothing items in Dad's bag, including the slicker raincoat. My homecoming was a momentous occasion and all were anxious to hear of my experiences. I was careful to limit my remarks to the more enjoyable times and to minimize the few hardships.

When I arrived at Ruth's apartment for dinner, it was raining and I was wearing the huge slicker raincoat over my uniform. It hung way down to my ankles, and when she answered the door she took one look at me and started laughing.

"I know it looks funny," I said, "but I'm dry." (That incident has survived over a half-century of memories and still earns a laugh).

Mrs. Wasson's specialty of roast prime rib of beef and Yorkshire pudding was a delightful contrast to the two weeks of Army fare I was learning to tolerate. Ruth's father was a tower-man for the Illinois Central, his schedule requiring him to be on the job this night. He was busy manning the switching controls that diverted rail traffic onto the South Shore-South Chicago branch at 67th Street. I sat next to Ruth at the table, facing her sister Alice and her mother. Their interest peaked when I described the Army's way of preparing food, the quantities dealt with, and the number of mouths being conditioned to receive it.

The roof on my car was still leaking when we left Ruth's house to go dancing at the Trianon. Without comment, she scooted over near me and under the protective cover of the umbrella. I was grateful for the rain and the umbrella. Ted Weems and his orchestra, along with Perry Como, Elmo Tanner the whistler, and Country Washburn were still holding forth, and all were at their best. We danced and sang to one another — so many of our favorite tunes of that Big Band era — had a Coke, talked and talked, and danced some more.

What was there about this girl that was different from all the others I had dated? That haunting question lurked in the background of my thoughts whenever we were together. I once tried enumerating those qualities that constantly drew me to her. She was certainly beautiful. She was impeccably groomed, and she used makeup to enhance her natural color and not to obliterate it. She was stylishly but not expensively attired, conservative in taste, fun loving, and had a hearty laugh, a ready smile, and an open countenance. Ruth was intelligent, honest, poised, and confident, and certainly unassuming; yet she was ambitious. She loved her family and they all loved her.

But there was something else that clanged like a bell within me that night. It was the realization that she was deeply interested in me. She was concerned for my welfare and what the future might hold — not just for herself, but for me.

When I held her in my arms at her door at the end of the evening, I knew I had fallen in love with her. "Will you be coming back next weekend?" she asked.

"Yes, of course, unless I get shipped out before then. It could happen," I said with a little hoarseness gathering in my throat.

I kissed her again, then unwillingly released her and turned to go. I stopped, stood for a moment holding her hands, my eyes feasting on her lovely face. Reaching out to her, I cupped her chin in my hand and planted a peck on her lips, then again embraced her. Almost whispering I said, "Ruthie, you must know that I love you very much. I couldn't leave you tonight without telling you."

She blushed, a hint of color creeping into her soft cheeks. Whatever response she intended, it stalled on her lips. She breathed deeply, then paused for a moment. "I'll be waiting for your call. Have a safe trip back to camp." I planted a final kiss, then turned and descended the stairs. She leaned over the bannister and looked down. When I reached ground level, I glanced up toward her. Our eyes met as we exchanged air-borne kisses, and her lips silently formed the word, "Goodnight." Sleep evaded me well into the wee hours.

Sunday dawned. An encore of Mother's breakfast art and an account of my first nine days in the Army mustered the whole family to the table. But even more apparent was their eagerness to hear about my date with Ruth. I answered their questions as honestly as I dared. "Was she glad to see you? What did Mrs. Wasson serve for dinner? How was the Trianon? Did the band play your favorite music? Did you dance a lot? Is Ruth a good dancer? And more seriously . . . do you think Ruth likes you?" To this, I gave an unqualified yes. Then finally, Margaret, with a star-lit twinkle in her eye teased, "Did you kiss her goodnight?" I guess I blushed a little, and without answering, pushed my chair back and said, "Hey, it's time to get ready for church!"

We walked together the six blocks to the First Presbyterian Church where we all belonged and attended since moving to the Southside. Actually, most of our memberships originated in the Woodlawn Park Presbyterian Church at the same location, but a merger occurred in about 1930 with the migrating First Church. At that time, a beautiful new Gothic structure was built and the two congregations merged into one. It would be the site of David's and my confirmation, our baptisms, and our church home membership.

Mother had partially prepared Sunday dinner before church and again served up one of my favorite meals. Her pan-fried chicken was superb, the tender morsels literally falling from the bone. She had rolled the pieces in a light coating of flour and turned them frequently in the frying pan, slightly crisping them to a golden brown in pure butter. The fluffy whipped potatoes with creamy gravy were topped off with her matchless Jonathan apple pie. I exaggerated a groan as I leaned back in my chair and told Mother that she was a true artist with skillet and pan. I knew that the finest ingredient in her food was the love she poured into it.

My time at home was running down and I gathered my things for the return trip to Camp Grant. I returned Dad's Gladstone bag to him and found a small drawstring bag to use. My GI Issue had included a musette bag, which I would be using in the future for smaller personal articles. At about 3:00, I answered the doorbell and greeted one of my closest friends, Dick Gentzler.

"Are you ready to go, Stewie?" I saw Jack Diehl waiting in Dick's 1932 Reo Royale sports coupe parked at the curb. They had volunteered to drive me back to camp. I hollered to the folks that it was time for me to go.

They all assembled on the porch, and we exchanged hugs and kisses. Again, they wished me well. This departure was not as emotional as the first one, but matched it in fervor. Dick and I walked to the car and I squeezed in next to Jack. As we pulled away from the curb, Dick gave a long blast of the twin trumpet-like horns mounted in front of the radiator, as if to say, "Farewell to the gallant warrior." I was reminded of Dad's description of the steam horns on the *Cedric* when it had cruised into New York harbor upon his arrival to America in 1904. The three of us in the sports coupe waved vigorously and the six on the porch reciprocated until we turned the corner and they were lost to our view.

The Draft had not yet become a threat to Dick and Jack, as they both had the deferments due to their poor eyesight. They had worn thick, heavy glasses for as long as I had known them. Dick had enrolled at Armour Tech (later to be named Illinois Institute of Technology) to pursue a degree in Civil Engineering. He and I had worked together at Cooper's and had left the same day. Jack was at Drake University and would hang on there as long as he could.

We arrived outside the gate at Camp Grant and I got out, grabbed my small kit bag, and we said our final goodbyes. I passed through the gate and showed my ID to the guard. I looked back. Dick was watching. He waved, and started off, again giving me a blast from those terrific horns.

Entering the barracks, I checked the bulletin board and was angered to find my name posted again for KP duty, starting at 6:00 Monday morning — angered, but powerless to do anything about it. I sought out the Sergeant and asked why. He grinned and said, "That's the way it goes. This is the Army. Tough luck, Stewart."

I served the three days without enthusiasm, finishing after supper on Wednesday. When I entered the barracks one of the guys said, "Hey Stewart, you better get your ass in gear and start packing. We're shipping out tomorrow morning. Go check the bulletin board to see where they're sending you." I scanned the long list and found I was assigned to Coast Artillery Basic Training at Camp Wallace, Texas. I and those assigned with me would depart on a troop train at 8:00 a.m. following breakfast. All men were to secure clean bedding from the supply room and make their beds before departure. Boy, I thought, how terse can you get?

Packing didn't present much of a challenge; the two large barracks bags easily held everything. But my first order of business was to call Ruth and the folks and give them the news. I placed the call to Ruth first and was glad that it went right through. "This is the moment I've been dreading, honey. I'm shipping out for Texas in the morning, Camp Wallace, down near the Gulf between Houston and Galveston. I was sure hoping we'd have one more dance together. Now it'll have to wait for another time." My voice was tense and a little higher in pitch than my normal baritone.

"Oh, I am sorry. But Alex, we knew this would come and soon. It's a disappointment, but not a surprise. Let's just be sure we write to each other every week and make the best of it." Her voice leveled out and its sweet confidence returned. We talked out the three-minute time limit and then said goodbye. I did not repeat the declaration of love I had made on the previous Saturday.

I jiggled the receiver and persuaded the operator to put through my call to Mother. "Please operator," I pleaded, "I am shipping out tomorrow and I need to talk to my Mother."

"I hear that all the time, soldier," she replied. "But I do believe you. Stand by." The connection was made and I delivered the same news to Mother that I had given to Ruth. "Oh-h, I see. Well Alex, it's no surprise. We've been expecting it, you know. Go with confidence and always do your best and God will bless you. Send us your address when you get there. We'll be writing to you and you be sure and write to us. Goodbye dear."

The messages were delivered. I returned to the barracks, packed my stuff, and made plans for an early morning short-sheeting of my cot. I didn't want its next occupant to be disappointed.

The blast of that infernal whistle jolted me from a sound sleep at 6:00 on Thursday. Like most of the others, I was ready to leave well ahead of the designated time. While waiting for the order to march to the train, we compared notes. Some were going to the Infantry, some to the Field Artillery, others to the Quartermaster Corps, the Medical Corps, or the Engineers, spreading out across the country to fill needs of the various Army branches. We would all board the same train at Camp Grant and ride to Chicago where we would be parceled out to the different railroads that would send us on our specific journeys.

The marching order came. We each shouldered our pair of barracks bags and musette bags and joined the gathering horde on the barracks street. No roll call was made. We did a left face and headed for the train yard. When all were aboard, the train gave a departing blast from its steam-powered whistle, the cars jerked as the tug of the engine took up the slack in the couplings, and we started to roll. I looked out at the mass of barracks, warehouses, and the huge water tower. I saw the columns of marching recruits and their ragged response to the rhythmic demands of their leaders. This was my fourteenth day in the service of Uncle Sam, but I held no nostalgic attachments to Camp Grant. I had spent six days on KP, one day on latrine duty, two days with sore feet, too many hours following the bare butts of others being physically examined, and had too many eyes scrutinizing my manliness.

The camp's one redeeming feature was its proximity to Chicago and the waiting arms of the girl that had plucked and strummed on the strings of my heart.

Camp Wallace may be a better camp but . . . it could never match that!

Chapter 8

Camp Wallace, Texas

HE TRAIN CRAWLED along on low throttle, maneuvering the track switches that would take us from the Camp Grant siding back onto the main line. An increase in speed finally signaled the end of our association with one of Ulysses S. Grant's namesakes and we were soon rolling along through the autumn-tinged countryside of northern Illinois. The trees were beginning to turn and the corn shocks stood in the fields, ready for gathering. The pumpkin crop had already been harvested and canners of the bright orange treat were competing with the carvers of jack-o'-lanterns for the best specimens. It was Thursday, October 9th, 1941. With an early snow this pastoral scene would be transformed into artistic inspiration for a hundred Christmas card designs.

We slowed a little for gated crossings in the small towns and villages and the rural wig-wag signals that demanded attention with the ding-ding-ding-ding of their warning bells. Cars and trucks and a few pedestrians were stopped, waiting for the train to pass before hurrying on. Strange, two weeks ago we came this way, unnoticed in our civilian clothes. Now transformed by the magic of mere olive drab, we were celebrities. Women and children waved and blew kisses to us. Men just waved. We answered them with equal vigor. They, too, had loved ones in uniform and surely, for a few minutes, we symbolically touched a void in their lives while adding a little stature to ours.

The Draft was universal and the rush to military preparedness affected everyone. Although Hitler's aggression had raged unchecked since his invasion of Poland in 1939, his attack on the USSR in June of 1941 and America's Lend-Lease program to supply armaments to England drew us closer to the specter of war. The Battle of Britain was taking a heavy toll on property and lives in the large industrial areas of London, Liverpool, and other cities. Families were being separated when children were evacuated to friends and relatives in the country. My father continued to communicate with his brother John and his family as well as many old and dear friends who kept him posted on the bombings and the hardships of life under siege.

Friends who had emigrated to America at the turn of the century had relatives who fell under the devastation wrought by German bombers. One of these was Alice Atkinson, wife of Reverend Ralph Atkinson, Dad's closest friend from boyhood. Having received word of the tragedy that befell Alice's family, Dad wrote to Alice in Pasadena, California:

Chicago, Illinois   September 5, 1941

Dear Alice,

A letter from England this morning brought the appalling word of the death of two of your sisters — one described as the blind sister and the other not identified. It also stated that the third was severely injured but recovering. This is indeed a bomb shell to us, and leaves us almost dreading the harrowing details.

As my acquaintance with your family was somewhat inactive, though always cordial, the description affords me only a hazy recollection of each one, so that at this distance I cannot distinguish them.

But Alice they are your sisters, and this is all I really need to know to assure you of our grief in the shock just received, and I am reminded of a line in my letter to Ralph just after his arrival in the States in which I expressed my sympathy with you in leaving sisters in England before the shooting began.

There is little need, Alice to remind you where solace is to be found, you have lived nearer to that Fount than most of us.

So here we are, one and all, joining with every friend of yours on earth which you have so much traversed, in fervent hopes of lasting comfort.

To Ralph and your family, and all that are near and dear to them our deepest sympathy.

Very sincerely,
Alex Stewart

As young people still floundering from the despair of the Depression, we had not been intimately concerned about the distant conflict. Communications were slow and sketchy, confined to the print media, movie newsreels, and abbreviated radio reports. Rolling through this lovely countryside, we all naively thought we would be homeward bound in a year.

Our train included one or two baggage cars containing our barracks bags, two kitchen cars where Army cooks prepared our meals on gasoline-powered field stoves, one Pullman sleeping car for commissioned and non-commissioned officers, and about 15 Pullman sleeping cars for the rest of us. Nearing Chicago, we would be shuffled from this branch of the Illinois Central to the southbound right-of-way of the Santa Fe. But that was of little concern to most of us. The complexity of the great railroad system in the Chicago area was beyond our comprehension. It was the job of the experts to get us to Texas.

I would learn that our country's new military forces were well manned with card players, readers, sleepers, letter writers, story tellers, Crap-shooters, artists, and just plain daydreamers, who all decided, as if on signal, to exercise their preferences. One-legged portable tables appeared from nowhere and their two steel lugs on one end attached to mating wall sockets below the train windows. Two opposing bench seats thus were converted to a booth, providing a perfect facility for most of our sedentary activities.

Poker and Black Jack were the most popular card games and never lacked participants. Players would come and go, and it wasn't hard to tell who was winning most of the money — they never left the tables. My card playing was limited to that of casual observer. I knew the gambling games but claimed no proficiency, had played for matchsticks, and once or twice for pennies, and had lost and then vowed never to risk hard-earned cash again. Perhaps it was my indifference. I never really enjoyed that type of competition. I hated to be bluffed, though I admired true finesse.

The clickety-clack of heavy, steel wheels impacting the rail joints ticked off the growing miles that were separating me from the source of heartbeat and heartthrob. The song of the road was tenacious, varying only when we slowed for a town or a track repair crew. Meals were served much like our first train ride to Camp Grant, only this time we had our own mess kits, flatware, and canteen drinking cups. After eating, we made a return trip to the kitchen car to dispose of leftovers and wash our utensils in the prescribed manner. Utensils were made with holes in the handles large enough to slip over the mess kit clamping handle. A thorough washing-swishing action of the assembled pieces in boiling soapy water, followed by three rinses each in clear boiling water did the trick. Held by the hinged clamping handle, everything cooled down and dried as we returned to our seats.

Soon after the evening meal, the civilian porter in his white jacket came in to make up the berths. Typical Army travel required that two men would occupy the lower berth and one man would get the upper. Of course, we all wanted the upper and drew cards for it. This was my only card game that ever paid off. I drew an Ace, and was glad for the solitude it provided. A few card games persisted and caused the porter to return a little later to complete his work. Contrary to regulations, a few half-pint bottles of clandestine whiskey surfaced. They had been brought on board in their brown-bag disguise and were consumed, leading to an escalation of the profanity and noise of both winners and losers. The Sergeant of the Guard soon entered the car and all games, drinking, and noise suddenly ended and the porter finished his job. (Most of the men admired and appreciated the work of the porters and, although we did not have money with which to tip them as they were accustomed to, we did give them candy bars and cigarettes. The porters always appreciated our gifts.)

I stretched out full length in the upper berth and retrieved my book, *Beau Geste*, by Percival Christopher Wren, from the net sling beside the bed. I had started it at Camp Grant. As a youth of 11 or 12, I shared in the Sunday evening family reading circle around our dining room table and remembered this story as one of my favorites. In the intervening decade, however, its details had become a fuzzy memory. On impulse, I took it from the bookcase in our back parlor and stuffed it into my bag. Now this re-read of three aristocratic English brothers, caught up in the mysterious disappearance of a valuable family sapphire called "The Blue Water," riveted my interest. The brothers had individually fled their home for service in the French Foreign Legion in North Africa, each casting suspicion on his declared innocence.

More than the mystery itself, I was drawn to their lives and their courage, as well as their love and devotion to their family, and especially to one another. I likened these qualities somewhat to the relationships I shared with Ray and David and occasionally addressed them as "Beau" in my letters. But even more, the Sahara Desert warfare with all its primitive aspects reminded me of the horrors of hand-to-hand combat. The reality of Pearl Harbor was yet to be, and I could not picture any of us in that framework.

The train rumbled on through the night. I had alternately read, fallen asleep, awakened with the book on my chest, thought about Ruth and the family, and wondered what Camp Wallace had in store for me. Thursday's routine was repeated on Friday, with the addition of an exercise period beside the train somewhere in Oklahoma. Jim Gordon, whom I had met at Camp Grant was one of two seat mates with whom I had some enjoyable conversation. I don't remember that our interests were similar, but our disinterests were comparable. He disliked Poker and the other gambling games, but favored Bridge. Unfortunately, I did not know the game nor was he able to find others with whom he could play. So we talked and read.

By Friday night in the upper berth I was ready for a change of scenery. Saturday dawned and it was announced that we had crossed the Red River and were now in the Lone Star State. The remaining 350 miles, without long delays, would put us into Camp Wallace in mid-afternoon. Many anticipated that every square foot of Texas would be covered with oil-well derricks, and cattle and cowboys riding the range would be a common sight. We did see a lot of cattle, a few cowboys and border collies working the herds, many acres of cotton stubble, and mowed hay fields with bales ready for gathering, but few if any oil wells. The part of Texas we saw just did not have any visible evidence of Black Gold production.

After lunch there was very little resumption of card games. By that time, most of the men were becoming better acquainted with their neighbors. Occasionally, one of the non-com escorts would come through the car and would be bombarded with questions about the Army. His answers were not always accurate, as we later learned, but were amusing.

The train slowed as we entered the Houston railroad yards, but did not stop. Camp Wallace was still about 35 miles south, near the town of Dickinson. The main entrance fronted on Route 3, the highway between Houston and Galveston.

We saw a scattered few oil wells and wondered why there were high, torch-like pipes extending skyward with large plumes of fire burning at their tips. It was later explained that this was the method of disposing of surplus natural gas occurring at the well heads. Whether or not this was an accurate statement, I lamented the fact that it was not being piped to Chicago as fuel to replace coal and gas manufactured from coal; its BTU rating was twice that of the manufactured product.

Our train finally slowed and was diverted onto the camp's siding. We chugged into its loading area, amazed at the large number of new two-story barracks neatly lining streets, paved not with gravel but with millions of crushed seashells. We would soon learn that rain water, whitened by seashell by-products, would make a mess of our highly polished shoes. The screech of steel against steel and hissing steam being expelled as brakes were applied told us that we had arrived at our new "home."

As at Camp Grant, noncoms instructed us to each find our barracks bags, which were being set in long rows beside the train. We had printed our names and serial numbers on heavy, manila string tags and attached them to the bags before leaving Grant. Mass confusion erupted as the search began, but in due course we located our belongings and were ready to "march" to our temporary barracks.

A week of testing and short interviews established our individual Military Occupational Specialties (MOS), which hopefully would be adhered to in our training assignments. From the Army's standpoint, my knowledge and experience with cars considerably exceeded that of many others and could be utilized in the repair and maintenance of military vehicles. My official classification was entered as "Truck Mechanic's Foreman," an indication that I would be trained Army-style to supervise the efforts of those who actually did the dirty work.

All those classified for motor vehicle work were assigned to the four batteries of the 29th Coast Artillery Training Battalion and relocated accordingly. Battery A, to which I was assigned, occupied the first of four barracks that faced a large open quadrangle. Three other battalions of varied designation occupied the other three sides of the quad. Most of the other groups were designated for training on big guns, the powerful anti-aircraft and other cannons that would protect American shores.

I moved to my new barracks and found a vacant cot on the second floor. Tossing my bags on the tightly stretched blanket, I looked across the room and to my complete surprise gazed into the sleepy face of George Bowman! He was already stretched out on his bed. This was our first encounter since we had parted in the train-boarding process at Chicago's Dearborn Street Station on September 26th. I wondered how George wound up in this group, as he admitted that he could hardly use so much as a screwdriver. However, he had worked as a clerk for a large trucking company in Chicago and was familiar with the paperwork and the nomenclature and function of practically every automotive device and part. And he could use a typewriter.

The next day being Sunday, we roamed the camp, went to the post movie theater, and spent a little cash in the PX (Post Exchange). A big item with the beer drinkers was the product with the 3.2 percent alcohol content. Those who complained of its weakness were nonetheless among those that staggered back to the barracks. What the "near beer" lacked in potency was compensated for with high-volume consumption. I think I had one bottle.

Monday came and was highlighted with an orientation lecture covering most of the aspects of our training. We would learn all the drill commands, manual-of-arms, stripping, cleaning, and reassembling of our rifles (.30-caliber British Enfields, later replaced with

.30-caliber Springfields, all bolt-action World War I leftovers), qualifying on the rifle range, military courtesy, and a host of other incidentals that were supposed to make fighting men out of a bunch of recalcitrants.

Sandwiched between these activities we would spend a good deal of training time on our occupational specialties. Unfortunately, the vehicles we learned about and trained on were units committed to the salvage yard and not representative of those modern machines we would encounter in actual operations. But the basics of repair and maintenance applied equally to old and new and we all became quite proficient.

A select group of 15 two-man teams were instructed to roam the salvage yard and collect all the components needed to build an operating vehicle. The rules required that it must be capable of starting and running and be driven around the yard. No bodies or seats were required, just the chassis and a box to sit on while driving. My partner and I found the basics, and although few components were from the original assembly, we improvised misfits and welded, cut, drilled, and bolted them into an operating pile of junk. I had concluded that this was what the instructor wanted and would accept. Was he not looking for our ability to create, make-do with what we could find, and to test our skills? I don't remember my partner's name, but he was a good welder and metal worker and did what I asked. He too was from Chicago.

We were the first to finish and ours was one of only four vehicles that met the test. We did excel on one point. Our vehicle could also be driven in reverse. Engines on several others would start, but could not be driven. The prize? A memo in our MOS files and a soon-to-be-served three-day tour of KP duty. No medals!

The KP assignment was on a Friday, Saturday, and Sunday. The work was similar to that required of us at Camp Grant, but on a much smaller scale. I performed a variety of tasks, from Dining Room Orderly to scrubbing out garbage cans on Friday and Saturday. Early on Sunday afternoon, the cook asked if any of us knew how to cut a pork loin into chops. I had seen Mr. Snapp, our butcher in Chicago, cut up dozens of them over the years, and decided I could do it. I had seen two pork loins lying on the meat block in the kitchen and the thought crossed my mind that I could cut them up in fairly short order and spend the rest of the afternoon before supper lounging on the back steps of the mess kitchen. I volunteered and was immediately put to work. The others were doing the dirty jobs while I hacked away at the loins.

In due course, I finished the two loins and found a shady spot on the steps. Soon the cook came out and hollered at me to finish the job. I told him I had done so and the chops from the two loins were in the refrigerator.

"You're not done yet. Get your ass in here," he ordered. He pulled a wire-bound wooden crate from under the meat block and revealed ten more loins. "These have to be ready for cooking for tonight's chow, so get going," he growled.

I couldn't believe it. George Bowman's sage words on the bus came to mind, "I guess the Army will be full of surprises, Alex." As I carved away on those loins for a couple more hours, two things were revealed to me. First, I became a pretty good butcher of pork chops, and second, I resolved that I would never volunteer for anything during the rest of my Army days. Meat cutting was never again presented to me, but on two occasions I was invited to volunteer for duties that could have been extremely hazardous or deadly.

Our training commenced at a reasonable pace, but it became apparent that considerable

Sergeant Strickland (l) and Alex Stewart at Camp Wallace, Texas, in November 1941, the second month in Basic Training.

time and effort was devoted to provoking us to anger. We would receive an order to "fall out" dressed in fatigue suits and hats. Then, as we were lined up in our permanent designated places, the Sergeant would loudly protest the disobeying of orders. "You are supposed to be wearing fatigues and leggings. You have five minutes to go back in and put on leggings." Back in formation after struggling with the awkward lacings of the leggings, the

Sergeant would make a casual inspection of the troops, then announce that the uniform order had been changed to Class A olive-drab shirts, pants, and black necktie, and to return to the barracks and change. *"And do it on the double!"*

The chorus of grumbling and profanity reached a high pitch during the uniform change. Everybody and everything was berated from the Commander-in-Chief all the way down to the Corporal doing paper work in the battery office. But in the end, the order was met and again we reassembled on the road in front of the barracks. Whatever the training mission was at the moment, our aggravation was soon replaced with that great youthful penchant for situation conversion as we devised our own unofficial, humorous, and ridiculous uniforms to suggest to the "Brass": "Fall out with leggings and jock straps," or "Fall out with rifles, ammo belts, and shorts," and — one of the best — "Fall out with barracks bags, jock straps, and overcoats!" Even the Sergeant tried, but failed to conceal his mirth.

Our leader, Sergeant Strickland, was approachable, and one day I asked him the purpose behind all this uniform change nonsense.

"It's in the official Army Training Manual, Stewart," he replied. "It states that a good soldier is an angry soldier and all this bullshit is designed to make you mad, pissed off."

Well, now I began to understand the Army a little better, and it ceased to bother me. Right or wrong, I didn't question his explanation.

Our training commenced on schedule and the regulation and discipline favorably affected most of the men. There were a few misfits who would always be in trouble and were dealt with accordingly. George Bowman and I became quite friendly and frequently went on pass together to Galveston or Houston. George liked to fortify these forays with some hard liquor and encouraged me to share in his refreshment at a liquor store at the "Y," an intersection where the road to Texas City branched east from Highway 3. I was ready to go on to Houston or Galveston after one or two short drinks, but George always said, "just one more." That usually lead to a half-dozen or more for George and one more for me. Sometimes we didn't make it into town at all, and I would hitch a ride for us back to camp.

The object of our time in town was to have a good steak dinner, perhaps go to a movie, or attend some sports events. The USO (United Service Organization) had not yet come into being, and the opportunities for affordable entertainment were few. On several occasions I went to Houston on Sunday with Jim Gordon and attended morning worship services at the First Presbyterian Church. We knew that our presence would be noted and would always produce an invitation for dinner at the home of one or more members. This was always an enjoyable time for me as it provided fellowship and good conversation along with a fine meal. It reminded me of home, and the graciousness of the hosts sometimes approached that of Mother and how she would provide for servicemen at her table.

The exchange of letters with Ruth and the folks became the constant that interrupted the monotony of my routine. They covered their day-to-day activities and gave me a glimpse into their lives I had not previously perceived. I saved every letter and formed the habit of sending a bundle of them home, especially when I had a change of station. Mother assured me that they would remain intact and would be stored away for safe keeping till I returned. They agreed to save all of my letters to them, as did Ruth.

Oddly, when I returned to civilian life, I was focused on family and career and I had little interest in claiming the letter collection. In Ruth's case, my letters to her had been stored in a basement locker of her apartment building and were destroyed when torrential rains flooded the basement. But when I closed out the old house in 1986, I found most of the letters I had sent to my parents.

The first Sunday in December 1941 dawned bright and clear in Texas, and all of us were enjoying a relaxed time around the camp and in the PX. After lunch, men out on pass were returning and blended into the on-going activities. There was a Craps game in full swing over in the corner of the barracks, and the Poker game on George Bowman's bunk was getting hotter as the pot grew in value. From my onlooker's vantage point I observed other men sleeping, reading, writing letters — and one with a small radio "glued" to his ear.

Suddenly, he spun the volume control, jumped up, and hollered, "Hey, the Japs bombed Pearl Harbor!"

The gamblers paused briefly. One of them asked, "Where the hell is Pearl Harbor?" The games resumed. But then, the awful portent of that announcement began to sink in as details of the enormity of the bombing began coming in. The games were over and a quiet, tense seriousness replaced bravado as the horror of what was happening hit each man in the pin-drop silence between each new declaration by the newscaster. Some well-chosen expletives were uttered and all doubts vanished.

WE WERE AT WAR.

As raw recruits in the eighth week of basic training, we had coveted the promise of one year's service. In an instant, that promise became history. Walking to the base theater that evening, sentries challenged us, live ammunition in their aged Springfields. We were so green and so surprised we didn't know how to respond. We learned fast. It was as though the enemy had made a landing on Galveston Island and everyone was suspect!

I had tried to call the family earlier, but the circuits were loaded. After returning from the theater, I finished my letters to Ruth and to the folks, knowing they would be anxious to have my response to the Japanese action and to know that I was all right. Although they had as much information as I did, I felt they would like to talk to me. I walked to the pay phone in the PX and finally succeeded in getting the call put through. As luck would have it, Ruth was there for a brief visit and I was able to talk to her, too. It was an unexpected treat after a shocking day.

There was much speculation by the men as to how we would be affected by this cataclysmic change in events and, of course, like all of them, I wondered where it would take me and what I would be doing. The night of December 7th, 1941, was a gloomy one at best, and the restlessness of many was evident by the number of trips made to the latrine. As usual, my last thoughts before falling asleep were of the family and Ruth and the anxiety that was surely gnawing at them.

At our first Monday-morning formation the Battalion Commander spoke to us of the impact of the Hawaiian tragedy on all our lives. He told us that a declaration of war by President Roosevelt would undoubtedly follow swiftly. We were encouraged to do our work well and learn as much as possible about our individual specialties. Of course, he didn't know anymore than we did; I felt that everyone in America was in the same boat.

On December 14th I received a letter from Dad, the first since my induction into the Army. When he initiated correspondence, he often wrote from his studio after his last lesson. Typically, Dad encouraged me by giving me a little taste of home. He chose to forward a description of one of Mother's fine dinners, arrayed on a white linen tablecloth, knowing that that would awaken fond memories.

920 Kimball Hall   Chicago. Dec.11-'41

Dear Alex,

Your first letter following the phone call Sunday night came this morning, and satisfied us that you were well acquainted with the new startling events of the last few days as we are. We entertained a fear that your superiors would endeavor to withhold current news, but we are glad the reverse is the truth.

Sunday afternoon we returned from church as usual and were soon served with one of Mother's masterpieces: on a nice white cloth we each received our portion of roast pork with apple-sauce, mashed potatoes, beans, mixed salad, dessert. You did not miss us at mess anymore than we missed you.

Your letter today reveals the spurt of activity that has taken hold of the men at camp, and while it makes life there more interesting it casts ominous clouds for ensuing days which will have to be met courageously. In this we shall not need to coach you, officers will see to that.

I am ready to encourage you in perfecting yourself along mechanical lines, they are safer than front lines. Do not be slow to advertise and even recommend your abilities in such directions, using showmanship in all your demonstrations, taking care not to betray cowardice or fear.

And lastly, remember that when you think of us we are thinking of you. We have never burdened you with precept, we have striven for practice.

I was expecting to send you some observations and perhaps corrections in your writing exhibits, but felt that this is hardly the time as you doubtless will be well occupied with military demands: but you can advise me on this point.

Meanwhile let it be just "good night," with hopes that we shall soon meet.

Affectionately, Dad, Mother & all

A few days later, I received a newsy letter from Ruth wherein she reported on work and activities at Cooper's, the robbery of tires at her brother Bud's service station, and the antics at Bud's birthday party by her two nieces Bonnie and Janet Wasson (Bud's children) and nephew Wayne Carlson (sister Viola's son) during Bud's birthday party, as well as her feelings about the war.

Sunday, December 13, 1941

Dear Alex,

. . . I have attempted to write to you before now, but I have felt so bad about the whole business I couldn't think of much to say. Although the war still has me very upset, I am beginning to feel normal again. I am really disappointed that you won't be home for Christmas, but I hope and imagine that before you are sent out of the States you will be allowed to come home, if it is at all possible.

Your description of guard duty was interesting and like you, I hope you don't have to use your rifle.

Your little camera certainly takes good pictures. Ray came over for a few minutes and showed them to me. You look wonderful in your uniform. I'll bet those Texas lassies whistle at you. Don't I rate any pictures?

You certainly do get a Christmas kiss without asking I'm sure. Those little things like that I rather like to do in person. But if no can do — I'll take the next best thing.

Love X X X

Ruth

As the war in the Pacific developed and the Japanese invasion of the Philippines took its toll of American forces and defenses, it was obvious that the enemy aggression following Pearl Harbor would be greatly accelerated.

On Monday, December 8th, 1941, President Roosevelt declared war on Japan, and it appeared to us that the first U.S. military action would be the establishing and strengthening of the defenses of American shores. This would certainly impact our Coast Artillery units and enlarge the forces of the American Defense Command. The West Coast was considered to be most vulnerable to attack by the Japanese.

Rumors at Camp Wallace started "flying around" like wind-blown feathers, and their accuracy was about as predictable. Those of us concerned basically with motor vehicle repair and maintenance realized we could fit into most any operational unit. Contingents of trainees from other battalions were being shipped out to coastal anti-aircraft batteries on the Pacific Coast from Seattle to San Diego to reinforce and enlarge those units. Some went to Alaska, others to Panama.

Around December 20th, some of our battalion was alerted for shipment to Camp Davis, North Carolina, near Wilmington. The men in this group would be assigned to a newly forming arm of the Coast Artillery, Barrage Balloons. George Bowman numbered among them and was as curious as we were as to the function and purpose of a barrage balloon. After two weeks of indoctrination and training at Camp Davis, George's contingent was sent to Michigan to establish a balloon barrage to protect the locks of the Sault Saint Marie

Canal on Saint Mary's River, where it links Lake Superior with Lake Huron. Although the canal and its locks were vital to wartime shipping on the Great Lakes, this seemed to be too far inland and too remote as a likely target for attack from either coast. Its proximity to Canada, however, might have presented problems to the strategists in Washington.

I received another newsy letter from Ruth on Tuesday, full of happenings at home and office and involvement with her family. She indicated that the needs of wartime production might divert materials from domestic manufacture, as we had earlier feared, having an impact on Cooper's inventory of merchandise and replacement of stocked items. R. Cooper, Jr. Inc. was a distributor and service company for General Electric appliances, and materials devoted to armaments would seriously curtail the making of products for civilian consumption. Cooper's, like many other firms sought government contracts for producing war products, and the employees were all on edge concerning their jobs. Ruth wrote:

Saturday, December 20, 1941

Dear Alex,

I am writing this letter on Saturday to make sure you get it on Tuesday. The Christmas mails are very heavy and it's hard to get letters into the boxes.

Well, our bonuses came through. Mr. Risch called me into his office and had me sit down. He told me that last year he had to mail my check because I was recovering from surgery, but was very happy that he could present it to me this year in person. I got $20.00 and have decided to invest it in a War Bond. He also advised me to brush up on my typing because our business is going to be bad and he would like to keep me as long as he can.

It has me a little on the fence. I don't know whether to stay there and wait or to go out and get another job while the getting is good. I do have an advantage — Risch does like me. . . .

My friend Mona Nelson took me to a Christmas party on Wednesday at 3000 North Sheridan Road (automatic elevators and a maid), really a classy affair. I enjoyed myself very much.

Thank goodness, my Christmas shopping is done, but I'm going downtown the day before Christmas, just because I want to. I love to see the people, the children and their excitement and of course the beautiful decorations, especially at Marshall Fields.

Ruth Hansen is always asking me what I hear from you. We compare information. She thinks you are swell. And so do I.

How is the guard duty going? How can you guard and write letters at the same time? Is George Bowman still in your barracks?

Commenting on your letter, I'd really like to be with you at the Trianon right now. They are playing Chattanooga Choo Choo and I really feel we could swing out on it. . . . Sure, I want some pictures. Those you sent your mother were really good . . . I certainly hope you don't get sent to the tropics, and I do hope Fort Sheridan, Illinois will invite you up there.

Ray says he expects to be called up shortly that will be very hard on your mother. I told him I hoped you would both be in the same camp.

I still hope you will get home soon. I keep saying "they can't do this to me." Then I answer myself, "Well, they are."

Well Alex, I'll close for now — wishing you a very Merry Christmas and a Happy New Year.

Love and many Christmas XXXX's
Ruth

I received this letter on Tuesday, December 23rd. I planned to use my leisure time that evening to answer it fully, but in late afternoon the balance of our battalion received word that we were shipping out the next day to Camp Davis, North Carolina, for formation of the 304th Barrage Balloon Battalion. After indoctrination and training, we would be sent to Seattle, Washington, to establish a balloon barrage around the Boeing Aircraft Factory. Caught up in the flurry of packing, I only had time to scratch out a short note to Ruth and to the folks, telling them of my impending departure from Camp Wallace. We had been cautioned (or warned) not to disclose our destination as this would be a breech of security. All I could say was that from Camp Davis I would be sent to the West Coast. It was the first instruction of its kind designed to conceal troop movement from the enemy, with the implication that the enemy or its sympathizers could be lurking most anywhere. To say the least, the requirement of secrecy left the home folks in the dark while adding a degree of urgency to our purpose.

Chapter 9

Camp Davis, North Carolina

HE THING I DREADED most was spending Christmas Eve and Christmas Day on a troop train. The joy and festivity of each of my previous celebrations had always highlighted our year of work and struggle, our achievements and failures, smoothing out the wrinkles and offering promise of better times. Now confronted with the dreariness of the mass movement of drab-clad men, each one burrowing deep into his individual memories of home and family and happier times, we settled into the aging Pullmans that would rock us into and out of restless slumber.

Throughout the weeks of disciplined maneuvers, the rules, the regulations, the training, and the recent and profound shock of Pearl Harbor, we were being shaped into men with a deep sense of mission — strong, resilient. These were the perceptions that followed me on this journey. We were young, and our disappointments and hardships were overshadowed by that sense of purpose born on December 7th.

The incidence of illicit spirits was greater than before, and even I had joined the ranks of the "smugglers." We had boarded the train in mid-afternoon and were well under way when supper was served. Following the meal, the half-pint bottles emerged from musette bags and were being shared with seat partners who had failed to secure their own provisions. Until my Army experience I had never tasted hard liquor and was not now particularly fond of it, though I had become aware of its soothing or slightly numbing effect when taken in reasonable quantity. I drank mine mixed with tap water from a folding paper cup.

There had been a group of ladies at Camp Wallace handing out cigarettes and candy to us as we boarded the train. Though not yet wearing gray uniforms, which would make them famous as the Red Cross Gray Ladies, they were doing their best to improve our Christmas for us. Now, rumbling along on our way out of Texas, an officer and his Sergeant aide marched through our car, handing out small gift packages of candy and chewing gum and wishing us a Merry Christmas "from the American Red Cross." Though not dressed like Santa Claus, they created the aura of the season with their corny Santa-like "*Ho, Ho, Ho's*" while they laughingly wished us a Merry Christmas.

Conversation among the men seemed to brighten, and family Christmas stories were exchanged. Presently, the lively strain of "Jingle Bells" echoed through the car, performed by a competent harmonica player. As the musician approached my seat, I started singing, and others joined in. Several fellows gathered around and we were soon pooling our talents on such favorites as "Away in a Manger," "Joy to the World," and "Silent Night," followed with an attempt at harmony on "Swing Low Sweet Chariot" and "Down by the Old Mill Stream." It soon became evident that many were tiring of the efforts of the few, and our "quartet" was ushered onto the platform between the cars. We kept our vocal chords lubricated with an occasional nip from our half-pints of Town Tavern and continued our harmonizing, which, to our way of thinking, was getting pretty good. Occasionally, an officer or noncom would pass from car to car and would be detained and enlisted in the group. One Second Lieutenant did oblige and gave out with an exceptionally fine tenor rendition of a familiar carol. Finally, the Sergeant of the Guard came through and ordered everyone to bed. It was 10:45 and all overhead lights were turned off at 11:00.

The gloomy prospect of spending Christmas Eve on a troop train somewhere in the hinterlands of Louisiana had been transformed into a heart-lifting time by the magic of music, such as it was. I had won the coin-toss with my seat mates and again enjoyed the solitude and comparative roominess of the upper berth. The route of our troop train would transport us across Louisiana, Mississippi, Alabama, Georgia, South Carolina, and the lower, eastern part of North Carolina. Surprisingly, the Army did its best in helping us celebrate Christmas. Roast turkey with the Army's scant version of all the fixin's was abundantly provided.

At various stops along the way, Red Cross ladies were out in force to meet the train, providing hot coffee, cakes, cookies, candy, and cigarettes. We were touched by a group of children at a station stop near Atlanta who were allowed to come through the cars and sing carols. Like the people in Illinois who had greeted us so warmly at road crossings, the folks down South met us with cheers and shouts of "Merry Christmas." Their fervor had no doubt been increased with the tragedy of Pearl Harbor and especially the declaration of war.

Late evening on Friday, December 26th, our train was diverted to a rail siding that extended into the heart of Camp Davis. With the exception of a few trackside exercise sessions, we had been confined to the cramped conditions of that train for well over 50 hours.

To several hundred strong, healthy young men, this confinement was a rather severe but necessary price to pay in order to cooperate with the Army's logistics.

Evacuation of the train and claiming of barracks bags was done in short order, in spite of the cold weather and the slippery conditions caused by four or five inches of new-fallen snow. This was no deterrent to those of us from the North, but rather an instant incentive to engage in our favorite winter sport of snowball fights. There was no choosing up of sides, just that innate urge to let loose on the closest victim. Everyone participated, including officers and noncoms, who became the most likely targets. When would we ever have another chance to bombard those of rank without severe reprimand or punishment? After about ten minutes of revelry, we had used up the best "packing snow" in the area and responded to the Sergeant's whistle, ending the games. Barracks were assigned to each of the four batteries and cots were claimed and occupied just before the 10:00 lights out.

Camp Davis was an older facility than Camp Wallace, and its age was evident in the condition and vintage of its structures and devices — especially the latrines, where long porcelain-lined troughs served as urinals rather than the more modern individual china-type we had known in Texas. The central heating system was also very inadequate and the men complained about being cold. We suffered through Saturday, voicing comments to the Sergeant about the near-frigid conditions, but to no avail. Apparently no service technicians were on duty because of the holiday. Sunday dawned, and most of the fellows returned from breakfast and continued to wear their field jackets or overcoats in the barracks. Some even huddled under blankets. This finally was intolerable to me. I felt there had to be something wrong with the heating system rather than inadequate of size. There was little difference in the temperature between inlet and outlet air.

I found the oil-fired furnace, located in a mechanical equipment room behind the latrine. The forced-air blower was running but the burner nozzles were intermittently firing and then shutting down. The firing chamber and flue passes were badly clogged with soot and the high-limit safety control was doing its job of short-cycling the burner. Another fellow came in and I enlisted his assistance. Together we cleaned the badly sooted devices. We found some brooms and mops and improvised tools to clean hard-to-reach areas. I climbed up on the roof, removed the flue cap, and rammed a mop down the pipe. It, too, was clogged with soot.

With the cleaning job complete, I energized the control circuit and the burner fired as it was designed to do. It was obvious that the soot was caused by improper adjustment of the oil supply, which made the flame yellow and smoky. I used the small screwdriver of my pocketknife to adjust the oil flow and produce a fine blue flame. We observed its operation for about ten minutes and decided it was doing its job. My limited experience with central heating systems, and especially oil burners, had paid off.

We were both pretty well covered with soot. Our blue denim fatigues were streaked with the black stuff, and our faces and hands were generously coated. We walked into the barracks and were greeted with cheers from everyone. The barracks temperature was beginning to climb and jackets and overcoats were coming off. A few remanents of half-pint Christmas bottles of cheer appeared. We were toasted and shared in the celebration.

On Monday morning, December 29th, for us the holidays were over. On that day we would begin to train in earnest for our career as barrage balloon specialists. Although New Year's Eve was just a few days away, there would be no celebration in Wilmington, and certainly not much at the camp. We were confined to the base for the duration of our stay.

On December 31st I received a letter from Dad, which I could only describe as a masterpiece of love. His description of the Christmas home scene resounded in the depths of my being, and while creating in me a healthy touch of homesickness, it nurtured a contentment in knowing that they were mine, that they were there, and that they were anxiously awaiting my return. The eloquence of my father's prose wrote indelibly on the slate of my memory.

920 Kimball Hall   Chicago.Dec.29,'41

Dear Alex,

Our concern regarding your removal from Texas was relieved today by the receipt of your latest letter, emblazoned in 8 red United States stamps.

Christmas festivity was slowed down somewhat, first by your actual absence and next by the circumstance of your unknown whereabouts. The letter today confirmed some of our guesses. Our celebration was quite unusual, and you missed little. The members of the family descended to the kitchen where breakfast was served a ala "short order," which interpreted means "any old time." A former decision made the Merit Cafeteria our dining hall, where we arrived about 2:30 or later.

No complaint or even criticism could be leveled at the provision of the visible bill of fare — the best was arrayed and we ate to contentment. Only one element was lacking and it needs no interpretation viz-atmosphere. Our home is modest, perhaps rather quaint, speaks more of contentment than luxury, but it has a wealth of family magnetism that challenges willful desertion and provides an outlet for unspeakable and oftimes unspoken love. Truth is more often expressed by silence than sound and this is undoubtedly true of our family and home.

Your queenly mother in her characteristic humility sought no head position at the table, partook of her allowance in quiet gratitude, thought and talked of you and Cameron, Rita and Sharron, and shared regrets with us all that vacant chairs, temporary or permanent are the common order of today.

I was looking at your picture in your mother's arms: you don't need reassurance that we miss you: you were born to the royal title of our love and only our flesh is separated: God gave us memory and we use it aright when we affectionately pronounce the words "each other."

So for the present our thoughts are dedicated to the absent sheep of our fold, away, but not lost either in body or soul, awaiting with some impatience the hour of sweet reunion.

Your affectionate father,
Dad

The next day I received a letter from Ruth, expressing her anxiety as to my whereabouts. It was written on her new stationery, imprinted with her initials RAW.

Tuesday, December 30, 1941

Dear Alex,

I was so happy to get your letter today. I was beginning to get worried. It was a shame that you had Christmas on a miserable troop train, but I guess that is the way of the Army for you. Why they send you to the west coast by way of North Carolina is beyond me. It is too bad you are not close enough to tear up here.

First of all, I want to thank you for the beautiful bracelet. I wear it all the time. You were so sweet to send it. The shoe shine kit I sent to you isn't exactly my idea of a gift, but I thought it would be better to give you something of Army regulation then something you could not take with you when transferred. Anyway, now every time you shine your shoes you can think of me.

Cooper's had a very nice Christmas party, including a delicious lunch. Everyone got prizes and I managed to get three of them. . . .

I spent Christmas eve at my sister's house and had a fun time with many of the family. Then on Christmas the whole family came home. On Friday I went to my cousin's house, went bowling with them (I kept the score) and stayed overnight. George had some moving pictures of me and the rest of the family. They were pretty good.

I received several very nice gifts, including your other package containing the records: "Concerto for Two" (Tommy Tucker's arrangement), Hal Kemp's "Heart of Stone," Eddie Duchin's "Stormy Weather" and "Chattanooga Choo Choo." I like them all very much. XXX.

I sent you a Christmas telegram but I don't know if they will send it on to you. I hope so though. Your snap shots were darn nice. I don't have any good ones but I'll enclose two that I think are the best. What is the Army Coast Artillery Barrage Balloon Battalion? Is it good? As long as they keep you on good old U.S. soil I won't worry too much. Looks like it will be a grim 1942.

I am going to wrap bandages and learn first aid from the Red Cross. They haven't everything organized yet so I'll have to wait until February to start. I'm listening to Fibber McGee and Molly. He just cracked a joke about war bonds. I'm going to buy a $100.00 one, I hope.

Well, "Swoose," I'll have to close now. The best of everything for you in the New Year — and do write soon.

Love,
Ruth

P.S. Thanks again for the bracelet.

P.S. " " " " pictures.
P.S. " " " " records.
P.S. Are the pictures okay?
P.S. Was your friend's name Bob Reynolds? He was killed about three weeks ago. I wasn't sure of his name but the address in the newspaper was his. I feel very badly about his death.

Love again,
Ruth

This was the first time that Ruth had used the casual nickname of "Swoose." She had extracted it from a new, popular song called "Alexander is a Swoose." The chorus line was worded, "Swoose, Swoose, Alexander is a Swoose. Half swan, half goose, Alexander is a silly Swoose." The name was originated by a B-17 pilot in the South Pacific who so named his plane. Words to the song didn't reflect the heroic exploits of the plane and crew, but an imaginative song writer picked up on the name and composed the lighthearted, rather silly little ditty.

I was glad that the chain of communication was intact and that the exchange of gifts and greetings were timely. Of course, the reality of next being shipped to the West Coast didn't add to my glee, and the fact that we were to become an arm of the American Defense Command raised questions as to when I would be able to get a furlough. Seattle was a long way from Chicago! And even if I did get a leave, where would I get the money for train fare, and how much of the leave time would be used up in round-trip travel? Surely the folks would send me the money, but I knew it would be a hardship for them to do so.

Barrage balloons were a far cry from the motorized vehicle training we had recently completed at Camp Wallace and the Mechanic's Foreman rating I had been awarded. However, I wasn't disappointed and felt there was potential for service more interesting and exciting than would be found in a motor-pool repair and service garage.

It was apparent that barrage balloon defenses were relatively new to American armed forces. We newcomers were assigned to training units manned by a cadre of noncoms with little or no balloon experience who had been gleaned from other Coast Artillery units. We soon learned that our barrage would consist of 72 balloons, to be strategically located near the outskirts of Seattle to protect the Boeing Aircraft plant against possible Japanese dive-bomber attack.

Manned observation balloons had been used as early as the American Civil War, and by the British, French, and Germans in World War I. By 1939, unmanned barrage balloons were being used as anti-aircraft defense. The balloon was tethered by a steel cable and rose above the dive-bomber's height of bomb release. A plane's wing impacting the cable at high speed could be severely damaged or even sheared off like a board in a table saw. If the cable became entangled in the plane's propeller, the result would mean total destruction of the enemy aircraft.

The British used balloons in multiple-unit formations strategically positioned around vital installations. Our first balloons, which were British made, had been used to elevate long-range radio antennae, besides functioning against attacks on shipping.

Our total purpose was to tow the ¼-inch steel cable to 7,000 feet, which was above the then-known release point of bombs from Japanese dive-bombers. Balloon site locations were mapped and selected to cover the most likely enemy bombing flight paths to the Boeing Plant #2 and Boeing Field airport. No sensible pilot would knowingly approach such a hazard. Balloons were therefore considered a very strong deterrent.

Our barrage of 72 balloons formed a large, staggering arc about two-thirds of the way around the target. The balloons carried no snagging nets. We didn't want the enemy to hit the balloons, only the cables.

Each inflated balloon, attached to its own ¼-inch steel cable, when released had the lifting capacity to raise the cable to 7,000 feet. The cable was stored on the spool of a heavy, skid-mounted winch, powered by a Hercules six-cylinder gasoline engine. Payout and retrieval of the cable was managed with a standard automobile-type clutch and stick-shift transmission.

The balloon was cigar-shaped, 80 feet long and 36 feet in diameter at its center. It had both horizontal and vertical stabilizers, similar to an airplane, an internal diaphragm separating the upper chamber from the lower chamber, and a large aluminum pressure-relief valve in the upper chamber. Tie-down ropes and lifting harness ropes were attached to its sides, with the lifting harness terminating in a central clevis ring on the underside. To this ring would be connected the mating device of a leader cable that would attach to the ¼-inch cable. The entire balloon envelope was fabricated from heavy, neoprene-impregnated cotton, with double reinforcement at seams and attachments.

In one of her letters, Ruth included a full-page Shell Oil Company advertisement she had taken from a magazine, perhaps an issue of *Life*, which depicted five barrage balloons in flight. The advertising copy described the effect of a chemical formula called toluene, developed in the Shell laboratories, which would dissolve synthetic rubber. When spread over the fabric of a barrage balloon, it made a helium-tight container. Unlike the slight porousness of natural rubber, the neoprene balloon was rendered virtually leakproof.

In training at Camp Davis, the balloons were inflated with high-cost helium because of its non-explosive safety feature. In actual field operations, they were inflated with the much cheaper hydrogen, which required daily sampling of the charge to determine the oxygen level. If the oxygen contamination reached 15 percent, causing a highly explosive mixture, the balloon had to be deflated and recharged with pure hydrogen.

During the training process, I qualified as a winch operator and learned the techniques of raising and lowering the balloon. During actual operations, the winch operator had total control of the balloon. All others on a balloon site were there to handle the ropes for release and tie-down. Special training classes were held for winch operators and gas technicians, designed to acquaint them with all aspects of their jobs. However, unforeseen situations would occur in Seattle that were never covered in the Camp Davis training exercises, as our instructors were slightly less green than we were and had not had any actual operational experience.

The Camp Davis training ended abruptly at noon on Saturday, January 11th, 1942. We

Helium is a Hellion to Hold

BARRAGE BALLOONS are made of sturdy cotton fabric coated with a rubber-like material which will hold *helium*—and this thin, buoyant gas is a Houdini for getting out of tight places.

Natural rubber won't do—helium seeps through its "pores." A dense, non-porous, *synthetic* rubber was found . . .

But it wouldn't dissolve in an ordinary rubber solvent. *How to apply it?*

Shell scientists came out of their laboratories with *toluene*. They had first produced toluene from petroleum to increase this country's production of TNT. And here was another use—it would dissolve the synthetic rubber so this could be spread over the fabric of the barrage balloon, making a helium-tight container.

As toluene is precious for explosives, the scientists weren't quite satisfied—yet. More experimenting, and they had a solvent of toluene and another material that is plentiful and low in cost.

Manufacturers of barrage balloons today are working with Shell-suggested formulas, and Shell scientists are continuing their research to conserve toluene. Barrage balloons, buoyed by helium or hydrogen, are mounting skyward on their vital mission.

This widening knowledge of petroleum molecules—what they will do, how they behave—today is "coming home" to you in dozens of ways. Already it has led to better food, better clothing at lower cost, more effective drugs, "beauty aids," plastics with scores of uses . . .

This scientific knowledge "carries over" to your motoring—in the Shell gasoline and motor oil you buy today.

"Oil is ammunition—use it wisely."

SHELL

The Shell Oil Company ad in *Life* Magazine, 1942. Shell developed toluene to contain balloon cases. (Reprinted with permission of Shell Oil Co.)

were instructed to pack our belongings and be ready to board the train for Seattle after breakfast on Sunday. I had come down with a bad head cold and went on sick-call, half hoping that I would be hospitalized for a few days. This might have afforded me the opportunity of avoiding troop-train travel in favor of private means on scheduled civilian passenger service. But no such luck. The doctor sprayed my throat and sinuses, a treatment that unplugged my eustachian tubes. He gave me a bottle of nose drops and some aspirin, and sent me on my way.

Before leaving, I told him of the crowded conditions on a troop train and the need for isolation from others to prevent spreading my germs, especially while sleeping. "Could I have some sort of note or prescription to give to the troop train Commander, instructing him to provide me with an upper berth?" I asked. The doctor thought it was a good idea and wrote out the brief order on his official Army paper. I figured my luck at drawing an upper berth for the third time was getting pretty slim, and besides, I really didn't relish the idea of sharing my coughs and sneezes.

I had written to the folks and to Ruth, telling of my departure for the West Coast. We were now permitted to identify our destination and new address: Battery A, 304 CABBB, APO 309, Fort Lewis, Washington. Eventually our mail would come directly to Seattle, avoiding the delay of first going to Fort Lewis, which was actually located near Tacoma.

Chapter 10

Seattle

M Y TWO SEAT MATES were congenial, though strangers to me. I did notice that they avoided direct conversation, and I did my best to keep my germs to myself. When the porter came into our car to make up the berths, my two companions told me to take the upper and they would share the lower. I never had to show the doctor's memo. Feeling somewhat like a leper, I thanked them, and again enjoyed the isolation. This time I really needed to be alone.

We settled in for the long journey that would traverse at least a dozen states and actually touch the Chicago area sometime in the middle of the second night. I learned from a trainman that our route would not include any mileage on the Illinois Central line that passed near our house, but would skirt south as it angled across Illinois toward Iowa. The folks and Ruth would be pleased in knowing that I was so close to home.

Because of my cold, I was not a happy traveler and took little interest in the passing scene. My seat mates were willing to let me spend time in the upper berth during the day, even though its down position somewhat cramped their headroom. I was glad that I had not been scheduled for KP duty in the kitchen cars, but did serve during the fourth day on guard duty in Montana. I enjoyed some of the scenery as we crossed the Rocky Mountains and viewed the snow-covered peaks in what I determined was Glacier National Park. The train moved slowly and darkness fell before we could get our fill of nature's wonders. We had a long stopover at the small depot at White Fish, where I got off on the platform and had a Red Cross Lady snap my picture. It was about 11:00 p.m., and I was surprised to find a few of these wonderful volunteers on duty at that hour. We guards, who were the only ones awake, benefited from their presence and partook heartily of their wares.

The final lap of our trip was on the right-of-way of the Great Northern Railroad, which angled slightly southwest from White Fish to Spokane and then west to Seattle, where we arrived in the rain in the late afternoon of Friday, January 16th, 1942. We had been train-bound for 5½ days and 5 nights.

After considerable switching and maneuvering, the train was finally positioned for our debarkation at the Seattle Municipal Auditorium. We entered a huge basement room where several hundred folding canvas cots awaited us. Other areas were set up for a kitchen, an infirmary, offices, and latrines. This would serve as a staging point for the formation of balloon-site crews and their disbursement to balloon locations around Boeing Aircraft Plant #2 at Boeing Field.

I was still suffering from my head cold, and felt its migration into my chest. I was just plain miserable. The medical technician in the infirmary gave me more aspirin and a jar of Vicks Vapo-rub, which I applied copiously to my chest. We had been issued long under-wear shirts and drawers at Camp Davis, and I was glad to use them now in this drafty room. I crawled under the blankets of my cot and dozed fitfully throughout the night.

Checking the bulletin board on Saturday morning, I saw that I was scheduled to drive a truck to deliver balloon crews and their equipment to established locations. I tried to beg off due to my cold, but to no avail. Equipped with à Seattle map, I searched a big chunk of the city before finding the vacant lot destination in a West Seattle neighborhood. My truck was loaded with tents and cots and other equipment for the 12-man crew that was waiting for me on the front porch of a house next to the lot. They unloaded the truck in record time, and I headed back toward the Auditorium, stopping at a drugstore to buy Bromo-Quinine. I found a liquor store and bought a half-pint bottle of whiskey. The entire trip took more than four hours, which earned me a reprimand from the dispatching Sergeant. I told him I probably shouldn't be on duty at all due to my illness and persuaded him to scratch me from further assignment so that I could go to bed.

I spent Sunday in and out of bed, taking the Bromo as directed, but all it seemed to do was make me sweat. Real relief from one of the worst infections of my life didn't happen. Nor did a nip of the whiskey help. I got indigestion.

In mid-afternoon on Monday the 19th, I was assigned to Balloon Site Number 12, a vacant lot located at the corner of Delridge Way SW and SW Holden Street. I joined 11 others, and we were delivered with our equipment to the muddy site, overgrown with weeds and grass. Our site Commander, Staff Sergeant Robert Norstad, directed and helped the erection of two pyramidal tents while the incessant rain and cold added to our misery. To make matters worse, the truck that was supposed to bring our supper in large Thermos containers was long overdue.

We assembled our folding canvas cots and arranged our belongings and bedding for the night with the light of a kerosene lantern. By that time, I was suffering with chills and

Alex Stewart was the winch operator with the 304th Barrage Balloon Battalion Site Number 12 at Webster Street and Delridge Way, Seattle, Washington, in April 1942.

fever. I removed my muddy boots and, fully clothed, including field jacket, bedded down on my cot, covered up with three wool blankets and a heavy comforter. The chow truck finally arrived with two Thermos containers, each one containing three stainless-steel pans about 4 inches deep and 15 inches in diameter. I had no appetite for the spaghetti and meatball menu, by then cool, and declined my share. Some of the others started a fire outside, using a dry shipping crate for kindling, and warmed their food. They were ready to eat most anything and soon devoured the whole offering.

Presently a tall, slim, gray-haired civilian gentleman of about 50 years of age entered our tent, looked around, and asked how we were getting along. The other five said they were doing fine, now that they had eaten. The man looked my way, walked over beside my cot, and asked, "What's wrong with you, young feller?" I told him of my lingering illness, and after feeling my forehead, he told me I had a fever. "This is no place for you. You put on your boots and come up to the house. I live next door. Ma and I can get you fixed up in no time," he commanded in a deep, friendly voice. I told him I couldn't leave without the Sergeant's okay, at which he went to the other tent. When he returned, he said, "Come on, let's go. Bob said it was okay."

I put on my boots as he introduced himself as Bill Gallagher. I told him my name as we shook hands. We walked about 100 feet to his small cottage, built on the side of a hill. The entrance was actually on the second floor where the two bedrooms and bath were located. The living area was at the bottom of a rather steep stairway.

Pointing to the spare bedroom, he told me to get undressed while he filled the bathtub. I sank into the great luxury of wonderful hot water for the first time since the winter of 1940 at home. "Put these on when you're ready, then come on downstairs and get some of Ma's beef stew," Bill ordered. And I did just that. Ma's name was Ada, a rather short stocky lady of about 45 with brown, bobbed hair. She had a friendly face and a hearty laugh as she said she hoped I was "feeling better." She was concerned, however, that I didn't have clean socks to go with "Pa's" old flannel PJs. I replied that everything was just wonderful and thanked them. Ma dished up a large bowl of delicious beef stew and I ate to contentment. The stew was followed by a large slice of boysenberry pie, as good as any pie I had ever eaten. Ma explained that though the berries were out of season, their bushes were prolific and she had canned enough to last them all winter.

The Gallaghers quizzed me about home, where I was from, and wanted to know all about my family. Finally, Pa said it was past time for me to get to bed. He led the way upstairs, gave me aspirin and water, turned back the featherbed, and told me to hop in. I obeyed and said goodnight as he closed the door, leaving it slightly ajar. I thought of these wonderful, generous, sweet people and saw in their kind deeds a reflection of Mother and Dad in a similar circumstance. I would also expect a like response from Ruth. These were my last thoughts before drifting off into the best sleep I had known in the new year.

I awoke at 6:00 and felt that I would survive. The rain had stopped, but it was still cloudy. I heard Ma and Pa down in the kitchen working on breakfast. After dashing water on my face and doing a rough combing job on my hair, I returned to the bedroom and found that Ma had dried my fatigues in front of their furnace and had washed my underwear and socks and had them laid out for me on the chair. I dressed and went down to the kitchen.

Pa had me sit down while he made a big pancake with a fried egg on top.

"How many can you eat?" he asked.

"Let's start out with two," I said, but before I could say, "No more, thank you," I had eaten five, with two cups of strong coffee. Ma sat there the whole time, sipping her coffee, watching me eat, and smiling. I thanked her for washing my clothes and for taking such good care of me.

Pa was a railroad engineer, working in the Seattle marshaling yards, switching cars and making-up and breaking-down trains. This particular week he was working days, driving an electric diesel locomotive. I thanked Ma for her kindnesses and left the house with Pa as he was leaving for work. I reported to Sergeant Norstad, telling him about my stay at the Gallaghers, and thanked him for letting me go. He was glad to see my improvement.

Sergeant Norstad was liked and respected by all the crew for his fairness and leadership.

Norstad had surveyed the site and started planning the layout for tents, balloon, and winch. He made note of the large pine trees close by and overhead wires, all of which could become hazards to balloon operations. After awhile, our Platoon Commander, Technical Sergeant Valluchi, a native of New York City, stopped by to see how we were doing. Bob pointed out the problems and inadequacies of the site, suggesting that if a better place could be found, we ought to pick up and relocate. Valluchi was to check it out and let him know.

It was Tuesday, January 20th, and mail was finally catching up with us. A driver from Headquarters stopped by in a weapons carrier with a pretty good load of letters. I received one from Ruth, and was surprised at her news.

Friday, January 16, 1942

Dear Alex,

It has been so long since I have written to you that I am just bursting with news. First, I will tell you the most important. I am no longer employed at Coopers'. I will start on Monday with the Pure Oil Company. They are located in the Pure Oil Building at Wacker Drive and Wabash Avenue on the 19th floor and the money is darn good. I will work 37½ hours a week and I will get two weeks vacation after a year's service. This is much better than Coopers' could do.

Two weeks ago I took my niece down to my alma mater, the Felt and Tarrant Comptometer school. She enrolled and will start right after high school graduation. While there, I talked to a couple of the Comptometer salesmen who told me Coopers' salary was too low. The following Thursday Mr. Manske with Pure Oil called me to come in for an interview. I went on Saturday, took a stiff comp test and was hired. I gave Coopers' a one week notice.

On my last day some of the gals took me out to lunch. The office gave me a beautiful black patent leather purse, which I didn't expect. Everyone was so nice to me, I almost cried. At first I dreaded leaving Coopers' but Alex, on Monday when I went to work everything was fine. On Tuesday the company was on its way out of business.

Someone started the rumor that household refrigerator production was going to be frozen by the government. So Coopers' wasted no time and shipped out everything in their warehouse, $90,000.00 worth in one day alone. The freezing hasn't started yet but today fifteen people were laid off. I felt badly for them as they all treated me so nice and they didn't get any severance pay.

Today I told Ruth Hansen about us. She wasn't surprised — and you know why. But I'm not angry. I can't stop you from bragging (hmmmm—). You don't have to worry about anyone calling you a wolf. I can assure you that you are not and that is a very commendable characteristic, and I am not kidding. With your pay increase to $70.00 a month as a corporal (when you get it) and my new job, we really could meet at the City Hall — hmmmmmm!! I consider every letter I get from you a date. When I don't get one I just pretend you are working nights.

I hope you like Seattle. Next year when I get my vacation I'll come and visit you.

Bye now,
Love, Ruth

P.S. Did you hear about the firefly who backed into a fan — he was delighted — no end.

A few days later we packed up and moved one block north and two or three blocks west to a partially wooded lot located at the foot of a hillside orchard. The gravel road had no name marker but could have been an unimproved section of SW Webster Street. The entire area is now the location of the West Seattle General Hospital.

The Army Brass had contacted the owner and negotiated the use of the land. Though there was considerable work in preparing the site, its size and location were ideal for our purpose.

We pitched our tents, dug a latrine, and covered it with an outhouse. Some obstructing trees were felled, old tree stumps were removed, brush and overgrowth were cleaned out, and eventually we built a small log mess hall and an underground food storage box. The balloon bed area required leveling and filling with sand. Underground drain "tiles" made from boards were installed to divert rain water coming down from the orchard.

Large, heavy logs with steel cables wrapped around them were buried about four feet deep and left with a cable loop protruding above the ground surface. Many of these were located in an oval pattern describing the perimeter of the balloon. They would serve as tie-down pickets. Finally, the winch was located near the southeast corner of the balloon bed and a trench dug from its cable discharge point to the center of the bed. Two or three large, heavy logs were buried about four feet in the ground to anchor a large pulley, called a snatch block. When the ¼-inch cable was extended the length of the trench from the winch, threaded through the pulley and attached to the balloon leader cable, the balloon would rise from and descend to the pulley location. The entire impacted sand surface of the bed was covered with canvas tarps to hold the sand and deflect rain water. Finally, two rows of logs were positioned at the side of the bed to hold perhaps 40 or 50 125-pound steel cylinders containing hydrogen.

Our balloon, winch, and a supply of hydrogen for the initial inflation were delivered. We accomplished the make-ready work in good time and busied ourselves with the improvement of the camp while waiting for trial flight orders. I spent time on the winch, raising the balloon 40 to 50 feet and then lowering it, getting a feel for its operation. Bob Butler, our gas technician had done a good job of inflating the balloon and now took daily samples of the gas from a tie-off appendix-like sleeve near the tail.

Hydrogen was purchased by the military from commercial distributors of pressurized gases and was picked up by Army men at distributor warehouses, loaded onto Army trucks, and transported to balloon sites.

One cold, rainy day I was assigned to a four-man work crew to secure a truckload of hydrogen-filled steel cylinders at Tacoma. In the loading process, a cylinder slipped from my grasp and caught the tip of my little finger on my left hand, smashing it between the bottom of the cylinder and the iron-reinforced concrete edge of the loading platform.

The impact was sufficient to rupture the finger pad, causing profuse bleeding and severe pain. I immediately wrapped the finger in my handkerchief and let the other men finish the work. I sat on the stacked cylinders for the ride back to Seattle and had the driver take me to the battery infirmary.

I unwrapped my finger and saw that the wound was still bleeding, and the throbbing pain persisted. The Army doctor, a short, skinny First Lieutenant from Mississippi, examining the injury, seemed to find it necessary to squeeze the finger several times. With every squeeze a fresh flow of blood came forth.

I was beginning to have doubts about his medical competency when he finally asked, in his Mississippi drawl, "Ah yew ah bleedah?" I didn't understand what he had asked. "Am I a what?" I probed. "Yew know, ah bleedah!" he repeated. I became slightly incensed and blurted out a rather insubordinate answer, "I never was before but I guess I am now, as long as you keep squeezing like that." Rather than receiving a reprimand, the doctor grinned, squeezed again, then had an enlisted medical corpsman disinfect the wound, apply a small splint, and bandage the finger.

Living in the restricted quarters of a pyramidal tent with six men and their belongings had its drawbacks. Light still came from a kerosene lantern and heat from a small, sheet-steel pot-bellied stove. It was crowded and hard to avoid invading another man's area. We were all subject to sentry duty, with the exception of Sergeant Norstad, and agreed to a simple schedule that called for a two-hour tour once per day for each of us. It was the job of those on night duty to keep the fire going in the stove of each tent while the rest of us slept.

It was also the unofficial job of the guards, when conditions warranted, to toss Private Hoffman's odoriferous socks into the fire. He was lax in donning clean ones at tolerable intervals and habitually hung his dirty, damp socks on the end of his cot to air out and, still rank, be ready for wear the next morning. This always brought a violent response from Hoffman and failed to effect his reformation.

Besides myself, the Site Number 12 personnel were an interesting, if odd, assortment of American youth. Their origins and ethnic backgrounds were as varied as their individual experiences. All names are not remembered, but their service is not forgotten.

- Staff Sergeant Robert Norstad — Oak Park, Illinois. Balloon site Commander and brother of Colonel Lauris Norstad (later to become U.S. Air Force General and Supreme Commander of Allied Powers in Europe).
- Corporal Robert Butler — Battle Creek, Michigan. Gas technician and formerly with the Weston Company.
- Corporal Elmer Davis — St. Louis, Missouri. Assistant winch operator.
- Private Francis Keenan — Chicago, Illinois.
- Private Joseph Moqua — Milwaukee, Wisconsin. Former long-distance bicycle racer and fire fighter.
- Private Sam Glorso — Chicago, Illinois. Truck driver. Former coal-truck driver. Served in Civilian Conservation Corps (CCC) in Santa Clara, California.
- Private James Irwin — Duluth, Minnesota. Formerly worked in open-pit iron mines of the Mesabi Iron Range in Minnesota.
- Private Ken Zimmerman — Wisconsin. Former farmer. Served in the CCC.
- Private Charles Hoffman — Wisconsin. Former farmer. Served in the CCC.

• Private Ernest Yoder — Detroit, Michigan.
• Private _____ _____. Name and origin not remembered.

The men who had served in the Civilian Conservation Corps were good workers and were especially experienced with the large two-man cross-cut saw and the double-bitted ax. They were quick to relieve me of either tool whenever I attempted to use it, deciding it was better for me not to learn the technique than to risk injury. And they were right. I was strong though, and did my share of the work load, moving dirt, sand, logs, and debris. Most of the others were as inept as I was with the tools.

Work around the site became somewhat routine and the usual Army discipline was enforced. Daily clean-up and improvement of facilities was ongoing. The Gallaghers' house and yard were visible from our new location, about a city block diagonally distant. The kindness they had rendered to me that first night was only a sample of their generosity. And their efforts were not restricted to me, for they soon practically adopted the whole crew of 12 men.

I was unhappy with the Army mail service and asked the Gallaghers if I could have letters from my folks sent to their address. They agreed, and when mail came for me, Ma would hang a dishtowel in a chosen location on her backyard clothes line. When our afternoon work was finished, and with Norstad's permission, I would walk over to pick up my letters. Ma always had cake or cookies or pie and a cup of coffee for me. We would sit in the kitchen and talk. They became known as Ma and Pa to all of us.

Ma told me she had a son by her first husband and thought he was somewhere in the San Francisco area, but she never heard from him. He was about my age and she said I reminded her so much of him. Surprisingly, his photo revealed that he was about my height and build and had the same hair and complexion coloring. Ma was a plain, uncomplicated person with a heart as big as all outdoors. Pa had a son, Bill, Jr., by his first marriage, who was a career Army man and had attained the rank of Master Sergeant. He was stationed at an Army fort near the Bremerton, Washington, Navy Yard.

Soon after we moved to the new location, Ma and Pa set up the routine where two of our men would go to their house on Saturday evening for a very nice sit-down supper. At the same time, the fellows back at camp ate from a large kettle of Ma's hot chili, beef stew, or vegetable soup. Delivered with this were two pies or a large sheet cake. This was a welcome replacement for the often tasteless fare delivered almost cold from the Army kitchen. They set up a rotational schedule, so that in a month and a half, all of us had an opportunity to put our feet under their table. In retrospect, I imagine Ma spent most of Saturday preparing our supper.

When food rationing was introduced and ration stamps for fresh meat, sugar, coffee, and other foods were required, we wondered how they managed. We could not supplement their supply of meat, but we did manage to keep them in sugar, butter, coffee, bacon, and eggs. We had persuaded the Brass to supply us with the raw food supplies and we would prepare our own meals. As a result, we had a reasonable surplus which we gave to the Gallaghers. We cooked over an open fire with an improvised grille while adhering to the military's sanitary requirements. The arrangement worked out very well, due in part to the experience of the men who had served in the CCC.

In return for the Gallaghers' kindnesses, we did odd jobs around their place and kept their firewood box filled. When Pa needed a hand with some job, everyone was ready to pitch in. This help was never solicited by them but was anticipated by us and provided during non-critical hours.

Mail service by this time had improved, and the interest of the folks at home in barrage balloons increased. I had given them detailed information on their purpose in defending the Boeing plant and the potential for attack by the enemy. Our work was hard and demanding of time and energy. We were pressured by Headquarters to get operational as soon as possible, and this led to longer work hours in the very wet Seattle weather.

In early February I received another letter from Dad. I believe it spoke more to his feelings and intellect than those he had written to date. I was deeply moved:

Chicago   Feb. 1st, 1942

Dear Alex,

Christmas has come again and gone. For many reasons it was not one of the Noels of yesteryear, but of course they are and always will be different. We like to hark back to the merry, merry time when all our hearts were young and our burdens light. With no war on our minds and hands we really did not know how well off we were.

We didn't set up a Christmas tree then to make us happy: rather it was the symbol of happiness, the sign of contentment, and perhaps the token of prosperity. But for various reasons attitude has changed. The tree induces reminiscence, and much of the joy of the present is somewhat blurred by the word "absence."

The child can never fully interpret the sentiments of parents, nor realize the depths that are sounded when changes arise. We would like things that are a delight to continue but we are not of that kind of world. It is said that in the world to come there will be no more sorrow nor sighing, no pain, no death and no crying: what a change! But what a dark river to cross. The early part of my life had few joys that have been yours, but the advent of your mother on the scene dimmed its memory and left it all forgotten. And that is the mother that is still the faithful one to you and to us all. They called her Pearl but she did not like the name. It bore nevertheless her true title and her worthy emblem.

Now she has one concern — the safety of her boys, one hope — their speedy return to her arms. Do you think your father is speaking for her only? To us there is no glory in war, yet its necessity has never been satisfactorily denied though sharply debated.

With your brother David, like the doctor of large practice, he is hardly ever home: eats and sleeps at the hospital, studying when he can. This reduces the once crowded home to two girls and parents. Our early days in this country were filled with joy and contentment: they are not unhappy now but promise of the kind of future remains dark. To do our duty as we see our duty is not simply material for contemplation but for instant practice. Mother and I shall not fail while breath continues.

The whole eight of us meet every day by the miracle of imagination. That same magic enables us to see our children as infants in arms, as romping playmates, as adolescents, as men and women in maturity. Our eyes grow dim and our skin wrinkles, but with these declining marks memory sparkles as ever and we are young again.

Your letters are meat and drink and consolation to us all. Your well being is our one obsession in the awful misfortunes of war. We share hatred with none and hope is our only light. Tucked away at eventide is a short prayer for all whom we love, and rest assured, Alex, you are not forgotten.

Your affectionate father,
Dad

Dad's eloquence touched me deeply, and I felt a surge of pride in his expression of patriotism when he said, "To do our duty as we see our duty is not simply material for contemplation but for instant practice. Mother and I shall not fail while breath continues." It was then I realized that this war would be won by the entire population, even aged people, soldiering on the home front.

Bob Butler supplied the hydrogen quantities required by the balloon and monitored its oxygen level accurately. I don't recall that we ever had to deflate the balloon due to excess oxygen level or for any other reason. With Elmer's help, I tended to the winch just as I would my automobile, changing oil, lubricating the spool bearings and other mechanisms.

Sometime in early March, all the balloon sites became operational, even while we continued to improve our living arrangements. We were informed that a barracks would be built for us in the near future, causing us to abandon plans for constructing wood floors in the tents. We had covered the ground with large sheets of corrugated cardboard, which had been scavenged from cartons. This we overlaid with boards of random length, placing the same in front of our cots and on walk areas, providing a little protection from dirt and the dampness that was ever present.

In due course, a civilian construction team arrived and proceeded to build a barracks for us. A 20- by 50-foot concrete slab was poured to support a one-story wood structure covered with black tar paper. A private room was provided for Sergeant Norstad at one end, across the passageway from a simple but adequate bathroom. It contained a wash basin, toilet, and 3-foot square sheet-metal shower. A gas-fired water heater was housed in an adjoining closet. Because there was no city sewer connection on our road, a septic system was installed. A natural gas supply was available for the water heater, and when a plumber failed to show up to pipe the gas from the meter, with Sergeant Norstad's permission, I secured the materials, borrowed tools, and completed the job. The expert sawyers and axemen were surprised that I possessed this plumbing know-how and cheerfully consented to allow me the privilege of taking the first hot-water shower. For more than 2½ months, we had ridden the truck with Sammy Glorso to a city fire station about two miles distant for our shower baths.

The new quarters were clean and dry and easy to maintain. Each man had his own clothes rack with a shelf above and sufficient space between cots for freedom of movement. Footlockers contained our small clothing and personal articles. I was glad to have the shelf where I could display Ruth's picture and see it when I stretched out on my bed. At first some of the fellows teased me about her, but that soon got old when I failed to react.

The unfailing kindness and generosity of the Gallaghers endeared them to us and sustained our spirits. I had written to Ruth and the folks about them and occasionally they corresponded with one another. Dad gave them high praise in another of his very perceptive letters.

920 Kimball Hall   May 14, 1942
Chicago, Illinois

Dear Alex,

Mother so completely fills the post of correspondent that she leaves little to be told. I have just finished reading Mrs. Gallagher's letter to mother, a rare example of unaffected generosity. Instead of calling on her to buy any bonds, the government should finance her tireless attentions to the military, decorate her with distinguished insignia and pension her and her husband for life. You have found a warm place in their hearts and home, and we are proud of their selection. They are the kind of people that made America the lovely land it is, but alien thinkers and actors, not necessarily foreign, will seek to destroy it from its foundations upwards.

While we are not happy with your enforced absence from our fireside, we are proud to be represented in the sacred duty and privilege of defense, for America must be saved. A realization of this feature will relieve the monotony of guard duty, the constant watch and eye strain, the restless alert of nerve and muscle, the constant expectation of attack. There is a day to which we are all looking, the day when arms are laid down, and the voices of loved ones cry "Home, Home." The fastest train on rails will seem slow in that dawning, food and rest will seem trivial and irksome, tears of joy will blur the reading and patience will be impossible to command.

But that day is not yet. Hell has still to be quenched, and the fury of Satan destroyed, because he is surely let loose in the earth.

The papers inform us that we are losing better than one ship a day to the submarines. This is faster than we can build and after all, ships are our strongest hope, especially in the Pacific effort.

Mother is still doing most of the heavier housework. I don't hold up like formerly. May 23 will see me entering the dreaded zone of time, the promises for which are never comforting. My studio class is small, rent and expenses high. But I am hoping for better health and hoping soon to see you.

Your affectionate father
Dad

Bob Butler bunked next to me, and we enjoyed listening to classical and popular music on his small radio. Bob was an avid reader of news-type magazines, and I believe he subscribed to *Time*, which he read from cover to cover. He was six years older than me, was a college graduate, and a member of a fraternity. He had secured a private pilot's license before entering the Army. In addition to his duties as gas technician, Bob manned the BAR — the Browning Automatic Rifle — which was assigned to our balloon site. The rest of us had the 30.03 Springfield rifles, until the arrival of the new .30-caliber Garrand semi-automatic. These were eventually replaced with the smaller, lightweight carbine.

Whether new or old, we dreaded the introduction of weapons, as the job of making them fit for use was an irritation. They were usually coated with a heavy layer of rust preventative known as Cosmoline, the trademark for a heavy grade of petrolatum. It was dark brown in color and had to be removed from every crack and crevice and screw hole, first to qualify for the Army's standard of cleanliness, and, second, to ensure that the brown stuff was not transferred to our clothing. And, of course, the hardest part was the cleaning of the firing chamber and the barrel with its spiral rifling grooves. An inspecting officer would literally snatch the rifle from your hands, peer into the barrel from the muzzle end, and check for a mirror-like shine. A dirty rifle was tantamount to other serious offenses and would earn a severe reprimand or penalty.

Our balloon operations became quite routine and were highlighted with practice alerts. During the day we would often fly them at 500 or 1,000 feet for several hours and then retrieve them to "close haul" for evening or night-time hours. Sometimes we would fly them at maximum altitude — 7,000 feet.

Meantime, the war in the Pacific raged on. After Pearl Harbor on December 7th, 1941, I followed the action of the Japanese and recorded these events:

- December 23 Wake Island surrenders to Japanese.
- December 25 Hong Kong surrenders to Japanese.
- January 2 Manila falls.
- January 23 Battle of Macassar Strait.
- January 31 U.S. Fleet attacks Marshall and Gilbert Islands.
- February 15 Singapore falls to Japanese.
- March 7 Dutch surrender Netherlands Indies.
- April 9 Japanese take Bataan.

- April 18 American B-25s bomb Tokyo — the famous Dolittle raid from the carrier *Hornet*.
- May 6 Corregidor falls to Japanese.
- May 4-9 Battle of the Coral Sea.
- June 3-5 Battle of Midway.

Part of the Japanese plan of action at Midway was a side attack on the Aleutian Islands — the only phase of the Midway Campaign that succeeded. On June 3rd, 1942, Japanese airplanes raided the American air and naval base at Dutch Harbor, Alaska. A few days later, Japanese troops occupied Attu and Kiska islands, more than 600 miles to the west. This action brought an alert to the entire American West Coast, and we were ordered to fly the balloons at 1,000 feet altitude. It was feared that the Alaska action would create a diversion and provide the Japanese an opportunity to attack our strategic industries, launching dive-bombers from their aircraft carriers. If the threat became reality, only a few minutes would be required to send the balloon to 7,000 feet.

One day in early June, darkness came and with it the threat of bad weather. With the balloon at 1,000 feet altitude, Elmer and I took turns manning the winch at two-hour intervals. I saw the storm clouds building and felt the wind off the coast intensify. This was no casual spring rain. I kept watch on the cable, where it rose vertically from the snatch block, and noted that it was now laying over at about 15 degrees. The force of the wind was pushing hard against the balloon. I kept my ear tuned to the field telephone at my side, expecting an order to haul down all balloons.

Presently, the phone crackled and all sites received the order to play out cable and fly balloons at maximum altitude. Were the Japanese dive-bombers on their way here and were we in for some action? . . . I was amazed at the order, but complied.

The balloon rapidly reached its max, and I gingerly applied the brake, fearful that a sudden and jerking stop might snap the cable, which was now laying over at about 45 degrees. The storm in progress was not a shallow rain scud but a full-blown front. I concluded that there were no Japanese bombers flying around in that mess, but that the Brass must have gambled that raising the balloons would put them above the storm, a conclusion that was later confirmed.

In the chaos, I heard a balloon site Commander, using the telephone code, call in to Battery Headquarters. Site Number 8 had just lost its balloon. In rather quick succession, Sites Number 6, 10, and 11 called in to report their balloons lost. I continued to listen to the phone, expecting to receive an order to haul everything down, and it was a short wait.

The order came. I got off the winch, cranked the engine into action, and climbed back into the seat. I pushed in the clutch, shifted to low gear, and slowly let the clutch out, applying as little throttle as possible but enough to overcome the pull of the balloon without killing the engine. I had rehearsed this procedure in my mind and in actual operations from day one, knowing how easy it would be to jerk the cable and snap it. The winch was equipped with three forward speeds, but I realized the hazard of shifting to a higher gear. Depressing the clutch to make the shift would allow the winch spool to go into a free-wheeling situation with the result that the lifting force of the balloon would cause the cable to play out. So, too, letting out the clutch in the higher gear would induce a sudden braking action of the rising balloon and cause the cable to snap. The safest and surest method was to operate in low gear at a minimum speed, thus keeping a steady, constant pull on the cable.

Sergeant Norstad had awakened all the men and had them prepare for seizing the tie-down ropes and securing them to the picketing hitches as soon as the balloon reached near "bedding level." The storm was now approaching its greatest force, the rain coming in torrents, propelled by powerful, gusting winds. Several men hollered at me to "step on the gas," to speed up, but I turned a deaf ear to them. Norstad also asked me to go faster, but I told him I didn't want to be the one to lose the balloon.

"No, no, that's okay. You're doing fine," he replied.

I told the Sergeant to have the men ready to grab the ropes as soon as they could. They needed to be threaded into the pickets before I applied the brake and stopped the descent.

We had color-coded the cable with paint rings every 100 feet of the first 500 feet to indicate the remaining elevation. I held a flashlight beam on the cable and when the 500-foot marker appeared, I called it out. Next it was 400 feet, then 300, then 200, and finally 100. The balloon emerged through the rain and darkness at about 150 feet, indicating the low level of the ceiling.

The men did as instructed, and our balloon was soon safely tied down to the canvas tarp-covered bed. I set the emergency brake on the winch and shut off the engine. I turned the crank on the field telephone and the GI operator on duty answered.

"Hello Genore, this is Site Number 12. Our balloon is all settled snug in bed and we're ready to do the same," I reported.

We were the last one to report in and the only one in our platoon that didn't lose the balloon. Each platoon had 9 balloons, 18 to a battery — in all, 72 to the battalion. It was reported the next morning that a total of 18 balloons had been lost from the battalion.

Early in the morning, retrieving crews were organized and dispatched to distant points where balloons had finally come down. Reports from the Air Corps, the Coast Guard, the Navy and the Defense Command poured into Headquarters, pinpointing locations. Most balloons were dragging several thousand feet of cable, some crossing high power lines and blacking out towns and villages. The errant balloons ranged far into Canada, and the retrieving crews brought back some wild tales.

One crew reported that a cable had contacted a high power line and the dangling end had dragged through a farm yard, causing the electrocution of a bunch of pigs in a mud-laden sty. Another report described a dragging cable contacting a high, wood power pole, wrapping itself around the pole near the tip and tying itself into what was determined to be a perfect bowline knot. The balloon was tethered to the pole until the local power company men and our crew could ascend above the wires and clamp the truck winch cable above the knot. The knot was then untied and the crew began the long process of reeling in 4,000 feet of cable in 100-foot increments, the capacity of the truck winch.

A weather analysis indicated that our platoon had been square in the eye of the storm and had caught its full fury. I was commended for my success in bringing our balloon home and was asked by the Battery Commander to write up a winch-operating procedure. I did so, and it was reproduced and circulated to all units. My work earned me a promotion, but Corporal was the top rating approved for winch operator. I had been hoping for Sergeant, but was pleased that my work qualified.

Some time during the early summer, Bob Butler had persuaded his mother to come to Seattle for a visit. Mrs. Butler stayed downtown at the Olympia Hotel, but was anxious to see the balloon and our crew in action. She came out by taxi and stayed overnight at the Gallaghers to be on hand to witness our early morning launching of the balloon. She stood just off the edge of our site property so as not to violate military regulations. After the launch, several of the men walked over and greeted her. She was a lovely and charming lady and was complimentary of the crew. Bob and I stood alone with her for a few minutes, at which time she invited me to come with Bob to the hotel that night for dinner.

I was somewhat dazzled by the beauty of the hotel's dining room — the service and the fine food. Many diners were in uniform, mostly officers, while others were in formal wear. In my short 22 years I had not experienced the luxury of such an occasion and wasn't sure of proper table manners. From the corner of my eye, I watched to see how Bob and Mrs. Butler ate their soup and nonchalantly applied the same technique. Back at our camp, Bob was just one of the boys and slurped just like the rest of us.

Mrs. Butler had casually glanced around the room and was surprised to spot General Knudson, former chairman of General Motors and now head of the War Production Board, seated at a nearby table. The General, like many industrialists, had been recruited to head up vital government departments. Mrs. Butler quietly called our attention to him and his three male aides. The General ate and, in between bites, talked at a rapid pace. Each of the aides had a clipboard, and quickly recorded about every word the General said. They had not been served any dinner and presumably ate later on in the hotel coffee shop.

Sometime in mid-summer, a series of U.S. Army commercials were aired on the radio, calling for men with flying training and experience to apply for service in the Glider Corps. They called for civilians, inactive reservists, National Guardsmen, and soldiers on active duty to apply for glider-pilot training with the promise of becoming flight officers. Bob Butler became intrigued with the invitation and suggested that he and I get passes and go to the Seattle recruiting station to check it out. Bob was a somewhat restless type, and when the balloon activity became a routine endeavor, he seemed to crave greater challenge. I think he felt his usefulness on balloons had peaked, and he could not see himself sitting out the war in a Seattle vacant lot.

Bob had flying experience. He held a private pilot's license, but I had never been higher than a ride in a Tilt-A-Whirl at a local amusement park. "Maybe they won't get enough applicants," he encouraged, "and they'll let you in."

The next day, we inquired at the recruiting office where Bob was told that they did not yet have a formal application blank but that he could use a "Powered Flight" form and hand write "Application for Glider-Pilot Training."

"As for you, Stewart," the recruiting Sergeant told me, "you don't qualify for gliders but you can apply for powered flight training." I reluctantly took the papers, but had little enthusiasm or zeal for completing them.

Back at camp, Bob filled out his form, then secured the required letters of recommendation attesting to his character and background and turned them into the Battalion Commander. I filled out my form as well, wrote for and received the recommendations from Dr. Harold Bowman, pastor of Chicago's First Presbyterian Church, from my uncle Henry Stewart, and from an old family friend and voice student of Dad's, Henri Marcy. I clipped the letters and application form together and tossed them into my footlocker. By that time, I had cooled to the idea and decided flying was just not for me, even though the educational requirements had been reduced to that of high school graduate.

Sometime, perhaps two or three weeks later, we were sacked out on our cots during the lunch break when Bob asked me if he could borrow some pipe tobacco. "It's in my footlocker, help yourself." Bob found the tobacco but also spied the Air Corps application and letters.

He exploded. "Goddamit, do you want to stay in this lousy outfit the rest of the war? If you don't turn these in to the CO, I'm going to turn them in for you. There are lots of guys a lot less qualified than you in this crazy Army doing more than rotting away playing nursemaid to a balloon."

His words stung me to action. He apparently saw more in me than I did in myself. I promised to turn them in the following day.

I called Headquarters and arranged to see the Battalion Commander at 10:00 the next morning. Sammy Glorso drove me over in the big truck, and I asked him to wait for me.

The clerk announced my arrival to the Colonel and ushered me into his office. Standing at rigid attention, I rendered my smartest salute and said, "Corporal Stewart reporting, Sir."

"At ease, Corporal. What can we do for you?" he asked.

I produced my application papers while explaining that I respectfully sought the Colonel's approval for my transfer to the Army Air Forces to enter pilot training. He scanned the papers briefly, then stated that they appeared to be in order and he would have them processed.

Then, leaning back in his big chair, he mused, "Corporal Stewart. Are you the Corporal Stewart that wrote the instructions for proper winch operation to launch and retrieve our balloons?"

"Yes, Sir," I answered.

The Colonel said he had read my report and had sent it to Coastal Command Headquarters, recommending that it be made a permanent part of procedure in all West Coast balloon units.

I was dumbfounded. Groping for words, all I could think to say was, "Well, Sir, at this point I don't know what more I can contribute to the success of the 304th or the American Defense Command. I feel my work here is completed and I now have this urge to move to new areas of service."

The Colonel smiled, then told me I would get orders in a few weeks to report for testing in downtown Seattle.

I thanked him, saluted, and departed.

Back in the truck, Sammy quizzed me. "How'd you make out? What'd the Colonel say?"

"He told me to get the hell out of here and take that crazy Italian truck driver with me," I grinned. Then I told him I wouldn't be risking my life in his damn truck much longer but would be taking off into the "Wild Blue Yonder." Sammy could drive that Army 6x6 truck like it was a Kiddy Kar, never clashing gears, double-clutching every time he shifted up or down, as smooth as silk. He was perfectly coordinated and would very likely have been a good pilot had his life's fortunes taken him in that direction. He crowded the Seattle speed limits getting us back to Delridge Way and Webster Street to tell about my interview. He made it sound almost as if he had intervened in my behalf!

Two weeks later, I reported to the Seattle recruiting office for physical and written examinations. Like the Draft Board in Chicago, this office was located on the second floor above some stores. In all, 36 men reported for Army Air Forces testing, several enlisted men in uniform, as I was, and the others civilians hoping to be accepted for air service rather than be drafted, as I had been. We sat at school-type desks and responded to 100 questions in a three-hour timed test. Passing required 70 correct answers. I completed mine in 2½ hours, then spent the remaining time double-checking my answers. Papers were collected at 12:00 and we were told to return from lunch at 1:00 p.m.

After lunch, the names of those who passed were read and I was glad to be among them, with a score of 91. In all, 24 of the 36 passed. Those failing were dismissed but were told they could reapply at a later date. The rest of us were then subjected to a thorough and rigid physical exam. I did well, except for one disturbing report. The doctor listening to my heart asked me if I had ever been diagnosed with a heart murmur. I had not.

"I can't be sure," he said. "I'll let you go on now but you may be stopped later down the line." Out of the 24 of us to take physicals, only 6 passed — and never was a heart murmur detected. I was walking on air as I made my way back to camp. Bob Butler and Sergeant Norstad were both delighted and generous with their congratulations.

I lost no time in writing to the folks and to Ruth with the news of my testing success and pending transfer to the Army Air Forces.

Several days later, I received a letter from Mother. She had recently received the news of the tragic death of Charles Hannish of Pawtucket, Rhode Island. Charles was the son of Mother's girlhood Omaha friend, Clara Nelson Hannish. Charles had been a flight instructor with the Royal Canadian Air Force; his plane had crashed in a training accident. Charles and I were the same age. But he was an only child, and Clara was devastated by the loss of her son. In a subsequent letter to Mother, Clara disclosed her ongoing illness and her total inability to reconcile her great loss. She had lost all desire to continue living. Her surrender to those illnesses would eventually take her life.

All of this had a very disturbing effect on Mother. In her letter she pleaded with me to abandon my plan to take up flying. She was consumed with the fear that I would meet the same fate as Charles, that I could not possibly survive. "Tell me now, Alex, that you will not go through with this. I beg this of you."

Of course I was shocked to learn of Charles' death and deeply concerned over Mother's fear. I reasoned that she could not see past it and her apparent assumption that all who flew airplanes were doomed to disaster. I tossed and turned most of the night after receiving her letter and struggled with the answer I would have to send her. This was so uncharacteristic of her, I thought. She was always such a positive force in our family life, encouraging us to meet opportunities and challenges if we truly felt they were of God's bidding. Her own life had been testimony to this posture. Then I concluded that the war and all its devastation was certainly clouding her optimistic resolve.

Fortunately, it was a letter I never had to write, a decision I never had to make. A day or two later I received another letter from Mother and could hardly believe the change that had come over her. She wrote simply. Like her other letters, this one, too was very newsy about the house, the family, friends, neighbors, and the problems and joys of life on the home front.

Dear Alex,

I was anxious to write to you again but you don't know how much I have to do around here. For one thing, I have been canning fruits and vegetables. Sharron has been here some, then Dad to take down to the studio and go for. You see those two trips alone take 3½ hours. It takes time to get him up to the 9th floor after getting him out of the car. I also have to take a lunch down after fixing it. I also have to pay bills, do repairs and quite a number of things that he used to do. The car has had no attention. We could have been ticketed on at least five counts: no state license, no city license, cracked and splintered windshield, leaking muffler and no safety sticker. I got desperate and had the two first attended to. David has had no time to give up to it either.

Well, Cam and Re are going to live at 86th & Bennett. Re was looking at another apartment at 83rd & Vernon for rent September 1st but it was taken. Sherry stayed all night Saturday and all day yesterday, then didn't want to go home.

I am glad you had the little trip to Vancouver. It does break the monotony of camp life doesn't it. There is nothing monotonous here. Chicago is alive with work and activity. Re called for me the other night and we drove down to see "Mrs. Miniver." It was just wonderful. It showed the bombing in England, the retreat at Dunkirk, and all the way through a pretty romance between two young people. The "Miniver family" was played beautifully by Walter Pigeon & Greer Garson. She certainly is beautiful and an unusual actress. Don't miss it.

The Marrs have returned from North Carolina where they visited Don at the Marine base. Tommy Shannon was killed in the Philippines. You will remember he was the son of Mrs. S. who ran the barber shop with her brother on Dorchester behind Vaslow's Pharmacy. He was a kid when some of you boys were young.

I believe Jack Everett has been rejected due to a bad ear. I don't know exactly. He has some spots on bronchial tubes also. They are long standing. He is a fine boy. He has been in lots of accidents. Dorothy Everett lives in Los Angeles and is going to help Mrs. Brown and Mary Anna when they come out there. Dorothy's husband is in service.

Well now about your work. I do hope you get the furlough. We are looking forward to it. Everybody has had a furlough but you. Do not think Alex that I was selfish in what I wrote to you about aviation. I was proud and happy that you passed all so well. I know it is partly your poise and personality and partly your abilities, and as I think of you, you just seem like an aviator. But of course, to have a shock like Charles, as well as so many of our boys being killed in training, it just seems that there could not possibly be a chance to escape.

I am very thoughtful too that there are some who are chosen by God to meet the great demands and go through it and come out unhurt. I also realize that there is great danger to do any kind of Army work. It just seems as though there is nothing to do but be very careful and take things as they come. I do believe that some or most do not have a proper idea of how fast they travel in a plane and how to control it when they meet an emergency. It may be you are the one that is going to see things through. I am not to say. As I have said before, it is for you to decide.

There was a Mrs. Burns here in the neighborhood. She was grieving over her boys going into the service. One of the boys went out one evening and was killed a few blocks from home.

I only know that I am not anxious for great position or fame from great accomplishment but rather for your safety and well being. I know I would not want you to be a coward nor shirker and I am extremely proud of your mental and physical ability. I am proud that I have raised such a perfect specimen of humanity. It is partly your dad too who is responsible for your fine physical condition. You were well born.

It is a great task our country has and now we are all in it. It is very evident around here. Everyone is talking of war, buying bonds, not caring about meatless days and everyone wants to be doing something. Dad is so disgusted to be laid up so long with his broken ankle.

Bernie Gold, you know, the grocer's son has been very sick. They have not even dared to Xray him. They do not know exactly what the trouble is but Jim has been there three or four weeks and will come home tonight. Bernie will be in the hospital three or four months. So you see it is not all aviation that brings trouble.

Now Alex, always remember that if you have a great call to go to the Air Corps I would not like to say you should hold back. I am only expressing my anxious feelings and perhaps if I should persuade you to flunk you might be killed some other way. It is for you to do as you think best. I know it is very hard and I know you would not want to fail. I am going to keep praying and thinking and with my great love I know you will come through.

Lovingly, Mother

P.S. The mother of Christ wept and grieved bitterly but what a grand result. To have been His Mother when he paid the price.

I will write again in two days.

Ah! That was the mother I knew, reasoning matters out in her mind, evaluating her concerns and fears, placing them in proper perspective, seeking and enumerating the positives and reinforcing them with her great faith and her love.

In my weekly letter to Ruth I had told her of the two letters I had received from Mother — first, the plea to abandon my flying plans, and second, her change of heart and encouragement to pursue them. Ruth's return letter was very heart-warming and I sensed her deeper feelings toward me. She used the salutation "Ace," a nickname I had acquired at Cooper's when Dick Gentzler misread my handwritten initials "ACS" on a service order.

RAW

Sunday, August 30th, 1942

Dear Ace,

Do you know what I'm doing? I'm pretending I'm having a date with you. Let's see, where shall we be? I know, let's make it Kennedy's Drug Store on 75th Street. They have the best banana splits. (I've been hungry for one for the past three weeks but haven't gotten one yet). We could do a lot of talking. I don't know when I have wanted to see anyone as much as I want to see you now. We would have a lot to talk about. Do you know, I think I have gotten to know you better by letter than I did when you were a 'courtin me (if I may use that expression) last summer. I suppose I'll have to reconcile myself to not seeing you this September. I planned on it. Oh boy, did I plan on it. When you get home for Christmas we can make up for lost time. Do you notice, I say when and not if. You just have to have something to look forward to.

This month was the fifth anniversary of our bridge club and we celebrated by breaking up. Too many girls were having families. We were always arguing about who worked the hardest, office girls or housewives and also, whether or not married men should be deferred from the service. The arguments became quite heated. I still don't think of it as a single man's war.

Gosh Ace, I'm mad about my new job. The work is so important. Thursday I did a few comparison statements of district 1 for the boss and he took them to Washington, D.C. I sure hope they were all correct. You would be surprised to see the effects of the gas rationing. We work on reports for the Office of Price Administration.

I heard a radio commentator say, "We did not lose one Flying Fortress in the 8 air raids to continental Europe." Makes you feel pretty good. The Japs and Germans haven't seen anything yet.

We had an eclipse here the other night. I expect you could see it too. It is rather hard to believe you can see the same moon when you are so far away. We have a notice printed on the wall at various points on the 19th floor of the Pure Oil Building: "This is not considered a refuge zone —

please use the stairway to the 14th floor." It was rather disturbing.

When on pass, the girls have discussions or rather bull sessions. We have discussed the possibility of the Japs bombing Chicago and various other points. Whenever Seattle is mentioned I always say. "I have a friend in Seattle and he will personally see to it that the Japs won't get there or any farther inland." I take quite a razzing on it . . . and I love it. They are going to be glad to hear you decided to transfer to the Air Corps, but so sad about your not getting a furlough. They like you. They have seen your picture and have given their approval.

Ace, I am just a bit speechless when it comes to commenting on your mother's reply. Nothing I can think of is worthy of such wonderful encouragement. It brought tears to my eyes. I am so glad she put her okay on it. There is something about mothers that when they don't approve of a thing, and no matter how right you think you are, you just can't enjoy yourself when you know they object.

Your mother must be a wonderful person. I think I have bragged on occasion about your being a perfect speciman of humanity. I feel very much the same as your mother but she has the advantage over me . . . she is your mother. I realize more than you know what this change means to you and now want to wish you the best possible success and pray that you will come out of the war unhurt.

Gosh, I'm in a talkative mood tonight. Maybe I should let you say something now. You are a wonderful conversationalist . . . didn't interrupt once. Wasn't the banana-split good?

Had a lovely time, Ace, 'night.

XXXX Ruth

Chapter 11

Santa Ana Classification

TRANSFER ORDERS DATED September 15th, 1942, were issued, ordering me to report to "DEML Sec SCU" (Detached Enlisted Men's List, Section Service Command Unit) 1907, Fort Lewis, Washington, near Tacoma. Two other transferees were in the command car that took us to the Fort, Corporal Robert Nowicki of Milwaukee, from Battery B, and Private First Class Stanley P. Zalewski from Battery A. Section SCU 1907 was known as a "casual" company, really a "way-station" or clearing point for men in transit from one status to another. Several were in the process of being discharged from the service for medical or family hardship reasons, some for unsuitability for military service, and many for transfer to other service branches, as we three were doing.

Departure from Seattle and the Site Number 12 balloon crew was without ceremony. Although I got along well with most all of the men, no warm, close friendships had developed, other than that which Bob Butler and I enjoyed. Bob's transfer to the Glider Corps had occurred several weeks before mine. And Sergeant Bob Norstad was a high-class gentleman, but rather quiet and reserved. He maintained his Commander status with dignity, was always friendly, but did not fraternize with any of us. Because of his brother's position as a full Colonel in the Army Air Forces and a member of General Eisenhower's staff, I thought Bob might have pursued a more aggressive place in the service. I asked him about that possibility, and he replied that he had no interest in a military career. His brother, Lauris Norstad, was a West Point man and was destined for greatness. Like the rest of us, Bob had been drafted into the Army.

When I saw the command car bouncing up our pockmarked road at 7:30 a.m., I made the rounds and shook hands with each man. We wished each other good luck and all of them came out to the car, one or two of them carrying my bags. In typical GI fashion, the farewell remarks were not of the sentimental variety but were well laced with a collection of ribald remarks and unsavory titles. Had it been otherwise, I would have been disappointed. In Army parlance, this revealed an unspoken and unexpressed fondness. To be ignored was akin to rejection. I climbed aboard the car and returned their waves as the driver meshed the gears and pulled slowly away.

As I took one last look at the encampment and the balloon, I saw Mrs. Gallagher running across the field, carrying a package and waving her pink dish towel, the one she had used those many months to signal to me the arrival of mail from home. The driver stopped and I met her in mid-field. She threw her arms around my neck and kissed me several times. Then she gave me the package which contained a decorated tin box filled with home-baked cookies. With tears streaming down her face, she handed me the dish towel, "to keep for old-times' sake and to remember us by."

I tucked the cookies under my arm and then with the dish towel I wiped the tears from her face . . . and from mine. With one more hug and kiss, we parted. We returned each other's waves till we turned from view on Delridge Way.

This farewell was quite unexpected as I had had dinner with Ma and Pa the night before, when we said our many goodbyes. We had promised each other we would keep in touch, which we did on a regular basis.

Before leaving Seattle I sent a telegram to Ruth, announcing my departure and giving her my new address. I didn't want an interruption in our correspondence. Her next letter, dated September 20th, 1942, told how her mother had called her at her office to tell of the telegram's arrival. She was glad that the Air Forces process had started and hoped my stay at Fort Lewis would be short, knowing how anxious I was to "get going."

Upon arrival at the Fort, we soon discovered that we would not be lounging around for a few weeks but would be assigned to Post Guard Duty, protecting vital elements of this vast establishment. I was to guard two huge water towers surrounded by an eight-foot-high chainlink fence high in the wooded hills a few miles from the barracks. Sentry duty schedule called for four hours on and eight hours off, around the clock. It was a lonely place, with powerful floodlights illuminating the enclosure.

During off times, and due to the experience I had acquired as a drill instructor when I was in Texas, I was recruited to conduct close-order drill for those whose physical difficulties prevented their service as guards. I would assemble the group in front of the barracks. The men all carried unloaded rifles, and I made quite a show of marching them around a few barracks before stopping for an extended rest behind the least conspicuous building. After 30 or 40 minutes of smoking and shooting the breeze, I would call the group to attention and march back to our barracks for dismissal. I was no more interested in close-order drill than they were.

Of all these medical hardship cases, one lingers in my memory. He was short, skinny, boney-faced, and always unshaven. He wore an overseas-type cap and a much-too-long heavy wool overcoat. He carried his rifle almost horizontally on his shoulder to relieve his frail, skinny arm of its weight and dragged his feet rather than walking or marching. His feet were in such bad shape that he could not lace his shoes but tied them halfway up. One day while drilling, he literally stepped right out of his shoes. After that, I excused him from drill and he sat out the session on the back steps of the barracks smoking hand-rolled cigarettes.

When eating, he was not a pretty sight. He had very bad teeth, which caused chewing and swallowing problems, and food would fall from his mouth back onto the plate. I asked myself and others how this poor guy was ever admitted into the Army. The only answer I got was that some how he just "slipped through the cracks" and his protests, if any, had been ignored along with his disabilities.

Guard duty required being armed with a sawed-off shotgun, the shells of which were to be removed before leaving the guarded post. One night about 2:00 a.m., a guard shift came off duty and some of their number stretched out on their cots, even before undressing. Dim lights burned in the stately old Army post barracks. Most of the 100 men in the room were asleep, but not for long.

We were suddenly jarred awake by the blast of both barrels from a gun about 30 feet away from me. The culprit had been lying on his back with one leg crossed over the other up-raised knee. He had taken aim at a fly crawling on the ceiling, squeezed both triggers, and blew a three-foot hole in the tile ceiling. He had forgotten to unload his gun. In the heat of the commotion, some wag had the temerity to ask if he had hit the fly. The man was a transferee to the Air Forces and we never did learn if he made it. His was a very serious and irresponsible offense, unbefitting that of a potential officer.

Bob Nowicki and I became quite friendly and made plans to travel together when our Aviation Cadet appointments were issued. After almost three weeks of guard duty and drill, the appointments came through with an effective date of October 15th, 1942. We were advised to travel to Santa Ana Army Air Base, Santa Ana, California, by public transportation and were allowed five days to make the trip. We turned in all work-type clothing, overcoats, and surplus uniforms that would not be needed in our new assignments. This reduced our luggage to one medium-sized canvas bag, finally ridding us of the blue-denim barracks bags. As Aviation Cadets, we would be issued all new uniforms of appropriate style and insignia.

On Saturday afternoon, October 9th, we rode the Army bus into Tacoma, registered for a room at the YMCA, secured train tickets for San Francisco, checked our luggage in a locker, then went to a bar that was very popular among servicemen. Bob had heard of a wine called *Alicante* that was supposed to be very good, and we were in the mood for a little celebration. We learned that *Alicante* was the name of the grape from which the wine was produced, was popular in Shakespearean days as a "tent" wine, and the grapes were grown in France, Italy, and now California. We planned to buy each other one drink, have a steak dinner, then go to our room at the "Y" for a good night's sleep. The wine indeed, was good and our resolve to each have one drink was soon forgotten, and we had another.

We became quite loquacious and other GIs and a few civilians were drawn into our conversation. The civilians were quite generous, providing drinks for us beyond our reasonable capacity. We learned that *Alicante* wine packed a stronger wallop than we had anticipated, and after several glasses, Bob and I began to "lose our memories." We later had no recollection of having eaten nor did we know how we got to our sleeping quarters.

I was awakened Sunday morning by the sound of a church organ playing the familiar tune to "Nearer My God to Thee." Blinking open, my eyes met the beautiful glow of the sun shining through stained-glass windows. I raised up on one elbow and looked around the room. Before my head cleared, I thought for a moment that something must have happened and I was now in heaven. This certainly was not the YMCA.

Who were all these other guys, all asleep on Army cots? Where was Bob? The fog in my head was beginning to lift, and I realized that we were in the balcony of a church and the music was coming from down below where the organist was practicing for the morning worship service. I soon spotted and awakened Bob, a Catholic, telling him he had altar boy duty and the mass was about to start. He became conscious in a hurry.

"Hey Alex, this isn't a Catholic church. Where the hell, oops, pardon me, where the heck are we?"

"I don't know," I told him, "but I hear people downstairs, and I think we better get dressed and out of here."

We pulled on our clothes and made our way downstairs where we found the restroom. After a dash of cold water in the face and a swipe at our snarled hair, we started to leave the church. But a deep, friendly voice stopped us and asked if we were ready for breakfast. We retreated to the kitchen next to the fellowship hall and were served a fine bacon and eggs meal by men who we learned were church elders. We were in the First Presbyterian Church of Tacoma, Washington, and this was their ministry to servicemen in town with no place to stay. They had removed the balcony pews to provide the sleeping quarters. Bob and I thanked them for their kindnesses and then headed for the train depot.

We rode to San Francisco, spent a day sightseeing, then hitchhiked to Los Angeles with a brief stopover in Bakersfield to visit another Air Forces transferee. We rented bicycles in Hollywood and toured the areas where many movie stars lived, then cycled to Beverly Hills and stopped at the Beverly Hills Hotel.

Entering the coffee shop, we saw four or five GIs sitting in a large circular booth, talking to a civilian with a microphone propped up in front of him. He called us to join in a live, remote radio interview and participate in a short quiz contest. The winner could name a movie star or starlet with whom he would like to have dinner and take to the Hollywood Canteen for dancing. The talk-show host would make the arrangements. All the participants were to receive some gifts, including a coupon for a free portrait at a Los Angeles studio.

Neither Bob nor I were winners but we did have our photos made and were each given four 8x10 enlargements. The copy I sent to Mother was promptly framed and displayed on our grand piano. It would soon be joined by photos of Ray and David.

The handsome winner of the radio contest expressed a preference for starlet Donna Reed as his dinner and dancing date for the evening. The rest of us preceded him at the

Hollywood Canteen and were delighted when he came in with Donna on his arm. She was very charming and we each got to dance with her. When I sent Ruth a copy of the photo, I told her of the Canteen episode, teasing her that Donna wanted my photo, but I refused to give her one.

The Hollywood Canteen was a favorite gathering place for servicemen in town on pass and as an outlet for the energies of many movie stars who sincerely committed themselves to serving and entertaining the troops. The night of our meeting Donna Reed, Fred MacMurray was busy bringing sandwiches and soft drinks to the many GIs seated at the tables. He wore an apron and kidded about having to be on KP duty. Actress Bette Davis also circulated among the guys and was generous in supplying her autograph. Hedy Lamarr just stood around and looked beautiful. I saw that her complexion was indeed ivory-like, as reported. She, too, was generous with her autograph. I still have them filed away.

October 15th dawned bright and clear in Southern California and Bob and I were ready to get on down to Santa Ana. We rode the interurban railway, arriving at the base about noon. We checked in at Headquarters and were assigned to a barracks that housed Squadron 8, our temporary testing and qualifying unit. Santa Ana Air Base was basically a tent city and we were surprised to be quartered in a barracks. Other recruits that were entering directly from civilian life were sent to tents, a row of which had been pitched alongside many of the barracks. Bob and I wondered if our status as GIs transferring to the Air Forces had anything to do with this arrangement. Each with a year of service, we felt a little preferential treatment was in order.

It was 384 days since I had been sworn into the Army at Draft Board 89 in Chicago. Back then, I was just another body, being forced to enter a way of life for which I had no desire or calling. Now I was launching into a strange, new, exciting experience of my own choosing, mentally and physically prepared for success without thought or fear of failure — or my eventual part in the war that was being carried around the world.

Chapter 12

Santa Ana Preflight School

HE FIVE-DAY TRAVEL interlude between Fort Lewis, Washington, and Santa Ana, California, was a poor substitute for a furlough. It was my first taste of independence in a year, and the break from daily Army regimentation was an enjoyable prelude to the rigors of the Army Air Forces training program that lay ahead.

Because of my accumulated service time, I had applied for a furlough at Seattle and again at Fort Lewis prior to my AAF assignment. I had been given some encouragement at Seattle, but my hopes were dashed when told that since my orders for transfer were in process and my status was tentative, the Coast Artillery no longer had jurisdiction. And, of course, the "Casual Company" at Fort Lewis produced a similar reply. I had told Ruth and the home folks that I was trying to get a leave, and it was disappointing for all when I wrote to them that my efforts had failed. I was to find the Army Air Forces to be equally adamant on the subject. Furloughs were granted only in cases of dire emergency, such as the very serious illness or death of an immediate family member. But I was determined that if all went well, I would get a leave after graduation from Advanced Flight School in July or August, ten months hence.

Making the way to our barracks, Bob and I walked past a row of tents and were observed by their occupants, who apparently noted that we were in uniform and still wore the Corporal chevrons on our shirt sleeves. They taunted us with the friendly greeting of "You'll be Sor-r-y-y."

To a man, they had not been in uniform for more than perhaps two or three days and had not yet been classified. We answered their calls with a wave and a smile. As it turned out, I found that my year of service proved to be an asset.

Military discipline held no surprises and I was well grounded in protocol. Close-order drill and marching formations were more precise than that practiced in the Coast Artillery. Emphasis was placed on very erect posture to enhance showy parades before the reviewing officers and visiting military and civilian dignitaries. I also sensed its effect on the cadets — the aura of pride that prevailed — that *esprit de corps* that did not exist in some other Service branches. We were dubbed by the press and the more vocal leadership to be "the cream of the crop" of America's youth, and most of the Aviation Cadets made every effort to sustain and reinforce that reputation.

I had learned close-order drill from regular Army men at Camp Wallace and was often called on to put a squad of inexperienced cadets through their paces. In many Sunday afternoon parades I was assigned the position of right guide, the man who sets the pace in time with the beat of the marching band and upon whom the entire squadron formation is keyed.

Physical training was rugged and demanding, requiring minimum numbers of push-ups and chin-ups. My average scores were passable, but well exceeded by some real "muscle-men." Each daily exercise period was concluded with a one- to two-mile run, and it was here that I struggled. I fared well on the dash or sprint, but faltered on the longer distances and seldom managed to exceed the mile. I became winded too soon and though I never had any breathing ailments, I determined that I did not know how to conserve breathing capacity or gain that so-called second wind. However, I was able to conceal any deficiency by slowing down on the back stretches out of sight of the instructors. I was never called down on this point, nor did I fall down as I made the effort.

Classification as a candidate for pilot training was the goal of most all of the incoming cadets, and apparently the only ones classified for bombardier or navigator were so assigned by their own choosing. In all cases, we were subjected to extensive psychological testing, hand-eye coordination, and finger dexterity, the most vivid remembrance being "the ability to place square pegs in square holes and round ones in their mating receptacles." Many tests of this nature were developed by a Dr. Johnson O'Conner, an expert in aptitude testing for the General Electric Company during the Depression. His methods helped GE to test and hire top-notch design engineering talent for the development of their products. One of our Army Air Forces tests was similar to his "Wiggly Block" exercise and is believed to have been adapted from his battery of examinations.

Physical examination was an all-day affair, and I felt like I had been put through a washing-machine wringer. Fortunately, no defects were found, and I was declared totally fit for the training. The "phantom" heart murmur that the Seattle doctor thought he heard was never detected. I was classified for pilot training and was assigned to Pilot Squadron 42, Class 43-G. The 43 designated the year and the G indicated the month in which I would graduate, G being the seventh letter of the alphabet corresponding to July, the seventh month of the year.

U.S. Army Air Forces Aviation Cadet Alexander C. Stewart transferred from the Coast Artillery, November 15, 1942.

Squadron 42, consisting of 180 cadets, was housed in barracks with an overflow portion going to tents located alongside the barracks. Having spent several months in the tent in Seattle, I was glad to be included in the barracks contingent. It was much easier living and more conducive to study and exchange of information.

I soon noted the ease that most of the college men had with the subjects that troubled me. My high school math only covered algebra and geometry, no trigonometry. It had been over six years since I had studied them, with no occasion for their application or practice. I had taken the general language curriculum, with those three years of Latin, and was never exposed to physics or chemistry. Now, with math and physics requirements, I needed all the help I could get.

Studies also included Morse Code, with a receiving requirement of eight words per minute. I had learned code in Boy Scouts and had practiced sending and receiving messages on my own battery-powered telegraph-type key and buzzer. To my surprise, much of it came back to me, and it proved to be one of my better subjects.

All cadets started out on the same level, with naval prerequisites, where we learned to identify the various classes of battleships, aircraft carriers, destroyers, and cruisers of both the Japanese and the United States. The Air Forces studies covered the identification of aircraft of the United States, Germany, and Japan, which we did from wood models and black silhouettes flashed on a movie screen.

I tested well in all studies except physics and had a barely passing grade in math. For about a week before final exams, some of my closer friends tutored me in the evenings, but to little avail. I received a 68 in physics and a 72 in math — 70 was a passing grade — which earned me a place in Holdover Squadron 65 where I repeated both physics and math and scored 91 and 94. I was glad for the opportunity and never had anymore trouble with ground school.

The Holdover Squadrons were made up of men with academic and repairable physical problems, such as broken bones. It was there, in Squadron 65, that I met Scotty Rohwer of Spangle, Washington, a graduate of Washington State University, suffering the discomforts and disabilities of a broken wrist incurred in a touch football game. Even at this early stage, the government had too much invested in each of us to justify a washout. The Holdover Squadrons gave us time to recover from our disabilities and go on to worthwhile service and training in the class of 43-H.

The letters from home and from Ruth continued with their usual regularity and were always newsy and encouraging. Brother Ray had entered the Army in October 1942 and was stationed with a medical training battalion of the Infantry at Camp Adair, Medford, Oregon.

Dad, Mother, Jean, Margaret, and David were coping with the difficulties borne by the civilian population. Rationing of meat, sugar, and other food essentials challenged Mother's resourcefulness in meal planning. But her experience of many years with the rearing and nourishing of a large family held sway and they managed quite nicely.

Dad's voice-teaching schedule was severely hampered by the shortages of time, money, and students, which the war imposed.

Jean continued her work at Scott-Foresman textbook publishers and was helpful in my remedial math work in the Holdover Squadron. I wrote to her on December 8, 1942, that I was having trouble with math and that the Army Air Forces books were inadequate and brief. Her company had published a refresher book entitled *Mathematics for the Emergency*, designed for servicemen who found themselves in this same fix! She sent me a copy, and it proved to be my lifesaver. A cadet friend, Bob Purcell, had a math need similar to mine, so I had Jean send him a copy of the book as well. His passing grade was 90.

Jean managed the correspondence department at Scott-Foresman, and by direction of the company president, reported our successes with the book in a bulletin sent to their agents all over the U.S. I was referred to as "Air Cadet Alex," with no last name mentioned. It was feared that some government regulation might be infringed and that Jean or I might be capitalizing on the notoriety. Several agents wrote letters of thanks to me for my testimonial and were using it in sales efforts in their local territories. They were quite gracious and had many compliments for Jean, whom they had known during her many years of service with the company.

Margaret was now teaching children in the First Grade at Yale Elementary School. She had sent me a Christmas card with a short message, the first correspondence I had received from her since my induction into the service.

David was now on scholarship in the pre-med school at the University of Chicago where he was an excellent student, working at this part-time job as an operating room orderly at the University's Billings Hospital. Though infrequent, David's letters were always a treat.

As promised, I had written to the Gallaghers in Seattle and was rewarded with a newsy and heartwarming answer on November 8, 1942, one letter from each of them. The balloon camp apparently was having quite a time with the weather. Pa noted that they had had a "65-mile wind" and seven balloons had been lost. The men at the balloon site ran out of heating oil for those two windy days and "nearly froze." Pa added that they had a big wood heater in the mess shack now, but had to buy it themselves for $5. The storm had done some $10,000 in damage to the city light company.

Ma was her usual cheerful self — she liked my "pretty" Air Forces writing paper, she said, adding, "We are so proud of you."

Some months later brother Ray managed a five-day leave from his base at Medford, Oregon, and visited me in California. I was able to get a weekend pass and we had a grand but short reunion in Los Angeles. We visited Mrs. Gallagher's niece and her husband in the beautiful former home of Douglas Fairbanks, and were especially impressed with their flower garden.

Like Mother, Ruth wrote to me almost every week. I replied promptly and gave her an ongoing description of my activities and camp life. When I sent her a copy of the portrait photo I had taken as a result of my Beverly Hills Hotel radio interview, I included a small pair of pilot's wings, gold rather than the customary silver. Her letter of November 23th, 1942, revealed her pleasure with both items:

Sunday 11/23/42

Dear Ace,

Hi beautiful, you sure take a good picture. The photographer did a grand job, considering the material he had to work with. 'Course I really don't mean that, but I can't let you get conceited. You have the place of honor in my room. Everytime I walk by I give out with my secret weapon, just to keep in practice. I wonder if it radiates to California. Can you feel it?

The little gold wings are my prized possession and I am going to wear them everyday. Thank you very much for both the wings and the photo. They came in the mail on Thursday when I was very much down in the dumps. They did a good job of restoring me to myself.

Oabye, the fellow that works in front of me at the office, said I was hard to work with before but now that I have the wings I am unbearable. He can't understand why you would send me the wings now that you have met Hedy Lamarr.

I was doing some computing for him and was stalled on an item that I just didn't know how to handle, so I said, "Hey Oabye, I'd like some advice, please step into my office." He got wound up on the subject of air cadets, said he was a married man, had never dated an air cadet and couldn't give me any advice. One of the other men butted in. He said he had never dated an air cadet but had heard they were "high-fliers." He (Mr. Wittmore) is quite a punster. He saw me rather absent mindedly scratching my head with a ruler and wanted to know if I was "inching up on them." Not bad, 'eh

The girls insist that I bring the photo and show it to them. They want to see what sort of character is sending me wings. I did want to show them the photo but not until they asked.

I hope you have received my package. Mother baked the cookies so I was able to send it sooner. I stuffed the dates. I hope you like dates — I mean stuffed ones. I really intend to send you boxes of goodies more often than I do. I have no excuse for not doing so.

Well Swoose, I hope you have a fine Thanksgiving. Thank you again for the wings and photo.

'Bye for now,
Love and kisses,
Ruth

I had to guess what Ruth meant by her "secret weapon" and concluded that it was her little mysterious way of telling me she loved me, but was not ready to say in so many words.

We did have a fine Thanksgiving at Santa Ana, with roasted turkey and all the trimmings. Our duties were modified to accommodate the day and the inclinations of most to relax or engage in touch football and other sports. But the next day our training continued, it seemed, with a vengeance. The Army was not in the habit of granting reprieves from its agenda.

Christmas was approaching, and most of the men spent their spare time writing cards they had purchased at the PX and buying and packaging gifts to mail to their families and sweethearts back home. I purchased a very nice bracelet for Ruth and sought a means of disguising the package so that its contents would not be too obvious. I tied the bracelet, contained in its own box, around the neck of a fair-sized Teddy bear and shipped it in a carton. It completely surprised her.

She was very pleased with the bracelet, but it was the Teddy bear that commanded unexpected attention! She named it "Chris" (for Christmas) and reported his status in the family, now occupying his own chair in the living room.

Preflight School at Santa Ana had been a new and challenging experience for me. I had been forewarned of the rigid discipline and the need for adherence to regulations, regardless of their occasional inanity. That was no surprise to me.

For some unexplained reason I was never called on for KP or latrine duty, or any other type of work detail there. When I did serve as a drill instructor, I was always *asked* to do so, never *ordered*, and I never refused. Unlike the work details, I enjoyed the drills and the precision performance I was able to achieve with the units of our squadron to which I was assigned. A marching and close-order drill contest was announced, and our squadron placed first and was awarded the "E" banner for excellence. The banner was ours to carry in all future parades, and the men really shaped up when passing in review.

The 3½ months at Santa Ana was a time of personal growth and assessment of my value to myself and to the Army.

Chapter 13

Primary Flight School
Ontario, California

*A*FTER 16 MONTHS OF SERVICE, my military file was stuffed with copies of fulfilled travel orders, immunization records, and incidental memos, spiced with unanticipated experiences. I had become accustomed to many of the Army's idiosyncrasies but still struggled with its disregard for the civilized timepiece. The impudence of the Sergeant's shrill whistle jarred us awake at 0230 hours on Sunday, January 31st, 1943, again confirming that this Army's war was a 24-hour-a-day business.

A meager 4½ hours of sleep, followed by the rude awakening, would ordinarily produce at least one hour of moans, groans, and derisive commentary. But this was a great day in our lives and the often-expressed fear that an airplane was something we would never see would soon be dispelled.

Showered, shaved, and dressed, we turned in at the group supply building all equipment and bedding that had been temporarily assigned to us. After a 0400 hours breakfast, we returned to the barracks and catnapped on the naked, cotton-filled mattresses that we had rolled up to the head end of our cots. Our "raring-to-go" energies had been quelled by a two-hour delay before the GI trucks arrived to haul us to the Santa Ana train station.

Euphoria erupted and soared to new heights as the 20 cadets in the lead truck burst into song, voicing our favorite marching chorus, "She Wore a Yellow Ribbon." Like a trail of ignited gunpowder, the tune traveled the length of the truck convoy as we all joined in singing:

> Around her neck she wore a yellow ribbon,
>   she wore it in the springtime and in the month of May,
> And when they asked her why the hell she wore it,
>   she wore it for her pilot who was far, far away.
> Oh far away, oh far away,
>   Oh she wore it for her pilot who was far, far away.

Pedestrian officers, enlisted men, and cadets lined our route and waved to each truckload, some of them raising two fingers in the "V" for "Victory" sign. Our spirits would not be restrained. As if on cue, we broke out with the stirring Air Corps Song:

> Off we go into the wild blue yonder,
>   Climbing high into the sun.
> Here they come, zooming to meet our thunder,
>   At 'em boys, give her the gun.
> Down we dive, spouting our flame from under,
>   Off with one hell-of-a-roar.
> We live in fame or go down in flame, hey,
>   Nothing can stop the Army Air Corps.

We had reached the main base entrance and the singing was replaced with a tremendous yell as each truck in turn passed through the Air Base gate.

Was it "goodbye and good riddance?" Perhaps for many. But for some, and especially for me, it was "Thanks for the memories!"

Because of my remedial schooling in the Holdover class, my stay at Santa Ana had been almost twice as long as most of the cadets, and for this I was grateful. I could not have had better treatment or more generous opportunity. Any self-deprecation I might have harbored had vanished, and I now felt I was equal to the best performers. Primary Flight School would be a new beginning for all of us and would produce an abundance of challenges and surprises.

The hum of GI truck tires on pavement seemed to be singing a new song as we rolled the few miles to the Santa Ana train station. None of us had yet to see our first Primary trainer, but the conversations between cadets were adequately illustrated with flying hand gestures and punctuated with companion noises to compete with the tires, while matching their make-believe maneuvers. Ours was now a "flight of fantasy," soon to become reality.

Rolling into the railway station, cadets began jumping off the trucks before the vehicles had come to a complete stop. Usually, such eagerness would only occur at the sight of a bevy of pretty girls or a lunch wagon, neither of which were in view. We impatiently lined up for roll call, then scrambled aboard the waiting train. Moments later, the train began to move, encouraged by another rousing cheer from 300 cadets waving their hats through open windows in a final farewell to Santa Ana.

We were put on hold several times before reaching Los Angeles, for a passing freight train, a troop train, a passenger train, two workmen on a hand-car, and a crew working to free a faulty switch. Each interruption gave birth to a chorus of groans and did not abate until the engines were changed and we had traveled east out of LA to within ten minutes of Ontario, the time span accurately announced by the conductor.

A fleet of buses painted the civilian colors of blue and yellow formed the shuttle that carried us south along Euclid Avenue with its large, beautiful, overhanging eucalyptus trees and the six miles to Cal-Aero Flight Academy, widely acclaimed to be the "country club of all Primary Flight Schools."

Our excitement and curiosity were not dulled by the lack of food, which we had endured since eating breakfast at 0400 hours. We were all ready for nourishment, and that proved to be the first order of business. It was now past 1500 hours (3:00 p.m.) when we assembled into ranks and marched to the mess hall where we devoured the best Army meal most of us had known since October 15th. Not a complaint was registered, and to our complete surprise, the meal was served by lovely, gracious ladies.

Our marching formation next made its way to the supply building where we received our flying togs — a coverall-type flying suit, a leather jacket, a khaki-colored cloth flying helmet with chin strap and aluminum-tube "elbows" protruding from each ear location, a pair of flying goggles, and other essentials. I soon learned that my instructor, occupying the front seat of the open-cockpit Stearman trainer, would talk to me, not through an intercom microphone but by the use of a "gosport," a small metal funnel device, connected to the helmet elbows with a ½-inch rubber hose. I was surprised to learn how well it worked, especially when he chewed me out for some infraction. The Primary trainers were not equipped with any radio or intercom devices. I answered the instructor's questions with head and hand gestures or the thumb and forefinger "O" high-sign.

Arms loaded with our new issue, we straggled to the rooms that had been assigned to us, listed on a personnel roster showing building and room numbers. What luxury; two cadets to a room, twin-sized civilian beds with innerspring mattresses, study desks with lamps, chairs, clothes-closets, and a bathroom separating two rooms to serve four cadets. The buildings were single-story, ranch-type with a wide overhang covering the concrete walk. They were beautifully landscaped with shrubs, trees, and lush lawns. Someone likened Cal-Aero to that of a girls' finishing school.

All but a few Primary Flight Schools in the United States were owned and operated by civilians who had contracted with the Army. Most were located in California, Arizona, and Texas, though some were also in the Southeastern area of the country. Cal-Aero at Ontario, Mira Loma Flight Academy at Oxnard, and one of two "civilian" Basic Training Schools — Polaris Flight Academy situated in the confines of War Eagle Field at Lancaster, California — were founded by a retired Air Corps Officer, Major C. C. Mosely. The other civilian contract Basic School was located in the Southeast.

Although the contract schools were owned and operated by civilians, they were supervised by and the cadets were commanded by U.S. Army Air Forces (USAAF) officers. Our flight instructors were civilian, but the check pilots who rode with us and approved or disapproved our proficiency were fully qualified and rated Army pilot officer/instructors.

Our living quarters at Cal-Aero Flight Academy, Ontario, California, 1943 — "The Country Club of all Primary Flight Schools."

We were subject to the same disciplines with the civilians as we were the military. Instructors and flight-training Commanders were addressed and saluted the same as officers and were readily afforded equal respect. Likewise, the instructors were gentlemen and had a deep concern and respect for and commitment to their students. There was no question that they sought to produce the best-trained pilots possible. The entire staff was dedicated to both safety and technical perfection.

Monday morning, February 1, 1943, dawned bright and clear at Ontario and the vast orange groves that covered most of the area over which we would fly. Fortified with a hearty breakfast, we marched to the flight line, dressed in our flying clothes and ready for the great adventure.

Our class of about 300 cadets was divided into six squadrons with a total of 62 instructors. Lined up in alphabetical order, we counted off by fives, and by some rare selection process, five cadets were assigned to each instructor. I was selected by Jack Gray Mathis, a native of Kingsville, Texas, and connected in some way with the vast King Ranch in south Texas. Others selected by Mathis were Tony Van Reswick, Howard Roehr, Robert Purcell, and Robert Helle. We were assigned to Squadron 2.

We gathered around Mathis and learned that the first item on the agenda was our "Dollar Ride," a 30-minute initiation into the wild blue yonder. When my turn came, I climbed into the rear cockpit, strapped on the seat-pack parachute that was being used by all of us this day, adjusted the seat level, fastened the seat belt, plugged in the gosport hoses, and gave the sign that I was ready. A lineman spun the propeller to start the engine, pulled the chocks away from the wheels, and we taxied out for takeoff.

Checking to see that everything was in order for flight, Mathis opened the throttle, and away we went. We climbed straight out to about 5,000 feet, the instructor talking slowly but constantly about everything he was doing. I held a light touch on the controls and followed through on all his maneuvers. He asked me how I was doing, and did I feel okay for inverted flight. He looked in his rear-view mirror for my nod.

The first aerobatic was a loop, and I registered surprise when the engine stalled in the top of the orbit. Mathis explained that the engine was equipped with a fuel-monitoring float-type carburetor, and when inverted, the float, working in reverse, shut off the fuel supply to the cylinders. Automobile carburetors were similarly equipped, and I understood the reason for the temporary malfunction. Regaining normal flight, and with the propeller still spinning, the engine restarted itself. Other maneuvers demonstrated included slow rolls, snap rolls, chandelles, Immelmans, lazy-eights, split-S's, spins, stalls, and simulated emergency engine-failure landings.

The emergency landing required the location of a potential clearing, the determination of wind direction, and the maneuvering for an upwind approach. Because much of our flying was over the vast orange groves, few clearings were available, and, thus, we were told to determine wind direction, turn into the wind, and line up the fuselage of the plane with the space between two rows of orange trees, hold back on the stick as long as possible just above the tree tops, and then let the plane stall to a stop as the wings were supported by the trees. This seemed like a reasonable procedure. I don't know if any in our class ever had to do it — hopefully not.

Landing at Cal-Aero after the Dollar Ride, I climbed out of the rear cockpit with the greatest feeling of exhilaration I had ever known. I was thrilled from head to toe and concluded that I was in the right place with the greatest opportunity of my life spread out before me. Whatever we did, wherever we were from that day forward, we would all be totally obsessed with the art and technique of flying.

The immediate goal of all the cadets was gaining sufficient profiency to qualify for that first solo flight. It was in this phase that the most washouts occurred. Men were disqualified due to chronic air-sickness, lack of coordination, insufficient progress, or some other uncorrectable deficiency. And some were just plain frightened, unable to conquer their fears. My progress was perhaps average. Mr. Mathis and I had landed and he had me stop near the edge of the very wide landing area. With the engine still running, he climbed out of the front cockpit and told me that this was the "magic moment — you're on your own." I gulped a lung-full of air, and he later told me that my face flushed red before breaking into a huge grin.

I taxied to the head of the ramp, revved the engine, checked the magnetos, adjusted my goggles, cleared the area for other aircraft, opened the throttle, and was soon airborne. That front cockpit looked mighty empty, and I suddenly realized this was the greatest test of my life. It was a rare feeling, and I wondered how this punk of a kid from the streets of

Alex Stewart, after his first solo flight, completed February 1943, Cal-Aero Flight Academy, Ontario, California.

Chicago could achieve such glory in 7½ hours of dual instruction. From that day forward, I may have questioned the wisdom but never my ability to achieve what I set out to do. Until that moment I had existed in some sort of flying fantasy. Now, it was total reality and my very life was in my own hands. I flew the prescribed first solo routine and came in for a perfect landing.

Training progressed well and I passed all Army check-rides without negative commentary or demerit. The one problem that many cadets experienced with the Stearman trainer was its propensity for ground looping when landing in a partial or full crosswind. We had practiced the corrective action to avoid the mishap, but still, collectively, we had many occurrences. I never did a ground loop, but I did slightly drag the left wing, which required a small repair to the fabric on the wingtip. A ground loop could incur structural damage, sometimes requiring replacement of a quarter-section of wing at a cost of $1,000. It was an instinctive tendency to apply right stick to gain lift in the left wing, but at this point in the landing procedure the airspeed was insufficient to produce the required lift. Applying slight right rudder would tend to crab into the wind, and the wing would come up. The scraped wingtip was the only damage I ever caused.

The need for physics and math were realized in ground school classes when we studied theory of flight, meteorology, and navigation. I was completely enthralled with this new knowledge and soaked up all the information I could get my hands on. My roommate, Bill Stevens, and I talked about it even as we stretched out in bed after lights out. Bill was a fine fellow and friend, a college graduate, but unable to learn to fly. He suffered both from chronic air-sickness and lack of coordination. Bill had been one of my tutors in the Holdover Squadron at Santa Ana. I believe he went to an aircraft mechanics school.

Jack Mathis, my instructor, was an unusual man, completely dedicated to his job of teaching us to fly. Early in our relationship, he invited us to stop by his house in Ontario in the evening for a visit, to have a beer and share in a batch of freshly popped corn. Flying was the only topic of conversation, and I am sure he answered as many of our questions at home as he did on the flight line. His lovely wife was there, but usually did not hang in with us to the hour of parting.

The home field of Cal-Aero was not large enough to handle the traffic of almost 150 planes in any single flying period. Auxiliary landing strips had been set up within a ten-mile radius to handle the overflow. Students who were waiting their turn to fly would go to the designated strip in a small bus while their instructors flew to the strip with the first students of the day. These times were pure luxury to me, and I felt very privileged. The beautiful California weather, the ride into the country atmosphere, and the pursuit of the dream of learning to fly was a little overwhelming. This, I thought, was the sport of the rich and here I was, being paid $75 a month, plus clothing, housing, and all the good food I could devour. Certainly, I was restricted and regimented like all the others, but I never felt deprived, only catered to. It was too early in my training to think about my eventual role in the air war that was rapidly maturing in the Pacific, in Europe, and in the Middle East.

Ruth's letters kept me abreast of some of the facets of war on the home front — the

Cal-Aero Flight Academy, Ontario, California, students and instructor — Alex Stewart (l), Howard Roehr, instructor Jack Mathis, and Tony Van Riswick.

rationing of meat, sugar, and other foods, facial and laundry soap, gasoline, tires, batteries, cigarettes, shoes, and a host of other necessities.

Civilian automobile production came to a complete halt in 1942, and the demand for replacement parts for all cars became high priority. It was a time of patch-up and make-do on the old models. Prices for used cars on the automobile rows of America became unreasonably high and often required more work and new parts than they were worth. The one redeeming factor was the limited accumulation of mileage, due to gasoline rationing. Car-pooling was the order of the day for local transport, and cross-country travel was done mostly by rail. Travel by commercial airliner was dominated by military and priority civilian war-production people, and fortunately afforded to servicemen racing home on emergency family leave.

I had dropped a suggestion to Ruth that I would be thrilled and honored to have her come out West to pin my silver wings on me when I graduated from Advanced Flight School. I did not know when that might be or where I would be, but assumed it would be in the Western Flying Training Command. She was intrigued by the idea and the prospect of such a trip would occupy a lot of space in her letters. She started saving for that trip and was able to get a rather broad time span in the Pure Oil Company vacation schedule. At the Primary training stage, we had no idea of where our Advanced training and graduation would occur, but we did know it would all happen in late August. Also, there was no way of knowing if we would get any time off after graduation and before reporting to our next assignment, or where that might be. We all hoped we would get enough time to make it home.

Time in the air, both dual and solo, commenced to polish our proficiency. My increase in confidence and knowledge closely matched the airborne hours, and my progress was on a par with most of the other cadets. Unfortunately, there were many who were unable to make the grade and the washout rate zoomed and eventually totaled about 30 percent at Cal-Aero.

The only tragedy during my assignment there occurred when two planes collided on the downwind leg of the traffic pattern. The propeller of the offending plane virtually chopped off the tail assembly of the victim's plane as he turned into the downwind leg from the 45-degree entry leg. The offending pilot's view of the victim's plane was blocked when he banked into the turn; he never saw the victim. Cadet pilot Boucher was killed instantly when he crashed from 500 feet. The cadet pilot of the errant plane struggled and managed to land his damaged aircraft. He was extremely shaken by the accident, given a rest leave of several days, then set back to Class 43-I to resume training at a different school. Of course, the entire Cal-Aero contingent was saddened, and we all became increasingly aware of the extreme importance of constant vigilance in the air. Our Commanders and instructors renewed their demands that we "keep our heads on a swivel" at all times and were quick to observe and reprimand when we failed or became lax.

As we accumulated air time and increased proficiency, we were introduced to cross-country flights. This was our first experience at flight planning and navigation and opened up a whole new and important phase of our training. Most of these flights were commonly termed "Round Robins," derived from the three legs of the 150-mile route plotted in the valley surrounded by the Santa Ana, San Jacinto, and San Bernardino Mountains. Each leg required its own compass heading, with special consideration given to the effect of wind direction on that heading. With the course calculated and plotted on a chart, we were able to check our progress and accuracy as we passed over designated checkpoints. Compass headings were altered to correct for any inaccuracies. This process was termed VFR (Visual Flight Rules) navigation.

By the first week in April 1943, our primary training came to a close. I had accumulated at least the required 60 hours of flying time, about half of which was solo, the other half dual. Some dual time was with another cadet, usually on a cross-country hop, the rest was with the instructor or with the Army check pilot. I was declared fully qualified for graduation from Primary and was to proceed on to Basic Flight Training. It was announced that we would be going to Polaris Flight Academy based at War Eagle Field near Lancaster, California, at the edge of the Mojave Desert. Everyone was delighted to be moving to another civilian-owned contract school and not to a full-fledged Army base.

It was time for some celebration, and the remaining 38 cadets in our squadron organized a dinner and dance party at the Pamona Country Club. Each cadet contributed $5 and invited our instructors, their wives, and our dates as guests. Most all of the fellows had dates. On one of my forays into Los Angeles with Bob Purcell, whose parents lived near Hollywood and had a Plymouth convertible that Bob frequently borrowed, I met and danced with a girl at the Hollywood Palladium. I had two or three dates with her, and she was happy to be invited to the squadron party. I had Bob pick her up for me when he went for the car and his date. When the evening was over, Bob insisted that I go with them back to LA; we would return to Ontario and Cal-Aero together in the wee hours of April 6th.

I had written to Ruth about the coming party and my date and she said she was glad that I would have some feminine companionship, . . . and that she was green with envy! I had met and had dates with girls in Houston, Seattle, and in California. They had all been very nice, and I had enjoyed the friendship and diversion they had provided, but none of them held a candle to Ruth.

Bob Purcell was quite a lady's man and often chided me, in a friendly way, for not having a more serious encounter with the girls I met when we were out on the town together. He loved to tell the guys at camp, "Here we were at the Palladium. My date had to go to the ladies room. I walk around among the tables and find Stew sitting there with this gorgeous woman and he's telling her all about his sweetheart back in Chicago."

Tuesday evening, April 6th, we attended our class graduation dinner in the mess hall. Our instructors were there and joined in the celebration. The highlight of the evening was the presentation of the Mosely Award, given to the cadet with the most "conspicuous conduct as a flier, student and gentleman." My good friend, Scotty Rohwer, was the winner. He was given a gold crash bracelet with his name and appropriate inscription engraved thereon.

Scotty had been valedictorian of his high school graduating class, had previous flight training in the Civilian Pilot Training program, had worked his way through Washington State University, and had been a cadet officer at Santa Ana and at Cal-Aero. I could think of no one more deserving of this honor.

We turned in our ground school books and materials and our flying clothes on Wednesday and were informed that we would leave Cal-Aero for Lancaster early on Friday, April 16th. The next eight days would provide some leisure, with two 48-hour passes and a few parades, including the full wing complement of 500 cadets marching in the graduation review. This gave me time to catch up on correspondence with family and friends back in Chicago, to write letters to the Gallaghers in Seattle, to my brother Ray in Oregon, to brother Cameron and his wife Rita in Chicago, and especially to brother David at the Delta Upsilon house at the University of Chicago.

Aside from learning to fly and all of its accessory knowledge, I was moved by the appearance and message of two celebrities who came to Cal-Aero and spoke to us. The first was Lieutenant Whittaker, copilot on the flight in which Eddie Rickenbacker was lost at sea in the South Pacific. His 90-minute talk, sprinkled with humor, covered their 21-day ordeal adrift in a small inflated life raft. He had lost over 50 pounds, but his two companions in the raft were in a poorer condition. They had drifted onto a small tropical island and struggled to walk for six days before they were rescued by natives. Each one, having had about the equivalent of two glasses of water and a few swallows of fish in the 21 days, could not get their legs to support them, so great was their weakness.

Whittaker was touring factories, seeking increased production of war goods. He told us that we were badly outnumbered in the Pacific Theater, and that we were now getting a

CAL-AERO ACADEMY
ONTARIO, CALIFORNIA

April 7, 1943

MEMORANDUM TO:

ALL CADETS CLASS 43-H

Your class has completed nine weeks of training at this school, but with more than ordinary trials and tribulations. Your reputation as a class in general has not been of the best; you have lost many good men, and your ranks are thin. History records many units under similar circumstances, rising to unparalleled heights. It is hoped that your experiences here will serve as an inspiration for each of you to take the initiative and make yourself and your class the finest outfit that ever existed in basic and advanced schools. We know you have the possibilities inside if only they are stirred.

Obey regulations, keep on the beam and go out of your way to do right. Coupled with this advice I add sincerely, "Good luck!"

LeGRANDE D. KELLY, Jr.
Captain Air Corps
Commandant of Cadets.

SLIPSTREAM is published by the Ontario Daily Report, a civilian enterprise, in the interests of The Second Army Air Force, Flying Training Detachment, Ontario, California. Address: 212 East B Street, Ontario, California. Field Advisor, Captain Kelly.

better flow of equipment but were in dire need of food, blood plasma, weapons, and aircraft. He had come to Cal-Aero at the invitation of an instructor friend.

Another great man that came to talk with us was Colonel Robert Lee Scott. He had just returned from China, where he had served with General Claire L. Chennault and the AVG (American Volunteer Group), commonly known as the Flying Tigers. After Pearl Harbor, the AVG was integrated into the U.S. Army Air Forces, and Colonel Scott became one of the first American "Ace" fighter pilots. His visit to Cal-Aero was part of a tour he made to Army Air Forces installations around the country to boost morale and encourage dedication to the cause for which we were fighting.

Colonel Scott gave a detailed account of his combat experiences and the will of the foe to destroy us. Following his talk, he sat with us in a large informal gathering and answered the cadets' many questions. I was especially impressed with his sincerity and his emphasis on our preparedness for the job we would undertake within the next year. "The enemy pilots are skilled and treacherous. You have to become better and smarter than they are" — his concluding words.

A few days before leaving Cal-Aero we received a journal called *Slipstream*. It was a once-per-class periodical published by the Ontario *Daily Report*, a civilian enterprise, in the interests of the AAF's 2nd Army Air Force, Flying Training Detachment, Ontario, California. It contained photos of the students and their instructors, photos of the academy features, stories, and reminders of our many experiences.

In his "Memorandum to All Cadets Class 43-H," Commandant of Cadets Captain LeGrande D. Kelly wrote:

> Your class has completed nine weeks of training at this school, but with more than ordinary trials and tribulations. Your reputation as a class in general has not been of the best: you have lost many good men, and your ranks are thin. History records many units under similar circumstances, rising to unparalleled heights. It is hoped that your experiences here will serve as inspiration for each of you to take the initiative and make yourself and your class the finest outfit that ever existed in basic and advanced schools. We know you have the possibilities inside if only they are stirred.
>
> Obey regulations, keep on the beam and go out of your way to do right. Coupled with this advice I add sincerely, "Good luck!"

This issue of *Slipstream* was dedicated to Cadet Boucher, who had been killed in the mid-air collision:

> The heav'ns are grey and somber,
> And weeping gently today;
> Mute are the trees in their sighing,
> For one not content to stay.
>
> He lived among the stars,
> The sky a mantle of light,
> He talked with those in the heart of God,
> He's not afraid of the night.

In a cloistered knoll he's resting,
Where robins pause to sing,
And sentinel oaks are guarding,
The bird with the broken wing.

And finally, on the inside back cover of *Slipstream* was the poem "High Flight," written by British Royal Air Force Pilot Officer John Gillespie Magee, Jr., killed in action, December 1941.

Oh! I have slipped the surly bonds of earth
   And danced the skies on laughter-silvered wings;
Sunward I've climbed and joined the tumbling mirth
   Of sun-split clouds — and done a hundred things
You have not dreamed of — wheeled and soared and swung
   High in the sunlit silence. Hov'ring there
I've chased the shouting wind along and flung
   My eager craft through footless halls of air

Up, up the long, delirious, burning blue
   I've topped the wind-swept heights with easy grace
Where never lark, or even eagle flew —
   And, while with silent lifting mind I've trod
The untrespassed sanctity of space
   Put out my hand and touched the face of God.

Primary Flight School at Cal-Aero Flight Academy proved to be much more than that simple title implied, "learning to fly"! When it was over and the experience was behind me, I was a transformed person. I had always had a desire to do well in whatever I set my hand to accomplish, but now I wanted more — much more. I wanted to excel. My desire to now ascend was fueled by indelible impressions and observations drawn from this initial period of flight training.

The Cal-Aero experience would be remembered for many facets — the lesson in human endurance and the struggle to survive, to live to fight another day, as witnessed by Lieutenant Whittaker and Eddie Rickenbacker adrift in the vast Pacific Ocean; the courage and dedication of a humble Colonel Scott and his heroic action against the Japanese; Captain Kelly's vision of greatness held before the men of our class 43-H; our determination to avenge the death of Cadet Boucher by being the best that we could be; the reverence granted to God's creation and the art of flying so eloquently recorded by John Magee in "High Flight"; and, finally, on the most direct, personal level, the faith that my instructor, Jack Gray Mathis, had in me.

"Stew," he said on my last night in Ontario, "you are good, you're going to do just fine."

Chapter 14

Basic Flight School
Lancaster, California

HE MOJAVE DESERT IS approximately 15,000 square miles of barren mountains and flat valleys in Southern California, south of the Sierra Nevada. Borax and gold deposits have been found there. "Dry" lakes, undrained and encrusted with alkali, where water is seen only in wet seasons, dot this vast wasteland. Death Valley National Monument is in the northern part. The Salton Sea, 235 feet below sea level, is to the south. Its reptilian habitation includes a wide variety of snakes, lizards, and turtles that seek shelter from the blazing sun under rocks, cactus, and an inventory of seasonally beautiful wildflowers.

A combination of terrain, an almost cloudless sky, and a record of superb flying weather made the Mojave Desert an ideal venue for the heavier, faster, more powerful craft designated for Basic Flight Training, the Vultee BT-13.

Dubbed by other Army branches as "Eager Beavers," we who were to train with this aircraft strived to maintain some level of decorum as we arrived in the town of Lancaster on the western edge of the desert. Surface transportation had become very boring.

We paid little attention to the small, visible segment of the 2,300 sun-baked souls that called Lancaster home when we rolled to a stop at the remote train depot and landed on terra firma before the conductors could plant their stepstools. We had ridden the blue-and-yellow buses from Cal-Aero into Ontario, switched to the waiting train for the trip to Los Angeles, climbed aboard another train for Lancaster, and then scrambled aboard buses for the seven-mile jaunt to Polaris Flight Academy. The bleakness of the terrain, contrasted with the lushness of San Bernardino and Orange Counties, caused the cadets to be a little less than enthusiastic about their new surroundings. But attitudes soon changed when the buses wheeled through the main gate of Polaris and stopped before a large quadrangle of attractive cottages situated around two large swimming pools, all nestled in a carpet of lush, green lawns. What an oasis!

Each cottage contained four rooms, which were equipped with bunk-style beds, study desks and lamps, chairs, footlockers, and clothes racks with shelves above. We would live three men to a room and share a large central bath with the occupants of the three cottages. Though a little more Spartan than Cal-Aero, the arrangements were very adequate and suitable for our nine weeks of Basic Flight School.

Still being dealt with in alphabetical order, I was assigned quarters with others whose last names started with R and S. My friend from the Santa Ana Holdover Squadrons and the Cal-Aero Mosely Award winner, Scotty Rohwer, would bunk in my cottage. Also assigned with us was Arlin Stockberger from the Holdovers, a rather enthusiastic fellow from Santa Barbara who would enlist Scotty as his best man when he married his California sweetheart shortly before leaving Lancaster for Advanced Flight School. It was good to be with Scotty, as we shared the same passions for achievement. Such friendships were developed under the specter of separation, for according to demands elsewhere, the Army Air Forces would chop up the roster of cadets and send us off in different directions.

Time was of the essence, and our knowledge of meteorology and navigation was put to a lengthy written test on Saturday morning, followed by a clean-up of our rooms. Sunday's schedule called for an inspection of our quarters, clothing, lockers, latrine, and our personal appearance. Later we had an arduous session of close-order drill and physical exercises, followed by a refreshing swim. On Monday, we were assembled for a hike, which was officially described as an "initiation." It was a snap when compared with the 20-mile hikes with full field pack that I had experienced in basic training at Camp Wallace, Texas.

We were to be confined to the post for the first two weeks; after that we would have inspections and drill on Saturday mornings and then be off from Saturday noon until 9:00 p.m. on Sunday. Lancaster did not have much to offer in the way of entertainment or anything else, and it appeared we would make tracks for the 65-mile hitchhike to Los Angeles.

My introduction to the BT-13 commenced with several hours on Monday and Tuesday of "hangar" flying. Actual flying would commence on Wednesday, but in the meantime we sat in the cockpits of immobile planes and became familiar with the controls and instruments. The BT-13 was an all-metal, two-seater, enclosed cockpit with sliding Plexiglas canopy low-wing monoplane with a 450 hp Pratt & Whitney radial engine, two-position adjustable-pitch propeller, flaps, two-way radio and intercom, landing and position lights for night flying, and an array of instruments not found in Primary trainers. It had a cruising speed of 135 mph.

A. U.S. Army Air Forces 450 hp Vultee Basic Trainer, the BT-13, at Lancaster, California, April 1943.

I had my initial orientation flight on Wednesday, April 21st, with my instructor, James McCarthy, a short, stocky man of about 35 years of age. I learned that he had several thousand hours in the air and had been a bush-pilot in Alaska for a number of years before the war. He claimed he had made more landings on arctic lakes with pontoons and on ice with skis than he had with wheels on land. I believed him when I experienced the smoothest landings of my life with him manning the controls.

McCarthy wasted no time in having me take the stick. With his guidance from the rear cockpit, I taxied to the takeoff position, cleared the engine and checked the mags, checked instruments and controls for takeoff position, and cleared the area for incoming aircraft. He asked if my seat belt was fastened, and was I ready. I told him I was ready if he was. He gave a little laugh, as if he had been preparing all his life for this moment, then said, "Lets go!"

I opened the throttle and felt a surge of power I had not known in a Stearman. With sufficient speed, I pushed forward lightly on the stick, then harder to raise the tail when I felt the greater BT-13 resistance. I eyed the airspeed indicator at about the moment we lifted off, then eased back on the stick to establish a climbing attitude. All the while McCarthy had been talking to me and occasionally applied corrective pressure to the stick or rudder. At the same time, he announced the necessary throttle and prop-pitch settings and other observations needing my attention. His methods were those of "learning by doing" and "that starts now."

Landing was a little trickier than takeoff. I leveled off a little too high above the runway, whereupon he applied some throttle and eased down to the desired level and told me to land it. I did so. It was a little rough but satisfactory.

I progressed well with McCarthy and soloed the BT-13 after 4 hours and 45 minutes of dual instruction. Much of the pre-solo time was spent taking off and landing on Rosemond Dry Lake, 10 miles east, and on Rogers Dry Lake, about 20 miles northeast of Polaris. The dry lake beds served well as auxiliary fields and because of their length it was possible to make a series of straight-ahead touch-and-go landings without flying around a traffic pattern.

On the north edge of the Mojave there existed the embryo of an Army facility, later to be named Edwards Air Force Base. We never interacted with anyone there, and it seemed as though the Base's activity was quite limited. I don't remember any official announcement of its purpose, but it was rumored that it was a test site for experimental aircraft. The Mojave was an ideal place for such activity.

The BT-13 was much heavier than the Stearman and the pressures on stick and rudder were greater. It would take time and practice to get the feel of the plane and to be able to handle it rather than it handling me, an essential in the flying of all aircraft. That natural transition came about almost without being aware of becoming its master. I would later experience this sensation in the flying of combat aircraft. Until reaching that level of proficiency, the instructor often had unkind words, but never threats, for difficulties and repeated foul-ups.

Cross-country flights were added to our agenda and included the technique of flying the "beam," a radio signal that was transmitted from a radio-range station, which was usually located at an airfield. With the radio tuned into the range-station frequency, a steady humming tone was emitted at the center of the signal: deviation to the right, the signal would become a "dot-dash" beep; deviation to the left, a "dash-dot" beep would be heard. The goal of the pilot was to bracket the steady signal by gradually reducing the degree of correction till the constant hum prevailed and guided the pilot directly over the range station.

This device and technique was often employed while practicing instrument flying. With a black hood drawn over the student so that only the instrument panel and controls were visible, the instructor would dictate an instrument flight problem over the intercom. The student would fly the prescribed compass heading, altitude, and airspeed, make the changes and adjustments voiced by the instructor, intercept and bracket the beam, and then at the moment of arrival over the station, change to the station's radio voice frequency and announce his altitude, heading, and time to the ground-station controller. All this was done without visual reference to the ground, the horizon, or other external objects. The instructor's job was to constantly observe for other aircraft and to monitor the student's actions.

An adjunct to instrument flying was the Link trainer, a one-seater, platform-mounted instrument flight simulator manned by trainer operators seated at control consoles. The trainer had all the controls and instruments found in the BT-13. A hinged opaque canopy closed over the student while he executed the faux maneuvers. The flight sensations were often deceiving and imagined corrections or maneuvers were sometimes deemed unnecessary or even hazardous. The Link trainer was an outstanding training device and we all had to achieve proficiency. The instrument flight problems prescribed by the operator were similar to those we practiced in the air, and our performance was duly graded by the operator. I did a little better than average at both.

Polaris had a special building housing 12 of the Link trainer units.

Formation flying was as critical to our training as most of the other requirements. Flying off the wing of a leader, the student had to maintain constant watch for changes in altitude, direction, and speed. The wingman flew a little above and behind the lead plane with wingtips about even with each other. Constant throttle adjustment was necessary to avoid lagging behind or over-running the number-one plane. Various maneuvers were practiced, such as changing position with another wingman, crossing under or over the leader, or even taking over the leader's position. Due to the proximity of other aircraft, the demands of formation flying required intense concentration, producing exhilaration and the later side effect of fatigue.

My progress at Polaris was perhaps average or a little above average. Many fell by the wayside. The washout rate escalated and would reach close to a 50 percent total in our class. The schedule was intense, the discipline rigid, the pace rapid, and the expectations high. Mental alertness and clear thinking were a prerequisite, allowing for no carelessness or sloppy performance. This applied to all phases of our schooling, and these rigorous standards existed to transform us into top-notch pilots to assume our future positions in the air war.

Leisure time was held to a minimum, and the 65 miles between the base and Los Angeles was often a deterrent in our quest for entertainment. Sometimes Scotty and I would go into Lancaster to the USO dance or to a movie. We also went to movies at the base theater.

Bob Purcell and I went to LA together on a few weekend passes and usually wound up at the Hollywood Palladium. His access to his father's car eased our transportation problems. We would share a twin bedroom at the St. Paul Hotel near downtown.

I was piling up the flying hours, both dual and solo, and time was marching on. My correspondence with the folks, with Ray and David, and with Ruth continued on a fairly regular basis. An unusual lull in Ruth's letter writing occurred in early May, and I was somewhat concerned as she had been so faithful in keeping me posted on her life in Chicago. I continued to write to her and waited patiently for a reply. In her letter of April 25th, she told me of her father's ruptured appendix and the rush to the hospital, his operation, the application of sulfa powders to the exposed area before closing of the incision, and his pending recovery.

And then a telegram arrived, followed a few days later by her letter, telling of Mr. Wasson's death on May 1st, 1943, at the age of 60. Peritonitis resulting from the infectious appendix took its toll, and medications of the day were ineffective. Ruth was deeply grieved at the loss of her father. They were very close, and it was obvious that many changes would occur in the lives of Ruth, sister Alice, and their mother.

William Wasson, called Bill by his friends, more exclusively Will by his wife Clara, had been a kind and gentle family man who had worked for the Illinois Central Railroad for over 35 years. He had advanced from signalman, through a variety of track jobs, and finally had become a towerman, an important and demanding position.

At the 67th Street split, where some commuter trains diverted east onto the 71st Street line to serve South Shore and South Chicago, while others continued on south to the far suburbs of Matteson and Blue Island, Will controlled the track switches that governed their destinations from a narrow, elevated masonry building squeezed between sections of track right-of-way. A large electrified position board with dozens of blinking red, yellow, and green lights identified train and switch locations. The board was suspended above a long row of switch levers that extended four feet up from their floor mountings.

In the early days, the levers were directly connected to the track switches by cables and rods encased in conduits and were manually operated by the towerman. Later, they were powered pneumatically, making the job much easier. Ruth told me she had visited the tower on many occasions when she was a child, and her father let her pull on the switch levers. She said she also entertained her Dad and his assistant by turning cartwheels in the long narrow room.

Like most railroad jobs, the towerman was never paid what he was worth, and for many years Will worked seven days a week. To be sure he would have off on Christmas, he had to apply for the holiday early in January. The family always lived close to his tower location so that he could walk to and from work.

Will and Clara both came from large families, which supplied a host of aunts, uncles, and cousins. But it was during the war years that Ruth drew very close to her folks and would carefully plan their weekly trip to the movies. She was her Dad's companion when the others could not attend.

Though Will's free time was limited by his work schedule, he managed to be aware of the hazards that often confronted his daughters. Once when Ruth was about 12 years old, she reported to her father that an over-attentive gatekeeper at the 67th Street crossing always chased her through the viaduct when she came from school. Ruth was quick to note that a new gatekeeper was on the job the next day.

Later, when Ruth worked in a far Westside office, she was sometimes bothered by her supervisor. Will told her that she didn't have to tolerate his seamy behavior even if it meant quitting her job. When the next offense occurred and the supervisor ignored her protests, Ruth marched into the general manager's office and voiced her complaint. She demanded that either she or the supervisor be assigned to another department or she would find another job. The next day the supervisor was gone. Ruth had learned valuable lessons from Will.

With her father's death, Ruth's plans to come West for my graduation from Flight School had to be abandoned due to all the unforeseen expenses. I wrote, offering to pay her way when the time came, but she could not accept the offer. I wanted to talk with her, to hear her voice, and named a time on the following Sunday evening of June 13th that I would call her.

I placed the order with the long-distance operator and confirmed the call for 9:00 p.m. Chicago time. I was using a pay phone in the recreation room in the PX and stood close by to keep other cadets from using it when my time approached. The phone rang almost on the stroke of 7:00 p.m. California time. I fed the coin slot from a stack of quarters in front of me to cover the cost of the three-minute time limit, then heard that sweet, trembling voice say, "Hello Ace, you Swoose you!"

The wartime limits on long-distance calls did not allow for much conversation. The usual salutations, health, work, and family inquiries could claim the allotted time, questions which were generally covered in our exchange of letters.

But ink on paper could not transmit voice inflections. Words appearing on a page could not set the heart to pounding as could words spoken. Ruth's voice assured me of her caring, her sincerity, her love, and I felt her warmth as the cadence of her voice came dancing along the wires spanning the 2,000 miles that separated us.

All too soon, the operator interrupted us. In her next letter, Ruth wrote, "You sounded almost shy. What has the Air Force done to you?"

I left the PX after our call, stopped by the orderly room to check the bulletin board, and saw my name scheduled for an Army check-ride at 8:00 a.m. on Monday. But before falling asleep after "lights out," my thoughts were tugged between the memory of Ruth's voice and the uncertainty of the check pilot's appraisal of my ability at flying the BT-13, just ten hours away. The parting words of Jack Mathis at Cal-Aero rang in my ears, "Stew, you're going to do just fine!" I slept well all night.

The check-ride went off without a hitch. The Army officer check pilots were not long on praise but were capable of harsh evaluation if there was less than a satisfactory performance. My check pilot's silence seemed to echo Jack's prediction.

A cadet's total Flight School experience was sprinkled with demerits given for infractions of a considerable collection of rules: for being late for a formation, overstaying a pass, soiled clothing, poorly shined shoes, buttons on hanging clothing being unbuttoned or in improper order on the rod, footlocker contents not arranged per regulation, dirty rifle, bed improperly made, and a host of others. Demerits were recorded on a weekly basis and when the total exceeded a stated minimum, the cadet was awarded the punishment of walking a one-hour tour in prevailing dress uniform, with his shouldered 30.06 rifle, in strict parade-like posture for each excess violation. I had prided myself in never exceeding the minimum at Santa Ana, at Cal-Aero, and now at Polaris, but could not be certain my luck would hold indefinitely.

One day we came from a ground-school session and were unexpectedly ordered to change clothes and fall out immediately for calisthenics and swimming, rush-rush, on the double. Most of us tossed our books on our bunks, removed our clothes and laid them on the bunks, left unlaced and untied shoes on the floor in disarray, dressed in the required attire, and raced out to the formation seconds ahead of the "fall-in" whistle.

The physical training exercise completed, we returned to our rooms and discovered that a surprise inspection had taken place during our absence. All the violations were posted on our gig sheets. We were allowed four gigs without punishment, but mine totaled seven, which meant "three tours," or three hours of marching with the rifle in front of Headquarters on Saturday afternoon. Many others were in the same boat. We voiced our complaints to one another, especially the unfairness of the inspection and penalties imposed without the benefit of sufficient time to put our rooms in order. When I informally questioned the officer of the day, he replied that we should know by this late date that our quarters and belongings were subject to inspection without advanced warning, at anytime. We all realized that there would be no sympathy given by anyone in authority and grudgingly accepted our due.

I realized as I marched and sweated with my rifle on Saturday afternoon that this was all part of the training process. Adhering to regulations and obeying orders, as well as failing to do so, extracted a price. In the case in point, I had made a date to go dancing with a girl at the Hollywood Palladium. Now I would have to break it. On a ten-minute break, out of each hour of marching, I called Los Angeles and explained the unfortunate situation, which prevented me from following through.

At any rate, our time at Polaris was running out and questions concerning our future was foremost on our minds. We each had been given the opportunity of stating our preference for the type of aircraft we wished to fly in the future: single- or multi-engined. Some felt the call to get into fighters, while many of us preferred multi-engined bombers or transports. Most of us would no doubt be directed toward combat-type planes where the greatest need existed. Because of my correspondence with old Chicago friend, Bob Saxton, I had developed a fondness for the B-25 Mitchell bomber. This was the path Bob had followed and he was presently in B-25 combat training in South Carolina. I was not too enthusiastic about four-engined aircraft such as the B-17 Flying Fortress and B-24 Liberator.

I still had Advanced Flight School to conquer and requested a multi-engine assignment. In our final week at Lancaster I finished the formation, cross-country, and night-flying requirements, thus completing the prescribed 80 hours of total time. On Friday, June 18th, I received word that I would be going to Yuma Army Air Base, Arizona. It was not considered to be very glamorous, and we knew it was about as hot there in July and August as any other spot in the country, but it was a twin-engine Advanced School. That evening we had our graduation dinner with graduation exercises scheduled for Saturday morning, followed by a parade. We had the rest of the weekend off and spent Monday turning in temporary clothing and flying gear, packing our belongings, and writing or wiring home about our Advanced Schools.

Basic training at Lancaster had been good for me. I felt I had become quite proficient in the BT-13 and was confident that I could handle just about anything that was made available to me. My instructor had been an inspiration, although we shared no particular camaraderie. In this respect, Basic was different than Primary. His only words to me at the graduation dinner were, "I enjoyed having you as one of my students, Stewart, good luck." We shook hands and never saw each other again.

Chapter 15

Advanced Flight School
Yuma, Arizona

T HE THINNING OUT OF OUR CLASS began first at Cal-Aero, when about 30 percent of the cadets washed out of flight training for various reasons. Another 20 percent were eliminated at Polaris, and we assumed that the rest of us were "home safe" and that Advanced would be a snap. I don't recall any washouts, but we saw our numbers dwindle and divide up when the cadets were given the aircraft types of their choice. Many of those who chose single-engine fighters went to Luke Field near Phoenix; some asked for and were sent to start further training on twin-engine pursuits (P-38s) at Williams Field at Chandler, Arizona; and others, who chose multi-engine bombardment, went to Williams Field. For the first time since we had we met at Santa Ana, Scotty Rohwer and I were separated. He went to Williams and I went to Yuma.

Our contingent bound for Yuma thus was greatly reduced in number. Because of the washouts in Primary and Basic, fewer Advanced Schools were needed. Other Basic Schools also were sending cadets to Yuma, and that swelled our class to full strength.

We arrived at Yuma from Lancaster in the wee hours of June 23rd, 1943, aboard the slowest-moving train we had known to date. The truck drivers that came to town to pick us up were about as groggy as we were for want of sleep. There was practically no conversation on the ride to the air base, just yawns and grunts and occasional derisive expletives aimed at what would appear to be the "sexual deviances" of the train. The ten-hour ride had done little for our beleaguered dispositions, further frustrated for want of an audience.

We were hardly enthralled at first glimpse of the barracks in which we would be housed — row upon row of temporary GI buildings, one-story affairs covered with black tar paper retained with wooden slats. We cussed the guy that invented the black stuff and the Army for not having more imagination in selecting a waterproof wall covering. Black, more than any color, would absorb about every BTU of heat the sun could deliver. Why did it never occur to the housing planners to use the heat-reflective qualities of white or light-colored material? Our Eden-like days at Ontario and Lancaster were now ancient history. My mother would have voiced her stock appraisal of these previous luxuries as being "too much of a good thing."

As new arrivals, our first stop was in front of a complex of these ineptly named barracks. A Sergeant appeared and posted our assignments: two men to a room, steel cots with cotton-filled mattresses, a clothes rack with shelf and footlockers. As if the black wall-covering wasn't bad enough, they had to divide the total space into rooms, thus eliminating open cross-ventilation. Lying very still after a long, hard day, we did, however, sleep.

The one concession to regulations was the procurement from the mess kitchen by each cadet of a one-gallon wide-mouthed jar resembling a pickle container. Each evening after supper we would fill our jars with chunks of ice from a bunker at the rear of the mess hall and return them to convenient places next to our cots. Sometimes we added water to the ice and were assured of an adequate supply of cold drinking water to satisfy our needs during the night.

Seldom did we use more than a top sheet for cover as we slept. By morning, the bottom sheet was well soaked with perspiration. This was the first and only Army post I was ever on where making the bed every morning was not a requirement. I propped the sheet up with my now empty ice jar to allow air to circulate to dry the sheet, as well as the damp mattress cover below.

The food was remarkably good at Yuma. Served cafeteria-style on stainless-steel, compartmented trays, the enlisted-man purveyor of dessert splashed a huge paddle-scoop of ice cream into a compartment too small to accommodate the generous portion. Melted ice cream soon mixed in with the mashed potatoes and string beans and spoiled our appetites for either. I found a supply of large cereal bowls and solved the problem of migrating cream, while claiming a double portion of the delicacy. Soon all the cadets were using the bowls and calling for the extra scoop. The increased consumption of ice cream was never criticized, but the complaints from the dishwashing detail rose in a chorus of protestations. But we prevailed, and to my knowledge, all future servings of ice cream were in cereal bowls. Cadet friends were quick to dub them "Stewart bowls."

A few days after our arrival, we were introduced to the AT-17 Bobcat twin-engined Advanced training plane. Made by Cessna, it was a fabric-covered low-wing monoplane with two 250 hp engines, fixed-pitch laminated wood propellers, hydraulic flaps, retractable landing gear, and pivoting rear tail wheel. It had a left seat for the pilot, right seat for the copilot (or instructor), and a bench seat behind them for two or three passengers or other cadets scheduled for instruction. Rather than a stick, the AT-17 had a wheel with which to control ailerons and elevators. The wing structure was of laminated wood, and the fuselage was a wood-clad metal framework, designed to accept the dope-impregnated fabric. We sometimes described it as a "Siamese Stearman" — that is, two joined primary trainers. It also became known as the "Gingham Bomber."

Instrumentation-wise, the AT-17 only lacked a prop-pitch control, as the props were a fixed position and had no pitch selection. The AT-17 was good for procedure and handled well. Its orientation to the horizon was similar to our previous trainers and presented no tricky characteristics. The Curtiss AT-9 that we had used for instrument training was much different, as it was all metal and much heavier; in it, I was a little slower in soloing. Some schools used the AT-9 exclusively, and I felt it was to their advantage as it simulated more closely the combat-type aircraft we would be flying. Scotty Rohwer learned twin-engined flying in AT-9s at Williams Field.

I welcomed the challenge of the AT-17 and soloed it in about 4½ hours. Our procedure was confined to level flight and rather shallow maneuvers. The AT-17 was not stressed as highly as the AT-9.

We also checked out in the 600 hp single-engine North American AT-6 Texan low-wing monoplane. It was an excellent aircraft, highly maneuverable, and well suited to aerial gunnery training with its lone .50-caliber machine gun firing through the propeller. A gun site was mounted in front of the wind screen, and aiming the gun was done by aiming the plane itself. The gun trigger was mounted in the stick.

Gunnery training was held over the desert, where we dove the AT-6 and fired at ground targets, bottoming out of the dives at about 100 feet. Aerial gunnery involved firing at a sleeve-type target towed at a safe distance behind another AT-6 at several thousand feet of altitude. Our training in this activity was held to a minimum, and I recall that only a few days were devoted to it.

In due course, we started formation flying and found it to be similar to that of the Basic trainer. Eventually, we would form into larger groups and sometimes do a fly-over for the Saturday morning parade.

Night flying was soon scheduled, and we became keenly aware of the darkness and shortage of reference to the ground or to the horizon. In all these activities we were qualified by the instructor before flying the aircraft solo. On solo flights, we always had another cadet in the right seat as copilot. It was his job to raise and lower the landing gear and flaps when signaled by the pilot to do so. He also operated the radio, monitored the engine-operating instruments, and watched for other aircraft.

My instructor, First Lieutenant Ken Jones, was a taskmaster and never signed off on a cadet's performance unless he was totally satisfied that the student knew what he was doing — and could prove it by doing it!

Our schedules were grueling. We were up and dressed at 5:15 a.m., and we trained without a break through till 9:00 p.m. Sometimes our night-flying schedules lasted until 11:00 p.m. or midnight.

Yuma was known for its intense heat, and there was no getting used to it. Some days in

August topped out at 125 degrees, and one Sunday a medical officer measured the radiated heat 12 inches above the tarmac at 178 degrees. We all became very lean and brown. Water in our showers was never heated, as the temperature at the spray head was at least 85 degrees. Someone once started the rumor that the heat was so intense it melted the glue that held the wooden wing structure together in the AT-17!

During the first half of our training at Yuma we attended ground school and were drilled in recognizing our own and enemy aircraft and shipping. The same methods were used in all schools. We also planned the navigation for our several cross-country flights, most of which were "Round Robins" of 200 to 300 miles. When the class of 43-G graduated, we became upperclassmen and were exempted from any further ground school. We then devoted all our time to flying and getting in the required total of 85 hours.

Two disturbing incidents occurred during this time, one of which affected, perhaps unfairly, our squadron.

As upperclassmen, we had just finished a flying period and would soon assemble outside the ready-room for the customary dismissal by the squadron Commander, Captain Stapleton. Word spread that one of our number had cracked the wing of his plane against the wing of a parked plane while taxiing toward his parking area. The accident inflicted damage to both aircraft. We waited for 15 or 20 minutes in an at-ease formation for Captain Stapleton's appearance.

Finally, he came through the door and our cadet Commander called us to rigid attention. Captain Stapleton walked back and forth in front of our formation, hands on hips, a deep scowl creasing his face. The only sounds came from taxiing planes out on the ramp.

Then, with venom in his voice, he commanded, "Alright you Misters, bail out!" No one moved a muscle. He paced again.

"Don't you Misters know what you are supposed to do when ordered to bail out?" A loud cadet chorus shouted, "No, Sir!"

Then Stapleton continued, "Lieutenant Jones, would you please demonstrate to these Misters what they are to do when ordered to bail out."

Lieutenant Jones, who happened to be my instructor, stepped forward and explained as he demonstrated: "At the command of 'bail out' you simulate pulling the rip-cord by slapping your left chest with your right hand. Then you immediately assume a squatting position and raise your arms up as if you are holding onto the shroud lines of your parachute. You must stress your legs so that your buttocks do not touch your heels. You hold that position until you receive the command to stand up."

"Thank you, Lieutenant Jones. Do all of you Misters now know what to do when you receive the command to bail out?" asked Stapleton.

The loud chorus answered, "Yes, Sir!"

"All right then you Misters, *bail out!*"

With that, we all *bailed out* and held the position while Stapleton blew his stack about the cracked-wing accident. It seemed like an eternity, and I am certain we were in that strained squatting mode for at least ten minutes. The officer instructors walked up and down behind us to see if anyone was letting their buttocks rest on their heels. A few were and they were forced backward off balance and instructed to repeat the bail-out procedure.

Finally Stapleton ordered us to stand. I couldn't straighten my legs and had to fall forward onto my hands and stretch my legs behind me. Only then was I able to get up.

Captain Stapleton confronted me. "What is the matter Mr. Stewart?" I replied, "I couldn't make my legs work. I had a cramp in my left leg, Sir."

"We have a cure for that Mr. Stewart. Do a double-time run down to the end of the ramp and back, now!"

The ramp was almost one mile long and it was 118 degrees in the blazing sun. The round-trip took me 10 or 12 minutes, and I was soaking wet with sweat and breathing heavily when I resumed my place in line. The others were still being lectured as they stood in rigid formation.

Stapleton again gave the order to bail out, but this time it only lasted about five minutes. Then he issued his final blow.

"You Misters will double-time to and from the flight line for the duration of your stay at Yuma. This should burn into your minds everyday that carelessness and accidents will not be tolerated. You are dismissed!"

And double-time we did until the last day of flying sessions before graduation.

Regrettably, a second accident involved the same cadet. While night flying in the area, he had throttled back his engines to perform a shallow spiral let-down from about 5,000 feet to the 1,000-foot traffic pattern altitude. He reached the 1,000-foot level and opened the throttles. The two engines sputtered and coughed, then died. They would not restart.

Faced with a serious dilemma, he glided straight ahead, turned on his landing lights, and hoped he could make a belly landing in the desert. The ground came up before him and he flared out for the landing. Suddenly a huge concrete drainage ditch loomed, and he saw that he might crash into it. He pulled back on the stick to stretch his glide and pancaked safely but hard on the sandy soil beyond the ditch.

The cadet suffered a cut on his nose; his copilot was okay. But the plane was badly damaged. However, he had also flown over the border into Mexico, which could have complicated matters, though apparently there was no problem in getting Mexico to release the plane for return to Yuma.

What had caused the engines to fail? Carburetor ice. When descending from altitude with idling engines, especially at night, it was necessary to rev the engines after each 360-degree turn to clear them and prevent carburetor ice from forming. The ice would occur in the air intake ventures. The cadet had failed to clear his engines during the entire descent — something we had learned on our first or second flight in Primary.

We all thought our cadet would get washed out. He didn't, though we assumed that he had learned an expensive lesson and would certainly never repeat the error. He graduated and was commissioned a Second Lieutenant. We never heard where he was sent.

The last week of school arrived, and we used it to good advantage in accumulating our total hours requirement. Flying schedules were posted on the bulletin board, designating crews, plane numbers, and exercise to be practiced, such as formation. On one of these, I was designated to lead a three-ship flight up the Mojave to the Salton Sea and other points and then return.

I set the course, and the wingmen took their positions. When we approached the Salton Sea from the north, 235 feet below sea level, I nosed down and flew low, about 30 feet above the water for the length of the Sea. With the wingmen still in position, I pulled up to about 1,500 feet and headed back to Yuma Air Base. All had gone well, and I was enjoying the flight. Looking through my left pilot's window toward the left engine, my eye was attracted to what appeared as a silver-colored object swirling out about four or five inches in front of the propeller hub. I looked at the right propeller and saw no silver-colored object. I couldn't tell what the object was, but it surely looked suspicious.

I called it to the attention of the wingmen and told them I was returning at once to base. They stayed with me as escorts. I called the tower, requesting a straight-in approach due to apparent trouble and was granted clearance. I lined up with the runway and made a good landing. With the throttles closed and the strain off the propellers, the left engine started a violent vibration. I quickly cut the switch and coasted to the edge of the runway. I looked again at the prop hub and saw the trouble before calling the tower for a tow jeep. We climbed out of the plane and examined the problem.

The wooden propeller was designed to be mounted on a cast aluminum hub with a wide flange on one end. A mating flange on the opposite end fit over the hub where it extended through the prop. Splines on the hub matched the splines on the engine shaft. Eight studs, each about eight inches long and threaded on both ends, penetrated the hub, mating flange, and eight propeller holes for perfect alignment. "Castle nuts" anchored the entire assembly and were to be safety wired through holes in the studs and the notches in the nuts.

I was stunned when I saw our situation. Two studs were gone, two were missing castle nuts and had receded past the flange into the wood, two were still in place, and two — those that had created the silver swirl — were extending out forward from the prop about six inches. Our margin of disaster was the two studs, doing a fair job for the other six. I was incensed!

We rode up to the flight line in the tow jeep, and I immediately filled out a malfunction report. The maintenance officer came by and asked what had happened. I described the situation and then asked him what he was going to do about it. We had been told that a cadet pilot whose life was endangered by apparent careless maintenance had jurisdiction in demanding investigation and appropriate discipline.

The officer shrugged his shoulders and gave me a dumb grin before saying, "You're here and you ain't hurt, so what's the problem?"

I felt an uncontrollable fury surge up within me. I grabbed a fist full of his shirt front and pushed him against the wall, ready to flatten his nose. The color left his face when he saw my rage.

At that moment one of his maintenance Sergeants entered the ready room, saw the cringing officer in my grasp, and stepped between us to push me away without uttering a word.

The Sergeant remained in place; the officer did not move away from the wall and said nothing.

"What kind of a worm are you, Lieutenant?" I growled. "You know what could've happened if I lost that prop!"

"You could cut the switch and shut the engine down," he meekly answered.

"And what would've happened if the vibration tore the engine out of its mounts or tore the wing off before I could cut the switch? Tell me, Lieutenant," I again demanded.

He did not answer.

"I'm filing this report. It'll tell your stupid remarks about me being here and not hurt, and I'll tell them how I was ready to redo your face."

The flush of my anger began to subside as I continued to stand there with the Sergeant keeping his silent vigil between us.

As I turned and sat down at the picnic-style table, the Lieutenant walked toward the door, then delivered his parting threat, "I'll see you at your court-martial."

Still smoldering, I reached for a heavy glass ash-tray but refrained from throwing it at him.

I sat for several minutes, calming down and collecting my thoughts. I reasoned out how a lost propeller would affect engine operation.

In all internal combustion engines there must be a balance between energy generated and energy expended. The weight of the propeller and the load it creates by virtually pulling the plane through the air compensates for the power output of the engine. Reduce the speed of the engine and the work required of the propeller is lessened. The speed of the plane is slowed.

Lose the propeller and its compensating force and the engine runs wild. There is no place for that energy to be used as it revs up and exceeds its design limitations. Severe vibration occurs as the engine wildly tears itself and its mountings apart.

A similar function is found in an automobile engine, and its energy compensator is the fly-wheel. Engage the transmission, and that energy is transferred to the wheels and the car moves.

Remove the fan blade from a household electric fan, and the motor will run wild. Remove the belt from the small pulley on a sewing machine, and the motor will exceed its design speed limitations. Its energy compensator is the machine driving the needle and the drag of thread and material being sewn.

The more I thought about it, the more I was incensed with the careless maintenance and, especially, my close brush with disaster. But even more, I was troubled by the inexcusable attitude of the maintenance officer, its effect on his maintenance staff and, above all, the lives of the cadets.

I finished writing the report then sought out Captain Stapleton. After relating the entire story to him, he told me not to worry about it and that he would take care of the matter. I asked for and the Captain assured me that I would receive a complete report of the incident and the action taken. There would also be an official letter in my 201 file, vindicating me of any violence taken against the officer.

Captain Stapleton was no doubt sincere in his promise to get the matter resolved and appropriate action taken against the maintenance officer, but time ran out for me to learn of its final outcome. I was also disappointed that no letter made it to my file. My cadet days ended 96 hours later when the goal for which I had struggled became a reality and Yuma would be no more than an overheated memory.

Within the next three days we completed our flying requirements and prepared for graduation. We had purchased our officers' uniforms at the PX with the $250 clothing allowance. The PX was out of my size in the officer's pink-gray dress pants. I would have to purchase them at my next duty station or at a civilian department or clothing store.

The graduation party was held on Sunday, August 29th, and we were treated to a fine steak dinner at the Officers Club, a departure from custom we had not expected. A few lighthearted speeches were made by some squadron Commanders, including Captain Stapleton. When he had finished, by prearrangement, our squadron rose en masse and with one loud voice hollered, "Awright Captain, *bail out!*" And smiling good-naturedly, he did.

On Monday, August 30th, 1943, the graduation was held in the base theater building. The ceremony included a short speech by the Base Commander with congratulations for achieving the status of U.S. Army Air Forces Pilot and his wishes for success in our future assignments and service to our country. I had learned several days earlier that I would be commissioned as a Second Lieutenant in the Army of the United States and I had bought extra gold bars at the PX. Our future assignments were also issued and, joy of all joys, a ten-day delay en route to the new station was to be granted.

When we had entered the theater for the graduation ceremony we were each given a large, brown envelope. Mine contained a pair of silver wings, two gold bars, my discharge as an enlisted man/cadet from the Army, the official Army officer appointment with the imprint signature of President Franklin Delano Roosevelt, my official military 201 file, immunization records, and, finally, those longed-for travel orders that would allow me the time to go home after my 23-month absence from kith and kin.

I made train travel reservations on the Rock Island Line, purchased tickets, and would share a Pullman bedroom with August Strey and Henry Sydejko. I would leave them when I arrived in Chicago, while they continued on to their homes in Wisconsin.

I had long envisioned my mother or Ruth being on hand to pin those coveted silver wings to my uniform, but time, health, and resources had waylaid those hopes and plans, and I now faced what I thought might be the more sterile process of being pinned by the cadet sitting next to me, as I did for him.

We performed the process, threatening to pierce one another's flesh with the sharp-pointed pin of the wings, pinned the gold bars on one another's shirt colors, shook hands, and rendered to each other our first salute. Meaningful? It surely was, honoring and being honored by a brethren, united in the cause of freedom, in which we would soon present our very lives for possible sacrifice.

Leaving the theater, we were immediately confronted by a solid row of cadets and enlisted men lining the walkway and street, each snapping to attention and rendering their sharpest salutes as we passed. I returned their greetings, not with a feeling of superiority but as a gesture of respect for them and their membership in that same cause in which we all were engaged.

Following lunch in our cadet mess hall, I returned to the barracks and finished packing for the trip home. We were all excited as we compared notes on our new assignments. I believe everyone got what he had requested. At least, I didn't remember anyone registering disappointment. Home addresses of close friends were recorded on our new, engraved calling cards ("*Alexander C. Stewart, Lieutenant, U.S. Army Air Forces*") and some favorite snapshots were exchanged along with warm handshakes.

The final hour had struck; it was time to leave. We rode buses to the Yuma station, never looking back at the receding mass of black tar-paper barracks, but eyes were forward drinking in the desert we had ceased to hate. Over that horizon was home and that was all that mattered now.

The train stood ready for boarding at the Yuma platform. Hank and Augie and I found our bedroom compartment, agreed on our bunk selections, stored our gear, then settled in for the long ride. Conversation revolved around home, our families, and our waiting sweethearts.

"Are you going to get married, Alex?" asked Hank.

"No. I love Ruth very much but marriage has never been on my mind. Maybe someday after the war. The subject has never come up, Hank."

Hank was satisfied with my answer. I really didn't care to engage in a detailed explanation about Ruth's and my relationship and felt a simple answer was adequate. He seemed satisfied and did not pursue the matter.

I sat back, thoughts drifting to my pending reunion with Ruth, and wondered about the events that had changed the course of our lives.

Before I started dating Ruth I had been dating a very lovely girl for three years. We didn't go steady and each was aware that we dated others. I was very fond of her. She came from a fine family, was high principled, and a lot of fun. We were just out of high school when we met, and the country was still in the throes of the Depression. And I had progressed from job pay starting at $12.50 per week in 1938 to $22.50 per week when I left for the Army in 1941.

In the spring of 1941 she supposedly went on a vacation with her mother and sister to Washington, D.C., and married a Navy ensign she had been dating in Chicago. I was quite surprised even though our relationship had never gone much beyond that of platonic. Falling seriously in love and getting married, for me, was unthinkable. I simply had not advanced to that level.

During these same times, Ruth was going through a similar experience with a fellow she had dated for three years. He was perhaps a little older, had learned to fly, and had secured a pilot's license. In early 1941 he became a flight instructor and was hired to train Army cadets in a civilian primary school in Georgia.

Theirs had also been strictly a dating relationship that had no serious implications. Like mine, there was no thought of marriage. After a few months in Georgia, he wrote to Ruth that he had met and was now married to an Atlanta girl.

Ruth apparently was disillusioned, perhaps disenchanted of men, and thus was resistant to any serious involvement when we started dating in the summer of 1941.

In essence, we were both on the rebound. Since we both worked in the same office, we had many common interests and social contacts. We enjoyed dancing, movies, good music, family gatherings, and parties with mutual friends.

In late summer, I sensed my deepening fondness for Ruth, a kind of caring I had never known before. But with the specter of military service hanging over me and the reality of separation that plagued us, a barrier of resistance clouded the possibility of a serious relationship. Then shortly before my day of induction into the Army, I realized I had fallen in love with her. And now I was on a train steaming eastward to pick up where we had left off 23 months ago.

I told Ruth when I last saw her that I loved her, but she didn't tell me that she loved me, nor had we so expressed ourselves to one another in all those wonderful letters. I felt I had made the initial declaration and was not going to try to extract a response from her through the unromantic vehicle of the U.S. Mails. It was up to her to make the next move, and I felt she must have a good reason for not doing so.

I did sense her deep interest in and caring for me, which became especially evident when she acknowledged my gift of the small gold wings and the framed studio portrait of me taken in Los Angeles on the day of my entry into the Army Air Forces. She appeared to be very happy and proud to receive them.

Ruth wrote that the wings had precipitated an ongoing exchange between her and her office friend, Milly. Milly quizzed Ruth on the whereabouts of the wings when they were not in evidence on her outer clothing. Ruth replied that on those days the wings were pinned to her slip to bring them closer to her heart.

This prompted me to write and tell Ruth that a safety pin would fasten a broken shoulder strap better than the wings would. Then Ruth replied that the straps on her slips were not broken. I was intrigued with this rather subtle response.

I knew that Ruth had kept my photo on her dresser, and that everytime she looked at it, as she said, she "gave out with her secret weapon."

My mother, had she been privy to these goings-on, might have referred to this as "reading between the lines," and this I did.

I felt all that remained was to hear those three little words flow from Ruth's sweet lips as they sprang from a loving heart, in flight on a pair of golden wings.

The motion and clickety-clack of the train played a tune on my senses and I nodded off to sleep, having sealed thoughts of marriage in a time-capsule compartment of my mind. I could not stretch my imagination beyond that moment of first embrace.

After about 70 hours of rolling countryside, our train entered the southern outskirts of Chicago. I was eager to identify familiar landmarks as we chugged through the neighborhoods and factory complexes, noting the buzz of war production activity by civilian guardians soldiering on the home front. The train finally slowed, then came to a smooth stop, wheels squealing as brakes were applied. The conductor called out, "Englewood Station. Next stop, LaSalle Street Station."

Quickly, I shook hands with Augie and Hank, grabbed my B-4 Val-Pak and musette bags, scrambled through the car to the platform, and stepped out onto the wood deck of the old station. My eyes at once picked Mother, Dad, Margaret, and Jean out of the crowd. They were standing in a row as they would for a photo. Off to one side, a few steps behind them stood Ruth, smiling, eyes glistening, as she demurely yielded greeting priorities to the others.

All the disappointments of unrealized furloughs faded into oblivion as I embraced Mother, then Dad, then Margaret and Jean, then all of them together, their tears of joy flowing, as did mine. Then Mother, ever aware of the needs of others, called to Ruth, "Come dear, it's your turn." The four released me into the arms of my beloved.

Chapter 16

Home Again
Chicago, 1943

AD, NOW 71, climbed in behind the wheel of Ray's 1935 Dodge, which he had parked on the street outside the station. In his old familiar gesture, he pushed the steering wheel upward with both hands from the bottom of its arc, and drove the Dodge remarkably well, though the car's claim of five passenger capacity was considerably overcrowded with six adults. Ruth happily accepted my invitation to sit on my lap for the two-mile ride to the house.

With my musette bag in place in the car's small, narrow trunk, and the B-4 bag still suspended by its heavy wire hook from the trunk handle, we arrived Gypsy-style (minus pots and pans) in the driveway of the old house. Ruth's 110 pounds seemed to be feather-light against my lean, muscular thighs, and I was sure we both enjoyed the warmth of that innocent intimacy.

I stood in the yard for a few moments, drinking in the scene of my departure in 1941. It had not changed, but it seemed to be smaller than before. Homes and a smattering of apartment buildings occupied single-width 40-foot lots, larger buildings on double-width 80-foot lots. Construction designs, restricted in width, were enhanced with added height and depth, features of the old inner-city developments consistent with land-use economy, street right-of-ways and utility capacities. I noticed all this, as I had become accustomed to the wide-open spaces and the modern practices of suburban America in the West.

But the striped canvas awning overhanging the seven heavy wooden steps, the swing, and the porch's lattice skirt, were all intact, still shadowing the under-porch sand where as children we maneuvered tiny cars and trucks while imitating their shifting gears with lip-tickling sputters over imaginary roads. At long last, I was home!

Gathered in the living room for an hour or so, we were sipping Mother's fresh lemonade and exchanging answers to long-postponed questions and concerns about relatives, friends, neighbors, our church, and the war, when brother Cameron and his wife Rita arrived. Much of what had been said was then repeated for their benefit. Mother, Margaret, and Jean went to the kitchen to complete supper preparations, occasionally drifting back to listen or add commentary or just to see if they were missing out on something. We were soon seated at the long dining room table, its smooth, stark-white linen accented with sparkling colorful candles — Mother's festive touch for this memorable occasion — and were partaking of her roast beef masterpiece.

Time and the meal's lulling contentment took its toll on conversation as a few yawns were stifled and all agreed that the events of two years could not be covered in one evening. With Ruth seated by my side, our hands met and clasped beneath the table, signaling our pleas to one another for solitude. Cameron had offered us the use of his car for the remainder of the evening.

My old friend from high school days, Dick Gentzler, had notified me that he was coming to Chicago on furlough and asked if he could stay at our house for a few nights. He planned to arrive about 10:00 p.m. Mother said she would put him up in the small west bedroom.

Ruth and I drove Cam and Rita to their apartment at 85th Street and Constance Avenue, then turned north to 79th Street, where a favorite ice cream parlor was still dispensing excellent hot fudge concoctions, and indulged ourselves in two sundaes. Very happy and content, we drove east to South Shore Drive, turned north to Jackson Park, and stopped in a parking space facing Lake Michigan behind the rock breakwater at 67th Street.

The rising moon had ignited the shimmering waters, bewitching us with its eternal magic for lovers since time immemorial. What more could a young man ask for, deeply in love, with the girl of his dreams at his side? We sat in silence breathing in the balm of the night. We kissed, tenderly, her deep golden hair glistening in the reflected light of the water.

We talked about the war, the Army Air Forces, my newly acquired flying career, my potential future service and how it could impact my life — our lives. War-bred uncertainties dominated the backdrop of every nuance of our conversation.

The Police Safety Patrol came by and announced the hour of midnight and the closing of the Park, and we thanked him for his diligence. I started the engine and drove to Ruth's apartment at 1808 East 72nd Street where I parked the car and we continued with our talk. Finally, we were beginning to run out of words. But we were not ready to end the evening.

The declaration of love I had made on our last night together two years previous had been roosting in the recesses of my thoughts and was now begging again for release.

"Ruthie, you do remember that I told you two years ago that I love you very much, don't you?" I asked, a slight quiver in my voice.

She answered, "Yes, I remember."

I forged ahead. "You must know now that my feelings have never changed but have grown ever stronger and I find myself head over heels in love with you!"My whisper sought her ear and my lips brushed her lovely tresses.

Ruthie encircled my neck with her arms, drew me close and whispered into my ear those "secret weapon words" I had been waiting so long to hear, "I love you too, Alex. I love you very much!"

After celebrating our confessions with lingering kisses, I posed the question my heart demanded I ask: "Ruthie. Will you marry me?"

"Yes, a hundred times yes!" There was laughter and joy, merriment and excitement in her reply. More kisses, sealing our revelations.

Suddenly, the enormity of what we were sharing sobered me. I certainly had not planned for events to overtake me as they had tonight. But I asked her when she would like to be married, assuming we might marry after the war — that would be most suitable.

"Well," she said. "Today is Thursday — no, it's now Friday! You have to leave on Tuesday for California, so the only day left for our wedding would be Saturday."

I gulped. "Saturday?" I faltered. In wartime, everything bore the mantle of urgency, and I supposed that our two years of letter writing might be loosely interpreted as a long engagement.

"Why not?" she asked brightly. I thought all of 30 seconds on that one, then said, "Yes, why not!"

We sealed the decision with a kiss, set aside planning until in the morning, and said good night at her door.

I drove home in a daze. I had only now begun to think about the reaction of the family to this sudden turn of events.

I climbed the squeaky stairs to the second floor and awakened the snoring Gentzler. He groggily came to life; I told him about our impending marriage. In characteristic Gentzler fashion, he shook hands and congratulated me, and then told me to get the hell out of there so he could get some sleep.

It was past 3:00 before I too finally drifted off. I was awake and up at 7:00. I found Mother in the kitchen getting ready for breakfast. As she asked about my evening with Ruth, and if I had slept well, I put my arms around her and told her that I had proposed marriage and that Ruth had accepted. We were to be married on Saturday afternoon.

I felt a slight tremor in Mother's body before a sweet smile brightened her face. Her eyes teared slightly before she responded. "Alex, this is so sudden — and unexpected." She paused, breathed rather deeply, perhaps gathering her thoughts. "Alex," she continued, "I know Ruth is the right girl for you. I have said all along that the man who marries Ruth will be the luckiest man in the world and I am so glad you are to be that man." She took my face in her hands and kissed me.

I held Mother tightly and told her how much I loved them all, and how happy I was that she loved Ruth too.

"We don't know what the future will bring," I added, "but we're ready to face it together.

I see many of those qualities in Ruth that I think Dad saw in you when you set out together and left Omaha for Chicago, and I want them all!"

Mother gave us her blessing, then kissed me again and turned to her wonderful breakfast preparations.

Ruth's phone call initiated a flurry of preparations for the big event 36 hours hence. By law, she was required to get a pre-marital physical examination. She feigned being miffed that such was not required of me just because I was declared to be "an officer and a gentleman."

Since her sister Alice was working and there were no other women available with a car to take her shopping, Dick Gentzler was enlisted for the job to drive her to the stores on 71st Street for a new street-length dress, new shoes, and, I presumed, new "unmentionables." I had asked my brother Cam to be my best man; we would both need haircuts and could take care of it together with a trip to the barber. On my agenda was a call to Dr. Harold Bowman, minister of the First Presbyterian Church, to schedule the wedding for 4:00 p.m. on Saturday, September 4th, and to arrange a meeting with him that day for Ruth and me to cover ceremonial details.

Saturday morning was reserved for a trip downtown to purchase the marriage license, Ruth's wedding ring, and my gold band at Lebolt Jewelers, and a pair of officer's pink-gray pants at Marshall Field's Mens Store. We arranged to meet at the 67th Street station of the Illinois Central electric commuter train for the trip downtown, and Cameron agreed to meet us when we returned and take us to our homes. Cameron and I were to drive together to the church. Ruth's brother Bud guaranteed to have her there on time and not let her back out on the deal!

All came off as planned. Another wedding had been scheduled for 7:00 p.m., and Dr. Bowman had received permission for us to use the communion table flowers, which were to be placed by the florist in early afternoon.

We agreed on the wedding vows that we each in turn would repeat, and we covered a few details of procedure and the music that Dr. Prosser, long-time organist and choir director, would play. David and I had been members of Dr. Prosser's children's choir for several years until our voices started changing.

The trip downtown went as planned. We selected our rings at a total cost of $60. Marshall Field's altered my pants while we had lunch in their cafeteria, then we walked the short distance to the Randolph Street IC Station. While waiting for a South Shore Express, Ruth excused herself to make a phone call in a nearby booth.

Two or three days later, I remembered her making the call and asked her who she had to call at that moment.

"Oh," she replied rather casually, "I had to break a date I had made for that night!"

We laughed.

While all this was going on, Ruth's family was burning up the phone lines, making detailed arrangements. Though Ruth had not said so, I was sure she had a moment of quiet in thinking about her Dad, on this of all days and him not being there to give her away.

All appeared in place when Dr. Prosser struck the first notes on the McWilliams Memorial Chapel organ. I stood with Dr. Bowman in the chancel in front of the beautiful borrowed flowers, Cameron at my side. Ruth's sister Alice, her maid of honor, stepped forward and took her place on the right. Then Dr. Prosser pulled out all the stops on Lohengrin's "Wedding March," signaling the start down the aisle of my stunning bride on the arm of her beloved brother William W. (Bud) Wasson. The congregation arose, greeting her with loving smiles as she passed each pew.

Ruth took her place at my side, the vows were spoken, the rings were blessed by Dr. Bowman, the pronouncement given. Ready for the kiss, I lifted her veil, and caught its edge on the tip of her nose. We both giggled, the congregation giggled, as did Cameron and Alice. It got a smile from Dr. Bowman. I finished the job in true Air Forces perfectionist style, then we scurried up the aisle.

The many well-wishers gathered outside the chapel door on the 64th Street side of the church pelted us with a hail of rice as we emerged wreathed in smiles. We acknowledged the cheers of the small crowd, mostly relatives, then joined Cameron and Alice in the car to go to the Ray Studio on 63rd Street for two photographs, one of Ruth and me together, the other with the four of us.

Ruth's brother had arranged for a wonderful dinner for 29 in a private dining room at the Windermere East Hotel on 57th Street, opposite the famous Museum of Science and Industry. Both Ruth's and my immediate families, some other close relatives, and a few select friends attended.

My father, a teetotaler, probably didn't approve of the wine that was served, but he toasted us with water in his glass. Ruth, having long ago observed alcohol's effects on the behavior of some people and deciding she always wanted to be in control of her actions, did not drink any alcoholic beverages. I refrained from drinking any wine in deference to Ruth. Together we acknowledged the many eloquent toasts.

Dick Gentzler was sitting next to Ruth and happily received the gift of her wine. The waiter was quick to keep their glasses filled and each time, her full wine glass was traded for Dick's empty. No one was keeping track of how many glasses of wine Dick obtained and enjoyed in this manner, but Ruth wondered, apprehensively, if my father had seen the waiter's attentiveness but failed to see Dick as the lone imbiber.

Our next stop was at the home of Bud and Ruth Wasson for a reception. It was a "come and go" affair, with most guests coming but few going. They all partook generously of the delicious buffet of select ham, cheeses, and cold cuts provided by Cameron and Rita, and the fancy salads and other delicacies that had been prepared by Ruth's mother and sister Viola Carlson. There were Swedish breads and tiny rolls provided by the Carlson family bakery, all beautifully arrayed on the dining room table.

My relatives and the older members of Ruth's family gathered in the living room. Ruth and I cut the cake, a rich, large, lower section of a tiered whipped cream wedding confection, a specialty from the popular Dressel's Bakery on West 79th Street. It was complete with inscription and topped with a statuette of a white-gowned bride and her groom in Air Forces uniform. Such statuettes had become commonplace decorations in these times.

The less-inhibited migrated to the basement, where copious drafts of their favorite libations were dispensed. A player piano provided accompaniment to their vocal attempts and the muffled party atmosphere echoed up the stairs. Newcomers quickly chose their venue and many never circulated among those living-room stalwarts.

When the mantel clock struck ten, I whispered to Ruth, "Let's get out of here." Earlier we had recruited Dick to drive us to our hotel, but now he didn't want to leave. When Bud told him he could come back for more gaiety, he acquiesced.

Ruth kissed her mother, her sisters Alice and Viola and Bud. I kissed Mother, Jean, and Margaret, and shook hands with Dad and my Uncle Henry. Ruth and I said our goodbyes to all, and we departed amidst a chorus of cheers and wishes for "many happy years."

Dick drove us to the Country Club Hotel Apartments at 69th Street and South Shore Drive. Cameron's wife, Rita, had undertaken to engage a one-room efficiency apartment in this high-rise condominium, which was regularly used as temporary quarters for an apartment owner's use while his own unit was being decorated.

I secured the key from the night attendant who also served as the elevator operator. We got off at the third floor, found our number, and unlocked and opened the door. I started to enter, when Ruth tugged at my sleeve with the gentle suggestion. Was I going to carry her across the threshold? Without a word, I picked her up in the prescribed manner and carried her into the room. I had the idea of dropping her on the bed, but there was no bed! Ruth was mystified too! I guessed that the two large doors on the far wall concealed a Murphy bed, and my hunch was right. I soon had the bed lowered to the floor in its most appropriate and welcome mode.

"Well aren't you smart," she said.

"Smart enough to marry the most beautiful girl in the world," I said as I reached up and fumbled around searching for the pin that held her large corsage of orchids to her dress.

"What are you doing, Alex?" she asked as she touched my hand.

"Just trying to locate that little pair of gold pilot's wings," I smiled, kissing her.

I found the pin, removed it, and placed the corsage in the refrigerator in the tiny kitchen. Then I stepped over to the apartment entry. I hung the DO NOT DISTURB SIGN on the doorknob, and quietly closed and locked the door.

Since my arrival in Chicago, I hadn't been able to contact David in boot camp at Great Lakes Naval Training Station, north of Chicago, near Glenview. He had no knowledge of our marriage, but it was unlikely that he could have been granted leave to attend the wedding. I had written to him from Arizona, telling of my graduation and my leave time at home; we had planned to see him on Sunday, September 5th.

Ruth and I rode to Glenview with Cameron and Rita early Sunday afternoon, located the visitor's center, and were walking up the road when we spotted one another. We closed the distance with a fast trot, into each other's arms. The remembrance of our long separation was assuaged the moment we laid eyes on each other. How I loved this kid brother; we had always been so close! I recognized the depth and breadth of that love in that wonderful moment of coming together again.

As children, David and I had been inseparable, never viewing any exaggerated attention

2nd Lieutenant Alexander C. Stewart and Ruth Anna Wasson Stewart, on their wedding day, September 4th, 1943.

by parents or older siblings as partiality toward one or the other. Our personalities jibed. He admired my friendliness and loyalty to family and friends. He emulated what Mother described as my "industriousness," and an odd combination of generosity and thrift in my make-up.

And I, in turn, admired David for his intellect, his sensitivity toward people, and — especially — his musical genius. He possessed perfect pitch and astounded his listeners with rare interpretation of dramatic rhapsodies and concertos at the grand piano. He had been a budding concert pianist until he had begun his medical education. Ironically, the beat of war drums, the lives of men being slaughtered in battle and visions of his service in the saving of lives, drew the curtain on his passion for the concert stage and his medical training. After two years of Pre-Med at the University of Chicago, he found himself in Navy Boot Camp and from there as a combat company medical aide man destined to be transferred to the Fourth Marine Division in the Pacific.

But now in these brief hours of reunion, I was anticipating a rare opportunity to savor again the superb art of my "little brown brother." He had grown three inches in two years and now glanced downward in order for our eyes to meet.

David did not notice the wedding corsage Ruth had again pinned on that morning, but then, suddenly, a light came on. His eyes dropped and connected with the sparkle of tiny diamonds on the finger of her left hand. His quizzical smile spread to a huge grin as he half-shouted, "You two are married!" He encircled Ruth with his powerful arms and planted a kiss to be remembered on her waiting lips. A description of the wedding and the events leading up to it satisfied his immediate inquiry, and then we started for the Visitor's Center.

We chose our Sunday dinners from the large selection of tasty dishes arrayed in the cafeteria, sat at a remote table for easy conversation, and ate with satisfaction, praising the Navy for the unexpected quality of the fare. Conversation centered on the war and our potential involvement in it. My future service was cut out for me — the flying of medium bombers in Europe or in the Pacific Theater. David was focused on medical treatment of fallen infantrymen in the battle against the Japanese. Neither of us relished the prospects we faced, but realized we had put our hands to the plow.

Time was too short that day to be used speculating on our futures. We had wanted the master of the keyboard to "entertain the troops." David walked over to the concert grand piano. It was mounted on a raised island-like platform to allow guests a full view of instrument and artist as well as the close-in gathering of the more intense listeners. David teased us with a few runs and arpeggios, then launched into a simple version of "Chop Sticks," and finally performed his own concert improvisation of the same number.

Switching to the sublime, he played Brahms' *Lullaby*, then followed immediately with a crashing entry into Liszt's *Second Hungarian Rhapsody*, never giving the audience an opportunity to applaud. Hundreds of sailors and their guests had gathered close to the piano, standing or sitting on the edge of the platform and on the floor. As if an Admiral had entered the room, the huge crowd arose as one body, venting their emotions with thunderous applause, shouts of bravo, shrieking whistles, and loud cheers.

David smiled, nodded his acknowledgment of their appreciation, and then struck the opening bars of the most stirring movement of Grieg's *Second Piano Concerto*. The crowd settled down and listened intently as David played the intricacies of this great work. When he reached the concluding passage, the audience was on its feet before he had struck the final notes. And, again, a tumultuous ovation.

David had played for almost a full hour without music, all from memory. As a tribute to his fellows in arms, he launched into "Anchors Away." The crowd joined in singing their famous service song, then again cheered at its conclusion. David motioned to me and Ruth to come and stand next to the piano, and after a flourishing musical introduction, he struck the stirring notes of the "Army Air Corps Song." The crowd joined in and we all sang. At its conclusion, David jumped up from the piano, stood before me, and rendered the best salute I had ever received. I returned the greeting while the crowd cheered their approval. Then, to include Ruth in the celebration, he embraced her and delivered a true, body-bending, sailor-style kiss.

With the impromptu concert over, the people began to drift back to their chairs throughout the hall. We rejoined Cameron and Rita, and spent the balance of our time in conversation. Visiting hours were drawing to a close, and we very reluctantly parted. David continued to wave as we exited the parking lot and turned from view onto southbound Sheridan Road. The fortunes, or misfortunes, of war would dictate the time of our next meeting. We were both in the hands of others who would decide the immediate course of our lives.

Our route to Mother and Dad's led through the North Shore suburbs near Lake Michigan, picking up Highway 41, which became the Outer Drive south of downtown Chicago. We exited at 57th Street and passed the Windermere East hotel, site of our wedding dinner, then through Jackson Park to 64th Street, passed our old Walter Scott Grammar School, and then on home.

Gathered with the family for Sunday evening supper, all were anxious to hear about our visit with David. They were not surprised at the thrill he had brought to the crowd at the Visitor's Center, as they had witnessed many similar spur-of-the-moment occasions during recent times.

On Monday, Ruth and I visited several of her relatives, saw her niece Bonnie Wasson (Bud's little daughter), where she was confined to La Rabida Sanitarium with rheumatic fever, and had supper with Ruth's mother and a gathering of her immediate family, then returned to our hotel.

Tuesday, September 7th, would be our last day together for three weeks. Ruth had promised Pure Oil Company two weeks notice before leaving her job. She had become a valuable employee and was needed to help train her replacement. Then she needed time to get her clothes in order for her new life as a soldier's wife, accompanying him to his various duty stations around the country.

My new assignment was at the B-25 bomber transition school, located at Mather Field near Sacramento, California, and my orders specified that I report there on September 10th. We checked out of the honeymoon apartment, had breakfast with Ruth's mother and a late lunch with Bud and his wife, "Big Ruth" (my bride had always been referred to by her family as "Little Ruth"). Serving as our chauffeur, Bud stopped at my house for a goodbye visit with Mother, Dad, Jean, and Margaret before heading downtown to the Chicago and Northwestern Railroad Station.

With several minutes remaining before time for my boarding the train, Ruth and I stood off to one side next to a large steel roof support column, exchanging our newly acquired words of love, punctuated with a steady stream of kisses. Just as we turned toward the train, we heard some enthusiastic clapping and cheers. We looked back at the train on the track next to mine and saw a dozen soldiers hanging out of their windows, applauding our romantic performance. We laughed; Ruth blushed and I bowed to them from the waist. They were still cheering as we walked down the platform to my Pullman car. Ruth told me later that Bud, who had been standing some distance away, said he hadn't seen that much necking in a long time!

I stood on the car's platform next to the conductor, exchanging goodbyes with Ruth, when the train started to move. I held that place, leaning and waving through the upper half of the door, till we passed from view. I entered the car and found my reserved seat and settled down for the 2,000-mile journey.

My time at home had been an exciting — a thrilling — episode in my life, so spontaneous, so unexpected, yet so welcome. In spite of the war, I felt I was sitting on top of the world. I had advanced from being a Private/Draftee, with few skills useful to the Army, to a candidate for training as a military combat pilot in the greatest air force in the world. I had achieved the initial stages in preparation for advancement to operational aircraft, my introduction to which would commence in a few days.

And in all my travels and endeavors, I had felt a presence, a confidence that empowered my resolve, now to be fortified by and shared with God's beautiful gift to me, Ruth Anna Wasson Stewart.

Chapter 17

B-25 Transition
Mather Field, California

T HE OLD SAYING "Join the Navy and see the world" had nothing on the Army and its penchant for inflicting travel on the troops. In two years I had gone from Chicago to Rockford, Illinois, to Texas, to North Carolina, to Washington State, to California, to Arizona, to Chicago, and now back to California. And I had yet to fire a shot in anger or drop a bomb containing explosives instead of sand. I was assured, however, that this make-believe warfare would come to an end sooner than I wished.

It was a long trip westward, touching Des Moines, Omaha, North Platte, Cheyenne, the long causeway across the Great Salt Lake, then on to Reno, and the final lap into Sacramento. Three nights and the better part of three days had elapsed since we had steamed out of Chicago, when I had exchanged a volley of airborne kisses with my bride. Now, we faced a three-week separation before I would meet her at the very depot we were now approaching to take her to our first home as husband and wife. And just where that would be, I didn't know.

I boarded a city bus for the 12-mile ride to Mather Field, registered in at Headquarters, and was assigned a comfortable room in the BOQ, the Bachelor Officers Quarters. About 125 pilots, half of our class at Yuma, had been assigned to Mather for B-25 Transition training and were now showing up for the nine-week indoctrination. The other half had been sent to B-26 medium bombardment and A-20 attack bomber twin-engine schools and to four-engine heavy bombardment training in B-24s and B-17s.

Hank Sydejko was one of my first encounters and couldn't believe that I was now married. I had trouble convincing him that the whole affair was born *after* our train trip into Chicago.

Of course, my first order of personal business was to find a place for Ruth and me to live, and this search would have to be sandwiched in with a rather daunting duty schedule.

I phoned some furnished apartment ads in the newspaper, but none was suitable in size, location, or affordability. Rooms in private homes and rooming houses were generally appropriate for single renters, most of whom worked in war plants and other industrial areas. Ruth and I had hoped to find a room and private bath with kitchen privileges.

After several attempts, I responded to an ad by Mrs. Carol Taylor, a housewife with two young children. Her husband was a professor at the local college. They lived in a fairly new pre-war, Spanish-style stucco home at 2815 Land Park Drive. For a reasonable cost, they had a very nice front bedroom with an adjoining bath and a semi-private outside entrance. The only hitch was that we could not have full kitchen privileges, but Mrs. Taylor thought a satisfactory arrangement could be worked out. I decided it would be as good a start as we could find and told Mrs. Taylor that I would call my wife that evening and would get back with her right away.

Ruth approved of the choice, at least as a starter. She agreed that we could relocate if something better could be found, and so I gave Mrs. Taylor a payment covering the first three weeks. I could have lived there before Ruth's arrival but decided to wait as the BOQ was more convenient — it was close to the Officers Club and mess hall — and I knew my duty schedule would be better served during this initial period if I remained there.

As officers, our work load was as heavy as it was when we were cadets, but it lacked the regimentation. There was no marching to classes or to the flight line, and schedules were met on an independent basis. On Saturday, September 11th, the day after my arrival, an orientation meeting was held, outlining the nature of our training. Our ground school classes would emphasize navigation, meteorology, and everything there was to know about the B-25. Flight training would include formation and instrument flying (leading to an instrument rating), high-altitude flights with the use of oxygen, and several cross-country flights.

Ground school classes consumed six hours a day of the first ten days, plus an hour a day for athletics. I finally got close to a B-25 on Saturday, September 24th, and had my first 55-minute ride as a passenger with my instructor, First Lieutenant W. J. Brown. By the following Friday, the 30th, I had logged 5 hours and 20 minutes and had qualified as a limited copilot.

I was finished with my duties at noon and was looking forward to meeting Ruth's train in at 3:00 that afternoon. I packed my belongings and checked out of the BOQ, rode the city bus to the train station, and had a one-hour wait before her train arrived. I walked toward the far end of the platform where the sleeping cars would be located when the train would come to a stop. After looking at my watch for the hundredth time, I finally heard the rumble of iron wheels on the tracks. The mammoth engine soon loomed into view, slowed, then stopped a few feet short of its track-end barrier. I was only one car distant from where Ruth disembarked. The porter was quick to unload the luggage and set it in a row in the middle of the platform. Ruth was the first passenger to descend the steps.

We spotted each other at the same time. She waved both arms, calling out. After an exchange of hugs and kisses, she leaned her head back a little and coyly asked, "Did you miss me?"

Mimicking her gesture, I leaned back a little and replied, "Naw! Why would I do that?"

This would evolve into our standard greeting of one another after any overnight separation.

I stood for a few moments, holding her at arm's length, admiring her child-like complexion with its slight tint of color, her golden hair, the cut of her light-blue linen suit and white tailored blouse and her navy-blue and white spectator pumps. Now past Labor Day, they may have been out of season in Chicago but were perfect for warm California.

Even after the long train ride, Ruth looked like she had just stepped out of the display window of Saks Fifth Avenue. I would learn that she was not extravagant, she simply chose her attire carefully and often from the sale rack. She had an eye for conservative fashion that was stable and enduring, colorful to complement the season, and always feminine.

I carried her two large suitcases into the depot, claimed my B-4 and musette bags from the locker where I had left them during my wait for the train, and had a Red Cap tote them out to the taxi stand. The first cab in the line pulled up, the driver loaded our bags into the trunk, and we were soon on our way to Land Park Drive.

When we arrived, Ruth was impressed with the clean, neat, tan-colored stucco *casa*. Its red tile roof and the stucco wall enclosed an entrance garden that extended from our front bedroom on the right to a wrought-iron gate next to the front-access garage on the left. A flagstone walk led to the semi-private entrance, which opened into a short hallway leading to our room. The taxi driver deposited our bags on the walk near the entrance, accepted his fare and tip, and departed.

Mrs. Taylor answered the door and graciously received us. I had called her earlier to tell her of Ruth's pending arrival. She was prepared and had the room in order, including a vase of flowers from her front garden. Ruth noted her thoughtfulness and thanked her.

We unpacked our things and were grateful for the large closet and ample drawer space in the large walnut dresser. Mrs. Taylor invited us to the living room for coffee and cookies and a brief discussion on kitchen arrangements.

Because of my early-morning training schedule I would not be eating breakfast or lunch there. Ruth could have her breakfast after the Taylors had eaten and left for the day. She could use the kitchen for her lunch, and occasionally, by special arrangement, prepare supper for the two of us when the Taylors would be out for the evening. Most days Ruth would ride the bus to Mather Field and join me for supper at the officer's mess. Many nights she would take the bus home, as I would be on a late-night flying schedule. Sometimes she would visit with other wives in the Officers Club if my flying schedule ended before 10:00; then we would bus home together. On some of the nights when I had no duty schedule, Ruth and I would be able to eat supper at a small restaurant within walking distance.

On the first night that we were granted use of the kitchen, Ruth prepared the first meal of our married life. She had shopped for the ingredients in the afternoon and was quick to brief me on the menu when I came through the door. We were to have grilled pork chops, mashed potatoes, fresh shelled peas, lettuce and tomato salad, and ice cream for dessert.

The breakfast-room table was set and a pair of candles were ready for lighting. Ruth was busy at the electric stove, trying to get it adjusted for the proper heat setting; she was accustomed to the gas-fired stoves we had in Chicago.

I lit the candles, poured our drinking water, and found a supply of paper napkins. I tuned the radio to a popular network station, hoping for some favorite music.

Suddenly Ruth realized that the pork chops were burning and the peas were already scorched. A hefty cloud of smoke was rising above the stove as she rescued the pans from the burners and made a jab at the knobs to turn off the heat.

As if on signal, Glenn Miller and his orchestra, playing from the famous Trianon Ballroom in Chicago, boomed out on the radio with his great theme song "Moonlight Serenade."

That was all Ruth could handle. The dam broke and she burst into tears, totally frustrated.

After a few minutes, I took over. I scrapped the peas, dished up the potatoes and salad, and trimmed out a few small edible portions of the pork chops. We picked away at the charred remains and supplemented them with some toast and fried eggs borrowed from Mrs. Taylor's supply.

Ruth lamented that she couldn't even cook that first simple meal for her husband without messing it up. But we concluded that the nostalgic music coming from Chicago lit a spark of homesickness that had turned on the tears and thoroughly blamed the electric stove for its insensitivity toward a potential home economics dropout who had interned on the fortunes of the Peoples Gas, Light and Coke Company of Chicago!

All in all, the living arrangement worked out fairly well at Taylors, only lacking the convenience and privacy that a self-contained apartment would provide.

By October 11th, I had 15 hours flight time in the B-25 and qualified as a copilot. On October 16th, with 26 hours and 10 minutes, I soloed and was qualified as a limited B-25 pilot for local day flying only. We had been told that about 35 hours were required to solo, so I felt confident that my progress was satisfactory.

A certificate of proficiency covering the use and familiarization with equipment was a companion to the actual act of soloing and was certified by the Checking Officer, Captain Norwood Forte. The checklist, dated October 16th, covered a total of about 75 items dealing with:

All Instruments	Power Plant	Flying Characteristics
Flight Controls	Propellers	Hydraulics
Electrical System	Fuel System	Oil System
Communications	Emergencies	Miscellaneous

A Pilot's Transition Progress and Qualification Record itemized all pilot proficiency requirements commensurate with each level of achievement. The instructor and/or qualifying officer would certify the attainment of the proficiency and the flight time required to do so. I had progressed from Limited Copilot on September 30th through the seven classifications required to attain Unlimited Pilot status on November 13th, 1943.

Our graduation from B-25 Transition School was set for Monday, November 15th. It was a simple ceremony with the Mather Field band playing, a short talk by a Captain who had recently returned from combat, and diploma distribution by Post Commander Colonel Pyle.

While most of our class received assignments to B-25 combat training units at Columbia and Greenville, South Carolina, 36 of us were retained at Mather to serve as instructors in the B-25 for at least one month. We learned that a squadron of WASPs — Women's Air Service Pilots — had arrived to learn to fly the B-25. When qualified, they would be disbursed throughout the country to ferry planes from the factories to staging points for distribution to combat crews. They would also perform other Stateside flights, thus relieving male pilots for combat service.

At this time a new group of men also arrived in Class 43-I who would go through B-25 Transition, just as we had done. Some of the 36 retainees would instruct these men and some would be assigned to teach the women. I was assigned three women students and ordered to commence instructing the next day, Tuesday, November 16th. The instructor status, due to a temporary back-up in the system of too many pilots, would last for one month.

Because of the departure of almost 200 pilots to their new bases, a quantity of housekeeping rental units that had been occupied by married officers was vacated in Sacramento. Ruth and I rented a one-room fifth-floor apartment with bath and efficiency kitchen in a nice high-rise elevator-equipped building.

We had enjoyed our stay at the Taylor's but were glad for the privacy of the new facility. Though I had "lived with roomers" for the early years of my life, it had been the first such experience for Ruth and the Taylors. Mrs. Taylor indicated that she would not re-let our room as the length of stay of military people was too uncertain and was somewhat of a strain on her family.

We packed our belongings and moved into our apartment on Tuesday evening, the 16th. We were located a little closer to downtown, more convenient to stores, to entertainment, and to the bus line, which afforded Ruth more opportunity to see the city and its facilities. As a short-term instructor, the demands on my time were not as great as they had been as a student and there would be no night flying.

The three women assigned to me to learn the ropes of flying the B-25 were all quite experienced pilots and had flown small twin-engined aircraft as I had done. And, as I had been when introduced to the B-25, they were somewhat in awe of its size and the complexity of its systems, its instruments, and its controls. My first session with them was one of orientation, describing controls, devices, and their functions. I had no difficulty in determining which of the three that would eventually qualify. Two of them were very attentive, asked reasonable and sensible questions, and seemed to respect me and what I had to say. The third seemed bent on trying to embarrass me with unsavory language whenever posing a question. She was tough and indifferent, with no zeal for learning.

When I reported for duty on Wednesday, November 17th, I was told that the WASP training program was being discontinued nationally and that the women at Mather were in the process of being shipped out. This came as quite a surprise to us, but we realized that the entire pilot recruiting and training program was being reduced. We speculated that estimated needs were now not as great as they had been and that a sufficient number of male pilots would be available to fill all the slots.

I would be assigned to instruct some of the new men of Class 43-I, but that would not commence for a few days. In the meantime, I was to fly several men down to Santa Ana Air Base (not the Preflight School) for testing and training in a high-altitude chamber.

I had not had the high-altitude chamber experience and was included in the group to be tested. The process was designed to acquaint the pilots with the effects of reduced oxygen on the human body. We entered the large tank-like chamber through a door that locked tightly from the inside. The pilots sat on long benches on either side, though the instructor and I sat on a short bench at the far end. We were each equipped with an oxygen mask and shown how to wear it. The instructor talked by intercom with the technicians outside the chamber.

The chamber was decompressed to a pressure equal to that at 30,000 to 35,000 feet. When we reached that "altitude," the instructor asked for a volunteer to remove his mask for a few moments to show the effects of interrupted oxygen supply on the body. No one was willing to volunteer, so I said I would do it. On signal, the instructor removed my mask but held it close to my face for quick reapplication. In a matter of a few seconds, I began to black out and the mask was immediately replaced. I fully recovered in about a minute and felt no ill effects from the ordeal. It was an impressive and valuable demonstration.

We all had lunch at the officer's mess, during which time I met Captain Stapleton, my "bail-out" squadron Commander at Yuma. When I told him I was instructing student officers at Mather, he told me how lucky I was, and that he was still in that "God-forsaken" Yuma desert. Jokingly I told him that he was being punished for making us do all those "bail-outs" and making me run the two-mile round trip on the ramp in 118 degrees. What else could we do but have a good laugh? That was history! I gathered my charges and enjoyed the return flight to Mather.

The next day, I was assigned to take a B-25 down to the North American Aircraft factory at Burbank, California, for some sort of experimental modification and return in another B-25 that had been there for two weeks of modification work. My copilot had just qualified as Limited Copilot and was eager for the trip.

While we waited for takeoff clearance from the tower for the return flight to Mather, we saw what was probably one of the first radio-controlled, pilotless "drone" planes make a takeoff — a small craft, about half the size of a fighter plane that looked very strange as it taxied to the head of the runway. As it opened the throttle, it lifted off like a fighter plane. We were impressed and wondered about its future application.

On December 2nd, I finally started work as an instructor, which continued almost daily through December 16th. During that time I had flown 23 hours and had made 31 landings and enjoyed breaking in my three students. But my instructor days ended, and the time had come for we 36 "Holdovers" to leave Mather and go on to combat training.

My orders were dated December 17th, 1943, and indicated that I would proceed to Columbia Army Air Base, Columbia, South Carolina, reporting there on January 1, 1944. I called Ruth and told her to start packing. After reserving a bedroom compartment on the train for Chicago, I made the rounds of all the facilities on the base where I could have been indebted: the Officers Club, the PX, the dry cleaners, etc., secured their signatures on the clearance form, and filed it with Headquarters. As I was leaving the Headquarters office I was approached and stopped by a Brigadier General.

"Are you just signing in or are you signing out, Lieutenant?"

"I'm signing out and leaving for B-25 combat training in South Carolina, Sir," I replied.

"Lieutenant, I am seeking volunteer pilots to fly the P-61 Black Widow twin-engined fighters to form a night-fighter group to train and go to England. The Germans are giving us hell over there and we need to stop them. Are you interested?"

I was a little amazed at the informality of the recruiting method for so vital and dangerous an assignment. But I reasoned that he hadn't become a General in the Army Air Forces by being cautious or indecisive. He was dead serious and had the authority to apply whatever methods he chose to get the job done.

"Sir," I answered, "I have been in the service for over two years. Early in my basic training I volunteered for a duty that backfired on me, and I vowed at that time that I would accept whatever assignment the Army would impose, but that I would not volunteer for anything. I have felt the Army's judgment of my abilities surpassed mine. I respectfully decline your invitation, *Sir!*"

I was glad he didn't ask me what it was that I had volunteered for. It would have been hard to tell him of my unhappy experience with cutting up pork chops at Camp Wallace, Texas.

I didn't regret my decision, as many of those who formed his night-fighter group were later slaughtered by highly skilled German fighter pilots over France and the English Channel.

Finally, I bid farewell to the people I had worked with at Mather, before boarding a city bus for the ride into Sacramento and to our apartment. Ruth met me at the door with the greeting that we would need to go out and buy another suitcase as the ones we had would not hold all of our belongings. I surveyed her efforts and decided a repacking job was in order. I unpacked everything then methodically folded, rolled, and packed our clothing to best wrinkle-free advantage, filling her two suitcases, my B-4 bag, and the musette bag, which also accommodated her cosmetics and toilet articles. She was impressed with my work, but it wasn't until we had left Chicago for Columbia on December 30th that I inherited all future packing chores. She vowed it was an art or skill that she was incapable of learning and henceforth was honoring me with the assignment!

Having cleared our departure and rental obligations with the building manager in Sacramento, we rode with bag and baggage to the depot, boarded our train, and settled in for another 2,000-mile journey. I had acquired an olive-drab green canvas portfolio zipper case in which to carry my increasing volume of paperwork. It fit well into one of the large side pockets of the B-4 bag and was accessible for reference during the long ride.

The transition from twin-engined training planes at Yuma to the B-25 combat-type aircraft had been a dramatic undertaking. The B-25 was much more complex, was seven times more powerful than the AT-17, and was equipped with a multiplicity of instruments, controls, and emergency devices. All of these had been part of our training at Mather and would be expanded in the upcoming combat expertise we would acquire in South Carolina. I used much of the travel time in reviewing all the data and shared some of it with Ruth, hoping it would help her in understanding the nature of my work and improve her knowledge for conversation with other Air Forces wives.

Our stopover in Chicago on our way to Columbia allowed for ten days of visiting with friends and relatives and celebrating the Christmas holidays in a fashion I hadn't known since 1940. David was still stationed at Great Lakes Naval Training Station and Ray was coming in on furlough from Oregon. It was the chance of a lifetime for all of us to be together once more. The war clouds hung heavy over our heads but did not dampen our spirits.

So much of our time in the service was spent in training and preparation for the crucial aspects of war that there was no doubt that my eventual destination was one of the war zones, Europe or the Pacific. Ray was a confirmed medical technician with the 96th Infantry Division, which was assigned to the Pacific Theater of Operations with an island-invading force. David had been rated Pharmacist Mate Third Class with the Navy, and he and those who trained with him were scheduled to continue their training also in South Carolina. He could serve as a Corpsman on ship or could be drafted as a Corpsman by the Marines and join an invasion force for a future Pacific island landing.

David's superb musical talent and great artistry at the piano, once discovered and made general knowledge, put him in considerable demand by the Special Forces for entertaining the troops. His name was on the lips of both rank and file at Great Lakes and there were many opportunities for him to minister to the morale of the men. Had he chosen to pursue a safe haven, it was there for the asking.

What a rare combination of gifts and callings were his! Some of those who knew of his accomplishments were amazed that so much talent could be bestowed on one individual.

Our first big celebration at home that December of 1943 was a feast with the whole family in attendance. Whatever lit the fire of hilarity, of razzing and sibling cut-up, the contagion spread rapidly and became general. The exaggerated reaction to a simple remark would set off a flood of commentary that could not be resolved with words. The exchange would commence between two of us, progress into a tussle on the back-parlor floor, and climax with all four of us in a wild, head-locking free-for-all rassle — four grown brothers, ranging in age from 21 to 34, carrying on like kids, in the end all laughing ourselves silly.

Mother, Dad, Jean, Margaret, Rita, and Ruth were the cheering audience, delighted with the antics as well as our feeding of long-suppressed hunger for "fellowship" with one another, a mock renewal of adolescent rivalries. Because of our physical prowess gained in the military, we three were quite evenly matched, though Cameron was no slouch and held his own in our "every man for himself" contest.

A dinner party was planned for an evening in the Walnut Room of the Bismarck Hotel in downtown Chicago and included David and Ray with their dates, Cameron and Rita,

Alex Stewart's younger brother, Pharmacist Mate Third Class, U.S. Navy, David Barton Stewart. He was drafted by the Marines as a Medical Corpsman.

Ruth's brother Bud and his wife "Big Ruth," and Ruth and me. We enjoyed a fine meal and more than adequate drinks and dancing to the music of Jimmy Joy and his orchestra.

When the musicians broke for an intermission, we encouraged David to play for us on the Walnut Room's grand piano. Dressed in his Navy Blues, David gave out with some of his finest. The patrons packing the room were thrilled and urged him on with applause and cheers. Presently, the maitre d' came over to our table and begged me to have David stop.

"The union [meaning the American Federation of Musician's union] will shut us down!" He threatened to call the Shore Patrol.

"But the crowd is loving my brother's playing," I told him. "The union wouldn't have the nerve to shut you down with a sailor from the United States Navy playing like that.

What harm is he doing? I can't make him stop. Call in the Shore Patrol and see what happens," I countered. I had seen Jimmy Joy and the orchestra members standing behind a curtain off stage, laughing and enjoying the whole episode.

The maitre d' left and a few minutes later two big Shore Patrolmen entered the room, went to the piano, and allowed David to finish the song he was playing. He prolonged the conclusion with many grandiose flourishes, intricate runs up and down the keyboard, and finally several crashing, double-handed chords.

Then the SPs each took one of David's arms, had him stand, then slowly escorted him from the room, all the while David feigning a struggle for freedom and head bowed in phony repentance.

I followed them out to the lobby and found all three of them laughing about the incident. David introduced me to the SPs, who were friends of his, and when I returned to our table, the orchestra had again started playing. When David came sauntering in, grinning from ear to ear, the crowd gave him a standing ovation. David bowed.

There was nothing brash or conceited about my brother. He was an outstanding musician and he knew it. People loved to hear him play and he loved to make them happy. And with his vast repertoire, he could astound any audience. That evening at the Bismark Hotel was to be remembered and recalled many, many times.

During that December Christmas visit, Ruth and I were almost swamped with party invitations from relatives and friends, and we had a difficult time working them all in. Several combined their celebrations, and I believe we managed to cover most of them.

Time was running out and we prepared to leave for South Carolina. I knew that I was destined for a war zone and that at least a year or more would pass before I might see all these wonderful, loving people again.

Wartime seemed like it was made up entirely of hello's and goodbye's. The hello's were always joyful, the goodbye's most always carried a disguised note of melancholy. Perhaps it didn't appear in the consciously tailored words or voice of the well wisher, but it most always showed in the eyes.

Ruth and I boarded the New York Central at the 12th Street Station, also referred to as Central Station, on Wednesday morning, December 29th, 1943. Because we would change trains at Cincinnati, then continue on the Southern Railroad south to Columbia, there was no opportunity to ride in a Pullman sleeping car. The trip to Cincinnati was in a comfortable coach, with reclining seats, but we were in for a let-down on the trip to Columbia.

It appeared that the Southern Railroad had restored to wartime service some old coach cars that we claimed were leftovers from the Civil War! The car exteriors were made of tongue and groove wood boards known as "car-siding," which had once been painted a very ugly dark green but were now a worn and peeled smoke-charred black. The train was crowded and we found two seats facing a similar pair, which were occupied by two soldiers.

The seats were fixed, non-adjustable, and were covered with a dark green, scratchy, velvet-like fabric with a worn, diamond-shape embossed pattern. Our only luggage was my musette bag, as we had checked our other luggage through to Columbia. Ruth carried her old seal-skin fur coat in a shopping bag, as it was winter and she thought she might need it. The soldiers were very nice and accommodating, and kept calling me "Sir."

Alex Stewart's older brother, Sergeant Raymond R. Stewart, Medical Technician, 321st Medical Battalion, 96th Infantry Division.

I told them I had probably ridden more troop trains than they knew existed, that we were all in this "cattle-car" together, that I had been an enlisted man for a year before I went to flying school, that my name was Alex and this was my wife Ruth, that they were not under my command, that we would be knocking each others' knees all night, and to can the "Sir" stuff! They laughed and agreed to the terms. Ruth's mother had packed a lunch for us to eat on the train and we shared our sandwiches with our cordial companions.

Sleep was slow in coming on the Southern railcar and didn't last long when it did arrive. Oddly, a refreshment vendor came through about every hour, loudly calling out for collection of empty soda-pop bottles; yet I never knew him or anyone else to ever come through selling the stuff.

Ruth observed that there was no running water in the lady's restroom and that she was glad for the small tube of cold cream she carried in her purse for use on face and hands.

High above our heads over the aisle was a bare light bulb, suspended from a single wire. It swayed continually with the less than rhythmic motion of the creaky old train, and its glare was a constant source of annoyance. I found the control switch, and turned it off, only to have the conductor relight it. I thought I had solved the problem when I stood up on the arms of our seat and unscrewed the bulb enough for it to go out, but on his next pass through our car, the conductor noticed that the light was off and got a small ladder from a closet and screwed it back in. This happened twice, when I decided there was only one solution. I removed the bulb and stored it in the musette bag.

We arrived in Columbia, South Carolina, on Thursday, not knowing where we would stay. It was December 30th. I phoned and reserved #1100, a corner room on the 11th floor of The Hotel Columbia. I was informed that we could only stay there three nights and that the rate was $7 per night. We then went to the baggage claim for our luggage, and low and behold, it wasn't there. When we had transferred at Cincinnati, our bags were taken off the New York train but did not get put on the Southern train. The bags were to arrive in Columbia the next day on the evening train. And so we spent New Year's Eve in the hotel room, washing out our underwear in the wash basin.

On New Year's Day, which fell on a Saturday, Ruth scanned the newspaper ads for a place to live while I went to an Army store and bought a new sun-tan shirt and pair of pants. I felt travel-stained from the long train trip and did not want to report in at the air base looking disheveled. When I returned from checking in at the base, Ruth told me of a room contact she had made and that if we went right away, the party would be on hand to show the place to us.

It was a nice split-level home located on a street of well-kept homes. The available room was actually in the basement next to the garage. It was clean and well furnished but did have a rather damp, musty odor. It was equipped with a small refrigerator and a two-burner gas laundry-type stove. There was an adjoining bath with tub, but no shower. The lady owner was very nice and we decided to take it. We checked out of the hotel on the morning of the 2nd and moved into the basement room. We had reclaimed our baggage on January 1st, and I was now ready for work.

My friend Scotty Rohwer and another pilot, Art Nomland of Grand Forks, North Dakota, and I had all been transferred on the same set of orders from Mather Field to Columbia and with the same reporting dates. Scotty and Art and Art's wife Millie came in a car that Scotty and Art had bought together in Sacramento. They were the first people I encountered at Columbia Air Base on January 2nd. We were assigned to the Replacement Depot, pending assignment to a bomb group and squadron for training purposes.

We all submitted to the routine physical examinations and were reviewed by the Medical Board to be qualified for overseas duty. Our personal affairs regarding pay, allotments, life insurance, and wills were attended to, and necessary forms were completed. We were also given a short course in camouflage and tested on it. I got a grade of 92. Actually, this was the first, and I believe the only, time I ever received camouflage training.

We were required to attend many other classes on a variety of subjects, but few of them dealt with the B-25 or bore relevance to our purpose for being there. We spent time at the Officers Club playing cards, while others played the slot machines. I was not a good card player and usually lost a few dollars to Art Nomland playing Poker or Black Jack. I avoided the slots, while Art usually spent his card winnings feeding the one-armed bandits. This routine went on without interruption for about two weeks.

We had every assurance that we would soon be assigned to a training unit there at Columbia, which prompted Ruth and me to seek a more desirable place to live. In mid-January a newspaper ad led us to the rather large two-story home of a widow who recently had decided to rent four upstairs bedrooms, each with use of an upstairs kitchen and one bathroom. Three enlisted men and their wives were already occupying three of the rooms. Ruth and I rented the fourth. I assured the landlady that we intended to be there for three to four months.

The arrangement worked out quite well as the enlisted men were required to be at the air base very early in the morning. There was little conflict in the kitchen or the bathroom, and the wives found common ground for conversation, meal preparation, and other interests. My schedule was not very demanding, and we were able to dovetail our use of common space quite nicely.

Then, without notice, on January 26th, 14 pilots and 5 bombardiers were issued orders transferring them 101 miles northwest to Greenville Army Air Base, Greenville, South Carolina. My name was on the list. I broke the news to our landlady who did not happily accept the situation because of the assurances I had given her that Ruth and I would be staying put for at least three months.

We packed our stuff and rode with Scotty, Art, and Millie to Greenville to what we hoped would be the beginning of the end of our long training for our ultimate purpose in the war effort.

Chapter 18

Combat Training Depot
Greenville, South Carolina

URING THE 100-MILE DRIVE TO Greenville on the 28th, we discussed housing possibilities for Art and Millie Nomland and Ruth and me. Scotty would live in the BOQ at the Air Base. We considered the likelihood of renting a house together and sharing expenses and housework, and decided to look into it as soon as possible. But in the meantime, we would stay in a Greenville hotel.

When we checked in at the Greenville Air Base on the 29th, we were told that our training unit was not quite ready for activation and that we were free to fill in about a week's waiting period in whatever manner we chose. This was an excellent opportunity for the three of us to apply for a five-day leave before we started training — possibly our last before going overseas. The leave was granted.

Scotty's brother Earl and neighbor Dick Denny, from Spangle, Washington, had left the farm for a few winter months to travel with Scotty and the Nomlands to Columbia, South Carolina. From there, Earl and Dick continued on their own to Jacksonville, Florida, and found temporary jobs in a shipyard. Scotty notified them that he, the Stewarts, and the Nomlands were heading for Jacksonville at once and that we would be there early in the morning of February 1st. Earl and Dick took off from work on the 2nd, 3rd, and 4th, and we all rented ocean-front cabins at Jacksonville Beach.

Scotty, Earl, and Dick shared a cabin, and the Nomlands and Ruth and I had cabins next to the others. We enjoyed a fun and relaxing time trout fishing, walking the beach, and playing cards in the bachelors' cabin. One evening we all went out for dinner, dancing, and the floor show at the Embassy Club near Jacksonville. Then Earl and Dick went back to work on the 5th, and the rest of us drove back to Greenville.

One disturbing incident occurred on the beach. Ruth and Millie were out walking in the sand, picking up seashells and enjoying the relaxation wrought by the surf and the constant onshore breezes. We five men were in the bachelors' cabin playing cards.

Suddenly we heard the unmistakable roar of a Navy fighter plane buzzing the beach. I jumped up and looked out the window in time to see the plane hedgehopping northward toward the Jacksonville Naval Air Station. The girls came running toward the cabin and exploded through the door frightened and breathless. The plane had come so low over them that they had to drop to the sand for fear of being struck by its propeller. It was obvious that the pilot had intended to give them a scare. We were incensed that he would pull such a fool stunt and threaten their lives!

We obtained the phone number of the Naval Air Station and reported the infraction to their flight operations. Unfortunately, we didn't have any telling numbers of the plane and therefore questioned whether they would be able to identify the culprit. We couldn't pursue the matter further, and our opinion of the whole Navy Air Corps took a nose dive due to the recklessness of one of its members.

On Monday, February 7th, Scotty, Art, and I, assigned to the 472nd Bomb Squadron, 334th Bomb Group, prepared to commence the final phase of training in preparation for combat. We attended ground school classes on the 8th and for the balance of the week. Finally, on Tuesday, February 15th, I made my first flight since leaving Mather Field on December 16th. I flew four hours of qualified dual, one hour of which was on instruments, piloting under the hood. I made two landings. That night I flew four hours as first pilot and made four practice landings. It became obvious that we were going to be making up for some lost time. The schedule was intense. In ten days of flying in late February, I flew a total of 31 hours.

We were fortunate in being able to rent a four-room framed cottage with the Nomlands, two bedrooms, a bath, and combination living room-dining room and kitchen. There was a large pot-bellied heating stove in the hall dividing the bedrooms as well as a wood-burning heating-cook stove in the kitchen. There was also a gas cooking stove that was used in the warmer weather.

Art and I had no time for housework so it was up to Ruth and Millie to do the clean-up, and the house really needed it. The real estate agent happened by when the girls were scrubbing the floors on hands and knees and commented that it was the first time he had ever seen a white woman on her knees scrubbing a floor. Millie, being a farm girl, was very energetic and thought nothing of the work involved. When they finished, she changed clothes and went shopping in downtown Greenville. Ruth took a bath and went to bed!

The next day, the girls went shopping together and bought some fabric on sale to make curtains for the living-dining room and to upholster the couch and two easy chairs. They borrowed a neighbor's sewing machine, and Art and I helped them do the furniture. When finished, the place looked pretty good, and the owner was amazed at the transformation. Her husband was away in the Navy, and she had several children that consumed her time and energy. She decided that when we vacated the house she would probably move back in — but we couldn't get her to pay for the curtain and upholstery material.

Contrary to common belief, it does get cold down South. The Stewarts and Nomlands took turns making the fires in the stoves each morning. During the week that it was the Nomlands' turn, Millie got up early and had them blazing away in a matter of a few minutes. When it was Stewarts' turn, I had the fire-lighting chores. Ruth, I don't believe, had ever struck a match in her life. I had plenty of experience and equaled Millie's skills.

In mid-February I witnessed what was said to be the worst military flight training disaster in the history of the Army Air Forces. About 1,000 officers and men were assembled on the runway in parade formation on a Saturday morning. A flight of 24 B-25s made a low fly-over at about 300 feet in close formation. I thought at the time that they were too low. They had just passed our formation when three of the aircraft collided in mid-air. They crashed in a huge ball of fire beyond the end of the runway.

There were seven men in each plane. We were all shocked, almost with disbelief that 21 lives could be snuffed out in a matter of seconds in a useless demonstration. I was deeply saddened when I learned that Hank Sydejko, my train companion from Yuma to Chicago, was one of the pilots. His death brought home for me the danger and risk of what we were about.

After the crash, we immediately marched back to our squadron areas and were dismissed. Everyone was stunned. It had a very sobering effect on all the men. The wire services picked up the story, and the news went across the country, even to Scotty's hometown near Spokane. Ruth had heard the report on the radio and was, of course, relieved to see me when I came home at noon.

Although I had seen my brother David the day following Ruth's and my wedding, and on several occasions during our Christmas-time leave in Chicago before coming to South Carolina, we had not met or even talked about any girls that he might have been dating. And for that matter, he had only told me of some get-togethers he had had with our long-time neighbor friend, Dorothy, and their evenings spent with Cameron and Rita at their home.

Whatever might have been David's current romantic pursuits, he was not sharing them with me. He was aware of the undercurrent of disappointment that the suddenness of my marriage had brought to my sisters and to Dad, depriving them of time they had anticipated spending with me during those many months of our separation. If Mother shared their disillusionment, she never revealed it. I suspected that should David contemplate a trip down the aisle, he would play out the scene differently than I did.

When I was at Santa Ana, he had introduced me by mail to Jane, a girl he was very fond of and had dated in Chicago while she was a student at the University. She was now living at her family home in Santa Monica. At his suggestion, I called Jane and took her out several times, usually dancing and Cokes at the Hollywood Palladium. She was my date at the Cal-Aero Primary Flight School graduation party at Ontario. She was a very nice girl, and I was pleased with David's taste in women. I had written about her to Ruth, and that was when she had replied that she was green with envy. I also wrote about her to David, and he jokingly threatened to date Ruth if I got too serious with Jane.

There was never any question about David's charisma, a special quality of leadership that captured the popular imagination and inspired allegiance as a youth, a special charm or allure that fostered fascination or devotion as an emerging adult. His physical persona — a very handsome, well-built man of 6 feet, 2 inches — his superb musical talent, and his outgoing fun-loving nature were rather awesome, drawing people of all ages to him.

Gifted musician that my father was, he was astounded at the talents that had been passed on to his youngest, and proclaimed them to far surpass his own. The family readily shared in this perception and acknowledged David's potential for greatness. My mother saw a prodigy destined for the concert stage, and, as I remember, a role for herself in directing him toward the fulfillment of that promise.

As the youngest, he probably enjoyed the limelight accorded him, but never allowed it to color his attitude toward any of us. He was totally devoted to me and was quick to champion my efforts. As he matured, the limelight became a smothering burden, which he sought to shed when he entered college. He was determined to be his own person. None of us was ever jealous of David. We were his greatest admirers.

Ruth and I had seen David on December 30, when we said our farewells at the Central Station Depot, and we knew about Dorothy and Jane, but had no inkling of any serious romantic interest in his life. In spite of our lifetime closeness as brothers, there never seemed to be any exchange of information or casual conversation about our girlfriends. For no established reason, that just seemed to automatically be off limits. And, until my marriage to Ruth in September 1943, the marriage of Cameron to Rita in 1938 was the only romantic incident to occur in our family. My sisters Margaret and Jean dated very little and I don't recall any men friends calling on them. They were attractive, well educated, intelligent, and musically talented. Margaret, a grade school teacher in the Chicago Public Schools, was a "walking encyclopedia" of classical music and opera and an enthusiastic fan of the great musical artists and orchestras of the time. And Jean studied voice with my father at his studio in the evenings, after her work at Scott-Foresman textbook publishers, and became an outstanding coloratura soprano. She sang some minor solo roles with a Chicago Opera Company. But neither of the sisters ever married.

Our home and the lifestyle of our father precluded casual or frequent entertaining of our dates, and seldom was there even a gathering of family friends. Dad's voice-teaching schedule occupied most of his evenings at his studio in the Auditorium Building, and the burden of running the household for six grown and fast-growing children with varied jobs, schools, and activities was carried by Mother. To entertain anyone was a major undertaking which we boys refrained from imposing on the family, and especially on Mother.

Ruth and I were therefore not prepared for the news from home about David's marriage on March 2nd, 1944, to a girl named Beverly. It came as a complete surprise.

I received a letter from Mother telling me of the private ceremony performed by a Baptist Minister in his church study, located near the University of Chicago campus, with

David's and Beverly's friends as witnesses. After the wedding, the couple went to our house and broke the news to the family, and it was then that they met Beverly for the first time.

David had been in medical training at Great Lakes since his entry into the Navy, advancing from Apprentice Seaman to Pharmacist Mate Third Class, a rating equal to that of Sergeant in the Army. He was soon to be shipped out to Medical Field Service School at Camp Lejeune, North Carolina, near Wilmington. I saw the possibility of our getting together for a few hours sometime before I would leave for overseas.

About March 4th I was named as one of four first pilots in our particular flight; another four were designated as copilots. I had progressed from limited copilot to unlimited pilot, approved by my instructor Captain Harrison A. Epperson, check-pilot Captain W. D. Decker, a combat returnee, and final check-pilot Captain Charles Seamans. The Pilot's Transition Progress and Qualification Card contained an exhaustive list of requirements that covered almost everything we needed to know, except what would occur when we were being fired upon by the enemy. That could be learned only in actual combat operations.

We first pilots were all afforded the opportunity of selecting the men who would serve as our crewmen — a rather touchy process as we had no prior knowledge of their qualifications. But I assumed that these men wouldn't be here if they had not been trained, tested, and approved for the jobs they were each to perform.

I selected Lieutenant Joseph Nuessle of San Antonio, Texas, as my copilot. Joe had graduated from law school and proved to be quite talkative. He earned the nickname of "Judge," and it was not unusual to have him expound on some judicial decision or recite some rule of law when we were on a cross-country flight. He was about equal to my height of 5 feet 11 inches and had light brown hair. His face was rather narrow and he wore a neatly trimmed mustache. He had a pleasing personality, an easy smile, and a prominent Adam's Apple that became quite active when he exercised his resonant voice. Joe was a good pilot, but lacked the hours and ratings in a B-25 that would qualify him for the pilot's left seat. The Army Air Forces had discontinued the use of B-25 Transition Schools such as Mather Field and was now training the upperclassmen in B-25s at some of the twin-engine Advanced Flight Schools. Joe was an early product of one of those schools.

At one time, the designations of bombardier and navigator were separate individual ratings, and those men trained as fully qualified celestial navigators remained as such. However, since much of our training and operational flights did not require the skills of a celestial navigator, the Army Air Forces created the rating of bombardier/navigator. Men with this rating were trained in VFR (Visual Flight Rules) and dead-reckoning navigation, which were also afforded pilots. Knowledge of and reference to celestial bodies with a sextant was not a requirement, as would be for flights over the ocean.

Dead-reckoning navigation consisted mainly of the plotting of a course from point A to point B, while adjusting for the influence of wind velocity, wind direction, and the effect of indicated airspeed to determine elapsed time en route. Depending on the wind velocity and direction, the ground speed — the actual speed being made over the ground — would establish the ETA, the Estimated Time of Arrival. Wind-drift observations while in flight and reports from ground stations along the way could dictate a change in compass headings and ETAs. VFR navigation was enabled by the ability to refer to the terrain without the shield of cloud cover. Other aspects of navigation were also included in the training.

I selected as my bombardier/navigator Lieutenant Herbert Robinson of Birmingham, Alabama. Robbie had a rather sunny disposition that oozed from his round, rosy-cheeked face. He seemed to be younger than most men of his job and rank, and I privately placed him in the style and demeanor of "Mark Tidd," a teen-age storybook character from the era of Tom Swift. He never referred to his mother but always to "my Mamie," which I attributed to his Southern origin. His physique was somewhat plump — more baby-fat than the product of over eating. Robbie was a very nice, clean-cut young man and tried hard to do his job right. He had worked as an accountant before the war and was meticulous with his navigational paperwork.

My choice for engineer/turret gunner was Sergeant Robert Caruth of Ramona, Texas, a small town just north of Denison. Bob was a good-looking Texan with long eyelashes and brown hair that he slicked back and then crushed into waves. He talked with a genuine Texas twang that descended in volume as he neared the end of a sentence and gave the false impression that he was finished speaking. He was dedicated to his job and knew the mechanical intricacies of the B-25. He also had a good rating in his turret-gun performance.

Sergeant Paul Wheeler of Bealsville, Ohio, was my choice for radio operator/waist gunner. He had excellent training in all radio systems and appeared to be mature and serious in the approach to his assignments. Paul was close to six feet tall, had light brown hair, rather delicate-looking skin, and a pleasant personality. He looked intently into your eyes when spoken to. He, too, ranked well in gunnery.

The sixth man of the crew was armorer/tail gunner Sergeant Russell Scott of Richmond, Virginia. Scotty was short and thin, real assets for the space allotted to his job in the B-25, and an infectious smile. As armorer, he was responsible for the ammunition and proper operation of all 12 .50-caliber machine guns on our plane. In our training mode, there were few demands on his gun expertise, but he was always quick to assist Bob Caruth in the refueling and preflighting of our aircraft, always without being asked. He was a worthy exponent of the team spirit I sought to establish.

At the time of the crew appointments, an administrative Second Lieutenant lectured the first pilots on crew discipline and how we should require them to conduct themselves when on duty. His suggestions emphasized an attitude of strict military behavior and courtesy, calling for their gathering in rigid attention in front of the aircraft before each training flight, and saluting the pilot as each one rendered a report on the condition and readiness of the equipment or duty with which he was assigned.

I had experienced enough of this in my days as an enlisted man and as a cadet and decided on methods I thought to be appropriate when commanding a small, close-knit group of men. I instituted a more relaxed approach in a context similar to a football huddle, gathering them in a loose, at-ease circle while I checked with each man on his personal appearance, flying uniform, parachute, and other equipment, and anything I needed to know about his area of responsibility. There were no salutes, but I did shake hands with each of them and emphasized that if they had any problems or if they didn't understand something to be sure to let me know. "We're not puppets," I told them. "We're men with a job to do and we each depend on the actions of one another. I may be your Commander, but I'm also your friend."

I couldn't have hoped for a better bunch of guys!

In the course of my entire training process, instructors and seasoned leaders dispensed wisdom that bore fruit in my development as a combat-ready pilot. My Basic Training instructor had taught me to practice "an awareness of the unknown — to be alert for the unexpected." This could apply to a sudden malfunction of the aircraft, the failure of support personnel to do their job, your own false move or error as a pilot, or possibly a sudden change in weather conditions imposing strange demands on the pilot or the plane. These were not rules consciously rehearsed before each flight but axioms that became etched in the subconscious.

It was a gray day in March 1944 when I was assigned to lead a three-plane formation on a cross-country mission from Greenville to a landing at Augusta, Georgia, followed by a continuing flight to Atlanta and the return flight to Greenville — a routine task.

Our planes sat at the ready out on the tarmac. The dull overcast ceiling was calm at 2,000 feet. The takeoff wind came straight down the runway at about 10 mph. I filed an instrument flight plan and registered our course with Operations, stating that we would fly above the overcast and observe Airways altitude regulations. After briefing the crews of the two planes flying in the formation with us on this practice mission, I confidently led the three crews out to our waiting planes.

On board at our respective crew stations, we went through the preflight checks, started engines, and checked their operations. Tuned to the tower frequency, I called for taxi and takeoff instructions, then checked for a readiness high-sign from the two wingmen. All in order, I gave the thumbs-up sign to the ground crew, and they responded by removing the wheel chocks. I released the brakes and started to roll, the others following close behind.

We each stopped at the head of the runway, checked magnetos, and lowered flaps to 15 degrees. I looked again at the solid layer of stratus clouds stretching over the land to the horizon and checked the windsock for confirmation of surface wind direction. I released the brakes, applied power, and turned into the wind, then gradually opened the throttles to 44 inches of mercury, our standard takeoff setting. We were soon airborne, wheels retracted, and climbing a gradual 180-degree turn to the right at 500 feet per minute (fpm). The air was smooth and the two wingmen followed me on schedule and joined up in a loose "V" formation. I turned to the compass heading for Augusta, and as we approached the overcast I issued the preplanned signal to the wingmen to initiate 45-degree turns, the left plane to the left and the plane on the right to the right. They were to hold this course for a minute and a half and then turn back 45 degrees and take up the heading to Augusta. Meantime, I held straight to the Augusta heading — so far, so good.

When we rose above the cloud covering we were to look for one another and regroup.

From below the overcast, there was no hint of unusual cloud formation activity above. I confidently entered the ceiling, climbing 500 feet per minute with an airspeed of 150 mph, a rate and speed designed to bring us all up through and out of the overcast in about a minute.

Within seconds after entering the overcast, our plane was seized and sucked into the vortex of a violent updraft. A hot charge of adrenaline jetted into my bloodstream, empowering me to react to my body's alarm system and then to act to meet the urgency of this crisis. With all of my senses on high alert, the hours of training and a generous dose of survival instinct kicked in. We were ascending as if catapulted upwards in a high-speed elevator at a rate of over 5,000 feet per minute — a vertical rise equal to 60 mph — while our forward rate dropped rapidly to about 110 mph. I pushed on the stick with every ounce of strength I could muster to bring the nose down and avoid an aerodynamic stall. We topped out at 12,000 feet.

I knew now that we were caught in the clutches of a thunderhead. Our meteorological training had taught that such a cloud formation could combine a series of powerful updrafts and downdrafts — something definitely to be avoided if possible.

But far from stabilized flight, we immediately entered a downdraft as severe as its rising sister and the instrument readings began to reverse. The rate-of-climb and descent indicator, also referred to as the vertical speed indicator, now registered a downward rate of over 5,000 feet per minute; the forward airspeed had climbed to about 250 mph.

Nature wasn't satisfied with just up and down action, but inflicted violent turbulence, tossing us into steep banks to the right or to the left — 25,000 pounds of aircraft bobbing like a cork in the churning cauldron of whitewater river rapids.

We bottomed out of the downdraft only to be seized by another violent updraft and compelled to repeat the earlier chaos. In the middle of this kaleidoscope of terror, the artificial horizon gave an 85-degree bank-to-the-right reading, although there were no significant body pressure feelings that confirmed this attitude. In a fleeting moment I wondered if the gyro-operated instrument had tumbled. Back to a basic instinct, I glanced at the needle and ball. The needle was hard to the right, the ball hard to the left. We were definitely in a steep, skidding turn to the right. I pushed hard on the left rudder while cranking the stick wheel to the left and regained a semblance of level flight, still riding to the peak of the vortex. The gyros had not failed.

But that malevolent thunderhead was not through with us yet! As quickly as before, we entered another downdraft as violent as the others, no time or instinct allowed for executing a possible escape from this monster. I repeated the previous process and as we descended, I suddenly spotted an opening in the clouds below me, permitting me to see the earth below. I shoved the stick hard and dived for that hole. We shot out underneath the overcast and leveled off at 2,000 feet. We had finally outrun the ogre, that sinister thunderhead that had been lurking above our air base from the moment of takeoff, waiting to seize and maul us and then administer the final blow!

I came away from the experience drenched with perspiration and with an enormous respect for cumulus clouds and their cousins, the thunderheads. We had been told and had observed thunderheads that reached to stratospheric heights, 50,000 to 60,000 feet. By that standard, ours was a baby, with drafts terminating at 12,000 feet, but perhaps no less violent.

Now to locate my wingmen. What had become of them? I soon found out. When they spread out before entering the overcast, one cruised past the thunderhead to the left while the other escaped to the right. One of us in the clutches of that rascal was enough. What a mess it could have been if two or three of us had been snared!

I called on the radio and got the location of the others, told them briefly of our roller-coaster ride, and then instructed them to put down at Augusta. We would meet them there, have coffee, and then proceed to Atlanta before heading back for Greenville.

Upon our return, I reported our experience to Captain Epperson, and he was relieved, of course, that we had survived it as well as we did. "You were caught by surprise; it could happen to anyone. Chalk it up to experience, learn from it."

Our training became more intense and included instruments, night flying, special fuel-conservation flights, a long-range cruise, cross-country and formation flying, and aerial gunnery and practice bombing.

The long-range cruise was designed for practice and testing of our navigational and fuel-conservation ability. The route of our flight was to extend from Greenville to Wilmington, North Carolina, then south to Nassau on New Providence Island in the Bahamas. We would land at Nassau, have lunch, then return to Greenville.

Our route for this training mission had been plotted on the aerial chart and our compass headings had been calculated after we were briefed on weather, winds, and altitude at which we would fly. I reviewed these figures, then made up my own flight plan as a counter-check. Earlier experience indicated that these calculations and Estimated Time of Arrival figures were not always accurate. We were required to check in by radio with specified ground stations along the way, and I didn't want any slip-ups.

We took off from Greenville as scheduled and flew first to Wilmington, about 250 air miles distant. As we turned from northeast to south, heading out over the ocean, I thought of brother David down there somewhere, just 8,000 feet below and of my two-week stay at Camp Davis in January 1942, training for barrage balloons. Where had those two-plus years vanished?

It was a bright clear day with no threat of adverse weather on our entire route. The B-25 was running smoothly, all engine and flight instruments indicating normal. The crew conversed freely over the intercom. I used this opportunity to review emergency procedures with them if trouble arose. We had checked in with the ground station at Wilmington and gave them our altitude and heading to Nassau. All seemed to be in order.

Suddenly, I became aware that the magnetic compass had ceased to function and was locked in a fixed position. I turned on the radio compass and got no reaction. I had Wheeler check the radios. He verified that they were all dead. I had Caruth, the engineer, check circuit breakers, and they appeared to be in order. It was clear to me that we could not proceed over the ocean with these malfunctions. I called Robinson, our navigator, to give me our estimated position. He checked his chart and said that we were just about 90 degrees east of Miami. But Miami was almost on a straight line west of Nassau; this meant it would be 2½ hours before we reached his estimated position. We were now only one hour south of Wilmington. I wasn't sure of Robinson's numbers.

I checked my own flight plan and chart and decided we were just about 90 degrees east of Charleston, South Carolina. I made a 90-degree turn to the right, guided by the Pilot Turn Indicator, and estimated we were about 150 miles out to sea. We should make landfall in about 45 minutes. I was greatly relieved when Charleston came into view three or four miles off our left wing.

Circling to the west of Charleston, I spotted the Army Air Base and the direction of their windsock. Flying downwind and parallel with their runway at 800 feet altitude, Joe Nuessle, the copilot, signaled an SOS to the control tower with the "biscuit gun," a Navy-type blinker signal light. The tower answered with a green light signal, indicating it was okay to land. I flew on past the runway, did a 180-degree turn, dropped wheels and flaps, and made a smooth landing. A jeep guided us to a parking place.

I reported our problem to the line chief and two technicians checked everything possible, searching for the trouble. They worked on the plane for over an hour, but could find nothing out of order. Nor could they get the radios or compass to work. There was no alternative but to return to Greenville. I would have to navigate by VFR (Visual Flight Rules), relying on ground landmarks such as highways, railroads, and rivers. The line chief loaned me his South Carolina road map to use as a check against our aerial chart, and I traced our visual route on it. I promised to mail it back to him, as road maps were very scarce during the war.

We took off, and I soon picked up the main highway that ran across the state northwest from Charleston to Greenville. It was about 175 miles and would take one hour.

Fifteen minutes into the flight the compass started working, as did the radios. I couldn't believe it! We continued on to Greenville, where I reported the trouble to maintenance and to the squadron Operations Officer. I was told that the long-range cruise would be rescheduled, but for some reason that assignment was overlooked, and we were soon to be shipped out of Greenville without having that experience.

Tales of a Bermuda Triangle had been circulating in 1944, and some of the fliers dismissed them, or categorized them as folklore on a par with the Loch Ness Monster. I neither believed nor disbelieved, but an experience like this gave one occasion to wonder. The Bermuda Triangle was described as an area in this region of the Atlantic Ocean where many ships and aircraft were reputed to have disappeared mysteriously. Someone suggested that we were probably the Triangle's marginal intended victims, as we were several hundred miles north of the region when we had our trouble. I had fun with the story and seized on it with feigned sincerity, my hearers listening with rapt attention and wonderment. It was as though we had tempted fate and beaten the odds.

On Thursday, March 23, I received a long-distance call from David, now stationed at Camp Lejeune, North Carolina, where he was in training in the Medical Field Service School. Our conversation centered on the possibility and the transportation available for a get-together. A roundtrip bus ride for him would take 26 hours out of a 30-hour weekend pass. He would inquire about landing facilities in his area should I succeed in getting a cross-country training flight out of Greenville. That night he wrote a letter, filling me in on details not covered on the phone.

CAMP LEJEUNE
NEW RIVER, N.C.

Thursday, Mar.23, 1944
2230 (10:30 PM)

Dear Al —

I am writing this in the head, the lights having been turned out, but — as Ray would say — what's a more suitable place to write your brother a letter? Sure was good to hear your familiar voice — this being away from home is a new experience for me.

If you have access to a N.C. road map you will locate Camp Lejeune at Hadnot Point on the coast south of Wilmington. I don't know where the closest air station would be but will attempt to find out. I want very much to have Beverly join me here and will try to do so before you and I meet. It would be great if all four of us could celebrate our new lives together, even for a few hours. Perhaps I can have Bev come by way of Greenville and I can meet her there.

There is a large trailer camp here on the base for the men's families to live in; I am trying to find a nice couple with whom we could share a large trailer and split expenses, making our rental cost $3.75 per week.

Our official medical training has not started, and they have us on mess-cook duty. I talked my way into a cook's job in the Officers' Mess and now have a chance to contact the gold-braid. They didn't waste any-time wearing us down; last week I was on a two day bivouac in the swamps in which we hiked 36 miles, dug foxholes, lived on "K" Rations, got gassed, made a landing in Henderson barges and in general — suffered miserably.

This outfit is too rugged, 93% casualty rate and too fast moving for my liking. The official course takes 6 weeks, and then you are shipped over — right into the theater of war.

If I can get my transfer to the 13th Defense Battalion, I will stick around here a long time. They are an F.M.F. (Fleet Marine Force) made up of Navy and Marines. There are only about three corpsmen in the outfit and they need more. They have a solid band and I really fit nice — they had just lost their pianist to V- 12 [the U.S. Navy college program].

I'm hoping I'll be here long enough to apply for V-12; I don't care to stick in a Marine outfit and I want very much to get my education while I'm still young. Incidentally, happy birthday, stinky!

Well, Al, I guess there's not much more to say. I'm very, very happy — I feel wonderful — and I feel that March 2nd opened up a new and beautiful chapter to my life. When I got my orders for sea duty, it suddenly knocked a lot of the nonsense — of which I am so full — out of my head. The realization came to me all at once that I was saying goodbye to one of the dearest of my treasures, and I knew then and there that — come what may — I was doing the right thing.

We are both young, very young, but what value does time have in this state of wholesale destruction? We are mutually agreed that I have a long course of study ahead of me — if and when I return, but the good at the end of it is our undivided ambition. Bev realized all this before we were married, and I know she is of sterling character that will be a source of inspiration to me in the hard years that lie ahead.

I must close now as I have to arise at 4:15 and make ready for an inspection tour of the M.F.S.S. I received a letter from Ray today offering his congratulations and best wishes — I'll never forget those happy days we all had together at Christmas. My love to Ruthie, and — as ever I remain

Your kid brother,
Dave

Three days later, I received a short letter from David saying Beverly was leaving Chicago for North Carolina on April 1st and that he would work to get a 72-hour pass on April 8th. In the meantime, I inquired into the possibility of getting a cross-country training flight to Wilmington. Captain Epperson did not give me much encouragement as our schedules were quite crowded with aerial gunnery, bombing practice, formation flying, and final check-rides. I emphasized that all I wanted was a day flight that would involve about three hours of flying time roundtrip and a few hours on the ground to spend with David and Beverly. Epperson said he would talk again to the squadron Commander.

Time was running on and the final days of our training schedule were crammed full. In the first 18 days of April there were only 12 days with weather suitable for flying, yet I had totaled 37 hours in the air in that time.

I was about to make one last appeal for a cross-country to either Cherry Point or Seymour Johnson Field, landing places that David had suggested in his letter that I received on April 20th, when I got notice that we were leaving for overseas on the 22nd.

David called me that evening and I had to break the news to him that I was shipping out and that the meeting we both had so much hoped and tried for just would not happen.

"Awe, Al, no kiddin'," the normal lilt of his voice was now tinged with disappointment. "Boy, I sure thought we could work something out to get together . . . well, we gave it a good try, didn't we?"

He surely could sense my disappointment as my own voice had gone flat. "I'd have given anything for a few hours together . . . and to meet Beverly."

The telephone was so impersonal — impaired voices sounding over the wilderness of a tangle of wires — no smiles, no handshakes, no love glistening in the eyes, no hugs and kisses like we did when we were little children . . . and now longed to do.

Now, we strained to say what must be said . . .

"We're both headed for the unknown — our lives aren't our own, at least not till this war's over. But we're not going alone, Al. Dad would set us straight on that score, wouldn't he!"

"Yeah, he sure would. They're praying for us. I think how hard all this is for them."

"I love you, Dave . . . like always. The greatest test of our lives is coming up. Whatever our fate, I pray God will be merciful — to us, to Mother and Dad, and to your Bev and my Ruthie. Always remember, I'm proud of you and what you've done. I'll pray for you and you pray for me."

He was sure right about Dad . . . he'd have told us to pack our kit and go . . . and trust in God and do our duty as we saw it, and he would support us with prayer all the way.

"I want you to know of my deepest love for you and my heartiest wishes that good fortune be yours wherever you go over there."

"And the same to you from me, Dave."

"Ruth sends her love — and our love to Beverly. Goodbye, Dave."

"God bless you and God bless Ruthie. . . . Goodbye, Al."

I held the receiver to my ear until I heard the disconnect bell that signaled the end of a long-distance call, perhaps expecting or hoping that David would come back on the line.

There had been one phrase in David's letter. His words, "if and when," etched themselves into my memory and lodged in my subconscious like an omen. He had struck a note of cold, hard reality. He was facing head-on the possibility of dying in this war, a possibility that had not entered my mind or conversation about my own future.

The next day we received our orders transferring us to the Third Air Force Staging Wing at Hunter Field near Savannah, Georgia, for assignment to overseas shipment. We were required to travel by train, and our wives were prohibited from accompanying us to Savannah, though they entertained the idea. There were three crews listed on the orders:

> Scotty Rohwer, Art Nomland and crew.
> Alex Stewart, Joseph Nuessle and crew.
> Edward Perry, Stanley Gerry and crew.

Ed Perry and Stan Gerry had trained with us all during our time at Greenville and had been in the contingent with us at Columbia. Their origin, however, was not by way of Mather Field but through other Advanced and Transition Schools on the West Coast. We had all become good friends and had many social gatherings with them. Ruth and Ed's wife Betty had become friendly and had agreed to ride together in the Perrys' car to Chicago when we shipped out. Betty would then continue on to their home in San Francisco.

We boarded the train in the early afternoon, and Betty and Ruth and Millie were at the depot to see us off. It was an emotional parting, with the full realization that our lives would be on the line in Europe or the Pacific. But we were a confident bunch and felt we could meet and succeed in any challenge. I felt we were well trained, and I had no qualms about the trip we would soon make to our overseas destination.

The purpose of the Third Air Force Staging Wing was to equip combat crews with aircraft, clothing, emergency devices, and other essential materials as well as navigation and meteorological information and supplies. Briefings were held to convey critical data that would impact our journey.

The inventory of aircraft at Hunter Field included twin-engine B-25, B-26, and A-20 and four-engine B-17 and B-24 bombers. The crews of all types of craft would receive the same equipment and briefings.

Included in the emergency equipment for each crew member was a "jungle kit" fitted with a large machete knife for hacking through jungle growth, a compass, a small first-aid kit, water purifying tablets, high-concentrate candy-like rations, matches in a waterproof case, a fishing kit with line, hooks, and an artificial lure (not too highly thought of by the fishermen in our midst), and a small flat roll of olive-drab-colored toilet paper. The kit was fitted in a flat olive-drab canvas backpack, to be fastened to our parachute harness. Since the crew wore either seat-pack or chest-pack parachutes, the jungle kit posed no wearing problems.

One of the most vital functions of our four-day stay at Hunter Field was the calibration of the instruments in the brand new B-25s assigned to each pilot. The plane assigned to me was B-25J, serial number 43-27661, a sleek polished aluminum beauty fresh from the factory at Kansas City, Kansas. I noted in its log book that it had been flown by only one other person, the pilot that had ferried it to Georgia from Kansas City. Of course, it had probably been flown at the factory by a test pilot before delivery to the Air Transport Service.

We made a three-hour flight on April 24th and calibrated all instruments that required fine-tuning adjustment. All radios and other navigational equipment were checked and adjusted. I wanted another opportunity to double-check the plane before leaving Hunter and managed another three-hour flight on the 25th. I was pleased and satisfied that everything appeared to be perfect and advised the crew of my confidence that all was shipshape for departure.

Though our stay at Hunter Field was short, it was productive and provided us with everything we would need to make the flight overseas. Each crew apparently was issued an individual order. My crew order was dated April 26th, 1944, directing us to proceed to Airport of Embarkation, Homestead Army Air Field, Florida, via the following specified route:

> Hunter Field, Georgia, to Homestead Army Air Field, Florida, via
> Savannah, Georgia, Jacksonville, Florida, Daytona Beach, Florida,
> Tampa, Florida, Fort Meyers, Florida, and West Palm Beach, Florida.

This was described as an extended route for practicing fuel conservation and I wondered at the time if my failure to make it to Nassau had finally caught up with me. Perhaps this was the reason for our crew to be on an individual travel order. The zig-zag route across Florida stretched our straight-line flight from about 450 miles to 650 miles.

Our actual flying time was four hours, two of which were on instruments, as we encountered some very bad weather. Thunderhead build-ups in a tropical front cut across our route, and I had to climb above the overcast and circumnavigate the bad stuff. I was able to make an instrument let-down through the overcast between Fort Meyers and West Palm Beach, then turned south toward Homestead in clear weather.

Darkness had fallen and as I approached Homestead, I called the tower for landing instructions. The tower operator assigned me a runway and warned that there were several planes in the area. I observed a whole string of C-47s at 1,000 feet in a very wide landing pattern with their downwind leg stretching out over the Atlantic Ocean. I made a tight turn well inside of their pattern onto the base leg, then another turn onto the final approach. I called the tower, reported my position, and flashed my landing lights.

"I see you Army 661. You are number two on the final, clear to land."

"Roger and thanks Homestead," I said. "For a minute or two I thought it was going to be a long night in a traffic jam."

"Those are C-47 students getting in some night local transition. You did all right Army 661. Roger and out."

The C-47 in front of me turned off the runway onto the taxi strip at the moment I flared out for a smooth landing.

I followed the jeep to a parking area, and we climbed down from our flight stations and reported in at Operations for assignment to quarters. It was reunion time again as we encountered our Greenville bunch, all of whom had taken a direct route from Savannah to Homestead. Our brief stay at Homestead would allow only enough time for navigation and weather briefings. Although our shipping orders were dated April 27th, our actual departure date would be dictated by the weather.

The rains came on the 27th and continued to exert their authority on the 28th and 29th, then finally cleared mid-day of the 30th. We were notified to attend a pre-dawn weather briefing on May 1st after loading our personal belongings aboard our planes.

Each plane was equipped with a "Tokyo Tank," an auxiliary fuel container suspended high in the bomb-bay to provide the range needed to fly from Natal, Brazil, to Ascension Island, a distance of about 1,600 miles. The tank had earned its name from that used in the 16 B-25s flown by Colonel Jimmy Doolittle and the Tokyo Raiders when they took off from the aircraft carrier *Hornet* on the first bombing of Tokyo in April 1942.

Suspended below this tank was a well-constructed wood-slat rack sized to receive the B-4 bag and barracks bag luggage of the entire crew. The luggage rack provided an efficient use of space by maintaining good weight and balance characteristics for the long trip.

We made a final inspection of Army B-25J 43-27661. I was supplied with the latest weather data, flight plans, and charts, and the all important sealed pouch containing our secret travel orders. I conferred with the ground crew who had already preflighted the engines, checked the Form 1 log for any recorded minor problems (and found none), then ordered the crew to board. I shook hands with the three ground technicians and thanked them for their good work, then climbed into the cockpit.

Joe Nuessle and I did a thorough cockpit check, reading from a printed checklist to avoid possible error. This was no time to become careless. The crew chief stood to one side of the plane, waiting for my signal to start the engines. I gave him the circular motion with my extended forefinger, and he answered with a thumbs-up all-clear motion. The engines each in turn sprang into life and the initial surge of power seemed to strain against the locked brakes and wheel chocks. I had the sensation that a jockey must have in the starting gate atop his eager steed.

I called the tower for a barometric pressure reading and adjusted the altimeter to show our pressure altitude. The tower gave me the takeoff runway number, and we were about ready to go. I called each crew member on the intercom for an individual readiness report and each responded, "Ready, Lieutenant." I gave a thumbs-up sign to the crew chief. He removed the chocks that were blocking the wheels, then stood off to one side. He came to rigid attention and delivered a very telling salute. He knew we were heading for the war zone, and his quiet formality seemed to shout out the desires of his heart: "Good luck, I wish you well, happy landings!" I returned his salute with equal respect. He smiled.

I released the brakes and eased out on to the taxi strip, then to the takeoff position of Runway 18, the 180-degree heading of the north-south runway. I revved the engines to check the drop of the magnetos, scanned the oil and hydraulic pressures, checked the cylinder-head temperatures, closed the cowl flaps, and lowered the wing flaps to 15 degrees. The tower radioed that I was cleared for takeoff.

The early light of May 1st, 1944, was just brimming the horizon. I released the brakes and gradually opened the throttles to 44 inches of manifold pressure as we began to roll. Our speed increased and I soon felt our wheels leave the runway. On signal, Joe raised the landing gear while I held the plane in level flight. I wanted to gain some extra flying speed before starting a climbing 360-degree turn over Homestead Field.

Satisfied that "661" was performing perfectly, I called the crew to take their last look at the "good old USA" for awhile. Continuing in our climb to the specified cruising altitude of 9,000 feet, I set our course for today's destination, Puerto Rico.

May 1st, 1944, was my "D-day" for that goal which I had set for myself 18½ months ago. Since that check-in day at Santa Ana on October 15th, 1942, I had been in a constant state of transition, a momentum building and ever so slowly rising in tempo from a complacent foot soldier to a highly trained and hopefully skilled airman tuned to the drums of war.

Was I ready? "God, I hope I am!" I prayed. "Please, dear God, watch over our loved ones and give them the courage to face these perilous times while we're away. And give me the strength and wisdom to see me through this day. Amen."

Chapter 19

"Our Purpose Defined"

"*PRECIOUS PRINCESS*? Who's that?" Copilot Joe Nuessle glanced at the flight log I had started in a stenographer's notebook that I kept in my open portfolio between our seats.

"You're riding in her, Joe. It's just a temporary name. Ruth and I saw a Cary Grant movie where he had named his boat *Precious Princess*, after his sweetheart."

I liked the name. In the early weeks of our marriage I called Ruth my "Precious Princess." If our plane got us where we were heading she really would be precious.

Joe laughed. "OK, but tell me, when're you going to open our orders to see where we're going?"

My instructions had been to open the papers after we had passed the point of no-return — some 2½ hours yet ahead of us. I told Joe I intend to go by the rules.

I called the crew on the intercom and gave them that same message. As their Commander, I felt they should know that I had orders that had to be obeyed just as I expected them to obey mine.

We were embarked on serious business now, flying over strange territory, endless open seas, and soon over some of the most dense jungle in the world. And this was the season for quick build-up of severe afternoon tropical storms, which meant we had to arrive at our daily destinations before 1:00 or 2:00 p.m. At the pre-dawn weather briefing at Homestead in Florida, we were adequately cautioned on this point and the treachery that these storms could produce. We had to be alert for any unforeseen circumstance.

It was a beautiful morning over the West Indies, and we could see the dim outline of distant islands on the horizon — Cuba on the right, the Florida Keys on the left. The *Princess* was performing perfectly. We were well past the Windward Passage, that point between the southern tip of Cuba and Haiti when I decided it was time to open the orders. I had Joe take the controls while I broke the seal and found the key words in the first paragraph: "Telergma, Algeria." At last we knew. We were going to fly combat in the Mediterranean Theater of Operations.

I was aware that the warfare in Europe was quite different from that in the Pacific. Bombing in Europe usually occurred at medium altitudes of 10,000 to 12,000 feet, and the targets were heavily defended by the infamous dual-purpose German 88-millimeter cannons that could be fired at both ground and aerial targets like tanks and planes. And in Europe, fighter opposition by the Messerschmitt 109 was as deadly as any in the world.

Pacific targets were said to be more strategic in nature. Bombing runs were often made at low level against Japanese airfields, fuel supply and ammunition dumps, bridges, shipping, and troop concentrations. Much of the Japanese defenses were from small-arms fire and smaller-sized cannons. Perhaps the greatest hazards were the long distances to be flown over ocean waters to engage the enemy and the shortage of emergency landing areas.

But I didn't know much about the Mediterranean area.

I called the crew on the intercom and told them we were going to Europe and would probably be based in the Mediterranean. Our reporting destination was the 2nd Bomb Training Wing at Telergma, Algeria, in North Africa, followed by assignment to a combat group. Everyone seemed pleased that we were not going to the Pacific.

The remainder of our flight to Puerto Rico was without incident. Scotty and his crew and several others took off from Florida within minutes of one another, and although we were in radio and occasional visual contact with them along the route, we did not fly in formation.

Five hours and twenty minutes after takeoff from Florida, we touched down at Borinquen Field, an elegant pre-war regular Army Air Corps facility. The control tower operator directed us to a transient aircraft parking area where we happily climbed down from our crew stations and stretched and exercised our stiff muscles.

Crew members had specific assignments, tasks to be performed at each stop on our journey. Engineer Caruth, assisted by armorer Scott would refuel the plane and check certain mechanical features and oil and hydraulic fluid levels, looking for any leaks.

Radio man Wheeler was charged with checking-in at the security desk our new classified portable automatic radio device designated as the IFF. The IFF — Identification Friend or Foe — sent out a signal to radar, enabling an aircraft to be identified. If there was no response from the IFF you assumed it was an enemy aircraft. The IFF was stored overnight in the security vault. The device was intended to secure password codes automatically from ground units to avoid accidental attack. And bombardier Lieutenant Robinson would check-in the new and still secret Norden Bomb Sight at the security desk for storage in the vault. Sabotage and the theft of classified material was still considered to be rampant throughout the world.

Copilot Lieutenant Nuessle meanwhile would inspect and check the work of the refueling men and record it in the flight log, designated as the "Form One."

During our training, I was frequently required to record the crew's names and serial numbers on various training documents. I had memorized each man's number and was able to fill in the papers at each stop along the way. While the men did their work, I signed them in, saving the time and nuisance of having to stand in line.

The Operations desks were always crowded with full crews waiting their turn. But my crew was among the first to get to the PX, the Officers Club, the NCO Club, or to stretch out for a rest. My men bragged on me to other crewmen. I never learned of another pilot who did this for his men, although any pilot could carry his crew's serial numbers on a slip of paper in his wallet and sign them all in.

The officers mess at Boringuen Field was beautiful, much like a hotel dining room, and the food was excellent. The enlisted members of the crew were well pleased with their facility. The big attraction was the PX, where cigarettes sold for 50 cents a carton, with a limit of one carton to each transit airman. High-quality liquors were also very reasonable. Ladies silk stockings were available, but not very cheap, about $8.50 per pair. Chanel No. 5 and Tabu perfumes were priced reasonably, causing us to wonder if it was the real thing. I did buy one pair of hose and perfume for Ruth, as well as a silver charm for the sterling bracelet I had given her for Christmas.

Leaving Boringuen Field at 6:00 a.m. on May 2nd, we ascended over the city of San Juan and leveled off at 9,000 feet on course to Atkinson Field, British Guiana. It was a beautiful clear morning, although we would encounter considerable cloud cover below for about two hours, just as we had on the previous day. Though we passed islands of the Lesser Antilles, most were obscured by the clouds. Our most significant check-point was Port of Spain, Trinidad.

We had flown past the overcast and fortunately the weather was clear over the rest of the route. I spotted Atkinson Field near Georgetown, received instructions from the tower, and made a smooth landing. Turning onto a taxiway near the end of the runway, I was surprised to find that the strip had been literally carved out of the jungle. The paving was narrow and the jungle growth had been cleared just a little more than was needed to allow the passage of the airplanes with the widest wing spans — the B-17s, B-24s, and C-54s. I concluded that this was a new taxiway to accommodate the increased wartime traffic.

Unlike the accommodations at Puerto Rico, at Atkinson we slept in tents with mosquito net suspended over each cot. We tucked the netting under the edge of the mattress, making us secure against the bite of "Annie" the malaria-bearing anopheles mosquito.

The crewmen had done their jobs, were well fed, and enjoyed swapping tales with the crews of the other planes. We had flown six hours and ten minutes from Puerto Rico to British Guiana. Following a good meal, I showered and shaved and was asleep before anyone turned out the lights.

We left Atkinson Field soon after dawn. A dense fog hung low over the jungle, though the field and flyway beyond the runway were clear. We were able to climb up to the recommended 9,000-foot altitude and set course for Belem, Brazil. It was May 3rd and the third day of our journey. The weather officer briefed us on conditions that we would encounter near the Amazon River. A heavy tropical front had moved in and extended out to sea on the east for about 150 miles. It also extended about the same distance to the west. The front was quite solid with a heavy accumulation of cumulonimbus clouds, better known as thunderheads. The weatherman felt we could find our way over the front between them, stay in the clear, and not exceed 10,000 feet.

The Amazon was still a hundred or more miles distant when I saw the outline of the weather front. As we approached that ominous cloud formation, I began a gradual climb to ever higher altitude. Joe and I searched for valleys between the billowing clouds that would provide a safe passage, but we had ascended to 16,000 feet without finding an opening. We were not equipped with oxygen, and I decided we had gone high enough and it was time to try another tack. I announced to the crew that I was turning back to descend over the mouth of the river and try for a route under the front.

At 500 feet above sea level I reached the bottom of the front and took up a compass heading for Belem. As we penetrated below the ceiling, we encountered some torrential thunderstorms. I zigzagged around them when I could, but by so doing I sometimes ran into a storm that I couldn't avoid and flew totally by instruments through the torrents. As we penetrated farther under the front, the ceiling forced us to fly as low as 300 feet.

On one occasion when we were on instruments in a thundershower at the 300-foot altitude, bombardier Robinson, who was riding in the "greenhouse" nose section, called me on the intercom and shouted, "Hey Stew, I think I just saw a dirigible."

"A dirigible? Robbie, what would a dirigible be doing down here under this stuff?" Nonetheless, Joe and I did a thorough scan of the area when we broke out of the shower. For the moment, I took Robbie seriously and had Joe call the Belem tower to learn if there was such a craft plotted or reported in the area. The tower reported none and was not aware of any such airships within several hundred miles. I decided that conditions were getting the better of Robbie and that his imagination was being fed by some strange-looking cloud formations.

We finally emerged from under the cloud bank into almost clear weather. Then, in the area of the Belem airfield, we encountered some rather large scattered cloud formations. I had climbed to 2,000 feet and called the Belem tower for landing instructions. The tower reported the clouds and told me that if I got caught in one to just circle for a few minutes and it would pass on out, and I could prepare to enter the pattern and land on runway 260.

Scanning the skies above me, I saw five or six thin clouds and could even see a B-25 circling in each one of them. The traffic pattern appeared to be clear. I dropped to 1,000 feet and turned onto the downwind leg, then onto the base leg. I called on the radio, "Belem tower, this is Army 661 turning on final approach."

"Roger, 661, you are clear to land, number one on final."

I wondered why those other planes were up so high and caught in clouds and concluded that somehow they had been able to find passage over the front and approached

Belem from a much higher altitude than I had. Again, we were early birds in the PX and the Officers Club. In spite of the delay caused by the change of altitude at the Amazon River, we completed this leg of our trip in 4 hours and 45 minutes.

Canvas cots and mosquito nets seemed to be standard from then on. The Belem facility was manned by American technicians but had native service people who spoke Portuguese. I bought a small, inexpensive English-Portuguese dictionary in the PX and tried to converse with one or two workers in the officers barracks. But it was almost impossible for us to make sense out of each other, though I had the feeling they understood me much better than I understood them.

When we reported for briefing in the early hours of May 4th, we were informed that a B-25 returning to the States from combat had crashed somewhere in the jungle between Belem and Natal and that all B-25s in our flight would be organized as a search team to try and locate the downed aircraft. A chart had been drawn with flight corridors, each one to be covered by a B-25. The planes would all fly the same heading on the true course to Natal and would space themselves one mile apart. This would provide a one-half-mile viewing area on either side of each plane. We were to fly at a minimum altitude for best viewing and would stay tuned to the Air/Sea Rescue radio frequency.

The low fog over the jungle forced us to fly at 300 to 400 feet, but it soon dissipated and we dropped about 100 feet. Within an hour the radio crackled and the plane to my right reported sighting the wreckage. He began to circle the area and kept the downed plane in sight until a fighter appeared to take up the vigil. A PBY-5 flying boat soon would come to drop emergency rations and medical supplies and would later be followed by a ground search party. The sighting plane then resumed his heading to Natal. He had reported that there were no signs of life around the crash site.

Our total flying time from Belem to Natal was 5 hours and 25 minutes. We were to remain at Natal for two nights to rest up for the long over-water trip to Ascension Island and to thoroughly check over the *Princess*. I spent about two hours with Caruth, Scott, and Wheeler going over the entire plane to be sure that everything was in top working order. The base mechanics did a 100-hour inspection even though less than 50 hours had been logged. The PX was well-stocked with gift-type merchandise, candy, cigarettes, and beer for consumption on the premises.

On May 5th, we were given a navigation briefing on the long Natal to Ascension flight. I had been concerned about the ability of Robinson and myself to navigate such a long distance over the South Atlantic. Neither of us had been trained, nor were we equipped, for celestial navigation. I did well at dead-reckoning and could probably succeed under normal weather conditions, but I couldn't believe that anything was ever normal over the ocean. I wondered how I could fly the plane, with Joe's help, and also concentrate on navigation.

But much to my relief, it was announced that those crews without a celestial navigator on board would follow a lead B-25 manned by an Air Transport Command crew. These fellows had made the flight many times, their crew consisting of pilot, copilot, engineer, and celestial navigator. Two or three B-25s were assigned to the very loose formation with the ATC plane leading. As soon as I could, I contacted my lead navigator and had him review his flight plan with me. He let me copy it into my *Princess* notebook, and I asked him to keep me informed of any changes he would make along the way. He would probably make wind-drift readings on the water as well as celestial sightings with the sextant.

Before going to bed that night I consulted our aerial chart and drew up my own dead-reckoning flight plan on a great circle route to Ascension. It matched the navigator's plan very closely. I was anxious to see how it would check out on the actual trip.

All was in order when I opened the throttles to 44 inches of mercury and a 2,600 rpm prop setting. Fuel/air mixture control was set at full rich, and flaps set at 30 degrees to add lift for the extra weight of the Tokyo Tank, now filled to capacity in the bomb bay. The weather was perfect, and everyone seemed eager to get on with the show.

My takeoff followed our ATC leader. Bob Merkel, a fellow Chicagoan and friend from cadets, from Mather, and from Greenville, followed me. Bob's plane was painted an olive-drab green, and mine and the leader's were polished aluminum. Bob had discovered that he could not maintain our 170 mph air speed with the same power settings we used and attributed the problem to the drag created by the rougher paint finish. His call letters were 067, and he and I had some fun calling and razzing each other occasionally. Because of his slower pace, I would call and request a "trailing weather report." I also told him I thought he had a lousy taste in colors. He in turn would tell me he was flying off to one side to avoid the clouds of smoke from my exhaust.

The flight had been virtually uneventful. We flew above an overcast for about three hours, which translated into instrument time and an opportunity to study wind-drift a few thousand feet below our 9,000-foot level.

Ascension Island was little more than a rock in the vastness of the ocean, 34 square miles in area. It could be compared to finding a needle in a haystack. We had flown about 1,600 miles with the help of favorable west to east winds and made a pass over the runway before circling around a small mountain of rock and dropping down into the traffic pattern at 1,000 feet.

We had been told at Natal that a hump was located near the center of the runway caused by the extreme hardness of the rock and the inability of the blasting crews and dynamite to get it level to meet the construction deadline. A two- or three-degree incline existed on the west end, while the same degree of decline was on the east end. As a result, when making a landing, the pilot's reference to the horizon was distorted and he might fail to pull back on the stick far enough, causing a hard landing. Or he could overcompensate and make a stalled landing too high above the surface and likewise hit rather hard.

I had mentally rehearsed this beforehand and visualized the amount of angle I would need to make a good landing. It was a matter of pride with most pilots that every landing they made should be as close to a "grease job" as possible.

The 7-hour, 35-minute flight over the vast South Atlantic came to an end when we touched down at Ascension Island. My landing wasn't perfect, but it was acceptable. I breathed a sigh of relief that the hardest leg of the trip was now a memory and that which lay ahead of us would be more routine. There was a big difference in aiming for and finding a tiny island in an endless ocean compared to making landfall on a huge continent.

Ascension Island was part of the British St. Helena colony, with very few inhabitants in its only settlement, Georgetown. It was more famous for its huge population of sooty terns, birds that had been dubbed with the name of Wideawake Birds. They posed a grave hazard when they flew up in massive numbers in front of bombers with noisy engines, such as the B-25 when taking off for the flight to Africa. It was perhaps the Air Transport Command personnel that unofficially named the place Wideawake Field. It was hard to imagine anyone living on Ascension Island permanently, and we wondered how long a tour of duty the ATC and ground service people could tolerate.

Gratefully, we took off in early morning of May 7th, but at the same time we were glad that the island was there and provided a way-station for planes with our limited range. It greatly facilitated the transport of aircraft and crews to the war zone.

With the constant flow of military planes going to and coming from Africa, the weather information supplied to the meteorologists at Ascension by the transient crews was current and accurate. We were instructed to fly under an equatorial front that would be evident at the equator soon after takeoff. The thick black clouds loomed before us, and I dropped down to 100 feet above the choppy seas without much ceiling clearance.

The drops of rain each seemed large enough to fill a tea cup as they transformed our windshield into a distorted viewing surface similar to the crinkled finish of a public bathroom window. B-25s, like most aircraft, were not equipped with windshield wipers as our speed of 150 to 200 mph would rapidly disburse the water into a rippled pattern and render wipers ineffective. Our windshield did have a small panel in its lower section that could be removed and by some strange airflow phenomenon would not admit rain into the cockpit. I had taken advantage of this feature a few times, viewing through it when making a landing in the rain. But our visibility was not now hampered sufficiently to use this option.

I was flying alternately between visual contact with the base of the clouds and water and on instruments. At 100 feet I realized this was only a shade more than the distance between homeplate and first base on a baseball diamond, and zero deviation from that altitude was an absolute must. I recalled my Greenville experience with thunderheads and had no desire for a repeat performance.

Five hours after leaving Ascension, the "dark continent" came into view and I was relieved to see that we were making landfall right on course at Roberts Field, Liberia, near the city of Monrovia. We did all our own navigating on this leg of the trip as our target was a huge continent and not a tiny island. Fifteen minutes after sighting Africa we touched down on the runway, which was clad with steel matting, and we had our first experience with the noise that the matting produced. It was a rather startling event, and I wondered if we had some sort of landing gear trouble. I had heard that if the matting was too loosely laid it could roll up in front of a plane's wheels high enough for the propellers to hit it. I cautiously applied the brakes and used all of the runway to slow down and turn onto the taxiway.

We were housed in screened-in huts with wood floors and wood wainscoting sides. The top cover was of canvas, like a tent. We slept on steel cots with mosquito netting and were quite comfortable. The facilities were manned by native boys, and I was amazed to see them carry large pottery-type water jugs on their heads. I looked out of our hut the next morning to see one of the boys, clad in a loose white shirt and white shorts, trot at a double-time speed down a walk, while balancing a large empty jug on his head. As his body swayed a little to the left, the jug swayed in the opposite direction, to his right and vice versa. He never missed a beat, never touched the jug with his hands; his rhythm and timing were perfectly coordinated, and he was very graceful.

When we returned from supper, the beat of drums was audible, and we thought it came from a gathering of natives across what we thought in the darkness to be a river. There was the glow of an open fire that shone through the trees and we guessed that they were performing a nightly dance ritual. Whatever the occasion, the drums, the sound of voices, and the fire's glow added to the intrigue. We did learn that Liberia was a republic and had been founded in 1822 by the American Colonization Society of Freed Slaves from the U.S. and that their chief language was English. Inland tribes were Moslem, whereas the coastal inhabitants were Christian. But our stay in Liberia was too short to learn very much about the tribes. As with all our stops on the trip, we were restricted to the bases and had no contact with natives other than base workers. The need to maintain security and avoid the potential for disease was strictly enforced.

Our next stop, on May 8th, was Dakar in Senegal, a territory of French West Africa. The air base was a very busy place as the four-engined B-17s and B-24s had sufficient range to fly direct from Natal and bypass Ascension Island.

Copilot Joe Nuessle had developed a slight ear infection and sought treatment by the local flight surgeon, causing us to stay two nights at Dakar. When we went for weather briefing on the morning of May 10th, I had a pleasant surprise. The weather officer who delivered the briefing was a redheaded fellow I had known in my class in high school, Lieutenant Charles Reilly. It was our first meeting since graduating from Hyde Park High in Chicago in 1938. A mutual friend of ours, Gregory Hedden, was also a weather officer somewhere in the China, Burma, India (CBI) Theater of Operations and with whom Charles had trained in meteorology. Small world!

Our flight on May 10th would take us through a hazardous mountain pass on our way to Marrakech. We would be traversing the northwestern edge of the Sahara Desert where sandstorms were in progress. Base maintenance had installed special filters in the carburetor air intakes on our engines as the storm-agitated sand could reach altitudes of 10,000 feet and higher. Robbie and I carefully planned our route and the time of our arrival in the mountain pass, which was in the Atlas Mountains near Marrakech. To make matters more intense, the weather through the pass was reported to be cloud-covered, and we were advised that flying on instruments might be required.

One of our check-points was Tindouf in Algeria, and as we passed over what I determined to be the edge of the city, I could barely see what looked like a French Foreign Legion fortress. We radioed our position, altitude, and heading to the ground station, which was acknowledged. The sandstorm was in full progress down there, and I wondered how anyone could tolerate those conditions for anything longer than a week at a time.

We landed at Marrakech after 6 hours and 25 minutes, and I was glad to stretch out for a rest before supper. This had been as trying a day as any. It probably wasn't as hazardous as I had taken it to be, but I felt a greater fatigue than I had experienced from Natal to Ascension.

Operations had told us that the air filters would be removed from our air intakes, and I asked Joe to be sure that this was done and to report the sand loading on the filters in the log. To say they were pretty tightly clogged was an understatement.

Marrakech was a famous and historic city and my interest was aroused when someone reported that a building we had passed as we were trucked into town from the airfield was the site of a recent war summit conference between Winston Churchill and President Roosevelt.

Day 11 dawned, and the end of our final flight lay 4 hours and 30 minutes to the northeast, the 2nd Bomb Training Wing at Telergma, Algeria. Telergma was just 30 miles south of Constantine, which was a few miles from the Mediterranean Sea. The weather was clear and the flight uneventful. Some exotic-sounding names were noted — Casablanca and Sidi-bel-Abbès the headquarters for the French Foreign Legion, which I had read about as a youth in the novel *Beau Geste*, and Oran and then Algiers, over which we flew on this final African leg — and now Telergma.

Immediately upon landing and while taxiing behind a jeep to a designated parking area, the tower operator instructed us to unload all of the personal belongings and equipment that had been assigned to us individually and to stand by. The jeep driver had me go with him to Operations where I signed in the crew and submitted my orders for processing. I was instructed to release the airplane to the wing and was given a receipt for it. We would be there for several days waiting for assignment to a wing in the combat zone. At that time I would be given another plane in which we would take to our new outfit and be assigned to an operational group and squadron.

A truck took me back to the plane to pick up the crew and all of our belongings. I had longed for a souvenir of the *Princess* and suddenly remembered the extra key that locked the lower access hatch. It was attached to a black plastic Bakelite tag with the plane's embossed serial number, and it was in my portfolio. In all my experience with B-25s or any other military plane, I never encountered a locked door or hatch, so I had no qualms about appropriating the extra key.

We were driven to "tent city" and unloaded our stuff into recently vacated tents. We were back to canvas cots, dirt floors, and mosquito nets. Nuessle, Robinson, and I wound up in the same tent with Scotty, Art Nomland, and Scotty's bombardier Jerry Rahatz. Six men to a tent was crowded, but we were only going to use them for sleeping and lounging around for a few days before heading for our permanent assignments.

A few ground school orientation classes were held to acquaint us with the region and the status of the war in the Mediterranean Theater. Sicily and most of the boot of Italy had been liberated, and the bomb line, that demarcation where the Allies were battling the Germans, was just south of Rome. The battle of the Anzio Beachhead still raged but was in its final days of German resistance. Army Air Forces bombing and fighter units were steadily on the move, advancing to new locations from which to launch their attacks against the enemy.

The German air force bombing activity seemed to be dying a slow death in the Mediterranean area. Its last major air offensive in this theater was reported on May 14th. The Luftwaffe had launched a devastating attack on one of our bomber bases on the 13th, destroying many planes and killing and wounding many of our men, mostly ground crews. The unit that received the brunt of the attack was not identified nor was its location announced.

On May 15th, Scotty and I rode the 30 miles in the back of an Army truck into the city of Constantine, Algeria. It was our first time to linger among a civilian population since we left Florida, and it was quite a rare experience. We walked up and down the narrow, dirty, smelly streets, took note of the Arab, French, and Jewish populace, and just monkeyed around in general. We went to the Army PX and bought all that our ration cards allowed. I purchased six packs of cigarettes, eight cigars, a tube each of toothpaste and shaving cream, two packs of gum, four candy bars, and two magazines. The magazines were almost a month old.

Leaving the PX, we walked down the street and looked into the window of a leather goods shop. We saw some leather wallets we wanted and were about to enter the shop when the French proprietor came to the door and handed me a piece of paper with some English words written on it: "Why do you boys sell your candy and tobacco to the Arabs? We can't get those things for our children."

We went inside and laid some candy, gum, toothpaste, a pack of cigarettes, and a cigar on the counter. Then Scotty and I each selected some wallets we wanted. Their cost totaled 470 francs ($9.40). In my best French (which proved to be pretty bad) I proceeded to make a deal. I asked the merchant how much he would give us for the candy, etc. He totaled it to 135 francs or $2.70 (it had cost us about 35 cents). I subtracted that from the total amount of our purchase and gave him 335 francs or $6.70. It wasn't what could be called a wonderful bargain, but the two wallets I got were very nice.

An English movie called *The Lady Vanishes*, with Paul Lucas, was next on our agenda — it was just fair.

Later on we met Nomland, Nuessle, and Rahatz and they related their tales of the day. We also attempted to converse with two soldiers of the Free French Army, but that was a failure. I wished I could have spoken the language, as it might have been interesting to talk with the natives. The few universal sentences I had learned in the Sunday evening sessions my Dad had held for us and some of our neighbors years ago helped, as the others knew not a word. But I found myself mixing French with the little Portuguese I had picked up in Brazil and decided my efforts to be a total failure.

Scotty and I were getting quite hungry around 8:00 p.m., so we took a taxi to an Army-operated cafe. They had finished serving, but the mess Sergeant got the Italian prisoner-cook to whip up some pork chops, corn, and coffee. It was an excellent meal, if not stylish or elaborate.

We hailed an Army truck that was heading back to the base and climbed aboard for the dirt-road trip, braking in our tent area in a huge cloud of Algerian dust. We were in bed by 11:00.

Reflecting on our day in Constantine, we observed that it was very dirty, the children were dirty, and very poor. About ten times each hour the kids asked us if we wanted a good chicken dinner. We didn't accept any of their invitations, though it was reported that the food was generally good and clean. They charged $3.00 per person.

We had noted how American Army goods wound up in civilian hands. Many Arabs wore white robes made from GI mattress covers and the funniest sight was that of a teen-age French boy being chased by other boys. He had cut holes for his legs in a GI blue denim barracks bag and tied the draw-strings about his waist. He wore no hat or shoes, the bag being his only garment. We speculated on his process for bladder relief and decided it had to be almost total exposure. Their resourcefulness was to be admired.

But perhaps the most startling of all were the young boys who constantly approached us, soliciting for their sisters. "Hey Joe, you want to meet my sister? She's pretty, Joe. Come on Joe, you like my sister." Of course their vocabulary was much more vivid than that.

We were all awake and hungry early in the morning. Soon after breakfast word came that we were to leave Telergma the next day, May 17th. Another B-25 was consigned to me, and I gathered the crew to check it out, to be sure that it was complete. I reviewed the Form One to see if there were any mechanical problems recorded. Whatever outfit to which I would be assigned, I wanted to be sure the aircraft was ready for the severe service it was to receive. All appeared in good order.

Later in the day, eight pilots were issued orders to report with their crews on or about May 16th to the 57th Bomb Wing. The location of the wing was not named in the order, as that would be a breach of security. We were told verbally that the 57th Headquarters was located at Ghisonaccia, on the island of Corsica, and that two B-25 groups were also located at the same base, the 310th and the 321st. We would check in at 57th Headquarters for assignments to groups in greatest need of replacements. I noted on the orders that Scotty was the only one I knew of the pilots. Again, I thought how strange it was that he and I continued to be together, with the exception of Advanced Flight School, on the same sets of orders or assignment to the same outfits since our first encounter at Santa Ana on October 15th, 1942.

When we lifted off from the Telergma runway in early afternoon on May 17th, every member of the crew was in good spirits. After almost a week of limited activity in the gritty atmosphere of North Africa, aggravated by the uncertainty of our combat assignment and the reported aggressiveness of the German air force bombing activity against Allied air bases, we were ready to get on with the purpose for which we had come. We climbed out over the blue Mediterranean in crystal-clear weather on a compass heading of almost due north.

It was a beautiful and easy flight from Telergma to Corsica. I routed the plane along the west coast of Sardinia, angled northeast over the Strait of Bonifacio to the east side of Corsica, and closed the remaining 40 miles to Ghisonaccia. If anyone was watching, I wanted to be sure to make a slick landing. While I was taxiing to the parking area, the tower operator answered my questions and told me where to report.

The Adjutant in 57th Headquarters said I was to go to the 340th Bomb Group, about 30 miles north. He recorded my name and checked off our crew on a copy of the orders. Scotty and his crew had been following close behind me, and they too were assigned to the 340th.

It was somewhere in this process that we learned that it was the 340th Bomb Group that had been bombed and strafed by the Germans four days before and suffered such great loss of aircraft and personnel. Now we could understand why the 340th needed so many replacements

My waiting crew climbed back into their positions, and we flew to the 340th at Alesan, about mid-point of the island. The group Operations Officer checked his manpower schedule and told me we were assigned to the 489th Bomb Squadron, as their current needs were the greatest. He told us to unload the plane of all personal belongings and that a truck from the 340th would soon take us the short distance up the road to the 489th Squadron area. Scotty and his crew were assigned to the 486th Bomb Squadron.

When I was told I was going to the 340th, I could hardly believe it as that was the group that my old friend Bob Saxton was in. Then when they put me in the 489th Squadron, I decided that the miracle of all miracles had occurred, as that was Bob's squadron. And now, waiting for the truck to haul us up to the tent city of the 489th, could it be that I was about to have a reunion with the one who had guided me through cadets and recommended that I go for B-25s? This was the same Bob Saxton that was part of that small band of high school friends hung together for three years after graduation until the war quickly dispersed us.

The truck came and we were soon deposited in front of the Headquarters tent of Major Alexander Parrish, Squadron Commander. I was anticipating a formal meeting with the exchange of salutes when the Major left a group of men with whom he had been talking, walked over to me, and said he was "Parrish, the Squadron Commander," and shook hands with me. I gave him my name, handed him our orders, and said we were glad to be in his squadron. With a grin, he said he wondered how glad we would be if we had anymore raids like the one they had a few nights before.

He added, "We sure need good men Stewart, and I hope you're as good as you look." He allowed that we didn't need any pep talks right then and suggested he get us all "a sack."

Someone directed the enlisted men to their area. Joe Nuessle who was a very thin Texan soon paired up with another newcomer, a big guy with a long twisted mustache named Ned Heilig, and they shared a two-man tent. Seen together, they soon earned the nicknames of Texas Slim and Dirty Dalton. Herb Robinson found a vacancy in a four-man tent and was welcomed in by its bombardier occupants.

I finally had the opportunity to inquire about Bob Saxton. He was over in Italy that day, and someone suggested I use his sack that night because he wouldn't be back until the next day. I walked over to Bob's tent and found a pilot named Ray Fitzgerald stretched out on his bunk, reading a magazine. I introduced myself, told him of my friendship with Bob, and asked when he would return.

Fitz was very friendly and invited me to sit down. He told me how Bob had blacked out when he was coming in for a landing from a mission, and the copilot had to land the plane. Physical exams showed that Bob had some sort of kidney ailment or injury that had caused the blackout problem and that he had been recommended by the squadron and group flight surgeons for rotation back to the States. Bob was now in Italy for appearance before the 12th Air Force Medical Disposition Board for evaluation and possible concurrence with Doc Nestor and Doc Brussells.

Ray also suggested I use Bob's sack and that some other arrangement could be made in the morning, should Bob be sent home, I could take his place in the tent, if the other guys approved.

At bedtime, I crawled into Bob's sleeping bag and lay there in the dark, retracing the events that had brought me to this time and place, to the very bed of my friend and some-time Army Air Forces mentor, destined perhaps to be his replacement in this damning but demanding war. It almost seemed like I was being groomed all these months for this singular purpose. The timing was incredible, to arrive here almost on the very eve of his health-induced departure.

The task ahead could and probably would be intimidating, but my resolve, at least for the moment, was dauntless!

Chapter 20

War Zone Reality
Corsica

RAY FITZGERALD THOUGHT I WAS still asleep. He grasped my left shoulder and rocked me back and forth, announcing in his Fall River, Massachusetts, accent the opportunity for a "medal-of-honor" breakfast.

"I'm awake," I growled, as I rolled over within the limitations of the old-style canvas sleeping bag with snaps (no zipper) and faced a pair of knobby knees on hairy legs that disappeared inside his olive-drab undershorts with the parachute seat.

"I was told that on the first day in a combat outfit I would be served breakfast in bed. Where's my eggs Benedict, Ray, and my champagne and orange juice?"

"Room Service is short of help today so you'll have to chow-down in the main dining room. Get dressed and wear a hat to cover that rag-mop head of yours. Say nothing about my legs, and I'll show you how to get the best in French cuisine," Ray ordered in his distinctive brogue. I wondered how many accents were spoken in Massachusetts.

Ray was a handsome, dark-haired Irishman with heavy eyebrows shading deep blue eyes. He laughed with his eyes, the wrinkles merging with his full, but not fat, face. He was always pleasant and had a ready comeback for any derisive remarks aimed at him in fun. He was a little shorter in stature than many, but well built and presented himself with an attitude of confidence. He was nearing the end of his tour of duty and anticipating a return to the States.

Yesterday's clothes were on a wire coat hanger where I had looped them through a tie-up tape on the side of the tent. I was dressed but still unbuttoned when I doused my face and swished my hair in cold water that I had poured from a GI can into an inverted steel helmet. The helmet was set into one of five sawed holes in boards salvaged from fragmentation bomb crates and crudely built into a long narrow wash stand, residing in a tarp-sheltered, dirt-floored entrance porch. A narrow shelf and back-bar board spanned the length of the wash stand and held toothbrushes and shaving mirrors. I decided these guys were not carpenters, but they were resourceful and inventive, and each tent occupant had his own helmet-labeled territory. I used Bob's.

"The guy that empties the water can has to refill it at the water wagon over there by the medic's tent." Ray pointed across the road.

I tied my shoes then took off with Ray to the mess tent, buttoning my shirt and zipping my pants as we walked.

Breakfast was not very exciting — a couple of pancakes, some watered-down syrup, watery scrambled eggs made from the dehydrated variety, and nondescript coffee. But hunger in the Army, and especially in the war zone, allowed for many concessions to food quality and preparation. I came away from my first morning meal on Corsica satisfied, though not enthralled. I'd had worse!

Ray was scheduled for a mission to destroy a railroad bridge at Viareggio, Italy, and told me he had to go "do batt'l with the Hun." I had not been contacted by anyone, and assumed I was free to get oriented to the outfit and learn the ropes. I saw no bulletin-board notice for me, but did see others of my crew busy getting settled in their respective areas. I picked up some equipment at the supply tent — a .45-caliber automatic pistol, bullets, coverall-type flying suit, fleece-lined leather jacket, pants, cap, and fleece-lined zippered boots. B-25s were no longer equipped with heaters, like earlier models, and temperatures at bombing altitudes often went to zero or below.

In the early afternoon I was in the orderly room tent talking with the squadron clerk when I looked out through the open flap and saw the unmistakable American Indian-like straight-footed stride of Bob Saxton walking up the road toward the tent. He had apparently just returned from Italy.

I walked up behind him and in a commanding tone asked, "Hey, fella, where the hell do you think you're going?"

Bob wheeled around, speechless for a moment, then broke into a huge grin.

We shook hands. We might have even exchanged a hug. We hadn't seen each another in over 2½ years. What a strange twist of fate it was to meet like this, in a USAAF combat outfit in a foreign land.

"From what I've heard, I guess I'm here to take over your sack. Man, you're a sight for sore eyes. Who'd ever have thought we'd wind up like this? Who will ever believe it?"

Bob said, "All I know, Al, is that I'm through with combat. They're sending me back to the States."

We walked over to his tent and I sat down on his cot. Bob found a bottle of bourbon in his footlocker and decided we needed to toast this crazy occasion. I found my canteen cup

Alex Stewart reunited with his high school friend, Bob Saxton, on Corsica, May 1944.

in the bottom of my newly acquired barracks bag, which was full of the equipment I had been issued in the morning. His cup was hanging on a nail over the wash stand just outside the tent.

Bob poured a generous portion of bourbon in each of our cups and offered it "straight or with a splash of water and no ice."

I opted for the water and because our canteens were empty, I helped him struggle with the five-gallon GI can, to anoint the spirits with just an ounce or two.

"Here's to old times, Al, and to your good luck here. Damn, I sure wish I was staying so we could fly together!"

We drank to his health, then toasted the other guys in our high school bunch, all of whom were now in the service — Jack Diehl, with poor eyesight, instructing in radio at Sioux Falls, South Dakota; Larry McBrearty working in personnel at Enid Army Air Field in Oklahoma; Dick Gentzler, in spite of poor eyesight in England, and soon to be serving as a combat engineer with Patton's Third Army in France and Germany; and Hale (Swede) Huddleston with Army Air Forces communications in Georgia.

With a swallow of bourbon for one another and for each of our old friends, we were ready for a refill. Bob then launched into the details of his experiences that were now forcing his return to the "zone of the interior."

He told me that the 340th Bomb Group recently had started experimentation with flying low-level bombing missions aimed at targets in Yugoslavia, Bulgaria, and Greece. The low-level approach was designed to avoid radar detection by the enemy and achieve surprise attacks on German-held airfields and ammunition and fuel dumps. The B-25s were manned by volunteer crew members and especially by pilots with low-level skills and experience.

Bob had been assigned to the number "3" position on a low-level mission to Greece. Our dirt runway was equipped with steel-mesh mats, each about 24 inches wide by 12 feet long, linked together to provide a surface suitable for takeoff and landing operations in all kinds of weather. With 4,000 pounds of bombs and a full load of 100-octane gasoline, he had taxied into takeoff position.

When his turn came, he had opened the throttles and was soon nearing the point of liftoff, about 100 mph, when the left tire of the main gear became entangled with the sharp edge of a stray steel mat. The mat curled up in front of the tire, shredding it and causing a blow-out. The plane veered hard to the left, and the wheel, minus the tire, hit a culvert. The impact was so severe that the plane literally did a cartwheel.

The left wing dipped and hit the ground, followed by the nose, then the right wing and engine, the fuselage, and the tail assembly. Finally the entire plane slid backwards about 100 feet along the side of the runway before stopping. It was totaled.

Bob suffered a severe wrenching of his back. The crew scrambled out through the escape hatches as fast as they could, for fear of fire or an explosion, but fortunately none happened. No one else was hurt.

The doctors checked him over, and after a few days rest, Bob was feeling pretty good and returned to flying status. On his next mission, however, he blacked out when they were coming in for the landing. His copilot grabbed the controls and landed the plane.

This time the doctors ran some tests and x-rays and determined he had an injury to one of his kidneys. There wasn't adequate equipment or testing facilities there in Corsica, or in Italy, so Docs Nestor and Brussell agreed that Bob should be sent back to the States for treatment. They had scheduled the appearance before the Medical Disposition Board at 12th Air Force Headquarters in Italy and the Board concurred with their findings and recommendations.

"So, here I am," Bob added. "I've flown 39 missions and was ready to go to 50 or 60. I guess my combat days are over."

Bob was a capable and respected pilot and the others knew he regretted not being able to complete his tour of combat duty. It was one thing to be disabled by enemy action, still another to be sidelined by the failure of an inanimate piece of ordnance. I reflected on my own potential for disaster, remembering the time when I almost lost a propeller at Yuma, Arizona.

Ray Fitzgerald, Bob's tent mate, returned from his mission and reported that our bombing had destroyed the large railroad bridge at Viareggio, though the Huns didn't give it up willingly. The flak was heavy and accurate and "we got a bunch of holes," Ray noted.

The three of us walked up to the officers mess tent for what turned out to be a less than satisfying supper. Bob and Ray explained that the quality and preparation of the food varied with its source. Currently, it was reportedly being supplied by the British, which usually included an abundance of "bully-beef," similar in form but inferior in taste and quality to that of American canned corned-beef.

I learned that quite often the cooks would resort to the American Army C-Rations, which included C-Ration stew, C-Ration hash, and C-Ration chili. The C-Rations also contained American-style cheese, which was packaged in cans with key-operated openers similar to those on sardine containers. It wasn't unusual to open a can that had been packed and sealed in Australia. And last but not least on our menus was the ever-present supply of Vienna Sausage, which required a real fit of hunger to consume with any degree of relish, and accompanied by soda crackers.

Eggs, milk, potatoes, lemons, and a few other items came in the dehydrated powdered form, which took some getting used to. Lemon powder mixed with water became the standard for mixed drinks and for lemonade. The bartender at the Officers Club would offer gin and juice, cognac and juice, or cherry-brandy and juice. The gin, cognac, and brandy were made and purchased in Italy. On rare occasion, American and British spirits were available in very limited quantities and would usually be consumed in one late afternoon by ground officers and fliers who were not on a mission, before those who were out on a mission came home.

Bread came in large, heavy loaves and was said to come from a central Army bakery in Bastia, the main city at the north end of Corsica. The facility supplied all of our military units on the island.

Green beans, peas, carrots, beets, pork and beans, sliced peaches, and sliced pineapple came in large cans and were prepared and served with little or no imagination, but then this was wartime. Quite often a B-25 courier plane was sent to Catania, Sicily, for a supply of fresh tomatoes, cucumbers, onions, and what were supposed to be fresh eggs. Everyone in the mess hall knew by the odor when a bad egg hit the hot griddle, and that was perhaps 10 to 15 percent of the time. The odor from the bad eggs caused us to be suspicious of the freshness of the whole shipment.

American cigarettes brought premium prices in Italy and Sicily and often were traded for the fresh foods. The pilots who flew the courier would collect one or two barracks bags full of cigarettes from all the men who had a surplus and were willing to part with them and use them for bartering.

On other rare occasions we would have grilled steaks and fried chicken. We guessed that somebody had made a deal with the U.S. Navy, trading a few captured enemy rifles or pistols for a cargo-net load of fresh provisions. (My brother Ray reported that one Japanese sword would buy at least one cargo-net load from the Navy shipboard refrigerators.)

Suffice it to say that we had enough food for proper nourishment, but I don't think anyone ever gained any weight and many of us lost several pounds.

Back in the tent, Bob and I continued to reminisce about our days before the war and again further reduced Bob's limited supply of bourbon. I had noticed the small, steel, pot-bellied stove in the middle of the tent and learned that 100-octane aviation gasoline was used for fuel. The 80-octane truck gas was not to be used, as its supply was limited.

The gasoline was contained in a five-gallon GI can mounted on a steel bomb-fin shipping crate outside at the back of the tent. A copper tube piped the fuel under the floor from the can to the ash-pit door of the stove. A hand valve controlled the flow of gas, allowing it to drip into a small pile of sand in the bottom of the stove. The sand dispersed the gas and created a very satisfactory burning surface.

Unfortunately, this was not a very efficient use of the fuel, and a considerable deposit of soot accumulated in the makeshift stovepipe. For some reason, stovepipes were not shipped overseas with the stoves, thus causing GI ingenuity to come into play. The fuses for our bombs were shipped in long metal cans, similar to those used for tennis balls, but a little smaller in diameter. A hand-operated can opener or tin snips were used to remove the bottom of the can, converting it to a pipe section about 14 inches long. About ten sections were then dove-tailed together to form a pipe long enough to carry the fumes out through the top opening of the tent.

About every third or fourth day the build-up of soot necessitated removal of the pipe for cleaning. Again, ingenuity came into play. Bob showed me how to use some tall weeds growing on the railroad embankment behind the tent as pipe cleaners. It was a simple, but dirty, job to run the pipe sections up and down on the weeds; the heavy foliage did a credible job of removing the soot. Rain would inevitably wash the soot from the weeds and keep us provided with clean pipe-cleaning implements.

Bob explained that the stove did a good job of heating the tent as well as heating water in a #10 fruit can for shaving. But best of all, it worked great for toasting cheese sandwiches for an evening snack.

"What are we waiting for," I said. "That supper we had is only a memory."

"Come with me," Bob commanded. "I'll teach you the ropes of after-hours requisition."

I followed him out of the tent and we walked up the hill to the mess tent kitchen. Bob knew where to find a loaf of bread, a pound of GI butter (a rather off-white color that seemed to be mixed with lard but tasted okay), and a can of cheese.

Back in the tent we fired up the stove, sliced the bread and cheese, and toasted one side of the bread while it lay on a crudely bent wire coat-hanger grille. Then we slathered the bread with butter, layered it with cheese, and finished the toasting process. Meanwhile, Ray had boiled water and brewed some coffee in a can. He poured it into our cups through a clean rag to strain out the grounds. Sugar was stored in a round pipe tobacco can, because it had a tight-fitting lid.

The "coffee strainer" was one of Ray's handkerchiefs, which he had donated to the cause. He rinsed it out and sterilized it in boiling water before hanging it up to dry. "Use it on your nose and you're through," he cautioned in an ascending version of his Kilarny tenor.

The cheese sandwiches and coffee were excellent supplements to the evening meal, and I saw possibilities for improvement if I could get Ruth to send me some non-perishable provisions.

One of the other occupants of the tent was on rest leave on the Isle of Capri, so I was able to use his cot until Bob left for the States. The bourbon and the sandwiches finally took their toll on the conversation, which was being replaced with yawns and drooping eyelids. We turned off the one dim, flickering, under-powered 100-watt light and the stove, and in a few moments the tent echoed with a harmony of snores.

Due to a head cold, I had not yet been scheduled to fly my first mission. This afforded me several days of extra time to spend with Bob while he awaited official orders to go home. His orders finally came through on Monday, May 22nd, and one of our courier planes took him to Naples where he would wait several days before boarding a ship for America. I hated to have him leave, but was glad he would get medical attention. He departed with a list of items he promised to convey to Ruth. I knew it would be a comfort to her to receive a firsthand report from Bob.

On May 24th, I was released by Doc Nestor for flying duty and copiloted for Ray Fitzgerald on a trip to Catania, Sicily, to get vegetables and eggs. We collected two barracks bags full of surplus cigarettes from the men and were able to make good trades for enough stuff to fill the rack adapted to the bomb bay. We assumed that the cigarettes landed on the black market and brought in excess of $20 per carton. Ray and I did our job and returned to Corsica.

The Operations Officer wasted no time in taking advantage of my flying status and scheduled me for my first mission for the next day, Thursday, May 25th. I saw my name posted on the bulletin board of a combat bomb squadron for the first time, 15 months and 9 days after my first flight in an airplane.

I listened to exaggerated accounts of combat by some pilots with a few missions, and I had been told by Bob to ignore them. "They're playing games, trying to scare you." I knew I would soon make my own judgment of combat, and I felt ready to face whatever fury it imposed on me.

The U.S. 12th Tactical Air Force, operating in the Mediterranean Theater, was made up of four twin-engine bomber groups — three B-25 and one B-26 — with the main purpose of interrupting and/or destroying the enemy's means of waging war. Our targets included road and railroad bridges, road blocks, tunnels, viaducts and marshaling yards, fuel and ammunition supply dumps, airfields and aircraft, power generating and transmission stations, troop concentrations, shore batteries, anti-aircraft gun positions, landslides created to block roads and railroads, and enemy shipping in harbors and on the sea.

Several P-47 fighter-bomber groups went after trains, their engines and freight cars, and the destruction of track — known as "post-holing," troop formations, truck convoys, and other targets. They also escorted bombers to ward off enemy fighters and engaged them in combat.

The 12th Air Force Service Command secured and supplied weather data, enemy movement, target data, and Intelligence information relative to the movement and progress of the war.

The U.S. 15th Strategic Air Force, operating out of bases in the Mediterranean Theater, was made up of the large, four-engine long-range bombers — B-24 Liberators and the B-17 Flying Fortresses. They ranged far and wide in the bombing of enemy factories and other strategic targets in Italy, France, Austria, Germany, and especially the Ploesti Oil Fields in Rumania.

The 15th also enjoyed the support of P-47 Thunderbolt ("the Jug") and P-51 Mustang fighters. Most of the unit's targets were bombed from altitudes above 20,000 feet, and with oxygen supplied at each crew station in the B-24 and B-17, the men could function for extended periods in the rarefied atmosphere. The German flak was not as accurate or as deadly against them, but the Messerschmidt 109 and Focke-Wulf 190 fighters took a considerable toll on the 15th Air Force bombers.

Prior to the German bombing of the 340th Bomb Group installation on Corsica on May 13, 1944, just before I had arrived, the German Luftwaffe was active in the Mediterranean area. But the raid on Corsica was its last major air offensive in our region.

Regardless of the wild combat stories told by the fun-seeking alarmists, I told myself that combat was not going to be a picnic, but as it turned out I was woefully unprepared for what the morrow had in store for me.

As with all the other flying personnel in the squadron, I checked the bulletin board, which was mounted on a wood framework and capped with a wide overhanging roof to protect it from wind and rain. I noted my name listed as copilot and recorded the names and positions of the other crew members in a small pocket notebook. The plane number and our position in the formation was also detailed, as well as the bomb load to be carried in each plane and the time set for the briefing session, which would be attended by all crew members.

The schedule was signed by the Assistant Operations Officer, First Lieutenant Jack Mair of Santa Ana, California. Jack was a cordial fellow with a subtle, dry, and quick wit, often laughing at his fumbled pronunciation of a difficult name at roll call.

MISSION #1

489th Bombardment Squadron (M) AAF

340th Bombardment Group (M) AAF

Stand Down Until Noon   APO 650 c/o Postmaster,
                                                         New York City, New York,

(Briefing—-1545)   25 May 1944

	101 9K	
	P. Haster,E.J.	
	CP. Parrish,A.H.	
	N. Hastings,J.F.	
041 9A	B. Scofield,F.W.	517 9L
P. Howard,W.L.	R. Vincent,T.R.	P. Crittenden,G.L
CP. Clinch,C.A.	G. Vance,C.L.	CP. Brassfield,W.H.
B. Bird,R.C.	TG. Brisudis,J.O.	B. Claussen,K.E.
R. Saxton,R.O.		R. Hunt,R.V.
G. Simpson,J.C.		G. Davis,H.D.
TG. Brown,C.H.		TG. Precoskey,L.F.

```
                              717 9H
                           P. Mitchell,J.L.
                           CP. Roesler,E.H.
       655 9M               B. Hollingsworth,W.B.        045 9T
   P. Stallone,M.J.         R. Winjum,H.E.           P. Hamilton,V.
   CP. Convis,W.D.          G. Hertel,R.L.           CP. Voss,F.R.
   B. Vargo,P.              TG. Frank,D.A.           B. Moerbe,W.V.
   R. Constantine,T.C.                               R. Hutton,H.A.
   G. Wakeland,R.F.                                  G. Carter,C.A.
   TG. Mallicoat,D.E.                                TG. Kelnhofer,H.J.


                              705 9H
                           P. Bowden,T.B.
                           CP. Keljik,V.
       516 9C               B. Turner,J.M.               485 9H
   P. Ellin,R.L.            N. O'Connell,W.F.         P. Robison,C.A.
   CP. King,G.B.            R. Bragg,C.K.            CP. Mullaney,V.E.
   B. Vargo,P.              G. Little,E.A.           B. Harper,F.G.
   R. Yocco,H.E.            TG. Galick,V.P.          R. Cooper,E.J.
   G. Wright,C.W.                                    G. Miller,R.N.
   TG. Scott,R.L.                                    TG. Fetherston,H.J.


                              659 9W
                           P. Insley,L.E.
                           CP. Bleimes,G.
       080 9S               B. Meridith,J.W.             687 9Z
   P. Montgomery,J.         R. Nicoli,J.A.           P. Thomas,B.
   CP. Stewart,A.C.         G. Renfro,D.P.           CP. Swanson,F.O.
   B. Nash,W.M.             TG. Suskind,P.           B. Brent,F.
   R. Harris,H.A.                                    R. Buchanen,J.J.
   G. Vaudry,F.A.                                    G. Pherson,F.D.
   TG. Shine,D.V.                                    TG. Williamson,W.F.


                              Stand By
                           P. Jones,A.S.
                           CP. McLain,J.L.
   Bomb Load               B. Ream,E.
   4-1,000 with            R. Wright,G.K.            Jack G. Mair
   1/10 nose-.025 T.       G. Bruegl,H.J.            1st Lt., Air Corps,
                           TG. Lewis,A.              Asst.Operations Off.
```

The mission schedule was made up to describe the position of each plane in the formation. The lead plane and its crew were centered at the top of the page while the wing planes were to the right and to the left and slightly below the leader. Each group of six planes formed a box and each box had a flight leader. Each "Vee" of three planes was termed an element. The six positions in each box were numbered:

```
                    # 1
         # 3              # 2

                    # 4
         # 6              # 5
```

The schedule posted on the bulletin board called for an afternoon mission with briefing time set at 1545 (3:45 p.m.). Those who were to fly the mission assembled in required attire and sat in the trucks at 1500 hours for roll call by the Operations Officer. The men answered with a variety of grunts, groans, and incompatible expletives attached to the words "here, present, and yeah." I had taken a place on the bench next to Russell Scott, the tail gunner on my crew. This was to be his second mission — and Mission #1 for me. None of the others of our crew were listed. Russell was flying with pilot Richard Ellin in 9C, the plane immediately in front of mine.

Our rough ride in the back of an Army 6x6 dodging some of the potholes in the gravel road soon ended in front of the quonset-type briefing building near group Headquarters. Inside the cramped room we sat on the ever-present supply of steel bomb-fin shipping crates, facing a platform where details of the mission would be described by several officers.

A large aerial chart mounted on an easel displayed the topography of the target area and the chart projection coordinates. Colored pins identified key enemy gun emplacements and a narrow red tape showed the flight corridor to be followed by our bombers in a plan to minimize exposure to the anti-aircraft shell bursts. The gun emplacements were determined by photos taken that morning or the previous afternoon by high-flying P-38 photo-reconnaissance planes, usually referred to as photo-recce's.

Weather data, direction of break off the target after bombs-away, fighter escort coverage, Air/Sea Rescue radio frequencies, mission leader and "wounded aboard" coded call signs, emergency airfield landing sites, and other items of general information were announced. Details pertinent to the actual target sighting, bombing, and navigation were given to the lead plane officers in a pre-briefing.

The last act was a time-hack, where everyone coordinated the time down to the second on their government-issue wristwatches. Then the group Commander, Colonel Willis Chapman, delivered a short pep-talk, wished us good luck, and told us to come back with a victory.

We filed out of the briefing room and piled into the trucks for delivery to our planes at the airfield dispersal area. As the truck stopped at plane #9-S, I wished good luck to Russell Scott and the six of our crew jumped down and proceeded with our assigned preflight checks. We all teamed together, three men on each propeller to "pull them through" to disburse any oil that migrated to the bottom cylinders of the inactive radial engines.

On board, the pilot, John (Jack) Montgomery of West Fargo, North Dakota, started the engines and positioned the plane to fall in line behind #9Z, piloted by Baxter Thomas

B-25s in loose "box" formation over Corsica, 1944. The front three planes were the "lead element," the rear three planes the "second element."

of South Pasadena, California, when he passed our revetment. Jack wheeled onto the taxi-strip and soon joined in the line-up stacking back from the takeoff position at the head of the runway.

The B-25s were taking off at 20-second intervals, alternating the use of each side of the runway to minimize encounter with the prop-wash from the preceding plane. The cross-wind was light and the prop-wash was slow in clearing, causing the next plane to get into its grip, dipping a wing, and creating a struggle for its pilot to temporarily maintain level flight.

We followed the join-up procedure, turning inside the leader to gain our position in the formation. All 12 planes together, we climbed on course toward the target, a railroad bridge 2½ miles southwest of Ficulle, Italy, near the city of Perugia and about one hour of flying time from our air base.

I looked straight down as we crossed the shoreline, the beautiful blue Mediterranean gently washing beaches here and rinsing rock abutments there. We were entering enemy territory, unwelcome intruders come to reclaim an ancient land for its rightful and historic owners, seeking peace by unpeaceful means.

"Dear God," I silently prayed, "Please give me the strength and wisdom to see me through this day."

The Apennine Mountains, with some peaks reaching over 9,000 feet, formed a back-drop for the tranquil scene of the Italian "boot" as viewed from our point of observation at 12,000 feet. Concentration on the job of flying in tight formation occupied Jack, while I kept my head on a constant swivel in search of enemy fighters. We couldn't afford the luxury of admiring the beauties of nature in the Italian countryside. We had no fighter escort today.

The lead plane located the Initial Point, a small town that would establish the starting point of the bomb run. The IP determined the axis of attack, that is, the compass direction to the target. Flying time from the IP to the target would be about five minutes, and our most vulnerable time for the enemy to launch his devastating barrage of 88-millimeter shells with all fuses timed to explode their projectiles in the midst of our formation.

It was during this time that our leader executed some mild evasive action, turning to the right or left, then returning to the required heading, with the hope of confusing and alter-ing the aiming point of the enemy guns. But success of the mission depended on our very strict need to hold straight and level at a constant speed with only minute aileron and rudder actions in concert with the leader as he responded to the lead bombardier's final bombsight adjustments. An exaggerated press on the rudder at moment of release could cause the plane to skid and throw the bombs far off target. This final, critical 20- to 30-second period was the supreme test of our skills, our commitment to our tasks, our ability to perform under the deadly threat of the experienced and determined firepower of Hitler's war machine.

The target was heavily defended, and the puffs of black smoke from four exploding shells did a range-finding stair-step in the heart of our formation. Satisfied that they had our range, the enemy fired the next volleys in rapid succession. The sky around us and all along our flight path erupted into a ragged trail of devastation. The concussive force of exploding shells beneath us caused our plane to rise or jump, like hitting a hard bump in the road. We heard the sound of shell fragments, shards of super-heated steel hitting the underside of the wings and fuselage. Some of them, those whose force was spent, made a noise like that of small rocks pinging against the fuselage. Others made a sharper, pierc-ing sound and we guessed that we would have holes to count when we returned to Cor-sica. But the most disturbing of all were those pieces of shrapnel that produced a harsh, airframe-jolting *KA-JUNG* sound, causing us to speculate that a large projectile had im-pacted on the aluminum skin where it was riveted to a structural rib or spar. The barrage was relentless.

The reign of terror was all around us now, bursts above, beside, and below, but we stayed on course without deviation. I wondered how much longer it would be before we got the final call to hold in tight and steady for the critical bomb run.

Jack was doing a good job of tucking in close to the #4 second-element leader, even though he was flying cross-cockpit as he looked past me through my side window at plane #9W in the #4 element leader position.

The call came and Jack appeared to almost freeze on the controls, tense and rigid, as if he had a stranglehold on a wrestling opponent. Moments later our bombardier called on the intercom, "Bomb-bay doors open." We could hear the rumbling noise caused by the rush of air as it streaked past the large belly opening of the bomb-bay at 200 miles per hour. There was no in-rush of air, as there were no openings in the B-25 that would cause a reduced interior pressure. There was little if any buffeting of the long narrow doors in their unnatural mode.

Finally, the bombardier called again on the intercom the magic 13 words we most wanted to hear on this wild journey. With his tense, high-pitched voice he announced, "Bombs away, bomb-bay doors closed. Let's get the hell out of here!"

At the moment of bomb release we felt the upward jolt of the plane as it was freed from the burden of 4,000 pounds of destruction. The flak was unceasing during the entire episode and continued as the leader took us into a steep diving turn to the left, which had been prescribed by the briefing officer.

Coming out of the turn we saw that 9C had been hit hard, a direct hit in the left wing. The plane fell out of formation and appeared to be in serious trouble. It went into a long, flat spiral and the pilot, Richard Ellin, was obviously unable to control it. He must have rung the bailout bell, as five parachutes were seen leaving the plane. Some speculated that he might have tried to crash-land in an Italian field.

I was suddenly struck with the fact that my tail gunner, Russell Scott, was on that plane. Was he one of those who was able to bail out? If he was, would he land safely or would the Germans shoot him and the others as they descended in their chutes? Or maybe he would be taken prisoner, or the fondest hope of all, he would be picked up and spirited away by the Partisans, the Italian guerrilla underground forces operating in the Apennine Mountains. When would we ever learn of their fate?

The downed crew consisted of pilot Lieutenant Richard L. Ellin of Flemington, New Jersey; copilot Garth B. King of Tyler, Texas; bombardier Staff Sergeant Pete Vargo of Brownsville, Pennsylvania; radio-gunner Tech Sergeant Henry E. Yocco of Windber, Pennsylvania; turret gunner Staff Sergeant Cecil W. Wright of Flint, Michigan; and tail gunner Sergeant Russell Scott of Richmond, Virginia.

"What a nasty business," I thought. We continued in our evasive mode as the entire formation high-tailed it for Corsica. One hour later, as we neared our home base, the first box of six planes formed into a stacked echelon, a stair-step formation stretching to the right, almost wingtip to wingtip and swept upwind, low over the runway. At the end of the runway the leader made a steep climbing 180-degree turn to the left and lowered his landing gear as he leveled out at 500 feet on the downwind leg. The other five in the formation followed his lead and spaced themselves in the traffic pattern for orderly landing.

Our box of five, now revealing that telltale "empty place against the sky" for the still unapprised ground brethren on hand to cheer our homecoming, formed its shortened stair-step echelon and mimicked the lead of the first box.

Although this procedure had its practical aspect of disbanding a formation for landing, there was something commanding and heroic about it that touched the minds and hearts of both its doers and observers.

The power and chorus of 12 mighty engines screaming in unison, the grace and beauty of an aircraft we all admired and loved, and the courage of men that had ridden her saddles through killing skies iced our tingling spines and gave birth to grateful tears.

But today there was no celebration. Victory came at a very high price, and that empty place against the sky melted our chills into a bonding memorial compassion.

With our planes all parked in their respective stalls, we boarded the truck and arrived at group Headquarters for coffee and donuts supplied by the American Red Cross girls assigned to our unit, followed by a session of interrogation by our squadron Intelligence officers. They wanted to know all important facts and observations concerning the mission — its success or failure — the enemy opposition, and particularly the loss of the plane and its crew.

We were all tired and still shaken from the mission and its vicious consequences, glad to climb aboard a truck for the short trip back to what we now referred to as "home."

Sleep came hard for me as I tossed, thinking about the lost men and their families, each of whom would be receiving that dreaded government telegram naming their Missing in Action son or brother or husband.

I thought, too, about the many long months of training I had received and endured and now realized I had no inkling of what I was actually training for or what combat was all about.

Today I had my "baptism-of-fire" . . . and it burned deep into my soul.

The 12th Air Force efforts were said to be accelerating as it was calling for increased activity from all of its units throughout the Mediterranean Theater. The Anzio Beachhead forces were about to join up with the main Fifth Army forces driving toward Rome, and the 340th Bomb Group scheduled two missions of 48 planes each for the next day, May 26th.

Flying again as copilot, but with a different pilot, I repeated yesterday's prayer as we crossed the shoreline. I wasn't asking God for any particular favors, no immunity from enemy fire, but just the physical strength and mental capacity to enable me to cope with whatever would befall me this day.

I had realized my responsibility to my crew 26 days ago when we left Florida for this maddening adventure, and I knew I would realize it on every mission, every flight that I would make. How casually they seemed to entrust their lives to my care, then and today. Even as copilot I had that same responsibility to the pilot, should he become disabled, and to the others.

26 May 1944 (First Mission) — Mission #2
Pilot: Lieutenant Gilbert Crittenden   Copilot: Lieutenant Alex Stewart
Target: Railroad Viaduct, Near Peteccio, Italy
12-Plane Formation — #5 First Box — Bomb Load: 8 500-pound

On the first mission of the 26th, the lead bombardier, Captain D. A. Whitcomb, planted the bombs of the first box square on the target, and the other boxes added to the destruction. The lack of fighter and flak opposition was a welcome relief from the heartbreaking loss the day before.

26 May 1944 (Second Mission) — Mission #3
Pilot: Lieutenant James McLain   Copilot: Lieutenant Alex Stewart
Target: Railroad Bridge East of Orvieto, Italy
12-Plane Formation — #6 Second Box — Bomb Load: 8 500-pound

The group flew a total of 48 planes, 12 from each of four squadrons on the 26th. The Anzio Beachhead forces and main ground forces joined up, and the bomb line finally moved. We all watched the situation map located outside the S-2 tent for Allied victories on the ground.

Our chief thrust was to destroy the supply lines that fed the enemy forces, which had become a very telling presence in the progress of our muddied countrymen slogging it out in foxholes. And to have two missions in one day without encountering enemy fighters or flak was more than anyone could hope for or expect.

Perhaps in gratitude for the lack of enemy opposition, at the moment of our bomb release I found myself silently praying that the target would be destroyed but that no one on the ground would be injured or killed by our bombs. I was perhaps still clinging to a philosophy of destroying the enemy's means of waging war and not destroying the enemy.

27 May 1944 — Mission #4
Pilot: Lieutenant Gilbert Crittenden   Copilot: Lieutenant Alex Stewart
Target: Railroad Bridge, Castiglione, Italy
12-Plane Formation — #4 Second Box — Bomb Load: 8 500-pound

May 27th was again a memorable day for the group with 96 planes launched. Captain Whitcomb did a credible job of bracketing a large railroad bridge. These three missions in a row without opposition were a real treat, known by our squadron as "milk runs." Scotty Rohwer, in the 486th Squadron, referred to them as "free rides."

Squadron Intelligence reported that "Jerry" was in full retreat with his bridges burned behind him. Over 12,000 German prisoners had been taken since the start of the offensive. It appeared that knocking out bridges instead of railroad marshaling yards was paying dividends.

Congratulations were sent to the 340th Bomb Group and its Commander, Colonel Chapman, from Lieutenant General Ira C. Eaker, Commander Mediterranean Allied Air Forces, from Major General John K. Cannon, Commander 12th Air Force, and from Brigadier General Robert D. Knapp, Commander 57th Bomb Wing.

28 May 1944 — Mission #5
Pilot: Lieutenant M. C. Lucas   Copilot: Lieutenant Alex Stewart
Target: Road and Railroad Bridge (W) Pisa, Italy
12-Plane Formation — #6 First Box — Bomb Load: 4 1,000-pound

Mission #5 was completed on May 28th, and I had not seen a burst of flak in the last four efforts. I was sure this was to be just a lull before the storm. Our bombing was successful, and I had a brief look at the Leaning Tower of Pisa. The weather had been beautiful. It was reported that our group was getting quite a bit of publicity back home, probably due to our bombing record and the kind words from the Generals.

With my first five missions under my belt in four days, I guessed that the Operations Officer decided I needed a rest. On May 29th, 1944, I flew a B-25 on the short trip to Naples to pick up some supplies. While there I located the Terme Hotel, an old-time hot mineral-water spa that had been converted to a staging center for American troops who were waiting to board ships for home. I was glad to see Bob Saxton one more time, knowing he would set sail in a day or two.

In my absence, the squadron participated with the group in bombing the north and south viaducts at Buccine, Italy.

My radio operator, Sergeant Paul Wheeler had been detained on a trip back to Telergma, Algeria, for some special radio schooling and was due to return to the squadron soon. The entire crew had not received any mail since we left the States, and Paul promised to look into it for us. We were anxiously waiting to see him.

On May 30th, I wrote to Ruth, telling her of my visit with Bob and that he would be bringing her a wallet I had bought in Africa. He would also be bringing information to her that could not be written in a letter due to security reasons. I brought her up-to-date on my clothing situation — the purchase of some sun-tan uniforms in Naples, the plan to ship unneeded stuff back home — and wondered where the Army got its dumb ideas for overseas clothing needs. I had no use for half the clothing I brought and a real need for some of that left behind.

I reported that Stan Gerry was flying everyday to make himself ready for check-out as a first pilot, and that my bombardier, Herbert Robinson, was being transferred to another squadron that had a bombardier shortage and because we had a surplus. I also told her I had seen Scotty the other night and that he had a mission or two less than I.

I spent another day of loafing on May 31st while the squadron flew a successful mission against some German troop concentrations east of Lake Albano, Italy. I felt all along that if we could cripple and destroy the Germans' ability to wage war by bombing their bridges, planes, airfields, fuel, and ordnance there would be little need for killing their people. I was especially concerned with our bombs injuring and killing innocent civilians and had to assume that they took cover when our planes made their appearance. I knew I was not being realistic and had determined that I would kill or be killed if I came face to face with that option.

I struggled with the biblical passage that admonishes us to "love our enemies." I doubted that our adversary had similar convictions, but I could not adopt his standards. It was for this reason that I favored flying the B-25 in a tactical operation, destroying his means of aggression.

We had frequent night alerts at this time, and presumed that high-flying unidentified aircraft were the cause. The Jerrys might be taking photos or just helping us to lose precious sleep. Nonetheless, we had improved our slit trenches since the terrible raid inflicted on the squadron on May 13th. Many of us added top cover on the trenches — boards spanning across the opening, then covered with a very thick layer of dirt.

On June 1st, the squadron flew a highly successful attack on a road bridge northeast of Orte, Italy. Direct hits were observed on the bridge and its approach.

I was assigned to fly a group of airmen to the island of Malta for a five-day rest leave, giving me one more day of respite from combat. It was an interesting trip to this bombed-out British colony fortress, once described as a virtual island paradise. Not a building had escaped the vicious bombings when the Germans were operating in North Africa and Sicily. We did have good food and drink, however, and a clean, friendly, English-speaking populace that welcomed our men and their money.

Lieutenant Alex Stewart in the cockpit of his B-25, Corsica, 1944.

2 June 1944 — Mission #6
Pilot: Lieutenant Alex Stewart   Copilot: Lieutenant Stanley Gerry
Target: Road and Railroad Bridge, North of Foligno, Italy
18-Plane Formation — #5 First Box — Bomb Load: 8 500-pound

Mission #6 on June 2nd, 1944, was my first as pilot. Flight leader Captain E. J. Haster took wild evasive action when four shells were fired from maximum range and burst in our formation, and his steep, hard right turn broke up the formation. I had responded in like manner to avoid possible collision with my leader of the second box, and several minutes were needed to reform. This was a phase of combat I was not prepared for and it unnerved me. I wondered about my survivability. But I learned that Haster was a new leader and would soon calm down. This was, nevertheless, a successful mission and again, no flak over the target.

3 June 1944 — Mission #7
Pilot: Lieutenant M. C. Lucas   Copilot: Lieutenant Alex Stewart
Target: Road Bridge, Castellana, Italy
6-Plane Formation — #3 First Box — Bomb Load: 8 500-pound

The June 3rd mission was routine but successful, with no enemy fighters or flak. The

RAF operated Spitfires from their base near the north end of Corsica, and their presence was always a comfort.

4 June 1944 — Mission #8
Pilot: Lieutenant Alex Stewart   Copilot: Lieutenant Stanley Gerry
Target: Road Bridge North of Orte, Italy
18-Plane Formation — #5 First Box — Bomb Load: 4 1,000-pound

On Mission #8, June 4th, again the noise of flak hitting the plane varied. Some shrapnel from enemy shells sounded like pebbles or rocks being thrown at our underside. Others made that vibrating *KA-JUNG*, perhaps striking against a metal seam at the point of its mounting to a structural framework member. It sounded deadly.

We counted 52 holes, no mechanical damage, no injuries.

5 June 1944 — Mission #9
Pilot: Lieutenant Alex Stewart   Copilot: Lieutenant Stanley Gerry
Target: Narni Factory Road Bridge, Italy
12-Plane Formation — #5 First Box — Bomb Load: 8 500-pound

June 5th marked my first but brief encounter with enemy fighters — six Messerschmidt 109s. Opposition from flak and fighters could be compared somewhat with that of a shotgun and a Tommy gun. The Tommy gun was fired with a readily controlled aim, whereas the shotgun sent a spray of pellets with the hope that one or more would hit the target. An attack by fighters had a more deadly potential and a sobering effect on all the crewmen. Our Spitfire escort pursued, preventing additional attack.

June 2nd-5th was a period of great activity. Six times the 489th Squadron struck at the enemy, blowing up his roads and bridges over which he moved his supplies, equipment, and troops to the front lines. The war in Italy assumed climactic proportions. On the evening of June 4th, Allied armies poured into Rome. The Germans evacuated the city without subjecting it to their customary destruction. At this stage of the conflict the Germans yielded to worldwide public opinion and left Rome intact — surprising in view of the fact that they had had no qualms in that respect in the past. The Allied capture of Rome was expected to have far-reaching effects on the progress of the war in Italy, and cause important political reactions in other Axis powers.

6 June 1944 — Mission #10
Pilot: Lieutenant Stanley Gerry   Copilot: Lieutenant Alex Stewart
Target: Road Bridge, Vetralla, Italy
18-Plane Formation — #5 First Box — Bomb Load: 8 500-pound

On June 6th, D-Day, toward which we had been looking for so long, became a reality. Early in the morning, a huge armada of Allied ships set out across the English Channel to storm Hitler's *Festung Europa*. An equally formidable armada of aircraft carried troops and supplies to be landed well behind the Channel Coast in France. Details of the invasion were not yet available for public consumption, but when they were revealed we were amazed at the magnitude of the operations. For a year, speculation had been rife as to when and where the mighty blows would be struck. Now we had the answers.

On June 6th, I wrote to Ruth.

> On my first mission as pilot, Stan Gerry was my copilot. He has been piling up missions as copilot and today I flew copilot for him on this his first mission as pilot. Stan is good.
>
> We usually fly in large formations. If you see any planes of our type in the Newsreels, they may be ours. I heard they were taking movies of us today. The morale in this outfit is high.
>
> Stan and Ed Perry are moving into my tent with me tomorrow. This tent is nicer and better located than theirs. We get along well together. Dave Fronfield, the former bombardier and now a supply officer lives here too. He's a nice guy. He had it rough in B-17's at Messina Straits at the tip of Italy. Now grounded.
>
> Major Alexander Parrish, 489th squadron commander is returning to the States for some specialized study. He is being replaced by Major Leonard Kaufmann, who has done a splendid job as Operations Officer and is qualified to be Commanding Officer. New crew replacements have been assigned to the squadron.

8 June 1944 — Mission #11
Pilot: Lieutenant John Mitchell   Copilot: Lieutenant Alex Stewart
Target: North Viaduct, Bucine, Italy
18-Plane Formation — #1 Third Box — Bomb Load: 4 1,000-pound

On June 8th, I flew my first mission as copilot in the lead plane of one of three boxes and was able firsthand to see the pilot and bombardier work as a team in positioning the six-plane box for a successful drop on the North Bucine Viaduct. Our training experience at dropping practice bombs back in Greenville was but an elementary exercise compared with what was being achieved this day.

Even with our capture of Rome and the Normandy invasion, we knew that to start with we could not look for large territorial gains. Our losses had thus far been less than expected during the initial landings, but the hardest battles were yet to come with Rommel rushing up with his mobile reserve divisions to the area of our assault.

The 340th Bomb Group had entered operations on April 19th, 1943. In less than 365 operational days we had flown a total of 400 missions. It was believed our total exceeded that of other groups in the 57th Wing, although they had been in operation longer.

From June 9th through June 13th, I was grounded due to a head cold. My eustachian tubes were so swollen that I was unable to equalize the pressure on either side of my eardrums. In our type of operations, with sudden and drastic changes in altitude, quick clearing of the ears was essential. Time and aspirin seemed to be the accepted remedy, assisted somewhat with the injection of sulfa powders by the flight surgeon into the back of the throat. I also used my mother's time-honored method of gargling with salt water. It seemed to work best of all.

14 June 1944 — Mission #12
Pilot: Lieutenant Alex Stewart   Copilot: Lieutenant George Bleimes
Target: Road Bridge. Pietrasanta, Italy
12-Plane Formation — #5 First Box — Bomb Load: 4 1,000-pound

Air activity over the east coast of Corsica continued with a fighter patrol keeping an eye on this vulnerable spot. Flying in pairs, they stood guard night and day. Throughout the day, C-47s had been winging up and down the island's shores, arousing our curiosity to know what they carried and where they went. For the previous week they had been making regular trips. We wondered if this could be the forerunner of an invasion.

On our June 14th mission, the flak attack was heavy and very accurate, and most planes were heavily holed.

15 June 1944 — Mission #13
Pilot: Lieutenant Art Harrison   Copilot: Lieutenant Alex Stewart
Target: Railroad Viaduct, Fabrica, Italy
12-Plane Formation — #5 Second Box — Bomb Load: 4 1,000-pound

June 15th was my first mission flying with Art Harrison. The flak was especially heavy and unrelenting, and we counted 61 holes when we returned to base. I wondered how we could have taken such penetration and not have had anyone wounded or have any mechanical failures. Pilots often reported damage to control cables or had important instruments shot out. I was sure my turn would come. Art and I worked well together, each anticipating the other's inquiry or need.

Significantly, B-25s often returned from a mission with badly shot-up wings, ailerons, flaps, stabilizers, elevators, and rudders. With inoperative rudders, a pilot would have to steer with the engines, increasing the power of the right engine to make a left turn and vice versa. Coping with the lost use of elevators was more difficult. Loss of hydraulics was another hazard that required special handling. Emergency manual systems were often employed to lower landing gear and flaps. And, of course, we dreaded having engine oil lines shot out, causing the loss of power and forcing continued flight on one engine. We were often in awe of the punishment the planes could endure and still stay in the air.

16 June 1944 — Mission #14
Pilot: Lieutenant Alex Stewart   Copilot: Lieutenant F. C. Swanson
Target: Road Bridge, Pietrasanta, Italy
12-Plane Formation — #5 First Box — Bomb Load: 4 1,000-pound

The June 16th mission was my first with Swanson as copilot. He seemed controlled under fire and did his job well. I believed we had confidence in one another and that was important in this business.

Just after nightfall, the big shore battery guns surrounding our airfield opened up with a terrific barrage. All hands hit the slit trenches while the guns maintained an almost continuous 15-minute bombardment, which was directed out to sea. We were relieved when the all-clear was sounded. In the morning, our ack-ack boys, the guardians manning our anti-aircraft guns, explained that an unidentified ship had failed to give the proper signals, and thus it was assumed to be an enemy vessel, as it probably was. Everyone was on edge and sleep came fitfully. I had heard the terrible noise of those type guns in Seattle in 1942, and a repeat performance was unwelcome. (Most Americans were unaware that our big shore batteries and 90-mm anti-aircraft guns were ever fired at unidentified planes or ships).

21 June 1944 — Mission #15
Pilot: Lieutenant Alex Stewart   Copilot: Lieutenant Fred Voss
Target: Road Bridge, Pietrasanta, Italy
12-Plane Formation — #6 First Box — Bomb Load: 4 1,000-pound

On June 21st, we again set out for the road bridge at Pietrasanta. The appearance of the same target on several mission plans did not necessarily imply that the target was missed a day or two before. The Germans had a terrific ability at repairing or rebuilding a bridge after it had been bombed. Sometimes they spanned a river with a quickly constructed pontoon bridge and were back in the business of supplying their forces. And they jealously protected their handiwork with heavy flak barrages.

On June 23rd, we were all pleasantly shocked. Three men whom we had never expected to see again suddenly made their appearance, walking in on us like ghosts. They were members of Lieutenant Richard Ellen's crew that had been shot down on May 25th and included Lieutenant King, and Sergeants Yocco and Vargo. They had been taken prisoner, but managed to escape and eventually reached the safety of friendly territory. They reported that all six had bailed out of 9C but that Lieutenant Ellen's chute failed to open. Sergeant Wright was shot and killed by Italian Fascists as he parachuted toward the earth. Sergeant Russell Scott, tail gunner on my crew when we had arrived on Corsica, reached ground safely but was taken prisoner. He had received a serious back injury when he bailed out and was probably hospitalized by the Germans. But I didn't learn of his safe return till after the war.

30 June 1944 — Mission #16
Pilot: Lieutenant John Mitchell   Copilot: Lieutenant Alex Stewart
Target: Railroad Bridge, Pietrasanta, Italy
12-Plane Formation — #1 Second Box — Bomb Load: 4 1,000-pound

From June 24th to the 30th, combat activity had been on a reduced scale. On the 27th,

Cherbourg, the third largest French port, fell before the Allied onslaught after many days of fierce fighting. Thus was completed the second phase in the great struggle for the liberation of Europe.

On the 29th and 30th, missions were flown to northern Italy, the first combat activity in about a week. I flew copilot with flight leader John Mitchell, and our bombs helped destroy the railroad bridge at Pietrasanta, Italy, in spite of heavy defenses. A *Special Accounts on Operations* reported that of 21 assigned targets, 15 were destroyed, 2 were missed, and near misses were made on 4.

With 16 missions to my credit, I guessed that I was about 25 percent on the way to finishing my tour of duty, but we never knew from day to day what constituted a finish. Russell Scott, my tail gunner, was finished after his second mission. I had encountered flak on nine missions to date and felt this was better than average. The uncertainty was always an underlying presence and contributed to a creeping anxiety that took its toll on my composure.

1 July 1944 — Mission #17
Pilot: Lieutenant John Mitchell   Copilot: Lieutenant Alex Stewart
Target: Railroad Tunnel, Prato, Italy
12-Plane Formation — #1 Second Box — Bomb Load: 6 1,000-pound

The B-25 Mitchell bomber was originally designed to carry a bomb load of 2,500 pounds. On July 1st, we carried 6,000 pounds — six 1,000-pound SAP (semi-armor piercing) bombs, long and slender, enabling them to be fitted into the bomb-bay. The SAP bomb was designed to partially penetrate the structure of the target before exploding. It was ideal for use against ships, storage tanks, and tunnels through rock formations. The heavy flak attack on the 1st, with our heavier-than-usual bomb load, was relentless.

2 July 1944 — Mission #18
Pilot: Lieutenant John Montgomery   Copilot: Lieutenant Alex Stewart
Target: Railroad Viaduct, Borgo San Lorenzo, Italy
6-Plane Formation — #4 First Box — Bomb Load: 4 1,000-pound

It was rare when only six planes attacked a target, but they were usually teamed with six-plane boxes from other squadrons to make up the striking force. Thus was the case on July 2nd, and photos show direct hits on the west approach to the railroad viaduct at Borgo San Lorenzo.

All squadrons had been running night transition flights, presumably for night missions. Night flying practice was essential for success, as the dark hours presented a different set of problems in takeoff, join-up, and formation flying.

About this time we had noted an improvement in our food, with more fresh meat and butter, and we finally moved into our new squadron mess hall. Made of logs, it was rustic, roomy, and comfortable with a large fireplace. Somebody said it was built by the officers, but I never had a hand in it. It contained a record player of sorts and a very small supply of records, though the only one I cared to listen to was a scratchy old 78 rpm recording of *Scheherazade* by Rimsky-Korsakov.

Legend had it that Sultan Shahriar, who lived in Baghdad, was so convinced of the unfaithfulness of women that he swore he would put to death every woman who had spent the preceding night with him. But beautiful Sheherazada told him such interesting stories that he had his executioner postpone her death so that he could hear more. The postponement went on for 1,001 nights, and he finally gave up his death plan and made Scheherazada his Sultana. Rimsky-Korsakov painted in tone the ferocity of the life in the Harem of Shahriar and, in contrast, the romantic beauty of Scheherazada and the mystery and suspense of the ancient legends.

The haunting themes and the ferocity of *Scheherazade* wove its spell as a few tired, frazzled airmen half-dozed in the warmth of the glowing embers in the new fireplace. And for a few moments, I tried to associate the beauty and mystery of the music with Africa. But such an exercise was futile. What I had seen in "the dark continent" could not be imagined in such a romantic setting. I decided to just listen to the music and forget the story.

3 July 1944 — Mission #19
Pilot: Lieutenant James McLain   Copilot: Lieutenant Alex Stewart
Target: Fuel Dump, Ferrara, Italy
12-Plane Formation — #6 First Box — Bomb Load: 8 250-pound

On July 3rd, the mission took us into the Po River Valley and some of the most fierce flak defenses any of us had seen. We had combined with planes from the 488th Squadron and dropped both demolition and incendiary bombs on vital German fuel supplies.

Besides the flak, we felt the wrath of four German Focke-Wulf 190 fighters that made a scathing attack at the 6 o'clock position — diving in on us from the rear. Our tail guns and top-turret guns opened up on them, and the stench of burnt gunpowder reached our nostrils. The cacophony of our guns and the crash of enemy bullets penetrating the fragile skin of our aircraft caused a chill to pass through me. I involuntarily visualized those deadly slugs dittoing up my spine. I wondered if this was my time to die.

The FW-190s made two passes at us before being engaged by a flight of our P-47 Thunderbolts and driven away from our formation.

But it all wasn't without tragedy. A plane from the 488th Squadron was shot down by flak a few moments later on the bomb run. Captain Crossman, the 340th Bomb Group's English Allied Liaison Officer, riding as an observer, went down with the plane. Technical Sergeant Hunt, a radio-gunner was seriously injured in the leg. And every plane in our squadron was holed. McClain and I counted 32 in our plane, 9M.

Theodore Roosevelt said:

> The Air Service in particular is one of such peril that membership in it is of itself a high distinction. Physical address, high training, entire fearlessness, iron nerve and fertile resourcefulness are needed in combination and to a degree hitherto unparalleled in war. The ordinary air fighter is an extraordinary man; and the extraordinary air fighter stands as one in a million among his fellows.

Roosevelt died soon after World War I in 1919 and was only familiar with the elementary achievements of air warfare up to that time. Like war methods and implements on the ground, air warfare had become much more sophisticated between 1919 and 1944. Surely we had it bad at times in the air, but I could not agree totally with his assessment. I never felt fearlessness, nor could I class my nerve as that of iron. Perhaps the only difference between the airman and the ground soldier was that in the air we had no place to seek cover, no place in which to dig a foxhole, yet in the air we were moving targets and perhaps harder to hit.

Our time of exposure to the massive German anti-aircraft barrages was limited to a few minutes — deadly, but short-lived, though with flak or fighters we had to face, unflinchingly, the fire intended to destroy us in order to accomplish our mission. Assuredly, we were scared. And it was this fear that sank into our subconscious and would eventually erode our ability for effective performance. In a discussion of the merits and demerits of the various Service branches, we were prone to resolve and dismiss the matter with the French paraphrase, "*c'est la guerre*" — this is war!

Although the Germans no longer flanked our island on the east, nevertheless they were still a dangerous menace. We were only a few minutes' flying time from enemy airfields in northern Italy and southern France. The previous night we were reminded just how close we still remained to the war. Shortly after midnight we were awakened by the earth-trembling concussion of big guns, and above this resounding noise could be heard the unsynchronized throb of twin-engine German fighter-bombers, interrupted frequently by the rapid fire of machine guns. Everyone was awakened by the commotion and expected an attack on our field momentarily, but none came. Apparently, it was a naval engagement not far offshore.

On American Independence Day, July 4th, 1944, it was "stand-down" for us, and many of the men went to the smooth, sandy, narrow beach. The BBC news reported that the Russians had captured Minsk, capital of White Russia. In Normandy, the American forces had started a new drive on the western side of the Cherbourg Peninsula against stubborn German resistance. In Italy, French troops of the Fifth Army occupied the city of Siena. More than 500 American bombers had been out again on the 3rd, pounding oil targets in Hungary, Rumania, and Yugoslavia. And in the Southwest Pacific, American troops had landed on Noemfoor Island in the Geelvink Bay area of Dutch New Guinea and had captured one of the airfields.

6 July 1944 — Mission #20
Pilot: Lieutenant R. W. Lang   Copilot: Lieutenant Alex Stewart
Target: Railroad Bridge, Parma, Italy
18-Plane Formation — #4 Second Box — Bomb Load: 4 1,000-pound

On our July 6th mission, 82 percent of our bombs fell within the target area — a highly successful mission. Targets in the Po Valley were heavily defended, with an accumulation of 88mm anti-aircraft guns that came from abandoned defenses in the south. We were encountering flak of increased volume and intensity and were reminded almost daily of the skill and accuracy of the German gunners. In spite of the withdrawal of German forces into mainland Italy, their resolve to destroy us had not lessened.

B-25s in various tactical formations, Corsica, 1944.   *From **History and Personnel, 489th, 340th Bomb Group**, 1947*

I was surprised to receive a graduation announcement from my Primary Flight School instructor Jack Mathis, the man who taught me to fly. Jack had hoped that when his instructor days were over he would be able to get into the Navy or Marine Air Corps and fly their fighters in the Pacific War. However, he expressed no disappointment or regret in his announcement that he was now a Flight Officer in the Air Transport Command.

8 July 1944 — Mission #21
Pilot: Lieutenant Alex Stewart   Copilot: James J. Walsh
Target: Oil Storage Tanks, Ostiglia, Italy
6-Plane Formation — #5 First Box — Bomb Load: 8 250-pound

Our mission of July 8th to the air storage tanks at Ostiglia was successful. Five of six planes dropped bombs. My aircraft, however, had a malfunction of our bomb rack and could not drop. Returning to base and landing with only 2,000 pounds of bombs was no problem. In this case, the bomb unit quantities more than tonnage were important; eight 250-pound bombs were all the bomb-bay could accommodate dimensionally.

Our Spitfire escort had engaged the German fighters before any damage could be inflicted; but the flak attack was mean.

The new Enlisted Mens Club opened the evening of the 8th, and liquor purchased in Italy was available in quantity. The celebration was noisy but orderly. At the same time, the new Officers Club had its official opening, which was more quiet, but with just as much enthusiasm.

Our mail to and from home had reached a level of normalcy, and I daily looked forward to a letter from Ruth and occasionally from one or more members of the family. Ruth always had an enthusiastic message and related the happenings at her office with the Pure Oil Company in Chicago. She often included the joke page from the in-house company newsletter. I liked a few of the war-related jokes and a choice selection of others:

> The story is told that Winston Churchill recently hailed a cab in London's West End and told the cabbie to drive him to BBC, where he was scheduled to make a speech to the world.
>
> "Sorry, sir," said the driver, "ye'll 'ave to get yourself another cab. I can't go that far."
>
> Mr. Churchill was somewhat surprised and asked the cabbie why his field of operations was so limited.
>
> "It hain't hordinarily, sir," apologized the driver, "but ye see, sir, Mr. Churchill is broadcasting in an hour and I wants to get 'ome to 'ear 'im."
>
> Churchill was so pleased he pulled out a pound note and handed it to the driver, who took one look at it and said, "Hop in, sir. T'hell with Mr. Churchill."

And then:

Mother: "I don't think the man upstairs likes Johnnie to play his drum."
Father: "What makes you think so?"
Mother: "Well, this afternoon he gave Johnnie a knife and asked him if he knew what was inside the drum."

And finally:

The Fuehrer and Goebbels, touring Naziland in an automobile, ran over a pig in front of a beer hall. Learning the dead porker belonged to the tavernkeeper, Goebbels stepped inside to break the news. An hour passed before Goebbels staggered out drunk. "What happened?" asked his Führer.

"I walked into the hall," Goebbels replied, "and said; 'Heil Hitler! The pig is dead!' And the bartender yelled: "*Gott sei dank*! The drinks are on me!"

On July 9th, at noon, the stand-down for the day became official. We flew another night practice mission at 2:00 a.m. It was being said that we soon would be striking the enemy at night. Meanwhile, we continued to reach any point in the Mediterranean almost every day on cross-country flights to Africa, Sicily, or Italy, on pleasure or business. A plane-load of men flew to Cairo, Egypt, for rest and recreation on the 9th.

10 July 1944 — Mission #22
Pilot: Captain Howard Taylor   Copilot: Lieutenant Alex Stewart
Target: Railroad Marshaling Yards, Rovigo, Italy
12-Plane Formation — #1 First Box — Bomb Load: 8 500-pound

On July 10th, the photographs of the day's bombing indicated that the mission was a success. The Rovigo marshaling yards near the Adige River southwest of Venice were heavily defended. Their vicinity to Ferarra had been an unhappy omen when the target was assigned to us at the morning briefing.

11 July 1944 — Mission #23
Pilot: Lieutenant Alex Stewart   Copilot: Lieutenant Anson Walker
Target: Railroad Bridge, Pietre Ligure, Italy
6-Plane Formation — #6 First Box — Bomb Load: 4 1,000-pound
Flak: Heavy, Accurate — Fighters: None, P-47 Escort

11 July 1944 — Mission #24
Pilot: Captain Lewis Insley   Copilot: Lieutenant Alex Stewart
Target: Railroad Bridge, Chiavari, Italy
18-Plane Formation — #1 Third Box — Bomb Load: 4 1,000-pound
Flak: Heavy, Accurate — Fighters: 16 Me-109s, P-47 Escort

On the 11th, a 489th plane with a full crew and two photographers took pictures of the bombing as they maneuvered with other planes of our group. Just prior to reaching the target, the photo plane trailing the formation was attacked by 16 Me-109s. Our waist and turret gunners shot down at least one of the enemy fighters.

On the afternoon of the 11th, a second 489th mission of the day, 18 planes flew to the Venice area to strike a railroad bridge at Chiavari. Possible hits were made on the bridge. Nearing the target, Lieutenant John Mitchell's 9B aircraft developed left engine trouble. As leader of the second box, he proceeded to the target and the bombardier dropped the bombs. Turning off the bomb run, the right engine failed while the left engine continued to miss badly. Over the Mediterranean, Mitchell could no longer hold altitude when the left engine died, forcing him to ditch the plane at sea. The five crew members in the front section were able to evacuate and climb into the larger life raft, which had been jettisoned from its storage compartment and automatically inflated.

Lieutenant Mitchell was apparently unaware and was stunned to learn that his radio operator/waist gunner Tech Sergeant R. E. Winjum and armorer/tail gunner Staff Sergeant W. E. McRitchie, seeing both propellers dead, had parachuted from the plane's rear section without instructions from the pilot to do so. Air/Sea Rescue planes were immediately dispatched to search for the two gunners but were unable to locate them. In the meantime, the Air/Sea Rescue Command raced to the lone raft to pick up the five survivors.

It was customary when a plane was downed at sea or disabled and forced to leave the formation and straggle back to base that one or two planes throttled back to become an escort for the stricken bomber. This provided a measure of protection against attacking enemy fighters or as an aid to the Rescue Service in locating the victims. Five men in a tiny raft in the vastness of the sea were sometimes very difficult to find.

Lieutenant Stanley B. Gerry, my tent-mate with whom I sometimes alternately shared copilot duties, was flying in the #3 position off Lieutenant Mitchell's lead plane when the ditching occurred. Stan immediately took up the position of escort and circled low over the sea, maintaining a constant vigil until the men were rescued.

13 July 1944 — Mission #25
Pilot: Captain Howard Taylor   Copilot: Lieutenant Alex Stewart
Target: Railroad and Road Bridge, Ferrara, Italy
18-Plane Formation — #1 Third Box — Bomb Load: 4 1,000-pound
Flak: Heavy, Accurate — Fighters: None

14 July 1944 — Mission #26
Pilot: Lieutenant W. S. Jones   Copilot: Lieutenant Alex Stewart
Target: Fuel Dump, Marina de Ror, Italy
12-Plane Formation — #3 Second Box — Bomb Load: 4 1,000-pound

On July 13th, approaching the railroad and road bridge Initial Point, we were jumped by four German Me-109 fighters. Pilot Jones, flying cross-cockpit was having difficulty holding our plane in a tight position next to the flight leader for most effective defense against the enemy. It was essential to concentrate greatest maximum firepower to bear on the attackers. I asked Jones and he agreed to have me take the controls and try to snuggle

The 489th Squadron encampment on Corsica. The Mediterranean Sea is on the horizon.
*From **History and Personnel, 489th, 340th Bomb Group**, 1947*

Tent mates on Corsica — all first lieutenants — Stanley Gerry, David Fronfield, Alex Stewart, and Edward Perry.
*From **History and Personnel, 489th, 340th Bomb Group**, 1947*

up close to the leader. I had no sooner done so when Jones called to me over the intercom, "Hold her in there tight Stew, we've got our ass full of fighters."

The attack came, four Messerschmidts peeling off from their formation and diving on us at six o'clock. Our tail guns and top-turret guns opened fire, answering the German overture of screeching, crashing devastation. The sound of bullets hitting and passing through the plane was different from the sound made by impacting flak, more like that of a sharp knife thrust into a tin can as opposed to that of the hammer-blow made by blunt pieces of shrapnel. But when the bullet hit a solid object in the plane, it felt like the whole hammer had arrived. Again, I had the chilling sensation of those bullets doing a dotted line right up my spine. And, again, in a mental flash, I wondered if my time had come.

The confrontation was over as quickly as it started. Our guns had ceased, the attackers were gone, now engaged by our P-47 escort. The gunpowder fumes were strong, their pungency caused a burning sensation in my eyes. Jones called for an injury report, and all hands responded, "Tail okay, radio okay, turret okay, bombardier okay." Then, still at the controls I piped in, "Copilot needs clean underwear."

Jones had me continue at the controls on the bomb run and through the diving break off the target and out of the flak zone. It was the first time I had flown a bomb run from the copilot's seat, but I found it made little difference. My concentration was intense, taking the leader's slight course adjustments in stride. When the final 30-second run came, I held position without a shred of deviation. Our drop was successful, and we were rewarded with a huge cloud of smoke rising from the ruptured, burning German fuel supply.

It occurred to me later that the copilot was usually at a disadvantage because he had nothing to do but watch the action and the engine instruments for possible deviation and impending trouble. His function as an observer was important, but didn't bear the immediacy required of the pilot. Like driving on a highway, I had learned in my earliest days at the wheel in our old 1927 Chrysler the point of reference of the hood ornament to the edge of the road in maintaining my position in the right lane of two-lane roads. Flying cross-cockpit in a B-25, I had established my points of reference during the first stages of formation training and assuming the position became automatic. It was reassuring, however, that in spite of the habits and idiosyncracies of each individual pilot, there seemed to be little variation in our flying ability. Many with whom I flew were less conservative than I was in the use of excessive engine power. I would reduce engine rpm as soon and as much as conditions would allow to minimize wear and increase my margin of safe performance. I wanted that reserve endurance when it was needed.

15 July 1944 — Mission #27
Pilot: Lieutenant Alex Stewart   Copilot: W. H. Brassfield
Target: Railroad Bridge, Villa Franca, Italy
12-Plane Formation — Standby — Bomb Load: 4 1,000-pound

On July 15th, 1944, we were scheduled as a Standby for a mission to the railroad bridge at Villa Franca, taking off after all the other planes and flying near the formation. We were ready to fill in should one of the planes be forced to drop out due to a mechanical failure or other emergency. If we didn't fill in for someone by the time we reached the enemy shores of the sea, we would return to the air base. For this we would be credited with combat flying time but would receive no credit for a mission.

On the 15th, however, we were needed, filling in for a drop-out from the 487th Squadron, and received mission credit and 3 hours and 35 minutes of combat flying time.

The 489th Squadron flew a total of four missions this day, the first that combined with the other three squadrons. The 486th was the only one to drop on the Ferrara road bridge; the other three squadrons opted for alternate targets, allegedly due to the intensity of flak at Ferrara. The 486th missed its target, however.

In spite of the heavy flak barrage protecting the railroad bridge at Villa Franca, our bombing as a fill-in for the 487th squadron was declared a success.

20 July 1944 — Mission #28
Pilot: Lieutenant Alex Stewart   Copilot: Lieutenant Robert Martin
Target: Railroad Bridge, Mantua, Italy
6-Plane Formation — #5 First Box — Bomb Load: 4 1,000-pound

On the 20th, again teamed with boxes from the other three squadrons, we destroyed the heavily defended railroad bridge at Mantua. We were the lead box in the formation with Lieutenant Insley as lead pilot and Captain Fred Dyer in the copilot's seat as mission Commander. Dyer was a veteran of many missions, bound to establish a record for longevity.

During the period from July 14th-20th, our squadron was unusually active as it struck hard and relentlessly at targets in northern Italy. On the evening of July 19th, Lieutenant Lewis Bulkley rejoined the squadron after spending 30 days at home. He was the first to return under the rotation plan that afforded some airmen the opportunity to go home after flying 50 missions and then return for a second tour of duty. Others in the plan included Captain Paul Neafus and Captain William Rittenhouse.

On July 21st, due to unfavorable weather conditions in Northern Italy, we had a stand-down all day. The S-2 Intelligence Section, receiving its information from several sources — the Armed Forces Radio Service, the BBC, the International News Service, the *Stars and Stripes* News Service, and tactical information from the 12th Air Force Intelligence Service — reported on events happening all over the world, events that were shaping the future course of the war. A bulletin board next to the S-2 tent showed on a map the frequent position gains being made by our ground forces on an almost daily basis at the Italian Front. When the Normandy Invasion was launched, the map was enlarged to include the war's progress on that new front. Detailed bulletins were posted for our perusal.

On the other side of the world, in Japan, there had been a shake-up in the War Cabinet. On July 18th, General Hideki Tojo was removed as Chief of the Japanese Imperial General Staff. The reason given for this change was the recent favorable turn of events for the Allies in the Central and Southwest Pacific.

In Germany, on the 20th, an attempt had been made to assassinate Hitler and some of his close henchmen. Hitler was only slightly injured. To assure the people that he was still alive, he spoke to them that night. Members of the military clique that had attempted this unsuccessful assassination had already been shot.

Within the previous few days, Ancona and Leghorn, important Italian ports, had fallen to the Allies, and the Russians were advancing on the Eastern Front at a pace unprecedented even for them. In Normandy, our troops were advancing against stiff resistance.

22 July 1944 — Mission #29
Pilot: Lieutenant Robert Martin   Copilot: Lieutenant Alex Stewart
Target: Road Bridge, Ronco Scriva, Italy
6-Plane Formation — #3 First Box — Bomb Load: 6 1,000-pound SAP

On the 22nd, the destruction of the bridge at Ronco Scriva, required the use of semi-armor piercing bombs, six of which could be accommodated in our bomb-bays because of their narrow shape. Captain Fred Dyer flew the lead plane, and the target was very effectively damaged. Although reveille was set for 6:30 a.m., we sat around until late afternoon before taking off. We were over the target at 6:30 p.m. and finally landed back on Corsica at 7:45, the sun having descended below the western mountain range.

In the midst of all this, food continued to be a topic of interest and importance to us. We had been doing better than usual, with some pretty good steak dinners about every week or ten days, and fried chicken about as often. Of course, none of it compared with that of home cooking, which just about everyone faintly recalled, but we were all aware of the huge task it was to feed several million men in every kind of circumstance thousands of miles from the food sources. Our cooks did a good job with the supplies made available to them.

Some time earlier I had asked Ruth to consult with my brother Cameron about sending me some salami. Earlier in the year, Cam had bought out a small grocery store and delicatessen at 85th Street and Stony Island Avenue and had stocked a variety of meats and cold-cuts, which did not require refrigeration. In due course, I received a package containing an excellent five-pound salami. It made a perfect complement to the palatable canned American-style cheese that came in K-Ration packages.

Tent-mates Ed Perry, Stan Gerry, Dave Fronfield, and Paul Neafus shared in the treat, and we frequently had very acceptable bedtime snacks. At one point, we had failed to properly wrap the remaining salami and discovered a few nights later that ants had found the open cut end of the meat and were having a feast. Ed's mouth was watering for a sandwich, and we decided that minor surgery on the salami loaf could resurrect the still generous remaining portion. A slice thick enough to separate the ants from their dinner but thin enough to preserve the maximum edible quantity was excised, and another feast was enjoyed by all. Ruth kept me well supplied with salami during most of my time on Corsica. We never tired of it.

26 July 1944 — Mission #30
Pilot: Lieutenant Alex Stewart   Copilot: Lieutenant James McLain
Target: Railroad Bridge, Ostiglia, Italy
12-Plane Formation — #6 Second Box — Bomb Load: 4 1,000-pound

We flew Mission #30 on July 26th. On the 27th, at noon, the 340th Group and all the other groups and forces on the island of Corsica were alerted for a possible invasion by the enemy from the air and the sea. Higher Allied Intelligence had acquired a certain knowledge indicating the imminence of a large-scale attack from southern France or from northern Italy.

We remained on a stand-down from the 27th through the 31st, the danger of an invasion of the island still present. Fighter planes raced back and forth over the island day and night, and we continued to carry guns and gas masks and remain alert for any emergency.

1 August 1944 — Mission #31
Pilot: Lieutenant Alex Stewart   Copilot: Lieutenant James McLain
Target: Road Bridge, Conneto S.Oglio, Italy
6-Plane Formation — #4 Second Box — Bomb Load: 4 1,000-pound
(Alternate: Filled in for 486th Squadron)

The several days spell of inactivity was broken on August 1st with the attack on a road and railroad bridge at Conneto San Oglio. We bracketed the target well, but failed to destroy it.

The 340th Bomb Group remained alert for a possible German invasion of the island. Packs of American Spitfires, P-51 Mustangs, and P-47 Thunderbolt fighters continued to rove the sky night and day. We were still under orders to carry arms, and our guard detail was at double strength.

I noted on the bulletin board that I was scheduled to fly a mission the next day, August 2nd. Although the target was never announced until we got to the briefing, rumor had it that we would be bombing in France. If the rumor was true it would be our first mission in that country.

With the earlier night practice flights, some of us had speculated that we were preparing for a possible invasion of southern France and not a change in strategy to bombing bridges at night. We could see no logical reason to do so and questioned whether we could be very effective. Those of longer experience who had participated in the invasions of Sicily and the Anzio Beachhead action remembered very early morning, pre-dawn take-offs. For this, night flying conditioning would be needed.

We still did not know how many missions constituted a tour of duty. The original goal of 50 had been replaced with an unofficial total of 60, but there was talk of the number going to 70. Regardless of what the final total would eventually reach, I figured I was somewhere near the halfway point. We had noted that many of the new replacement pilots coming into the squadron had limited experience in flying the B-25. The transition schools such as Mather Field, where Advanced Flight School graduates were sent for training in operational aircraft, were converting their efforts more to final combat phase training, such as we had experienced at Greenville, thus eliminating that one step in the process. Many pilots were introduced to the B-25 in the last half of Advanced Flight School.

In our evening bullsessions we reasoned that by stretching us to 70 or more missions, the experience gap could be filled, thus reducing the need for more pilots. Some of us had received word from friends back home that the recruitment of men for pilot training had been greatly trimmed. We figured that the high-command war strategists saw the end of the European war in their sights and that later needs in the Pacific could be filled with combat experienced airmen from the European Theater of War.

Assessing my own situation with 31 missions, I felt I was in good shape to go for the long haul. The casualty rate in our group was much lower than I had anticipated. From my first mission on May 25th to #31 on August 1st, we had lost only two planes from our squadron, one of those having been the one ditched in the sea, where five of seven men had been rescued. The injury rate was far less than I expected, and I was impressed with the large number of aircraft, badly damaged and crippled by both flak and fighters, that had limped back to base.

About this time, we saw what was described as combat fatigue beginning to creep into the psyche of some of the men, crippling their confidence and ability to cope with emergencies. In World War I, this phenomenon was identified as "shell shock." But in this modern day of more sophisticated terms, the medical community attached a more educated label known as psychoneurosis. These mental functional disorders were characterized by anxiety, compulsions, phobias, and depression.

For the layman, it was the daily mounting of the unknown, the wonder and fear feeding the doubts that rode on that unseen enemy shell, that would be his undoing. We saw the blackened sky of our bomb runs and heard the crash of the shrapnel on the delicate skins of our craft and somewhat casually dismissed them, after the fact, as annoying. But we were not fools, for we knew there was a determined enemy aching to mount our hides and our heads in his trophy rooms.

Would that unseen shell have our number on it?

Chapter 21

The Beginning of the End

B Y AUGUST 1944 THE PACE of the war had been increasing on a regular basis and the morale of the men took a corresponding jump. Everyone was closely following events, anticipating an early collapse of Hitler's Third Reich. The latest world news was broadcast to us many times a day over the loudspeakers located in the squadron area.

In Italy, the Allies were at the suburbs of Florence. In France, the Germans were falling back before the tremendous onslaught of the Americans, the English, and the Canadians. On the Russian fronts, troops of Stalin's armies were pressing on towards Germany proper. In the Central and the Southwest Pacific, the Allies continued to maintain their powerful offensive into Japan's inner defenses.

And here, in this small corner of the worldwide conflict, we were bombing targets in the southern sector of France. This was a departure from our long stretch of activity in the Italian boot and on critical targets in the Italian mainland. We had heard speculation about a possible invasion of southern France, but no confirmation. We had been aware of the build-up of troops and supplies on Corsica, and Ed Perry had made the unlikely observation that "if any more men and equipment were brought ashore, the island would sink." Many had considered Corsica to be a logical staging ground for an assault on the French Riviera. Such an action would be diversionary and cause the deployment of German troops from Italy and the northern France defenses. No one had encouraged our speculation, and we all realized that if an invasion was in the offing, we wouldn't know about it until the eve of its actual happening.

My first mission over France on August 2nd was also the first flown there by the 489th Squadron, the bombing of a railroad bridge east of Nice. The mission was declared unsuccessful, and we knew that we or others would soon be doing an encore. Failure had no place in our natures, and we felt that a duplication of effort was a waste of time, energy, and composure as well as a waste of needed matériel and equipment. Success was branded on our hides.

Early in the morning of the 2nd, about 200 heavy bombers of the 15th Strategic Air Force based in Italy had passed high overhead on their way to a target in France. It was a thrilling sight to see scores of bombers, their formations stringing out for miles as they droned by with their slick silver bodies flashing in the sky, and the realization that the might, the commitment, and the determination of the American people shone in this strategic relief. In spite of the hardships thrust upon us and our countrymen on the ground, we were determined to justify the sacrifices of those back home with nothing less than victorious performance. At the same time, we owed to one another the best of our capabilities and our determination to mount our winged steeds each day to bring the enemy to his knees with our costly, seasoned devastation.

2 August 1944 — Mission #32

Pilot: James McLain   Copilot: Lieutenant Alex Stewart

Target: Railroad Bridge, Nice, France

12-Plane Formation — #6 Second Box — Bomb Load: 4 1,000-pound

The accuracy of the German anti-aircraft defenses reminded us that the enemy took no holidays in France and that we gathered a worthy share of shrapnel tearing into the delicate aluminum membrane of our General Billy Mitchell namesakes. We were grateful for the added heavy armor plating that shielded our crew positions, at least partially protecting us from the cherry-red shards whose abstract forms were instantly crafted and superheated by the detonation and fire of their mother-loads.

The flak on August 2nd, Mission #32, was heavy, intense, and very accurate, but fortunately there were no fighter attacks. Our P-47 escort was on hand to deal with them should they come calling,

My fellow pilot and friend Bob Merkel, flying with the 486th Squadron, had occasion to ask when the aircraft manufacturers would invent a bulletproof or flakproof windshield. On a recent mission, a three-inch-long piece of ugly jagged flak had crashed through his Plexiglas, found a small unprotected gap at the edge of his flak vest, cut through his leather jacket, flying suit, shirt, and undershirt, and tore into the fleshy area in front of his armpit before falling down inside his undershirt and severely burning his belly.

From his hospital bed where he was recovering from surgery and repair of sliced flesh and severed muscles and tendons, he declared in his enlightened Irish manner, "Those damn burns from that hot flak hurt worse and have given me more trouble than this wound. I had one helluva time getting inside my clothes to get it out of there."

We told him he should be grateful that the red-hot flak had not descended further "south."

"Oh, my God," he moaned as he rolled his eyes heavenward.

"Think of having a second circumcision twenty-four years after the first surgery, Bob," my torturing words agonized his vivid imagination.

"Say no more, I can't stand it," he howled.

By this time, laughter mixed with his tears and he swore he would shoot us on sight the first chance he got.

The severity of the wound and the pending treatment were sufficient to end Bob's combat flying career, and he was returned to the States for therapy and rehabilitation.

6 August 1944 — Mission #33
Pilot: Lieutenant Alex Stewart   Copilot: Lieutenant George Bleimes
Target: Rhone River Bridge, Livron, France
6-Plane Formation — #6 First Box — Bomb Load: 4 1,000-pound

On August 6th, we flew Mission #33. Reveille was sounded at 5:45 a.m., allowing us only 45 minutes to dress, eat breakfast, and mount the trucks for roll call before our ride to Headquarters and a briefing at 7:00. Group Commander Colonel Willis Chapman was scheduled to serve as mission Commander, riding in the copilot's seat of the lead plane. Captain Roger MacLellan was lead pilot. In spite of the heavy, accurate flak attack, our mission efficiency was reported to be 96 percent.

An afternoon mission, however, did not do as well, with an efficiency of 32 percent reported. Efficiency was determined by the percentage of bombs landing in the designated target area. Movie cameras mounted in selected planes in each formation filmed the bomb drop from the moment the bombs left the bomb-bays until the exact film frames recorded the moment of impact and explosion. The photo lab was able to encircle the target area on an 8x10 enlargement of the appropriate frame and calculate the percentages.

On our return flight to Corsica from that rather early morning mission, we again saw and passed under the four-engine heavy bombers filling the sky for miles as they winged their way to France at altitudes almost twice that of ours, about 20,000 feet. What we lacked in altitude capabilities we made up for in speed and bombing accuracy. Our targets — such as bridges — required more pinpoint accuracy; the heavy bomber targets called for more general, blanket-pattern bombing, which was used against factories, airfields, and large troop concentrations.

7 August 1944 — Mission #34
Pilot: Lieutenant Joseph Nuessle   Copilot: Lieutenant Alex Stewart
Target: Drome River Railroad Bridge, Livron, France
12-Plane Formation — #6 Second Box — Bomb Load: 4 1,000-pound

On Mission #34, August 7th, I was teamed with Joe Nuessle; this was one of a very few missions that we flew together. Joe had been copilot on my original crew in the States and on our trip overseas to Corsica.

The Rhone River originates in the Alps, flowing from Lake Geneva southwest to Lyon before it follows the valley to Avignon and then to the sea. The Rhone meets the Drome, a small river originating in the foothills of the Maritime Alps between France and Italy, with targeted bridges crossing both rivers at Livron. The day before, on the 6th, we had scored the 96 percent bombing efficiency. On this mission we chalked up 100 percent efficiency and caught hell doing it. The heavy flak peppered our formation, and all six planes in our box were punctured with holes. We counted 37 in our plane.

The Air Intelligence Weekly Summary had given high praise for the 12th Tactical Air Force performance the past few recent months, quite an accomplishment in spite of much restrictive weather.

11 August 1944 — Mission #35
Pilot: Lieutenant Alex Stewart   Copilot: Lieutenant Arthur Harrison
Target: Shore Battery Installation, U546259, France
12-Plane Formation — #6 Second Box — Bomb Load: 8 500-pound
Flak: None — Fighters: None — No Escort

The first real indication that we were building for an invasion of France came on August 11th, Mission #35. It was the first attack that had been made against a shore battery, those big, long-range guns that were used against large naval vessels. The mission would be classified as part of the "softening up" exercise. Strangely, we had no opposition from shore battery installations.

12 August 1944 — Mission #36
Pilot: Lieutenant Arthur Harrison   Copilot: Lieutenant Alex Stewart
Target: Shore Battery Installation, Cannes, France
12-Plane Formation — #6 Second Box — Bomb Load: 8 500-pound

On August 11th, Art Harrison had been my copilot. On the 12th, Mission #36, we switched seats, and I copiloted for Art. Again we bombed a shore battery and recorded it as a "milk-run." It seemed strange to be bombing gun positions on the famous French Riviera.

14 August 1944 — Mission #37
Pilot: Lieutenant W. S. Jones   Copilot: Lieutenant Alex Stewart
Target: Shore Battery Installation, Cape Camerat, France
12-Plane Formation — #5 First Box — Bomb Load: 1 M76, 7 500-pound

On August 14th, we were in the alternate or standby rotation spot and filled in for a 488th Squadron plane that had to drop out and return to Corsica due to engine trouble. But because of poor visibility, we failed to demolish the target — a disappointment, as there was no flak or fighters hindering our efforts.

After supper, at a special meeting, we were told the awesome news that on the next morning, at 0800 hours, southern France was to be invaded. The 12th and 15th Air Forces would be out in full strength. Our group was scheduled to fly at least 72 planes.

15 August 1944 — Mission #38
Pilot: Captain John Mitchell   Copilot: Lieutenant Alex Stewart
Target: Gun Position — S. La Trayas, France
12-Plane Formation — #1 Second box — Bomb Load: 1 M76, 7 500-pound

We all had long anticipated the invasion. On the 15th, our mission briefing was set at 0435 hours, which meant we would be awakened no later than 0315. I was glad to be co-piloting for John Mitchell, one of my favorite lead pilots. And he told me at breakfast that he, too, was glad we were scheduled together. We had a lot of confidence in one another.

Our first targets at 0530 hours were against the gun positions where our invading forces would be landing at 0800 hours, 2½ hours after our drop. This mission fitted in with the intricate part of the huge invasion plan, and strangely, there was no flak opposition and our Spitfire escort turned toward its home base.

The most impressive sight of the invasion was the mass of hundreds of ships and land-ing craft that were scurrying in every direction delivering thousands of soldiers, supplies, and munitions to the shore before returning for another load. I later jotted in my diary that they appeared like a huge school of minnows. I did note that what I saw were the wakes that were being kicked up and not the crafts themselves. It was a very impressive sight, and we all tried to imagine how the June Normandy landings must have appeared and how they dwarfed this secondary effort.

15 August 1944 — Mission #39
Pilot: Lieutenant Arthur Harrison   Copilot: Lieutenant Alex Stewart
Target: Road Bridge, Avignon, France
18-Plane Formation — #3 First Box — Bomb Load: 8 500-pound

We had been told that we would probably all be scheduled for a second mission on the 15th, this "D-day," and to check the bulletin board upon our return from the early morn-ing foray. We were not spared. Again, I was scheduled as copilot for Art Harrison and was not disappointed, though I always preferred to be the pilot.

The bridges at Avignon were notorious, and it seemed that every mission flown there resulted in the group losing a plane or suffering badly damaged planes and wounded avi-ators. Those targets were as heavily defended as any within memory. The sky around us on our flight path was black with the smoke of hundreds of exploded German shells. The varied and now familiar sensations of shell fragments, crashing and piercing the high impact-strength aluminum, still carried its sinister voice, a never-to-be-forgotten sound.

Someone had penciled in on the schedule after that mission: "Avignon . . . We seen da light."

Baxter Thomas was piloting #9-P off the right wing of John Mitchell who was leading the third box on Mission #39. After dropping their bombs and heading for home, Thomas fell out of formation but remained under control, though he was rapidly losing altitude. He no doubt had a severe power loss and other troubles not visible to us. No other plane fell back to escort him, and he was soon lost from view. He probably reported to his leader the serious nature of his trouble and that the plane would not make it. It was later reported that Baxter's plane went into a spin and that the turret gunner, bombardier, copilot, and pilot were able to bail out of the forward section, but that the radio gunner and tail gunner for some unknown reason couldn't make it and went down with the plane.

The crew had consisted of pilot Lieutenant Baxter Thomas of South Pasadena, California; copilot Lieutenant Fred S. Swanson of Los Angeles, California; bombardier Lieutenant George H. England of Everett, Pennsylvania; turret gunner Tech Sergeant John J. Buchanan of Providence, Rhode Island; radio gunner Staff Sergeant William F. Williamson of Galesburg, Illinois; and armorer gunner Sergeant Luther S. Craver of Lexington, North Carolina.

16 August 1944 — Mission #40
Pilot: Lieutenant Alex Stewart   Copilot: Arthur Harrison
Target: Railroad Bridge, Lorio, France
18-Plane Formation — #5 Third Box — Bomb Load: 4 1,000-pound

At 0900 hours on August 16th, the BBC news from London reported over the loud speakers in our squadron area that Allied troops had landed in southern France the day before and were firmly established on beachheads between Marseilles and Nice. Substantial numbers of troops were ashore, and some of them had been pushing on to high ground inland. German opposition thus far had been weak.

Our flak opposition on Mission #40, August 16th, was heavy and very accurate, but there were no fighter attacks. Many planes were holed, and the sheet metal repairmen would be working through the night trimming the ragged edges of the holes and riveting in place their hand-cut patches, ready for the next day's mission.

The Russians had beaten off German counterattacks on the northeastern approaches to East Prussia and also near Warsaw. In Italy, Eighth Army patrols had crossed the Arno River into the northern part of Florence, as well as a little to the west of the city. And, again, Allied bombers had pounded the Japanese island base of Halmahera between New Guinea and the Philippines.

In our remote spot on Corsica we continued to be amazed at the communications and how we were kept informed of the war's progress throughout the world.

I had recently received word from my brother David that he had just arrived overseas. His letter identified his censored location as "somewhere in the Pacific" and I assumed he was in Hawaii. My older brother, Ray, had been overseas for sometime — in Hawaii, as a medical corpsman with the 96th Infantry Division and David was trying to locate him. Ray would work in a Company Aid Station, the first stop for wounded from the battlefield where they had received emergency first aid.

With his premedical training at the University of Chicago, David had quickly qualified for a Pharmacist Mate Third Class rating in the Navy and had been attached to the Marine Corps as a Medical Corpsman. He was assured of battlefield service with Pacific Island invasion forces.

In spite of the emotional burden of having three sons overseas at the same time, the family letters always seemed encouraging and optimistic. Mother, Dad, and sisters Margaret and Jean had their daily lives and work to keep them occupied. But I felt their concerns must have loomed large when they each dealt with those quiet evening hours, alone with their private thoughts.

Mother wrote in a letter that she would sometimes awaken in the night at the sound of high-flying planes and would think of me, and she would say a prayer for me and for those now flying overhead. She also reported that Dad sometimes preferred to stay later in the evening at the studio where it was quiet and he could write to us boys. They were pillars of faith and strength to us in our precarious situations.

In her letters, Ruth never voiced any fears but conveyed her confidence in me and my ability. She kept an unofficial count of my missions, which proved to be quite accurate.

18 August 1944 — Mission #41 (Scrapped Due to Bad Weather)
(Combat time only)
19 August 1944 — Mission #41
Pilot: Robert Martin   Copilot: Lieutenant Alex Stewart
Target: Road Bridge, Orange, France
Target: Road Bridge, Mount Faucon, France
18-Plane Formation — #3 Third Box — Bomb Load: 4 1,000-pound
Mission on 19th, different target, successful
(Combat time and mission credit)

Each day on Corsica was like the day before and described the next. Unchanging, with only slight variations, the days followed a set pattern. We flew combat missions, accepting the hazards and hardships of aerial warfare as the lot for which we had bargained through long months of rigorous training. We saw seasoned men retired to the States for rehabilitation while others less fortunate nursed their wounds. A few took up residence in the miserable confines of German prison camps, and some of their number paid the ultimate cost of freedom with their lives. Old-timers were replaced with younger-looking, refreshed men wearing new-style flight suits and nylon jackets with mouton-lamb collars. Some wondered how these "kids" would be able to do the job.

We ate, slept, read, wrote, played, and listened to war news. We speculated on how Germany would be defeated and when the war would probably end. Time passed slowly. Each day gone by was one less day to be endured.

Much rain fell around the middle of August, which caused a restlessness and uneasiness among us all. We were briefed for missions then returned to our quarters when weather over targets precluded failure. We had been airborne on Friday, August 18th, winging our way to trounce the enemy, when weather forced our return to Alesan. At least we got in a little practice. I noted that there always seemed to be a certain euphoria among the men, especially pilots, when they had been able to "pour the coal" to those two engines and conquer the forces of gravity, if only for a little while. The exhilaration born of flight was infectious and showed itself in a more relaxed, jovial camaraderie. Flying was exciting and fun without the enemy messing things up!

20 August 1944 — Mission #42
Pilot: Lieutenant W. S. Jones   Copilot: Lieutenant Alex Stewart
Target: Dispersal Area, Valence Tresorerie, France
12-Plane Formation — #5 Second Box — Bomb Load: Fragmentation

Loaded with clusters of fragmentation bombs, on August 20th we staged a successful attack on the important dispersal area at Valence Tresorerie and destroyed or severely damaged many enemy aircraft. About 65 miles north of Avignon, in the Rhone River Valley, we anticipated heavy flak concentrations and the Germans did not disappoint us. Fighter opposition was certainly expected, but none appeared. The P-47 escort maneuvered in the area out of the flak zone until we finished our work, then covered us till we got out over the sea and headed back to Corsica.

Several of us had been campaigning for a rest leave and a chance to spend a few days in Rome, on the Isle of Capri, an extended trip to Cairo, Egypt, or a chance to explore the famous island of Malta. Malta had been off limits for quite some time due to the indiscretions of two pilots from our squadron, which had caused an international incident. They had become acquainted with two Maltese girls who persuaded them to take them on a flying trip to Sicily. Their visit to that island to the north lasted a few hours, and there were no customs inspections of any kind when they landed at the airport at Catania. But upon their return to Malta, the British authorities arrested the pilots and charged them with illegally transporting citizens of Malta to a foreign country and in a military aircraft. After notifying our group authorities of the British intention to bring the offenders to trial, the men were released and returned to Corsica.

Sometime later, a court-martial was convened and Major Carl Kisselman, 340th Group Intelligence Officer and lawyer from New Jersey, represented our two pilots. Because there had been no complaint from Sicily and no evidence or testimony that they had actually landed there, Major Kisselman called for dismissal of the trail by the assembled court, and the problem was resolved.

The Major handled the matter skillfully and preserved an amiable relationship with the British so that Malta was again opened up to us for short periods of rest.

On August 22nd, orders were issued allowing eight of us to spend four days on this British Colony fortress. We were to leave on August 23rd, and a two-man crew had been assigned to fly us there in one of three B-25 courier planes, retirees from combat. Our group, all lieutenants, included pilots and bombardiers.

Malta had been the most heavily bombed island in the Mediterranean war. Its vulnerability to German attack stemmed from two sources: its British naval base was a constant target, as were its several British RAF fighter and bomber bases. The fame of its anti-aircraft batteries was widely acclaimed as having the most accurate marksmen in the world. But because of its location and limited access to ammunition supply, every shot had to count. The gunners would hold their fire until the German and Italian aerial attackers were well within range. They were allowed to fire only one volley of shells on each attacker — and that was cutting their performance opportunities pretty thin.

I likened this account to what we learned in grade school about the Battle of Bunker Hill in the Revolutionary War. Facing the British with a very limited supply of ammunition, the American soldiers were ordered not to fire their rifles on the enemy until they "saw the whites of their eyes." Gunners on Malta faced similar restrictions.

But the rationing of ammunition and superb marksmanship paid off, and Malta survived. Evidence of Axis bombing was everywhere, however, and it was said that there was not a building on the entire island that had escaped damage. Most, or perhaps all the buildings were constructed of white limestone, which had been quarried right there on the island. There were very few trees, mostly olive, and certainly none that would produce building lumber. We noted that many stone masons were busy rebuilding churches and larger municipal structures.

Malta, a British island possession in the Mediterranean between Sicily and Africa located about 400 miles southeast from our base on Corsica, had a pre-war population of 222,000 in 1938 and an area of 95 square miles. Two small islands lay adjacent, making it a fabled and picturesque oasis in the beautiful blue sea. It was annexed by the British in 1814. Its capital, Valetta, was a British naval and military base. The entire population of Malta was awarded a decoration for bravery in 1942 by King George VI.

And so it was in this historic setting that we relaxed for four days of late August 1944 in the warm sunshine of a quiet and interesting island in the Mediterranean. The people were friendly and welcomed Americans, perhaps as much for our money as they did for any other reason. We stayed in a dormitory-like room in the British Hotel in the city of Slema, but daily rode gondolas, propelled by gondoliers with their long poles, across the harbor to Valetta and its livelier activity.

One of our first stops was at a bar, run by an American Negro. It was reported that he had been a musician with a dance band playing on a cruise ship when the war broke out and was stranded there on Malta. He lived with his Maltese wife and young child in quarters behind the bar and lived off the proceeds of the business where he served both American and British spirits and sandwiches made by his wife. The big attraction to us was his considerable collection of American Big Band phonograph records. Not much could be said for the quality of his record player but that it was electric and not a hand-cranked manual contraption. Nonetheless, we managed to spend an hour or two each day in what I think we referred to as "Jim's Place," eating what he said was roast beef sandwiches (although there seemed to be a proliferation of goats in the area), drinking British beer or ale, or sometimes some authentic scotch or bourbon. All the while, we kept the record player going with our long-time favorite civilian dance music. "Jim" was always friendly and accommodating.

Slema had a fancier hotel that featured a dance band every evening during, and for an hour or two after, the dinner hour. It was the only place we could find that had a good evening meal available, and even then we were limited to a tasty cold roast beef plate with boiled potatoes and cold celery, carrots, cucumbers, onions, and pickles. There were less attractive and cheaper items on the limited menu, but we all ate the beef.

One evening we struck up conversation with some British Royal Air Force crewmen and noticed that they were not eating very much and limited their drinks to a slowly sipped glass of beer. It turned out that their pay scale did not provide funds sufficient for them to eat or drink much. We Americans decided it was time to have a party. We persuaded the

Brits to pull their tables close to ours and announced that the food and drinks were on us. "We have invaded your territory and need to pay reparations," we told them. At first they seemed embarrassed, but after a drink or two their resistance vanished and they demonstrated their ability to keep up with the rest of us.

For a bunch of hungry airmen, one rather skimpy roast beef cold plate was not enough, and we all reordered. We probably hadn't spend more than six or eight dollars each as our share for the whole evening. It was our first opportunity to use some of our savings in almost four months. I had a hunch that we had provided more business than that dining room had seen in a long time, and they were glad to see us return each night for supper.

Being inveterate souvenir hunters, most of us visited some of the small shops in Malta's narrow streets where building fronts showed gouges in the limestone caused by scraping wheel-hubs from passing carts, small cars, and trucks.

The prevailing religion on Malta was Roman Catholic, and it was apparent that some of the Church's support came from the sale of lace (shawls, doilies, table scarves, and full-size tablecloths), laboriously handmade by nuns of the Franciscan Order. I bought a four-foot square table scarf and about 18 doilies in two sizes for about $7. My purchase no doubt represented months of tedious work by nimble fingers of the saintly, hooded sisters.

At another shop I spotted a fine hunting knife that bore the trade name "NEST KNIFE," made in Sheffield, England, by Sluthern & Richardson. I had wanted such a knife, honed to razor sharpness, to wear in a leather sheath strapped to my leg under my boot when flying missions. If I was forced to bail out, especially over water, I could easily cut my way out of entangled parachute shroud lines. I bought the knife for $6 and wore it on every mission thereafter. The Army Air Forces supplied us with a rather large and awkward knife for no specified use, but it was not suitable for the purpose I intended.

We were interested in Malta's native language. Having been under British rule for well over 100 years, everyone spoke English, with a Middle-Eastern accent. The native Maltese language was a mystery, however, sounding more like an African aborigine tongue than anything we had heard. To our untrained ears, we didn't think it resembled Italian, French, or Spanish and wouldn't have been able to compare it to Greek or Arabic. But I had an opportunity to talk to a knowledgeable priest and he said Maltese was a combination or mixture of Italian and Arabic. Because of Malta's proximity to Sicily and Italy to the north, and the many Arabic countries of North Africa to the south, his explanation seemed reasonable.

Our rest leave passed too quickly, and we prepared to meet the B-25 that would take us back to Corsica and the remainder of our combat tour of duty. Several of us bought a few bottles of whiskey to reinforce the limited stash in each of our tents. Bob Helle of Oak Park, Illinois, an inveterate beer drinker, bought a case of British beer with the idea of hording it for his personal consumption in the privacy of his tent. He used the contents of a foam fire extinguisher to chill it down to satisfactory drinking temperature. However, word of his beer got out and the 24 quart bottles were gone in about an hour after our first night "home." Bob was a generous soul and hated to drink alone.

For a rest leave, our activity on Malta was far from sensational but it was a great diversion from the duty and combat routine we had been saddled with since May 1st, 1944, when we lifted off the Florida runway. We were not disappointed.

2 September 1944 — Mission #43
Pilot: Lieutenant Alex Stewart   Copilot: Lieutenant Robert Helle
Target: Railroad Bridge, Cassana D Adda, Italy
6-Plane Formation — #6 First Box — Bomb Load: 4 1,000-pound

On our next mission, September 2nd, east of Milan, the railroad bridge at Cassana D Adda was missed by all three flight boxes. The flak was excessive, which always proves to be distracting, but a wind shift at or close to the moment of bomb release was blamed.

4 September 1944 — Mission #44
Pilot: Captain E. J. Haster   Copilot: Lieutenant Alex Stewart
Target: Road and Railroad Bridge, Casale Monferrato, Italy
12-Plane Formation — #1 First Box — Bomb Load: 4 1,000-pound

On September 4th, our group sent up 62 planes against the critical road and railroad bridge target at Casale Monferrato. We flew ten boxes of six planes each plus two stand-bys. Photos of the drops showed the mission to be successful in spite of considerable haze over the target. The flak was very heavy and extremely accurate. We had a P-47 escort but encountered no fighter opposition.

The 4th was Ruth's and my first wedding anniversary and I fashioned a greeting on a sheet of plain white paper folded in four like a card and inscribed with the words, "Happy First Anniversary from the Enchanting Mediterranean Island of Corsica — Wish You Were Here!" One of our men was an excellent cartoonist and I had him draw a picture of me in a beach chair with a cool drink and surrounded by several bathing beauties. A few weeks later, I received a one-word letter from Ruth that read, "Huh!"

5 September 1944 — Mission #45
Pilot: Lieutenant Alex Stewart   Copilot: Lieutenant George Fitch
Target: Railroad Bridge, Canneto, Italy
12-Plane Formation — #2 Second Box — Bomb Load: 4 1,000-pound
Flak: Heavy, Accurate — Fighters: None, No escort

Following the mission of September 4th wherein I flew copilot in the lead plane for Captain Haster, I reported to Doc Nestor with a slight sore throat and stopped-up eustachian tubes. I was having trouble clearing my ears. The flight surgeon advised me not to fly, but perhaps failed to get word to Operations before the mission schedule for September 5th was typed and posted. I was listed as copilot for Bob Helle. I noted the error on the evening of the 4th and reported the problem to Jack Mair, the Operations Officer. Jack sought out George Fitch and had him replace me on the schedule in the copilot's slot.

The next morning, the 5th, the crews loaded up and went to the briefing, then on out to their planes. I was dressed, but relaxing in my tent, when Doc Nestor appeared to check on me. He reported that pilot Bob Helle had gotten sick while waiting to join the line-up for takeoff and could in no way fly the mission. The Operations Officer called Doc to see if I could possibly replace Bob. The entire group was in "maximum effort mode," and I was the only pilot available. Doc checked my throat, shot some sulfa powders into the back of my throat, and managed to get my ears cleared, equalizing the pressure on either side of my eardrums. I told him I didn't feel too bad but asked him what I should do if I couldn't clear my ears when there was a sudden change in altitude.

It was obvious that Doc had never been in a tight situation, though he had flown a few missions to have some understanding of what the flight crews went through. He suggested that if we went into a sudden loss of altitude mode I should pull out of formation and climb back up to relieve the pressure on my ear drums, then slowly descend as I cleared my ears on the way down.

"Doc," I said, "you don't pull out of formation in the thick of battle over a target when you're in a steep 350-mile-per-hour dive and become a sitting duck as you creep back up to an ear-clearing altitude and fumble along till you get your ears working right! But I think I'll be okay, though I won't leave the formation." He cleared me to fly the mission.

Doc called the Operations Officer to tell him I was on my way. He drove me in his jeep to the flight line, and I took my place in the pilot's seat vacated by Bob Helle. George Fitch had been to the briefing and filled me in on the target information and other mission details as I found and took our place in the line-up. We were flying in the #2 position off the right wing of the lead plane of the second box. Emil Roesler was the lead pilot. My other crew members were bombardier Lieutenant Hal Lynch, waist gunner Sergeant W. N. Stewart, turret gunner Sergeant Robert Carruth (of my original crew), and tail gunner Sergeant M. J. Walker.

Takeoff, join-up, and trip to the target were normal. My ears cleared okay as we gained altitude, and I felt confident that I would be able to complete the mission without problems.

Flak hit our formation shortly after crossing the Initial Point and continued in intensity for the full length of the bomb run. With bombs dropped and bomb-bay doors closed, Roesler led a rather severe break-off to the right from 325 mph, before turning hard left without regaining the lost altitude.

The pressure had built up in my right ear and I had tried everything I knew to relieve it. Suddenly I felt a pop and the immediate release of the pressure, followed by considerable pain inside my ear. I guessed that my eardrum had ruptured.

At the same time, the pressure in my left ear was giving me trouble, but I was finally able to clear it.

Immediately upon my return to Corsica I reported my mishap to Doc Nestor. He gave me a supply of aspirin for pain, had me gargle with salt water, sprayed some stuff in my ears and repeated the sulfa powder treatment to the eustachian tubes. I was taken off flying status until further notice. Doc checked and treated me daily, finally releasing me for flying status 13 days later. During that time there had been a spate of bad weather and few missions were being flown.

Doc reported that my ear was healing, and that the trouble had been small but nonetheless damaging. I believe he did the best for me that he could, with the limitations of therapy available to him. He did regret that he had allowed me to fly and swore he wouldn't do it again for anyone. He never did say that the drum had ruptured, but I drew my own conclusions.

B-25 pilots were very vulnerable to ear damage and hearing problems due to the plane's noise. Not only were the engine exhaust tubes short, offering no dampening of noise, but the tips of the propellers were in almost perfect alignment with the pilot's and copilot's ears.

At higher operational engine rpm's the tip-speed noise of the props reached a high decibel level and caused much damage to the nerves in our hearing mechanisms. Wearing earphones provided some protection, but I was very uncomfortable with both phones clamped to my ears. With the exception of those times on the bomb run or in another high flak attack when I wore a flak helmet with hinged ear flaps covering the earphones, I kept the right phone positioned behind my right ear when I was the pilot or behind my left ear when I was flying copilot.

There were times when conversation with the other pilot was needed without letting other crew members in on what was said. If, for example, the instruments showed that we had the potential for a serious malfunction, we might not have been ready to make that general announcement to the crew. Some men had been known to panic without provocation. In such instances the intercom was not used. And the exposure of the open ear to the full impact of the noise unknowingly did its damage.

18 September 1944 — Mission #46
Pilot: Lieutenant Robert Helle   Copilot: Lieutenant Alex Stewart
Target: Gun Positions-Supply Depot, Rimini, Italy
6-Plane Formation — #2 First Box — Bomb Load: 22 100-pound Demo

Although Bob Helle had been my copilot on the September 2nd mission, the September 18th mission was my first to fly as Bob's copilot. Bob and I first met in primary flight school at Ontario, California, in February 1943. And, again, on Mission #46, September 18th, we received a nasty taste of "Jerry's" revenge.

22 September 1944 — Mission #47
Pilot: Lieutenant Alex Stewart   Copilot: Lieutenant James Gittings
Target: Railroad Bridge, Nervessa Di Battaglia, Italy
12-Plane Formation — #2 Second Box — Bomb Load: 4 1,000-pound

On the 22nd, 12 planes dropped 48,000 pounds of bombs on the railroad bridge spanning the Piave River. The bridge was destroyed.

23 September 1944 — No Mission Credit
Pilot: Lieutenant Alex Stewart   Copilot: Lieutenant James Gittings
Target: Italian Light Cruiser *Taranto*, La Spezia, Italy
12-Plane Formation — Standby — Bomb Load: 6 1,000-pound SAP

On the 23rd, six planes from each of three other squadrons dropped a total of 108 1,000-pound semi-armor-piercing (SAP) bombs on the Italian ship *Taranto*, and it submerged, leaving no target for the 489th. Although I was flying "standby" and didn't fill in for anyone, I tagged along as #7 in the second box of the 489th, ready to drop our bombs rather than take them back to Corsica. We did not drop, nor did any of our squadron, but returned to base with a full load. I was credited with combat time but got no credit for a mission.

24 September 1944 — Mission #48
Pilot: Lieutenant Alex Stewart   Copilot: Lieutenant G. C. Gearhart
Target: Railroad Bridge, Citadella, Italy
12-Plane Formation — #5 First Box — Bomb Load: 4 1,000-pound

In spite of the heavy pounding we had been taking on many of our missions, I was amazed at the few losses we suffered. And miraculously, we had very few wounded men. Our planes, however, continued to return with badly damaged control surfaces, those fabric-covered devices that allowed us to turn and to rise or descend (ailerons, elevators, and rudders), horizontal and vertical stabilizers, shattered windshields, shot-out instruments, severed control cables, and punctured oil lines, which caused the homeward trip to be made on one engine.

26 September 1944 — Mission #49
Pilot: Lieutenant Alex Stewart   Copilot: Lieutenant G. C. Gearhart
Target: Railroad Bypass Bridge, Citadella, Italy
12-Plane Formation — #5 First Box — Bomb Load: 4 1,000-pound

September 26th, 1944, marked the third anniversary of my entrance into the Army. What a way to celebrate!

The mission that day, #49, was my first mission with Gayle Gearhart as my copilot. Gayle was from State College, Pennsylvania, and might be described as one of those types that most of us knew in grade school — "different." Remember the guy that always had a wad of twine in his pocket, or parts of an alarm clock, or some other contraption that he was working on to repair or convert to some other use? Well, Gayle fit into that mold. In September 1944, he was a rather recent addition to our squadron and had gathered with many of us in my tent on his first night on Corsica.

During our bull-session he became intrigued with my pot-bellied stove and the manner in which I had formed a length of ¼-inch copper tubing into a pinwheel-like circle with smaller circles graduating in size from the inside to the 10-inch diameter outer circle. I had drilled tiny holes about every two inches of tubing length from the inner to the outer circle. The idea was to create a generator where the gasoline in the heated turns of the tubing would pre-vaporize and cause a miniature "blow-torch" effect at each of the tiny holes. I had hoped to improve the efficiency of the stove and reduce the amount of soot generated, thus reducing the frequency of stove-pipe cleaning. But it never did work worth a darn.

Well, even before Gayle had been assigned to fly his first mission he fetched materials from the supply tent on the flight line and set about to fashion his own heating creation. He shared a two-man tent with his bombardier, James Clayton of Houston, Texas. Jim had no interest in the stove.

After a few days of work on his stove and several trial runs, which had been adequate to thoroughly soot up the stove pipe, Gayle decided he was ready to give it a real "shake-down" run. He opened the small gasoline supply valve, then began looking for a match. Finding none, he borrowed a book of matches from a guy in the next tent. He returned to his tent, bent over the stove, and struck a match. With the fumes that had accumulated in the stove while he had searched for matches, he had the makings of a piece of ordnance that might qualify for front-line routing of the enemy.

I had been sitting in my tent, 30 yards from his when I heard the explosion. I jumped up and ran out in time to see Gayle emerge from his tent, his face, arms, and hands blackened with soot. A closer look showed that he had burned off the hair from his arms, his eyebrows, and the front of his head. Fortunately, he was not burned otherwise. At first glance, he looked rather comical as he resembled the end man in a minstrel show.

In addition to his hairless condition, his tent was a mess. The explosion had caused the stove pipe to tumble down and coat everything with soot. His and Jim's clothes got the most liberal dose of the black stuff.

Suddenly, Jim became very interested in the stove. Gayle's stove-building days came to an abrupt halt, and they resorted to the normal stove operation. But Gayle never lived down his misguided stove adventure.

Gayle had been handed the nickname of "Gear Box" upon his arrival in the outfit. In the tradition of "Omar, the Tent Maker," Gayle's name was changed to: "Gear Box, the Stove Builder." And some of the guys called him "Smokey" — names that stuck as long as I was on Corsica.

30 September 1944 — Mission #50
Pilot: Lieutenant Alex Stewart   Copilot: Lieutenant James Gittings
Target: Railroad Bridge, Borgo Forte, Italy
12-Plane Formation — #4 Second Box — Bomb Load: 4 1,000-pound

Mission #50, on September 30th, was our first in five days of stand-downs due to rain. Major Berenson and his staff in Group Communications assisted in the development of radio release of bombs and we were among the first to use this new method.

Basically, when the lead plane released its bomb load, a radio signal was immediately transmitted and picked up by radio receivers in the other five planes in the box, which automatically released their bombs. This eliminated the short time lag that occurred when wing bombardiers toggled their bombs at the moment they saw the bombs of the lead plane leave its bomb-bay. Our bombing accuracy took a huge jump, much to the delight of Colonel Chapman and General Knapp, both of whom got our firsthand reports at interrogation that day.

Our target was the bridge that spanned the Po River. This was my first mission as first pilot flying in the #4 place in the formation, actually leading the second element. It was a difficult position and most pilots hated it as it required intense concentration on the lead plane and tended to put a crick in your neck. For some reason, I liked the spot and did very well at it.

1 October 1944 — Mission #51
Pilot: Lieutenant Alex Stewart   Copilot: Lieutenant K. B. Hancock
Target: Railroad Bridge, Magenta, Italy
12-Plane Formation — #2 First Box — Bomb Load: 4 1,000-pound
3-Plane Chaff Element — Bomb Load: 12 100-pound White Phosphorus

On October 1st, a three-plane chaff element preceded the other formations on the bomb run and over the target, throwing out paper-backed tinsel strips about 12 inches long to flutter down and form a radar-distorting window. The chaff element also bombed German 88mm gun positions with white-smoke phosphorus, to mark the emplacement for the following bombers.

3 October 1944 — Mission #52
Pilot: Lieutenant Alex Stewart   Copilot: Lieutenant Scott Herrin
Target: Railroad and Road Bridge, Magenta, Italy
12-Plane Formation — #4 First Box — Bomb Load: 4 1,000-pound

On the 3rd, once again we employed the radio-release technique and made a successful strike. This was my second mission as pilot in the #4 position. Flight leader John Mitchell, with Operations Officer Jack Mair flying as mission Commander in the copilot's seat, were both aware of my ability to hold a tight formation. With that and radio release, we had an especially compact bombing pattern.

Most planes collected a generous portion of flak holes, and one man in particular had a very close call. A gunner received the impact of a two-inch piece of flak that had penetrated his leather jacket and flying suit, but the flak was stopped by a small Bible with an "armor plated" cover that he carried in his left shirt pocket. After the mission, the gunner was riding on the same truck with my crew and some others on our way to interrogation. Joe Nuessle, also on the truck, examined the Bible, opening it to the page where the flak had made its last penetration. Joe read the item of scripture, and as I recall, it had no particular significance as far as its lifesaving role was concerned. But after that incident, an enterprising Bible salesman could have sold a few hundred armor-plated Bibles.

4 October 1944 — Mission #53
(No Mission — Bad Weather over target — One hour combat time credit)
Pilot: Lieutenant Alex Stewart   Copilot: Lieutenant Robert Helle
12-Plane Formation — #4 Second Box — Bomb Load: 4 1,000-pound
(Returned to base with all bombs)

For several weeks, we had very poor mail service from home, without any logical explanation. Our food situation also had not been very good, but, on the other hand, it hadn't been described as being very bad. We had been getting fresh meat and butter two or three times a week, but no fresh vegetables. The fresh produce was often purchased by men flying courier trips to Italy or Sicily. Most, if not all, vegetables and fruits coming from the States were either dried or canned.

In the late summer and fall months, we had been able to purchase fresh apples, pears, peaches, and some berries from the small Corsican farms, but the supply was limited. Somebody invaded the small orchard of a local grower and hauled away a goodly supply of peaches, only to be spotted and reported by the farmer to the squadron Commander. The culprit was quickly nabbed, ordered to return the loot to the farmer, and stiffly reprimanded. We were all informed that we had no right to these privately owned foods and were ordered to leave them alone.

Early October had been a period of stand-downs caused by heavy rains, high winds, and a time of long days and longer evenings. The dry river bed that had been the camp-site for many of the linemen became a raging torrent rushing along its course as it roared to the sea. The fickle elements of the weather had been a constant struggle for the old timers in the outfit who had endured the heat, cold, dust, sand, wind, and rain of Africa — all of which seemed to have conspired against them, with the possible exception of this summer on Corsica. With living conditions in makeshift accommodations and working in an occupation so dependent on favorable weather, we were acutely aware of the physical environment and its effect on everything we did.

Frequently the weather over Corsica was favorable, but conditions over the target areas were not conducive to bombing operations. Often at these times we engaged in practice missions, operating over the sea and sighting on familiar landmarks in the 340th Group area. These sessions were helpful to new replacement crews coming into the group learning join-up procedures and the finer points of formation flying as practiced in combat operations. And pilots who were trying out for lead-pilot positions had the opportunity to polish their skills.

Virtually everywhere in Europe the war had slowed to the proverbial snail's pace. Colonel Tolchenov, a Soviet writer, declared in a *Stars and Stripes* article: "The present period of military operations may be regarded as a period of accumulation of forces for the last decisive storming of Germany."

11 October 1944 — Mission #53
Pilot: Lieutenant Alex Stewart   Copilot: Lieutenant Robert Helle
Target: Railroad Bridge, Canneto, Italy
12-Plane Formation — #4 Second Box — Bomb Load: 4 1,000-pound

Because I had demonstrated an ability at flying the #4 position, the Operations Officer had been scheduling me in that spot quite frequently. He had learned that I was perhaps the odd-ball in the squadron that liked #4 and was determined to use me there as often as possible. Some of the flight leaders had expressed their preference for me there as my willingness to tuck in close on the bomb runs enhanced their bombing patterns. Actually, I found that I was able to respond quickly to their changes in altitude and direction and minimize what I termed "throttle pumping." John Mitchell once said that "I stuck to him like fly-paper." I never had a hankering to be a flight leader, but I felt I had found my long suit in the #4 spot. It didn't make much difference on our 53rd mission, however, on October 11th, as we encountered no opposition.

15 October 1944 — Mission #54
Pilot: Lieutenant Alex Stewart   Copilot: Lieutenant Joseph Nuessle
Target: Road Bridge, Galliate, Italy
12-Plane Formation — #4 First Box — Bomb Load: 4 1,000-pound

Mission #54, October 15th, occurred on a typical fall day on Corsica. There was a bit of a chill in the air, as the sun reluctantly hid behind a thin cloud cover. Corsican peasants were harvesting their grain, and the distant Mediterranean was placid, its blue color only somewhat less vivid than in the sunny weather. Returning from the mission, several of us played a noisy game of touch-football, relieving the tension induced by the morning combat and its heavy flak attack.

The roar of our B-25 engines could be heard as their crew chiefs serviced and checked operations. I had recently been assigned my own plane, 9C, which was crewed by a fine young man from Pennsylvania, Master Sergeant Ezra L. Baer. When we discovered we shared March 15 as our birthday, a further comparing of notes revealed who was the older — he having entered that world in the early morning hours of the 15th while I put in a tardy appearance mid-morning of the day. When he told me he weighed nine pounds at birth, I found the reason for my late coming was due to gaining another 1½ pounds, weighing in at 10½.

Our squadron artist, Michael ("Angelo"), painted on the nose of 9C the picture of the stunning bathing beauty from a Varga calender I had given him. I had named the plane *Ruthless Ruthie* but for some reason he left off *Ruthless*. I checked on it and found that the slip of paper I had given him bearing the name had been torn in two and only *Ruthie* had remained. So, *Ruthie* wasn't *Ruthless* after all. The real Ruthie certainly wasn't ruthless so I decided to just keep the plane in character with its namesake.

Crew Chief Ezra Baer's planes had a remarkable record of performance and had included at least four B-25s during his years of overseas operational service. *Ruthie* was perhaps under his care longer than the others. Her total wartime record showed that she had flown 108 missions, had downed one fighter to her credit, and only one early return, due to a mechanical malfunction.

We didn't always fly the plane assigned to us — sometimes it was grounded for periodic examination, sheet metal repairs, or some other requirement to keep it in top operational condition. But on those days when I came with my crew to fly 9C on a mission, I would sometimes ask Ezra if everything was okay and ready to go. He had one stock answer for me. "Get me a parachute and I'll go with you." That's all the assurance I needed, and I quit asking.

Soon after 9C had been assigned to me, Ezra told me that in all his time overseas and crewing for several pilots, he had never been given the opportunity to fly the B-25. I told him that we would soon correct that oversight, and we scheduled a time when Ezra and I could go off together and have some fun. Ezra was a good student, and I believe that had he been given the opportunity, he would have been an excellent pilot. He was smart and beautifully coordinated — and he knew the aircraft.

We flew three or four times together, and I was delighted to see how tickled he was for the opportunity and how well he responded to instruction. I had him do most of the flying

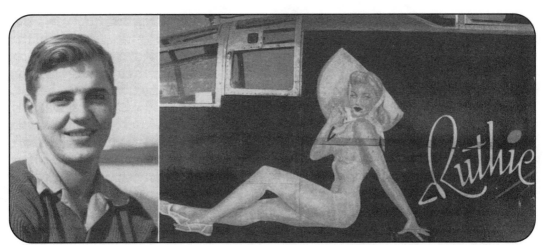

Master Sergeant Ezra L. Baer, of Somerset, Pennsylvania, crew chief of Stewart's B-25 9C *Ruthie.*
From **History and Personnel, 489th, 340th Bomb Group**, *1947*

while I kept a close touch on the controls, applying occasional pressures when he needed slight adjustments or corrections.

The last time we flew together I coached Ezra down to the final approach. He looked at me when he thought it was time for me to take over. I told him he was doing fine and to go ahead and land the plane. He said he wasn't ready for that yet, but I insisted he keep a light hold on the wheel and a light touch on the rudder pedals. I talked him down to the point of flare-out from descent to leveling out above the runway and he was able to feel the sensations and the required responses as I made the actual landing.

The B-25 had beautiful landing characteristics and most of the pilots exercised them to the utmost. With the approach established, the set-down spot selected, and the engines reduced to a full idling speed, the pilot would flare out to virtual straight-and-level flight a foot or two above the runway. As the plane lost flying speed, the pilot eased back on the stick, bringing the nose up into a shallow climbing attitude. Of course, with the reduced speed, the plane did not climb but commenced settling to earth.

By this time it had slowed to the stalling speed of about 95 mph, the main gear touched the earth, and the tires made a slight screeching sound as wheel rotation began. The pilot continued to hold the nose wheel off the ground as long as possible to effect maximum deceleration and minimize wear on the brake rotors and pads. Finally, the nose wheel would be lowered to the ground and brakes applied. A smooth landing like this was referred to as "a grease job."

Ezra Baer was delighted with his participation in our flight and landing. I pointed out to him that he was a part of the team that made our missions successful, enabling me to bring plane and crew safely home. I considered Ezra an equal, in spite of the fact that we wore different badges of rank identification for our respective Military Occupational Specialties, which in reality did little more than establish our varying receipts on payday. Our time together on Corsica forged an enduring respect and friendship.

Of course, I had been showing him, in a combat operational bomber, the fine points of flying and landing that I had started learning in a primary training plane and gradually had perfected in several types of aircraft during a period of two years and hundreds of flights.

I received much satisfaction at the pleasure he gained from the experience and wished I had spent more time with him. I helped him fill a longing that he had nurtured during those hectic years in training at Keesler Field, Mississippi, the fruitful time of learning every facet of the B-25 at the North American Aircraft Corporation School and the demanding work in war-torn North Africa, Sicily, Italy, and Corsica . . . keeping his charges flying! Besides his job as crew chief of 9C, Ezra was also flight chief of Flight C, where he advised on and supervised some of the work of several other crew chiefs. As a Master Sergeant, he had achieved the highest enlisted rank possible. Regrettably, there were no medals or awards given for his work.

Ezra became an intricate part of my service and took a place with a few others at the top of the list of comrades I most honored and loved.

18 October 1944 — Mission #55
Pilot: Lieutenant Alex Stewart   Copilot: Lieutenant Edward Perry
Target: Railroad Bridge, Magenta, Italy
12-Plane Formation — #4 Second Box — Bomb Load: 4 1,000-pound

Although Ed Perry and I had trained together in South Carolina and were in the same flight on our trip from Florida to Corsica — and even now were tent mates — Mission #55, on October 18th, was the first and only time we flew together.

This was one of those "off again-on again" days. We were on our way to the briefing when word came that a stand-down was declared for the rest of the day. But somewhere in the process, Wing changed its mind, and the call came just after lunch to stand-by. We soon returned to group Headquarters for the briefing before taking off for the target in northern Italy. Arriving at the Magenta railroad bridge, the sky was completely overcast, which caused us to return to Corsica with full bomb loads. Either the weather information had been faulty or the cloud cover had moved in while we were preparing for the mission.

20 October 1944 — Mission #56
Pilot: Lieutenant Alex Stewart   Copilot: Lieutenant John Daniels
Target: Railroad Bridge, Palazzolo, Italy (1st Box — Radio Release)
Railroad Bridge, Fornova, Italy (2nd Box)
12-Plane Formation — #4 First Box — Bomb Load: 4 1,000-pound
Flak: Heavy, Accurate — Fighters: None

Regardless of the circumstances, airplanes never cease to hold a fascination for those who fly in them as well as for the ground support personnel. On October 20th, Mission #56, I was impressed that members of Operations, the Intelligence people, and the ground maintenance men were on hand to watch us as we took off. They had climbed in our join-up procedure and observed our completed formation as we headed for Italy. They all had seen it happen dozens, even hundreds, of times and never tired of it.

There is a magic about the flashing silver-colored monsters maneuvering in orderly form against a backdrop of azure sky, bent on the common goal of forcing peace upon a world on fire.

And, with all of its dangers and uncertainty, I was proud to be a part of the conflict, even though the stress was taking its toll. I had now flown five more missions than our predecessors had, and that realization created a rather disquieting effect. The change in the number of missions to be flown from 50 to 60, then from 60 to 70, and then — the final blow — "There is no limit; you will fly until the flight surgeons decide you have had enough" hit many of us like a ton of bricks.

Our missions had escalated in intensity. Sometimes sleep came slow and hard, broken by wild dreams that exaggerated reality. Lying awake in the wee hours before dawn, my imagination sometimes exceeded reasonable limits and I envisioned disaster on the next day's mission. I would sit up and smoke a cigarette while I restored my mind to rationality and tried to regain perspective.

4 November 1944 — Mission #57
Pilot: Lieutenant Alex Stewart   Copilot: Lieutenant Scott Herrin
Target: Railroad Bridge, Casale Monferrato, Italy
6-Plane Formation — #4 First Box — Bomb Load: 4 1,000-pound
Flying third box of 488th Squadron formation

It seemed at times that the ill-fortunes of our bomb group came in deliberate segments and the tides of the war were aroused by renewed enemy vigor. Tales of miraculous incidents were common, such as that of the armor-plated Bible stopping a piece of deadly flak. At the same time, new tragedies were recorded that sometimes out-balanced the miracle score and left many of us in a state of shock and disbelief. I wasn't prepared for the blow that would hammer me and perhaps others into far-reaching submission.

The blare of the bugle echoed through the Corsican foothills and found its way back to the sleeping forms of about 400 Army airmen. There wasn't a bugler in the bunch but the scratchy phonograph record of Reveille, with the implied refrain of "I can't get 'em up, I can't get 'em up, I can't get 'em up in the morning" coming over the loud speakers was just as effective.

It was 6:30 a.m., Friday, November 4th, 1944, and I had, as usual, cheated the bugle by 30 minutes. I was facing my 57th bombing mission. As I stretched out the full length of my sleeping bag, I thought again of the phenomenon of warfare and the compelling, the propelling force that moved us to mount our daily assaults against the enemy, flying into a reign of terror, unwavering, to deliver our destruction. I thought about the foot soldiers storming a South Pacific Island beach, charging into the teeth of certain death, and never realizing how close to home such reality would become.

What was the force that powered us to do this, day after day? We used to say that we weren't required to be nuts, but it sure helped. And what about the enemy. Was he not faced with the same dilemma?

I doused my face and head with cool water from the inverted helmet wash basin, mopped with a towel long overdue at Maria's wash tub, then swiped at my hair with a comb that looked like it needed a set of dentures and hid it all under my overseas cap. A hot-water shave from the recycled #10 food can on the pot-bellied stove completed my morning ablutions, and off I trotted to the officers mess for a nondescript breakfast.

Garbed in the prescribed attire, ready to "do battle with the Hun," I boarded the waiting truck for roll call and a jarring trip to the airfield.

The potholes were large and deep and were often said to be the "hiding place for missing vehicles." They did little for the enthusiasm of 18 airmen being delivered in each of two Army trucks, bouncing along the narrow coastal road enroute to group Headquarters for a mission briefing. Other evidence of blustering military vehicles showed on the ancient cork oak trees lining the gravel thoroughfare. Never intended to accommodate more than burro-drawn farm carts, bicycles, and small French and Italian cars, the roadway was being eroded by the large American and British war machines, which were crudely pruning, debarking, and badly scarring the overhanging trees.

I had heard his name at roll call and now faced him as we tried to maintain our seats on the long, hard truck benches.

"Hey, Sydney," I hollered over the noise of the whining war-weary machine and the chatter of the others. "How come you're flying today? I thought you were all through and waiting for your orders to go home."

"Yeah! Well," he hollered back, "Turner was sick and couldn't fly, so Jack said he was short on bombardiers and asked me to go one more mission. So, I said, 'Yeah, just one more.' And, here I am."

The truck stopped in front of the group quonset-type building where mission briefings were held. The crews were glad to leave the vehicle and drag themselves inside to see what "fun" was in store for us this bright, clear fall day. The colorful conversations about what we would do to the Germans and the added number of missions we were expected to fly faded when we jumped from tailgate to inch-thick dust of the roadway. Cigarette smoke swirled around our heads as we walked to the quonset for the briefing, part of the blue haze hanging heavy inside the crowded room. The acrid smoke from still-burning butts in #10 recycled food cans was overwhelming, irritating our eyes.

We sat on four-legged steel stools, the major remnants of bomb-fin shipping crates, and listened to our leaders describe mission details. The target, marked in red on a large map of northern Italy, was a long railroad bridge spanning the Po River at Cassale Monferrato. It was surrounded by a formidable array of black dots, each designating a German 88mm anti-aircraft cannon, the most accurate and versatile of its type anywhere in the war. Camera-equipped high-flying P-38 photo reconnaissance planes had snapped pictures the day before and supplied the gun plots for the bombers. Though unstated, it appeared there were over 100 guns protecting the target and our likely route into and out of the target area.

A flight path to and from the target was charted in blue and the escape route designated, after "bombs away." We were to break to the right off the target to minimize exposure to gunfire. The bombing officer and the weather and Intelligence officers each spoke to their respective specialties, and we mentally noted their remarks. No written information was permitted to be carried on the mission by other than those in the lead plane.

Escape kits and high-energy concentrated emergency rations were issued and stored in the zippered leg pockets of our flying suits. "Glass Knob" was to be our radio call sign code name. We synchronized watches and listened to the Group Commander, Colonel

Willis Chapman, issue his final glorious message: "If you don't knock this goddamn bridge down today, remember, you're back every day till you do. Keep cool and good luck."

We again boarded the trucks and were delivered to our aircraft, 9C *Ruthie*, in the dispersal area. Each crew member pre-flighted his equipment, and I checked over the plane with the crew chief. The engines were fine-tuned, and I noted the pressures, temperatures, gas gauges, and controls as we taxied out for takeoff. Our turn came and I opened the throttles wide and synchronized engine speeds as we moved down the runway. Airborne, I signaled the copilot for wheels up and gradually "milked up" the flaps to help increase forward speed without sacrificing lift. I felt the prop-wash of the plane 20 seconds ahead of us and jogged slightly upwind to find smooth air. We joined the formation, climbed to 12,000 feet, and headed for the target.

At the moment of crossing the Italian coast near Genoa, I silently said my routine, fervent prayer, "Dear Lord, please give me the strength and wisdom to see me through this day. Amen."

We rendezvoused with our fighter escort, a squadron of 12 British Spitfires, also based on Corsica. They would fly well above us and engage any German fighters lurking in the sun, waiting for the chance to destroy us and our mission plans. The Spities would stay with us until we started our bomb run, then pull away, as would the German fighters, to avoid being hit by the anti-aircraft fire.

Our six-plane box was leading the entire group of 48 B-25s. I was the leader of the second "V," following the mission commander, and had been briefed to take over the mission if the leader was forced for any reason to abandon his role. As we neared the target area, the eight boxes of six maneuvered into single file. We crossed the IP and started the bomb run to the target. My two wing planes tightened the formation, and we were now wearing our heavy flak jackets and flak helmets.

Suddenly the first four customary shells burst right in the formation, stair-stepping up, *bump-bump-bump-bump*. The Jerrys sure had our range, and at this point we could take very little evasive action. Bombing success depended on perfect, straight-and-level flying, without deviations or skids. We were committed and had to endure this monotonous posture for about seven minutes.

Suddenly all hell broke loose. The sky became black with smoke from hundreds of exploding shells, acrid and sickening as some of the fumes seeped into the cockpit. Jagged shards of steel shrapnel rattled off the belly and wings, sounding like handfuls of thrown stones. Some pieces pierced the aluminum skin and made the deadly sound, the loud *KA-JUNG*. Others pierced the windows, and a section of my windshield was shattered. Fortunately, the sharp, dart-like pieces of Plexiglas went astray and didn't hit my face or the face of the copilot.

The German shelling was devastating. My job as leader of the second element required intense concentration on the lead plane. I held a position about 15 feet down and 15 feet behind the leader's tail. I didn't have time or inclination to observe the surrounding action.

Finally, the leader's bomb-bay doors opened. We all opened ours. Again, a radio signal from the lead plane would automatically trigger our bomb-release shackles and all six planes would drop their loads simultaneously, assuring bomb concentration on the target. Long seconds passed, then we felt the up-lift of the plane as its deadly cargo was released.

The bombardier called over the intercom, "Bombs away. Bomb-bay doors closed. Let's get the hell out of here."

The formation made a sharp, deep diving turn to the left, not to the right, as we had been instructed in briefing. Instantly, I realized the leader's error. I mashed the microphone button on my wheel and hollered, "Glass-Knob leader, break right, break right! Glass-Knob leader, you're going the wrong way, break right!"

He never seemed to hear me. I had a sudden impulse to break formation and take my element to the right. But that unbreakable rule of staying with the leader, with the formation, that had been pounded into us all during training and in combat, screamed at me to stay, and I didn't deviate. Our steep diving turn into the no-man's land of shell-fire, "right down flak alley," continued unrelentingly.

Ninety degrees into the turn, the turret gunner called over the intercom, "Rossler's been hit. Most of his left wing is gone. He's really coming apart. They're going into a spin."

Rossler was my left wingman. I took a quick look out of my left side window at the moment his right wing came up and they started into the spin, and as quickly, I returned to watching the leader's tail.

We finally bottomed out of the steep, diving turn and were going into a steep climbing turn to the right. We had clocked over 400 mph, 60 mph over the B-25 top-speed red line. The pressures on the ailerons, the elevators, and the rudders taxed my aching elongated muscles. We were flying bombers like they were fighter planes. The gravity force on our bodies was a thousand times worse than that of the steepest slide on a roller coaster. Facial skin and muscles stretched down against their will. Lower eyelids pulled down as if tugged by someone searching for specs of dirt. Neck and ear muscles merged with the shoulders. I felt like I weighed a ton and, technically, I probably did. I wondered if the aluminum skins of our planes would be rippled from the excess. Would we pop any rivets?

I called the crew to watch Rossler's plane and count parachutes, the one way we would know if anyone got out of that fractured capsule. The crew saw no chutes and watched as the plane met its ultimate doom, exploding in a huge ball of fire in the city of Alessandria.

We were finally headed out of the heavy flak zone, and I heaved a pained sigh of relief. At the same time, I had a sickening feeling over the loss of Rossler and his crew. I wondered who was flying with him, but this was no time or place for tears, as our flight responsibilities were all-consuming, ever-alert for the unexpected. We still had to get out of there and get back to Corsica. What other emergencies would we face? In combat, crises multiplied.

A frantic call suddenly sounded from the tail gunner. "One of the ships from the box behind us has lost an engine. He's feathered the prop and dropping down and back of the formation." I called the Glass-Knob leader for permission to escort him home. The leader granted the request, and instructed J. J. Walsh, my right wingman, to join his element in the #4 spot. I took up a right wing position on the crippled plane as he mushed along as my leader. We snuggled in close and slowed to match his 150 mph speed, lowering our flaps for needed lift in the slower flight mode.

With his left propeller feathered, I noted that the troubled plane, from the 488th Squadron, seemed to be losing power. He was losing altitude, unable to hold at a reasonably safe level and had descended to about 1,000 feet as we approached the Mediterranean coast. He obviously was struggling with an important decision. To continue over land, the likelihood of reaching an Allied landing field before he ran out of power and altitude was not very promising. To bail out or crash-land in enemy territory meant that they would all certainly be taken prisoner, suffer serious injury, or death.

If, on the other hand, he continued over the water toward Corsica and was forced to ditch in the sea, Air/Sea Rescue would be able to pick them up.

We talked by radio and I urged him to try for the water landing if he ran out of sky.

His good engine was failing, and we were at 1,000 feet when we crossed the coastline and headed out over the sea. Another ten miles and the engine finally quit. He feathered the prop and made a good ditched landing on the fairly calm water.

I immediately called Air/Sea Rescue on the emergency frequency, notifying them of the location of the downed B-25. We circled the sinking ship and saw the liferafts pop out of their outer-surface compartments. The six-man crew scrambled out, and buoyed by their Mae West life jackets, splashed their way to the rafts, tethered to the plane by ropes like umbilical cords. The four crewmen in front scrambled into the larger raft while the waist and tail gunners squeezed onto the smaller rear raft. At an altitude of about 100 feet, I continued to circle the downed men while their plane slowly filled with sea water and disappeared below the surface.

Suddenly the turret gunnner hollered over the intercom, "Fighters at six o'clock. I think they might be ours. Yeah, they're P-47s, four of them."

My heart did a flip-flop. First was that rush of dread, adrenaline flooding my brain, as I momentarily contemplated the potential encounter with a determined foe. Then the exhilaration, birthed by the presence of friends. I grinned, then wondered if those pilots included my Primary classmates Bob Purcell and Tony Van Riswick. They were based with a P-47 fighter group at Pisa.

The four P-47s dove down for a fly-by, then each in turn did a climbing roll greeting as they pulled up and retreated to the north. They were probably searching for targets of opportunity, saw us in our dilemma, and came by to check us out

. We continued to circle the liferafts until an Air/Sea Rescue fighter plane appeared to take over the vigil, waiting for the PBY-5 flying boat or the rescue launch.

I waggled our wings in gratitude, climbed from our 100-foot circling elevation to 1,000 feet, and turned toward home. Corsica sure looked good, and squadron Intelligence liked our report. But they were as saddened by the fate of Donny Rossler and his crew, as were all the men of the squadron.

I recited the details of Rossler's demise as best I could with other crewmen filling in. I knew Rossler's copilot was Gittings, but I didn't know who else was with him. Jack Casper scanned the schedule and read the names of the crew: pilot, Lieutenant Donald Rossler, Seattle, Washington; copilot, Lieutenant James Gittings, Louisville, Kentucky; bombardier, Lieutenant Sydney Newman, Dorchester, Massachusetts.

"Sydney Newman. Not Sydney?" I choked in disbelief. "He was ready to go home but agreed to fly one more mission 'cause Operations was short on bombardiers." I was stunned.

Jack read the names of the others: radio gunner, Sergeant Harris, Denver, Colorado; turret gunner, Sergeant Chester Corle, Baltimore, Maryland; and tail gunner, Sergeant Daniel Mallicoat, Monroe, Michigan. But I hardly heard these names; my mind was clinging to the fate of Sydney Newman, the man who rode with me on the truck that morning, having agreed to fly one more mission, though he didn't have to. The man whose wife had recently delivered their first child, and now that baby didn't have a daddy.

Sleep came slow and fitfully that night. I struggled with the reality of the situation. Could I have saved them from disaster by breaking our element to the right and leaving the formation? It was a question I could probably never answer.

There was something about the loss of comrades that dug deep below the surface of our day-to-day relationships with one another. We knew war was hell and, gratefully, we never forgot it.

5 November 1944 — Mission #58
Pilot: Lieutenant J. C. Hostetler   Copilot: Lieutenant Alex Stewart
Target: Railroad Bridge, Padua, Italy
12-Plane Formation — #4 First Box — Bomb Load: 4 1,000-pound

Back in the air after the tragedy of the 4th, we scored 83 percent bombing efficiency on November 5th's mission, due in part to the lack of opposition. This was my first mission with J. C. Hostetler, a top-notch pilot and soon to become a flight leader. We were from the same graduating class at Yuma Advanced Flight School.

6 November 1944 — Mission #59
Pilot: Lieutenant Alex Stewart   Copilot: R. Olsen
Target: Power Transformer Station, Trento, Italy
12-Plane Formation — #4 Second Box — Bomb Load: 8 500-pound

On November 5th, our bombing had been 83 percent efficient; on the 6th it was zero. Our bombs went astray and we completely missed the power transformer station at Trento, an important and key target well fortified with German 88mm guns.

10 November 1944 — Mission #60
Pilot: Lieutenant Alex Stewart   Copilot: Lieutenant Joseph Nuessle
Target: Railroad Bridge, Cassale Monferrato, Italy
12-Plane Formation — #4 First Box — Bomb Load: 4 1,000-pound

I couldn't believe that we were going back to bomb the same railroad bridge at Cassale Monferrato that had been the center of attention so many times. It was obviously a very important link in the German supply route, and they were putting forth great effort at rebuilding and defending it.

On November 10th, Mission #60, I was assigned the #4 spot in the formation, the second element leader behind flight leader Lieutenant Emil Roesler (not to be confused with Donny Rossler). We were flying in plane 9R, which was adorned with the nose-art of a small dog with a child, in a seated position, wearing a diaper and attempting to try on an Army officer's hat. The plane bore the name *Snot Nose* and was assigned to pilot Lieutenant William Brassfield. Its crew chief was Tech Sergeant Edward F. Bedell.

Lined up for takeoff, all systems checked out fine, and we were anxious to be on our way. I noted by the windsock that we had a strong cross headwind blowing in from the northwest. This assured me that prop-wash from the plane in front of me would be swept away to the right rather quickly, with little chance of our being caught in its turbulence. But I hated prop-wash and chose to use the left side of the runway and avoid any encounter with it. The control tower reported the wind at 22 mph.

Our turn came 20 seconds behind #3 plane piloted by Lieutenant Charles Clinch. Charlie and I had graduated from Yuma Advance School together; we both had learned to fly the B-25 at Mather Field, California. It was good to have men of his experience nearby.

I opened the throttles to the standard takeoff setting of 44 inches of mercury and became airborne a little sooner than usual due to the strong wind. Our join-up and flight to the target was normal, and the "fireworks" greeting we received on the bomb run showed us its usual generous, black, ugly face.

Our bomb drop appeared to be successful, though we wouldn't know for certain until the photos were developed. We made our standard diving turn, this time to the right, and soon cleared the flak zone. We had really caught hell, and I couldn't remember a mission when the flak concentration was this heavy. Per our standard procedure, we were checking all instruments for proper operation when Joe and I spotted the drop in the right engine oil pressure. At about the same moment, Harley Hutton of Marinette, Wisconsin, our radio operator, reported oil streaming out of the right engine, a sign that we would be limping home on one engine.

Joe poised his hand above the right propeller feathering button, waiting for my signal to feather, which I would do as soon as the propeller began to "run away." When an engine lost all its oil the pistons would seize and the engine would stop, but the propeller, void of any driving force would free-wheel and "run away."

Moments later the prop began its wind-up and Joe punched the button. The three blades of the propeller rotated in their sockets, geared to their master mechanism, and came to a stop in a perfect position, parallel to the line of flight. At the same time, the propeller stopped turning and all was quiet on the right wing.

I called to my two wingmen, Lieutenant Robert Helle, from Oak Park, Illinois, on the left in the #6 position and to Lieutenant James King, from Salisbury, North Carolina, in #5 on the right to stay with me as an escort back to Corsica. We had slowed to 150 mph and lowered flaps to maintain adequate lift. The wingmen did likewise.

I held at a comfortable altitude of 9,000 feet and maneuvered over the 50-mile land span to the coast just west of Genoa. Before reaching the coast, we picked up four bursts of flak in front of our small formation. We did a little evasive action, turning first to the left, then back to the right, then straight ahead, again on course. We must have been at the Germans' maximum range as no more flak greeted us.

We had about 125 miles over the sea to Corsica and then another 50 miles to our base on the east coast at Alesan. We crossed over water without incident and made it just opposite 8,900-foot Mt. Cinto, near the northern coast. I angled slightly to the left and felt we were just about home free. The mountains were falling away to the foothills and to the terraced orchards and gardens of the Corsican natives.

Then, without warning of any kind, the throttle control of the left engine, like a hammer-blow, slammed back into my hand. I immediately eased the control forward and the engine resumed its normal operation. But such an occurrence could not be taken lightly. It happened once, it could happen again. I guessed that the engine had backfired and something serious was wrong. I checked the fuel-air mixture control and it was at full-rich. In combat, we were seldom concerned with fuel conservation, as we opted for maximum performance. On long-distance missions we would sometimes lean out the mixture, but would restore it to full-rich while over enemy territory.

Moments later the engine backfired again, and I again eased the control forward to a near-normal setting. A hot charge of adrenalin flooded my head, coursed down my neck, and tingled throughout my body. I knew we were in trouble and hollered to Joe, who was as alarmed as I was. I called the crew. "We got trouble in the other engine. Be ready to bail out. Wait for the horn!"

I told Joe, "We can make it to the water but its too rough for ditching. We could get swamped and drown!"

Joe agreed. "There's no place for a belly landing here, all these terraces and orchards."

I hated to bail out. Someone always gets hurt or killed.

I voiced all these options in about five seconds. "Maybe we can make it to the runway."

Just then the engine backfired for the third time. I again eased the control forward, but it wouldn't take as much throttle as it had the other times. It coughed and sputtered so I settled for a lesser setting. We did fairly well, but couldn't hold altitude and still maintain a safe flying speed. All the while I kept the nose headed straight for the field.

I called the tower. "We lost our right engine by flak over the target. Now the left engine's backfiring and losing power. We're trying for the runway but we'll have to land downwind."

I knew we wouldn't have enough altitude to fly south of the field and land north into the wind.

"I repeat, we're coming in downwind."

The tower acknowledged; all was clear.

We had been blessed with only two more backfires for awhile and closed the distance to a point at 2,000 feet altitude and lined up with the runway.

Finally, with a violent, shuddering vibration, the engine gave out with a tremendous backfire, again slamming the throttle back into my hand with sledge hammer force and then died. I pushed on the throttle but there was no response. All the left engine instruments spun to zero, matching those of the right.

Joe immediately poised his hand above the left propeller feathering button, awaiting my signal. But for some unexplainable reason, I decided not to feather that propeller. I might have even reached up and pulled his hand away. My memory for such details in those frantic moments is quite vague. Joe might have thought I was nuts, but he didn't persist. We both knew that the propeller would reverse rotation and act like a windmill. And a windmilling propeller added a lot of resistance to flight. Of course, these were things we knew instinctively, and we were not consciously reasoning them out in these dire moments.

I told the tower we had two dead engines and were coming in "downwind, dead stick."

We had enough hydraulic pressure to lower the landing gear. The brakes were on a separate hydraulic system and the pressure gauge showed it to be okay. But I would be ready on the emergency air-brake system if the hydraulics failed.

We were descending with an indicated airspeed of 140 mph while the tailwind was boosting our actual speed over the ground to about 160 mph. We were too high and needed to lose some extra altitude before reaching the runway.

There were only two ways I could do this. I could "slip" the plane — push right rudder while dipping the left wing, putting the plane in a momentary aerodynamic stall, causing it to vertically descend more rapidly than it was doing in its forward "glide." I had practiced slipping a B-25 at safe altitudes and with full power available, but never in this condition. I didn't know what would happen with both engines dead, one propeller feathered, and the other propeller windmilling, full flaps down, and landing gear down and locked.

Could it flip over on its back? Would it descend too fast? Would I be able to recover to normal approach pattern in time for a controlled landing?

I decided slipping was too risky to try. I didn't know what could happen.

The surest way was to "stretch the glide" by making a short "S" turn. And I did. I gingerly made a shallow turn to the left toward the sea, held it for about 10 or 15 seconds, then turned back toward the mountains for about the same interval.

If people on the ground were watching, they would probably have thought I had lost my mind and wondered what that idiot was doing.

I finally turned back and realigned with the runway. I could have used a little longer "S" turn, as I was still a bit too high, which made the approach somewhat steeper at a higher speed. But I decided it was better than being short! And besides, how do you gauge the length of an "S" turn at a time like that? For me, it was total seat-of-the-pants guess-work — and I hoped I was right.

The runway came up to greet us. The airspeed indicator said we were doing 140 mph when I flared out for the landing. With the 22 mph cross tailwind, we were actually making 162 mph over the ground — all the more reason why I had wished for a lower airspeed. Landing into the same wind under normal circumstances would have produced a ground speed of about 110 mph.

Strangely, the cross tailwind was not causing us to drift off to the left of the runway, and I didn't have to make any correction to maintain straight flight.

With our excessive speed, we floated and floated, inches above the runway. When would we touch down? From the corner of my eye I saw us pass the control tower, which meant we had used up half the 5,800-foot runway. I had less then a half-mile to get that baby on the ground and stopped. I was trying for a stalled landing to reduce our speed to the minimum.

Finally, the main gear touched and held, no bounce. It was as smooth a landing as I had ever made. I held the nose wheel off the runway for as long as possible, knowing that at our speed it could collapse if the brakes grabbed too hard. Then I eased it down to the surface. I applied the brakes and felt them grab, then they began to fade as the hydraulic pressure dissipated.

I pulled up on the emergency air-brake lever to engage the 500 pounds of pressure in the steel-tank reservoir. Lowering it to the neutral position, I pulled up on the lever again to engage the air for its intended purpose. The compressed air shot into the hydraulic brake lines, and we finally came to a skidding, shuddering stop as our trail of runway dust and smoke from the scorched tires caught up with us before being whipped by the strong crosswind and carried out over the Mediterranean.

Amazingly, we had less than 100 feet of runway remaining before the terrain meandered off for another 100 feet into weeds, tree trunks, rubble, and then the sea. I had managed to stop 30,000 pounds of aircraft in 1,500 feet from 100 mph at touchdown, with a 22 mph tailwind pushing us.

We were home without adding further damage to the aircraft. We could blame our misfortune on the enemy and the accumulative effect of all his actions on the delicate, hair-line balance between good and evil.

A cletrac roared out, hooked onto our nose gear and towed us to a revetment. Other planes from the mission had been circling while all this was going on and were now anxious to land. Hatches flew open and the crew scrambled out, happy to get away from that crippled bird. Nothing seemed more dead than an airplane so mortally wounded that it could not be flown. This one couldn't even be taxied.

I sat there in a kind of stunned state. I was breathing hard and probably had no thoughts. Joe reached over and clapped me on the shoulder. Then in his usual lawyer-like baritone he said, "Nice work, Stew!"

With that, my cell-door of imprisoned emotion crashed open and I burst into tears, my sobbing shaking my body. I folded my arms over the control wheel and held my head as I continued to release the unrestrained flow.

Joe scrambled out of the copilot's seat and again clapped my shoulder as he descended down through the hatch.

Finally, somewhat recovered, I checked all the switches. Joe had flipped them off. I started to ease out of the seat when Major Leonard Kaufmann, our squadron Commander drove up in his jeep and stopped in front of the plane.

He called out to me, "What happened?"

Leaning out the side window, I tried to answer him but my jaw wouldn't work. I couldn't form any words. My voice wouldn't obey the demands of my brain. I gave up trying and began working my way out of the seat and to the hatch. My legs were shaking and my knees wouldn't hold me. I sat down with my legs dangling through the hatch opening and grasping built-in hand holds, I lowered myself to the ground. I crawled out from under the plane and sat in front of the left engine. That windmilling propeller, now in such innocent repose!

Crew members and Major Kaufmann knelt around me. I was still breathing hard and unable to talk. I tried reaching into the breast pocket of my flight suit for a cigarette, but my hand shook so much that I couldn't grasp the pack. Someone placed a lighted cigarette in my mouth and I took several deep drags. It must have been obvious to those around me that I was in some sort of shock.

After a few minutes my shaking eased and I tried my voice. I was finally able to tell the Major and the others what had happened. It was brief, each phrase abrupt, reinforced with a gasp-like breath.

"We lost an engine over the target. . . . The good engine started backfiring over Corsica. . . . It finally blew at 2,000 feet. . . . We were lined up with the runway. . . . We were too high so I made an "S" turn . . . to stretch the glide. . . . We were too hot and floated past the tower. . . . The brakes faded so I used the air brake."

The Major listened intently but didn't ask any questions. He told me I did a "helluva" job and he would tell Operations to give me a rest.

Major Leonard Kauffman, Commander, 489th Bomb Squadron.
*From **History and Personnel, 489th, 340th Bomb Group**, 1947*

The 9R crew chief was inspecting the left engine and saw where the #12 cylinder head had actually blown out through the engine cowling, leaving an oil-soaked rupture in the aluminum. Somewhere north of our runway there lay the errant cylinder head. Later on, someone photographed the ruptured cowling and the place on the engine where the cylinder head had been and gave me a print.

The truck came and we rode to Headquarters for interrogation. I detailed the experience for S-2 Intelligence Officer Captain Jack Casper. Jack was impressed with what we had done. "Stewart," he said, "I'm going to recommend you for the Silver Star. What you did exceeds the merits for the Distinguished Flying Cross."

I thought the Silver Star was awarded for gallantry in action and told him as much. "What kind of an award do you get for saving your own ass, for saving five great crewmen and for bringing a valuable airplane home?" I was back safe, even though not very sound. That was all I cared about.

Jack didn't have an answer for that but said, "You'll get something. You sure got it coming."

We soon finished the interrogation, grabbed several more donuts and a refill of coffee from the Red Cross girls in their little log refreshment stand, and rode the truck back to the 489th Squadron area.

I was still shaky from the experience as I stretched out on my cot, though not nearly as agitated as I had been out by the plane. I poured a double shot of bourbon from the bottle in my footlocker, added a little water, and slowly drank it down. The whiskey did have a soothing effect, and I soon felt myself begin to unwind.

As I was lying there, I reviewed everything in my mind, particularly the part about being able to keep 9R coming straight down the runway without any effort on my part. I was still asking myself why the cross tailwind didn't cause us to drift off the left side of the runway.

Captain Paul Neafus came into the tent and sat down on his cot. "I heard you had it pretty rough today, Stew. I wasn't on the mission but I heard you on the radio down at Group. That was some landing you made. How come you decided not to feather the left prop?"

"I can't answer that, Paul. I really don't know. Everything in the book says I should have, but there was some crazy instinct or somethin' told me not to. I was just thinking about that and wondering why the crosswind didn't blow me off the runway. I didn't have to crab into the wind or nothin'.

"Do you think maybe that windmilling prop gave me the resistance I needed to keep her straight down the runway? Maybe that resistance on the left side compensated for the crosswind and canceled out the drift?"

Paul pondered the situation. He agreed that the resistance caused by the windmilling prop sure hadn't hurt. "If you had feathered you would have been free as a bird and the crosswind would have blown you off the runway, unless you crabbed and corrected for the drift. And you sure didn't have much time to worry about that!"

Paul reasoned that the resistance on the left side actually *had* caused us to rotate to the left on the vertical axis. "Yeah, I believe the windmill saved your skinny little butt, all right."

He chuckled and grinned broadly. The sparkle in his eyes was contagious. He was known for his way of bringing humor into a tense situation, and while it got me to matching his grin, it wasn't quite enough to make me forget about our close call.

I had sensations that day that I had never felt before. It seemed like I could still feel the searing heat of the adrenaline charge that had coursed through me. At least I guessed it was adrenalin. And I never felt as alive and alert as I had during the whole emergency. I had no thoughts of failure, just a powerful intensity to do the job at hand.

Sometime later in reflective moments I recalled a portion of scripture that my Dad had paraphrased, "God sometimes works in strange and mysterious ways, His wonders to perform." He would tell me to accept this on faith, thank God for his gifts to me, and go on.

But my faith must have been quite fragile as the dead-stick experience produced some long, lingering negatives. I eventually realized that I had prayed for strength and wisdom to see me through that day, and I came to believe that God had answered my prayer. Where else could that wisdom have come from that caused me to not feather that left propeller? No question! That's what saved us!

But what about next time? Could I ever cope with another tough situation again? Had I

The ruptured cowling and cowl flap on the left engine of Alex Stewart's B-25 9R, where the #12 blown cylinder head exited as he made a downwind dead stick landing — his 60th mission, Corsica, November 10th, 1944.

run out my string on this one? These and other downers voiced by fellow pilots plagued me, and I felt I was losing my confidence. I had always thought I was a good pilot but I never felt I was superior. Flying copilot with many of the others, I observed their habits and performances and developed preferences. I guessed that many of us did such exercises.

This had been my 60th mission, and I was experiencing the accumulative effect of all the stress. I had seen and known about many men of faith that had been killed, not only in combat but also in training. I had come close to being a statistic many times. That growing record of emergencies in and out of combat was playing tricks with my mind. I thought my experiences were far exceeding the law of averages and probably felt my chances of survival were growing slimmer by the day.

For some unannounced reason, squadron flight surgeon Captain John Nestor paid me a visit in my tent on November 11th. I was alone when he came in and sat down on Ed Perry's cot. At first he quizzed me about my ears and my ability to clear them and asked if I was having anymore pain. Then he brought up my experience of the day before on the downwind-dead-stick landing. He asked how I felt I was doing now.

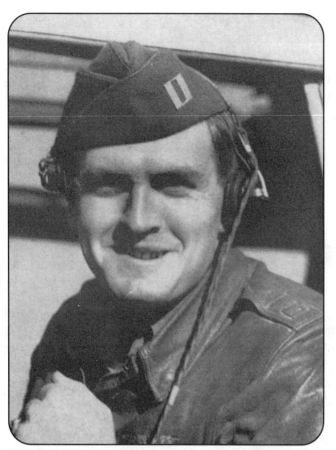

Major Paul B. Neafus, 489th Squadron Operations Officer.
From History and Personnel, 489th, 340th Bomb Group, 1947

I told him the details of the mission and the emotional trauma I had gone through, and how I felt it had really cramped my ability to function effectively. I told him how it had impaired confidence in myself and that I now seemed obsessed by it. I couldn't think of anything else.

"Well, Stewart, I really think you have had enough. You've had more than the usual share of serious upsets." Doc said he would be remiss if he were to advise my continuation in flying missions.

Of course, the decision to rotate me back to the States would not be his, but he would set up an appointment for me to see the group flight surgeon, Major Albert Brussell. Until the Major gave the word, Doc Nestor couldn't ground me, but he could have Operations limit my flying time.

I agreed with everything Doc Nestor said and hoped any additional missions would be milk runs. I looked forward to several days of rest, time away from the conflict, and an opportunity to explore the beautiful island we were presently calling home. A few of us talked about borrowing Scofield's jeep and driving into the mountain villages to visit with the natives and drink some of their very smooth and tasty Cap Corse wine. Captain F. W. Scofield was our chief bombing officer at the time and had the added perk of a jeep assigned to him. And he was one of the most generous men I ever met. Almost everyone asked to borrow his jeep at one time or another, and I had never heard of anyone being refused.

But Major Kaufmann's promise of a good rest somehow got lost in the shuffle or was not officially conveyed to Operations. We had a stand-down on November 11th due to rain and a mission of questionable results on the 12th. Checking the bulletin board on the evening of the 12th, I found I was scheduled to fly copilot for Jack Montgomery in the lead plane of the second box on the 13th. I was tempted but decided against protesting to Jack Mair, the Operations Officer. The squadron was putting 18 planes in the air for this mission and I knew they needed all the experienced hands they could muster. Several veteran pilots had recently been rotated back to the States and had been replaced by new men with little or no combat experience.

13 November 1944 — Mission #61
Pilot: Captain John Montgomery   Copilot: Lieutenant Alex Stewart
Target: Railroad Bridge, Faenza, Italy
18-Plane Formation — #1 Second Box — Bomb Load: 4 1,000-pound

Captain John O. "Doc" Nestor, M.D., 489th Squadron flight surgeon.
*From **History and Personnel, 489th, 340th Bomb Group**, 1947*

On November 13th, our mission was the railroad bridge at Faenza. A heavy cloud cover over the target made observation of the results impossible. Ironically, we had trouble finding the target but, with their radar the enemy had no trouble finding us and delivered a heavy dose of their 88mm shells. We high-tailed it for home with a considerable collection of flak holes. Fortunately no one was injured, and the planes received no serious damage.

My rest period finally kicked in, accompanied by several days of bad weather. On the 17th, six 489th planes went back to the Faenza bridge, located on the British Eighth Army Front, and inflicted considerable damage. On the 18th, the squadron led an 18-plane formation to the Novska railroad bridge in Yugoslavia with excellent results. This mission was longer than usual, lasting almost five hours.

While the mission was winging its way to and from Yugoslavia, I heard that Doc Nestor was leaving the 489th on orders to return to the States. I asked him about my appointment with Major Brussell, and he said that the Major was on a rest leave to Cairo but that he had written him a letter about me and his recommendations concerning my condition and asked him to contact me as soon as possible upon his return.

I thanked him for his care and help and wished him well on his homeward trip and his future assignments. As we shook hands, he grasped the back of my neck with his left hand and said, "I hope you do well Stewart, you're a good man and we need you."

Again, the Faenza area got pasted on November 22nd with clusters of fragmentation bombs. Then rain grounded our planes for three more days, ending November with a total of 13 missions. I had flown five of them, two of which had been the hardest of my combat career.

Mixed in with the wet weather were some dry days and chilly nights, which confined us to our tents and the comforting refuge of our gasoline-powered stoves. But in spite of the lower temperatures, the men sought entertainment and diversion at our makeshift open-air movie theater on the hillside about a block from our tent. Dressed in sheepskin-lined leather flight jackets, pants, boots, and caps with ear flaps, they huddled on the steel stools to watch the movies, some good and some not so good.

Finally on December 1st, the squadron put six planes into the air and sent them to Villavernia to bomb a bridge just outside of town. Instead of covering the bridge, the bomb pattern was laid directly across the town. The inhabitants probably paid dearly in destruction of property and possibly in loss of life due to the town's proximity to the bridge.

No mission was flown on December 2nd, but on December 3rd my name appeared on the schedule to fly copilot for Captain Gilbert Crittenden. This was my first since the long, wet and dreary interval from November 13th. I had no more enthusiasm for the adventure than I had had for several months, and my eagerness had been at zero as a result of the November 10th dead-stick episode.

3 December 1944 — Mission #62
Pilot: Captain Gilbert Crittenden   Copilot: Lieutenant Alex Stewart
Target: Railroad Bridge, Canneto, Italy
12-Plane Formation — #1 First Box — Bomb Load: 4 1,000-pound

There had been much uncertainty as to what our target would be on the December 3rd mission. At first, we were briefed to bomb a bridge on the Po River. Then we were recalled from our planes to Operations and briefed for a target in Yugoslavia. Then just prior to that briefing, orders came from our wing to bomb the bridge at Canneto in northern Italy.

The heavy drone of 96 engines from the 48 planes on the mission aroused the stay-at-homes as we came back and peeled off for the landing. It was somewhat of an epochal moment, as this was the 350th mission flown by our squadron. A contingent of Headquarters officers stood near the end of the runway taking pictures of the returning warriors. The weather was cold and penetrating, the skies were clear, and the sun delivered generous warmth. Our mission was successful, and in spite of the intolerance of the enemy, no one was injured. Gratitude for this was registered on the faces and in the jovial attitude of the flight surgeons and their crew of medical corpsmen and ambulance drivers. They were a dedicated and compassionate group of young men. Doc Nestor had not yet been replaced, so any needs of our squadron were referred to the flight surgeon of the 488th.

December 4th, 1944, was an eventful day in the life of the 340th Bomb Group. We were notified that Major General John K. Cannon, Commander of the 12th Air Force, and Brigadier General Robert D. Knapp, Commander of the 57th Bomb Wing, would make a presentation of the Presidential Unit Citation, awarded by President Franklin D. Roosevelt for the outstanding job performed by the 340th in the North African and Sicilian campaigns. This would be done at a formation of all personnel at Group Operations. Medals

Brigadier General Robert D. Knapp, Commander, 57th Bomb Wing, 12th Air Force. *From **History and Personnel, 489th, 340th Bomb Group**, 1947*

would also be awarded to some airmen. The bulletin board notice stated that all were to be on hand wearing dress uniforms. Bad weather in northern Italy prevented any combat operations, but the weather on Corsica was pleasant.

The four squadrons assembled and lined up in numerical order at the appointed time in a large mowed field near the briefing building. The officers lined up in rows in front of the enlisted men and the First Sergeant of each squadron instructed his men in dress-formation procedure, though there was to be no parade. I was the first officer, standing in the front row of the 489th. First Sergeant G. L. McAvoy asked me and I agreed to serve as right guide for our squadron. I stepped forward and took my position. The Generals had not yet arrived, and we all stood at ease, talking and smoking during a 15-minute wait.

Presently, a small L-4 observation plane came into view from the south. The pilot flew in over the tree tops, slipped down to within a few feet of the ground, flared out, and made a very skillful short-field landing, stopping about 50 feet from our formation. Out stepped the pilot, General Knapp, followed by General Cannon. Group Commander Colonel Willis Chapman greeted them with a sharp salute while voicing a few words of welcome.

As they approached our formation, they were joined by our Squadron Commander Major Leonard Kaufmann, Group Adjutant Major Dewitt Fields, and one or two ranking enlisted men. This assembly constituted the reviewing party. General Cannon chose to first award medals to the airmen, followed by the presentation of the Presidential Unit Citation. Our squadron was the first to be recognized, and due to my spot as right guide, I was the first to be approached by the reviewers. We all had been called to attention by McAvoy and stood in rigid readiness.

General Cannon led the party and stopped before me. I gave him my smartest salute.

Major Kaufmann was standing next to the General.

"General Cannon, this is Lieutenant Alexander C. Stewart. By authority of Headquarters 12th Air Force General Order #266, you have commanded that he be awarded the Distinguished Flying Cross." Someone handed the medal to the Major, who handed it to the General to pin onto my tunic. I was somewhat amazed, as I wasn't expecting to receive the DFC at this time, though I knew I might eventually receive it. A group photographer was on hand to record the event.

"How many missions have you flown, Lieutenant Stewart?"

"I have flown 62 missions, Sir," I replied.

"You're looking forward to going home soon?" he asked.

"I sure am, Sir. Very soon, I hope."

"Are you married, Lieutenant? Where is your home?"

"Yes, I am married. My home is in Chicago, Sir."

Then the General turned to one of the enlisted men and instructed him to get my home address.

Turning back to me, the General shook my hand and thanked me for the service I had performed for the war effort and said how glad he was that I had served in his command.

"Thank you General Cannon, Sir," I spoke as we exchanged salutes.

All the officers and enlisted men in the entourage shook my hand as they passed. The last in line took down my full name and home address, for what reason I did not know. They moved to the first man in the first row behind me and I thought that if the General took as much time with the others as he did with me, we would be there till midnight.

The balance of the review and perhaps a few other awards were made in rather quick succession, followed by General Cannon's short speech about the Presidential Citation. Then he and General Knapp boarded the tiny airplane and took off for Wing Headquarters 35 miles south at Ghisonaccia.

If there were other awards made that day, I wasn't aware of them. Later that afternoon, Major Kaufmann gave me the copy of General Order #266, and I was surprised to find that I was the only DFC recipient from our group on that order. This probably accounted for General Cannon's interest in my home address and marital status. It was not unusual for press releases to be sent to hometown newspapers.

We all had received the Air Medal, plus several Oak Leaf Clusters to the Air Medal, awarded without ceremony. I thus had the Air Medal plus seven clusters, each cluster representing another medal. The Air Medal was said to be awarded for each five successful missions flown, indicating I had flown 40 successes. The count was not totally accurate, but it perhaps reflected a reasonable average.

The Air Medal was not considered to be very significant and I did wonder about its importance and validity. At the time, we were aware that each one was worth five points toward our total military record and might prove of value when we were later discharged from the Service.

On December 7th, I was finally contacted by Major Brussell, instructing me to meet with him on the 8th in his office at Group Headquarters. We had a rather long talk about my experiences and I concluded by saying that I couldn't see how I could possibly fly as many as 70 missions, the number that some were reaching before being sent home.

"Some can do it and some can't," he said, noting that we were all made of different temperaments, and many had not experienced some of the rough missions that I had. He would recommend to the Medical Disposition Board at 12th Air Force Headquarters in Italy that I be grounded and returned to the States for treatment and rehabilitation.

"But don't get your hopes up too high," he told me. "They may say no."

It would take several days before the Major would get their answer. I shook hands with him and departed.

On December 9th, we had a stand-down due to bad weather over the target. That evening I checked the bulletin board and found my name listed as copilot for my tent mate, P. B. Neafus. I couldn't think of anyone I would rather fly with, but was not very intrigued with the prospect of the mission we were assigned.

10 December 1944 — Mission #63

Pilot: Captain Paul B. Neafus   Copilot: Lieutenant Alex Stewart

Bombardier: Captain F. W. Scofield   Radio Gunner: Sergeant H. A. Hutton

Turret Gunner: Sergeant R. H. Ledhal   Tail Gunner: Sergeant P. Suskind

Target: Railroad Rail Fill, Osseniga, Italy (Brenner Pass)

21-Plane Formation — Bomb Load: 4 1,000-pound in first 18 planes

Our 3-plane formation — Bomb Load: Chaff and White Phosphorus

On December 10th, reveille was set for 0720 hours, roll call at 0805, pre-briefing at 0805, and briefing at 0835. Our three-plane group was designated as a chaff element, carrying the usual white-smoke phosphorus bombs to be dropped on strategic gun positions and the chaff, the Christmas-like paper-backed tinsel that would be thrown out by the tail and radio gunners and flutter down to form a so-called window below our planes. The German gunners would set the fuses on their shells to explode at the altitude as indicated by the "window" on their radar screens.

When the chaff was thrown out into the planes' slipstreams, it would get blown back and spread over a considerable area, and the enemy shells would be set to burst at that altitude, well below our formation. And while the gunners were tossing chaff, the bombardier was zeroing in on the gun positions for bombing.

All this was done to reduce the accuracy and effectiveness of the enemy flak and help smooth the way for the boxes in the formation following us to hit the main target with their demolition bombs.

In effect, we were the bird-dogs and would receive the full force of the enemy shelling. The chaff was not expected to help us, and we were extremely vulnerable.

The main target was the first of its kind for me. It was named the Osseniga Rail Fill, deep into the Brenner Pass, the bombing out of a mountainside in the Dolomite Alps. This would cause a huge landslide of rock, dirt, trees, and debris to crash down on the railroad line, blocking the passage of trains loaded with supplies, ammunition, and troops. Seventy-two 1,000-pound bombs well placed could cause a real mess that would take much time and effort to clear before train passage could resume.

Our takeoff, join-up, and flight to the target were normal, and we arrived at the Initial

Point without incident. We maneuvered to cross the IP at the approach compass heading, and the other boxes fell in behind in their designated order. The crew had donned their flak jackets and helmets and were alert for the throwing of the chaff. Scofield was busy at the Norden Bombsight, and pilot Neafus had a fresh cigar clamped between his teeth in the corner of his mouth. He never did smoke them, and I seldom saw him with a cigar in the tent or the squadron area.

In short order, the first four shells arrived and burst right in our formation. We knew they would be there, but it was a sight for which we were never really prepared. These were followed in short order by several series of four bursts, then more and more, and the sky around us was filled with the huge spreading clouds of black smoke. Shards of ugly hot steel battered our planes and as the shells exploded, the familiar sounds grew louder and increased in volume.

Neafus was now working intently with Scofield who was adjusting the bombsight, causing the Pilot Direction Indicator to move in response to his corrections. Neafus responded to the needle in the PDI, bringing it back to a zero reading. On the earlier part of the run he had made some evasive action moves, but now he was holding the plane very steady.

Scofield told us over the intercom that he could not see the gun position but had set the bombsight on a particular formation of trees that looked exactly like the photograph from which he was working and the spot that was designated as the location of the camouflaged German guns. He was considered a remarkable bombardier and had earned the position of Chief Bombing Officer.

Finally, Scofield said he was locked in on the target. Long moments passed as we approached the point of release. Then, without further conversation or adjustment, we felt the uplift of the plane as the bombs left. Scofield called out, "Bombs away, bomb-bay doors closed, let's go home." Most bombardiers would say, "Let's get the hell out of here!" But I don't think I ever heard him swear.

Neafus did a steep, diving turn to the right, lost about 500 feet, and increased speed to 250 mph, then climbed back up to near bombing altitude and leveled off on a heading for Corsica. I was watching the engine instruments and saw the right engine oil pressure dropping. About that time, the radio/waist gunner Harley Hutton called and reported oil streaming out of the engine. I pointed to the pressure gauge and looked at Neafus. He had seen it at about the same moment. I poised my hand above the propeller feathering button and looked at Neafus, waiting for his nod to feather the prop. Presently, the prop began to "run-away" and its rotation rate rapidly increased. Neafus nodded and I pressed the button. The prop blades rotated, their leading edges now cutting straight into the line of flight, and then the prop stopped turning. Neafus cut the engine switches, lowered the flaps to 30 degrees, increased the left engine power settings to maintain level flight at 150 mph, then called our wingmen to be our escort.

We were heading toward the coast, and everything seemed to be running smoothly. One of the best B-25 pilots I had ever encountered was at the controls, and I felt he could handle any emergency. I had been in this situation several times before when I was the pilot and had managed to come through unscathed. But today seemed to be wrought with a foreboding, and I felt more than the usual anxiety that came with finding myself imprisoned in a crippled airplane. Undoubtedly, the after-effects of my dead-stick landing lingered below the surface of my awareness, and ever since that episode, I had decided never to fly over water on one engine again. I was rather obsessed with this posture, so posed the question to Neafus:

"P.B., are you planning to go back to Corsica or do you think we should land at an Allied field in Italy?"

He acted a little surprised at my question, "Oh, Stew, I think we're doing okay and can make it back all right."

I countered, "P.B., you know how I feel about flying over water on one engine. I decided I'd never do it again if I didn't have to. But, you're the boss." I let my plea hang there.

Neafus was silent for a few moments, then he said, "Let me ask the crew and see what they want to do." He called all hands on the intercom.

"I'm polling all you guys. Do you want to go on back to Corsica or should we make an emergency landing in Italy, probably at Pisa?"

Each of the four men answered that it was okay to return to Corsica.

I heard their reports and decided that I was outnumbered and that P.B. would go along with them.

But suddenly he called Scofield and asked for a compass heading to the P-47 fighter/bomber base at Pisa. Scofield checked his chart and gave him the heading he needed. P.B. made the turn and swung around to about 130 degrees.

I silently heaved a sigh of relief and did not ask him why he changed his mind. He offered no explanation.

He called the wingmen and told them what we were going to do and to stick with us, though the P-47 base probably would not let them land. Seeing us safely on the ground would be their reward. They would go on without us and would be happy to sleep in their own beds.

Approaching the fighter base, I called the tower, requesting emergency landing instructions and permission to land as we had only one engine operating.

The tower operator called back and said that we would have to circle for awhile, as they had some "chickens to get off." I looked down and saw several P-47s lined up at the head of the runway, waiting for their takeoff signal.

With a firm, positive voice, P.B. called back to the tower, "You better get your chickens off the road, we're coming in."

We were down to about 1,500 feet and lined up with the runway when P.B. told me to shoot some flares so that everyone around us in the air and on the ground would know where we were.

I took the Very pistol from its holster and placed a red flare in its muzzle. Then I inserted it in the locking port next to the Plexiglas roof above my head and fired. I grabbed another red flare and repeated the action. The flares shot upward in a high, brilliant arc and continued to glow for several hundred feet before falling to earth.

Out of red flares, I now shot two or three orange flares, then a couple of yellow and then green ones. The various colors had specific uses as signals, but I was only interested in being seen.

By this time, we were leveling out for the landing. Neafus made a beauty, rolled out, then stopped. A cletrac was there to tow us off the runway and clear the way for their planes to take off on their mission. The tower operator made some remark about the 4th of July and that we were five months late with the fireworks. I took a little razzing about my use of all the colors in the box of flares when the guys back on Corsica heard the story.

There was no argument with the tower or anyone else about our emergency landing ahead of their mission takeoff. The universal rule was that a plane and crew in distress took precedence over all other operations and should have landing priority.

I knew that my old Primary Flight School friend Bob Purcell was stationed there at Pisa, as a P-47 fighter/bomber pilot and I sought him out. We had quite a reunion, and he put us in touch with the right people to find us beds and food for the night. A plane would come from Corsica the next day to pick us up. We arranged for their maintenance to change the right engine and notify our outfit when it was ready.

We returned to Corsica the next day, and about a week later P.B. was flown back to Pisa to pick up the repaired B-25. But before heading back to Corsica, he decided to test-hop the plane and its new engine. He took off from the fighter field runway and had climbed to 300 feet when the left engine — the one that had brought us to Pisa — quit. It flat failed on takeoff. P.B. immediately feathered the propeller and brought it in on single engine. The plane was again towed off the runway with the cletrac and left there for another engine change. P.B. flew back to Corsica in the plane that had brought him. Another week passed and he returned to get the plane, by then sporting two new engines.

We had experienced a set of mystifying circumstances. First, my anxiety attack, then my voicing of my reservations about flying over water on one engine. Then P.B.'s decision to go against the wishes of the four crewmen and land at Pisa.

Our big question plagued us for some time: Would that left engine have brought us back to Corsica? Would it have withstood the strain of extra power demands for another hour or more? We would never know the answers.

P.B. speculated that the takeoff power demands from Pisa might have been the "straw that broke the camel's back." But in his quieter, personal moments with me he did say that he personally felt my anxiety and that spoke to him more than anything else.

There was another wrinkle to this Osseniga Rail Fill mission that soon surfaced and came as a big surprise to me. On December 11th, the day following Mission #63, Major Brussell sent his evaluation of me and the approval of my return to the States by the 12th Air Force Medical Disposition Board to Major Kaufmann. Kaufmann was doing a little checking on me, independent of Brussell, and had arranged with P.B. to have me fly co-pilot with him and observe my stability and actions under fire and give him his opinion. Because we were overnight at Pisa, P.B. had to wait until we got back on the 11th to report to Kaufmann.

P.B. told him the whole story. He had detected what he expressed as an extreme reluctance in me, a hesitancy that might prove to be critical in a tight situation. He felt that I had lost a lot of my confidence and that I had had enough combat.

"If it was my decision, I would send him home."

P.B. told me this after he had reported to Kaufmann.

On December 12th, Kaufmann called me into his tent office.

"Stewart, I was wondering if you'd like to take a rest leave to Cairo? Several others want to go and I think you could have a good time."

I was somewhat taken aback by this and felt he was trying to set me up for more missions. "Major, I don't want to go to Cairo. I just want to go home." I felt this huge lump well up in my throat; my eyes flooded with tears. The impact of his suggestion was more than I could conceal.

He could not miss the emotional reaction.

"Oh, you misunderstood me. I thought you might like to see that part of the world before you do go home. Major Brussell has sent me his recommendations and the approval of the 12th Air Force Medical Board. Neafus thinks you have had enough and so do I. You have been a real asset to the squadron. You have always done everything that was asked for or expected of you. You have the respect of all the men, and there are many of them that have often asked Operations to schedule them with you. You're a damn good pilot, and I'm sure going to miss you."

By that time, I had recovered my composure and my smile turned into a broad grin. I thanked the Major and departed his tent with a new spring in my step. I found Neafus and thanked him for his report to Kaufmann.

"That's okay Stew," he said. "How about a hand of Gin Rummy?"

P.B. and I had an ongoing game where we laid a paper bet of 1/10 of a cent per point. No money ever changed hands and the score sometimes indicated a debt to one or the other of several thousand dollars. This day I made sure he was the winner.

It was one thing to be approved for rotation back to the States and another for it to become a fact. I was told it would take three or four weeks for my orders to come through. Meantime, I was on my own to do whatever I wanted, no strings attached.

Winter had arrived, to the extent nature allowed on Corsica, and we received more than our share of rain. When good weather did come we took advantage of it and saw a good bit of the beautiful island.

The Corsican sky was spotted with low-hung cumulus clouds that drifted lazily over the jagged peaks. There was a chill in the air, but we were warmed by the sunshine. We noted the countryside with its leafless trees and the drabness that had replaced summer's green in the fields. Life seemed at a low ebb as nature rejuvenated the land and natives tended their flocks, perhaps feeding them silage and fence-line stubble. The farm-reared men in our midst would know about such things.

When weather permitted, our planes were out in force, pressing the enemy while absorbing an unhealthy share of his wrath. It was a strange feeling to now be among those who were still in flying mode, but no longer a part of the fraternity. I would hear their harrowing tales at mealtime and quiz them about their successes and hazards over a drink or two at the Officers Club.

In my own quiet, reflective times I sometimes found myself irrationally wishing I was up there with them. And I prayed for them. What a lousy business, this war! I thought about those who had given their lives for what we hoped was a cause worthy of such sacrifice.

I thought about Sergeant William Williamson of Galesburg, Illinois, the radio operator/gunner who had been in the back of Baxter Thomas' plane when they were shot down over Avignon, France, during the invasion. I had been appointed to serve as his Summary Courts Officer, charged with the responsibility of inventorying and packing his personal belongings for shipment home. There were small photos of his family, a collection of letters he had saved, which I did not invade, and several letters unopened that had arrived after his death.

I had toyed with the idea of writing a short letter of sympathy and condolence and inserting it in the shipment but decided that was something his family didn't need at the moment of unpacking his things. Instead, I wrote: "Lovingly packed for shipment by Summary Courts Officer Lieutenant Alexander C. Stewart of Chicago, Illinois." I had remembered my mother telling me how she wept when the civilian clothes of my brothers and I had been shipped home after we had received our uniforms upon entering the service. It was a personal thing, and all the recipients needed at the moment of unpacking was the comfort of Sergeant Williamson's personal items. They were his. He had worn them or touched them, or laughed or cried over their letters and snapshots, or maybe even kissed them.

Sydney Newman often came to mind, and I wondered how his wife and little baby were getting along. Times would certainly still be hard for her. The baby was too young, but would some day know of his daddy's fate — and be proud.

And that haunting question again surfaced, "Could I have broken formation and saved them from their doom?"

Once again, I pushed that thought back into the dark recesses of my mind. There was no answer.

Immediately upon receiving word from Major Kaufmann on December 12th that my combat days were over and that I would be going home, I wrote a long letter to Ruth. I was quite certain that I would go by troop transport, as there were few planes homeward bound via the South Atlantic route. I also learned that virtually the entire 319th Bomb Group, a sister outfit in the 57th Bomb Wing, was to be rotated back to the States. Rumor had it that they would retrain for heavy bombardment in the new B-29 Super-Fortress and be redeployed to the South Pacific for action against the Japanese. Perhaps we would all sail home on the same ship.

I estimated that it would be the middle of or late January before I arrived home, at which time I would be granted a 21-day delay en route before reporting to my new Stateside assignment. I would not know where that would be until I arrived at Fort Sheridan, Illinois, after docking on the East Coast.

Meantime, the wet weather continued to plague the Allied efforts throughout Europe, and Corsica was not spared. An occasional mission would get off and, as often as not, would return without making contact with the target. The airfield often was closed to all traffic as the sodden earth reached total absorption and the normally hard surface lost its resistance to the 15-ton aircraft.

On December 22nd, 1944, however, there was no rain, and a mission was launched against a railroad bridge north of Trento, Italy. For over three hours our crews and planes were tossed like children's kites by bitterly cold, high winds in sub-zero temperatures, but to no avail. Ground haze obliterated both primary and secondary targets, and all planes returned with a full bomb load. All crews were disgruntled. "It was one thing to be unable to bomb the target but still another to freeze your ass off in the process!"

Winter had definitely come to Corsica, borne on cold sweeping down from the north and bringing the first seasonal snows. The mountain barrier to the west became a solid white, and the skies were overcast, simulating those back home. But the snow didn't last long, as the persistence of rain overruled, and everybody holed up in their tents or lounged before the lively antics of the sputtering logs in the mess hall fireplace. In late afternoon the men braved the elements and sought relief and conviviality down the road in the group Officers Club.

Christmas Eve celebrations were waiting in the wings, but held little promise of creditable fulfillment. Someone had fashioned a Christmas tree of sorts and had decorated it with chaff. But it was stiff and hung on the scavenged branches of a denuded shrub like tiny, flat canes with half-hearted sparkle and no shimmering energy.

The drinks were warm and soothing but far from glamorous, and no match for the back-home stories and sentiments that were recounted and traded among gallant men whose bravery and daring had been borne on high spirits.

Yet Christmas was at hand and had a universal appeal. It fired the imaginations of the men of many faiths, and could not be quelled. Memories of peace-filled youths inspired a few attempts at Christmas carols, but earned protest from those intolerant of ragged harmony and discordant voice. Laughter replaced the errant music, but the lyrics were ennobled on moving but silent lips. Christmas, however, could carry its own weight. Its eternal story was a condition of the heart and needed no external embellishments. It was simply poised, ready to be shared.

"Merry Christmas!". . . was the command of the day.

Christmas Day was discharged with a better than expected dinner of roasted turkey, a tasty and well-seasoned dressing replete with English walnuts, and accompanied by canned cranberry sauce and many more trimmings.

Christmas parcels had come from home, laden with candies, cookies, and fruitcakes, shared and enjoyed by all. Ruth had sent me a fruitcake that my mother had made from her ancient family recipe, and I couldn't have been happier. Each morsel awakened memories of many Christmases, especially those late-evening suppers when we picked at remaining generous portions of the 25-pound turkey, the extra pan of crusty dressing, and slices of the fruitcake we had been too full to eat at the earlier grand dinner. Contentment was our password.

But our celebrations in Corsica were soon dampened by the news of the huge German counteroffensive that had been shuffled aside while we soaked up the joys and trappings of the holiday. The enemy crush had broken through the American First Army Western Front in Belgium, inflicting heavy losses of life and matériel. Allied nations had been advised of the gravity of the situation, and there was a great deal of speculation as to its appreciable lengthening of the war. The planned Russian winter offensive was said to be more than a month late. Activity on the Italian Front had come to a virtual standstill due to poor weather. But the American offensive in the Philippines was going along according to plan. And our mission to the Brenner Pass on December 27th was highly successful, completely destroying a railroad bridge at Calliano.

A news item in the *Stars and Stripes* newspaper revealed some startling statistics in a congratulatory message described by General Ira C. Eaker. The 12th Army Air Force had completed 350,000 sorties in 25 months of operations and was said to be the scourge of the German soldier in the Mediterranean. The 12th had severed enemy lines of supply and had attacked its troop concentrations and equipment in the front lines, as well as

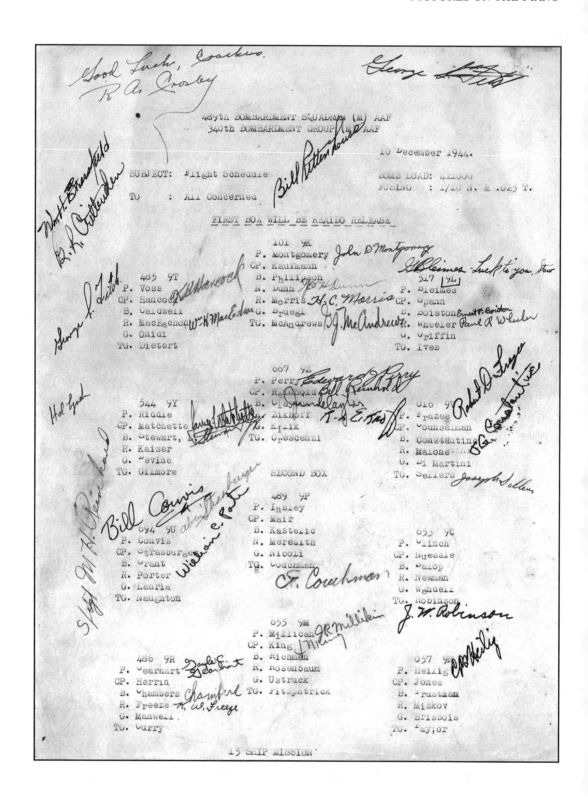

Good Luck, Crackers.
R. A. Crosley

George A. [signature]

Wm. H. Bransfield
B. A. Crittenden

George A. Lilly

Bill Rittenhouse

489th BOMBARDMENT SQUADRON (M) AAF
340th BOMBARDMENT GROUP (M) AAF

10 December 1944.

SUBJECT: Flight Schedule BOMB LOAD: 4X1000
To : All Concerned FUSING : 1/10 N. & .025 T.

FIRST BOX WILL BE RADIO RELEASE

101 9K
P. Montgomery *John D Montgomery*
CP. Kaufmann
B. Phillipson *G. Bleimes – Luck to you, New*
N. Dunn *J. H. Dunn* 517 9L
R. Morris *H. C. Morris* P. Bleimes
G. Bruegl CP. Spann
TG. McAndrews *S. J. McAndrews* B. Boiston *Ernest P. Boiston*
  R. Wheeler *Paul R Wheeler*
  G. Griffin
  TG. Ives

485 9T
P. Voss *R. L. Hancock*
CP. Hancock
B. Caldwell *Wm. H. MacEachon*
R. MacEachon
G. Onidi
TG. Dietert

Hal Good

687 9Z
P. Perry *Edward J. Perry*
CP. Reinhold *Bill Reinhold*
B. Clayton *James Clayton*
N. Eikhoff *R. J. Eikhoff*
G. Kilik
TG. Crescenzi

544 9Y
P. Riddle
CP. Matchette *Larry Matchette*
B. Stewart, R. *Stewart*
R. Kaiser
G. Devine
TG. Gilmore

616 9V
P. Frazee *Robert D. Frazee*
CP. Counselman
B. Constantine *Constantine*
R. Malone
G. Di Martini
TG. Sellers *Joseph Sellers*

SECOND BOX

Bill Convis *Lou Strasburger*

489 9P
P. Insley
CP. Mair
B. Kastelic
N. Meredith
G. Nicoli
TG. Couchman *C. F. Couchman*

694 9U
P. Convis *William E. Porter*
CP. Strasburger
B. Grant
R. Porter
G. Lauria
TG. Naughton

655 9C
P. Clinch
CP. Nuessle
B. Dalop
R. Newman
G. Wendell
TG. Robinson *J. W. Robinson*

S/Sgt Wm. H. Rawsbeard

655 9M
P. Millican *J. R. Millikin*
CP. King
B. Richman
R. Rosenbaum
G. Ustruck
TG. Fitzpatrick

657 9[?] *E. P. Heilig*
P. Heilig
CP. Jones
B. Trustman
R. Miskov
G. Brisbois
TG. Taylor

486 9R *Dayle Gearhart*
P. Gearhart
CP. Herrin
B. Chambers *Chambers*
R. Freeze *R. W. Freeze*
G. Manwell
TG. Curry

15 SHIP MISSION

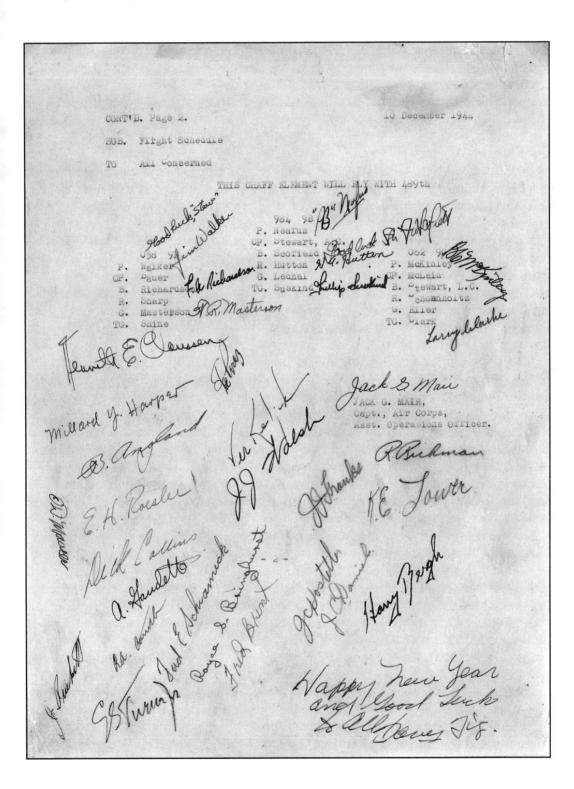

CONT'D. Page 2.   10 December 1944

SUB.   Flight Schedule

TO   All Concerned

THIS CHAFF ELEMENT WILL FLY WITH 489th

984 9B
P. Nearus
CP. Stewart, A.
B. Scofield
R. Hutton
G. Lednal
TG. Suskind

058 9
P. Walker
CP. Bauer
B. Richardson
R. Sharp
G. Masterson
TG. Shine

062 9
P. McKinley
CP. McLain
B. Stewart, L.C.
R. Schoenholtz
G. Eller
TG. Clark

JACK G. MAIR,
Capt., Air Corps,
Asst. Operations Officer.

destroying or damaging a total of 4,914 enemy aircraft. During its more than two years of operations, the 12th AAF had operated in Africa, Sicily, Italy, Sardinia, Corsica, and southern France, and had dropped 175,000 tons of bombs on enemy targets in 12 countries. In this period, the 12th AAF suffered losses of 2,277 American planes.

On December 29th, some Allied military strategists tentatively added three to six months to their estimates of the time required for victory in Europe as a result of the present Nazi counteroffensive. The 489th had five new crews fresh from the States assigned to it, and lost a like number being rotated back home.

New Year's Eve 1944 arrived with little fanfare and less than expected plans for celebration. I had received no word as to the status of my rotation orders, which were to come from 12th Air Force Headquarters in Italy, but I had reduced my belongings to fit into a B-4 Val-Pak-type wardrobe zippered bag, with a musette bag for toilet articles and other small items, and was prepared for an easy getaway when departure time arrived. I left room for one bottle of bourbon, which I hoped would survive the New Year welcoming party.

A few of us borrowed a jeep and ascended to a mountain village and purchased a few bottles of Cap Corse wine, which we used to compliment my remaining salami and a chunk of Wisconsin cheddar cheese I had been hoarding for the occasion. None of us were heavy drinkers, and I don't remember a time when any from our tent over-indulged. Even with the wine, we sipped in moderation and grew sleepy at the hour and not from excess libation. We exchanged stories of past New Year's celebrations, and in true Army tradition extolled the virtues of our respective hometowns.

Ed Perry enjoyed telling about San Francisco and how he and Betty highlighted their fare with 'chokes — artichokes steamed and served with some sort of sauce. I don't think I had ever seen an artichoke, much less taste one.

Stan Gerry was from Sacramento and had much to say about its advantages. And when I raved about Chicago, I thought the tent would cave in with derision. Stan broke the back of all commentary when he howled, "*Chicago*? That's the only place I have ever been where they have black ice and snow. Don't tell me about Chicago!" And to some degree, he was correct. Railroad trains were still being powered by coal-burning steam engines and emitted coal dust and cinders along their road beds. Coal was also still the popular fuel for heating homes, buildings, and industry, and it left its mark on two-day old snow.

I saw that I couldn't score on the Chicago tale, so switched to reminding them of the best fruitcake they admittedly had ever eaten and that it came from the best cook in the best kitchen — in Chicago — my mother and her famous recipe. The hometown debate drifted into oblivion as we sipped a nightcap of Cap Corse and one by one surrendered to the warmth of our innards and the toasting of the sputtering stove. It was 10:00 p.m.

January 1st, 2nd, and 3rd, 1945, were all bitterly cold, or wet, or cold and windy, and activity was restricted to two attempts at missions but sabotaged by the weather on Corsica or over the target areas. My preparations for departure were complete, and only final check-ins of bedding, pistol and ammunition, and a few government odds and ends that I had no need were to be surrendered.

Finally, in late afternoon of January 4th, I received my travel orders from the 12th Air Force. They were dated January 3rd. I noted that the 101 officers and enlisted men of the 319th Bomb Group headed the list — the earlier rumors proved to be correct.

Next were listed 20 officers and enlisted men of the 340th Bomb Group and included:

> First Lieutenant Scotty Rohwer - 486th Squadron
> First Lieutenant William Brassfield - 489th Squadron
> First Lieutenant Fred Brent - 489th Squadron
> First Lieutenant Alexander Stewart - 489th Squadron
> First Lieutenant Joseph Heller - 488th Squadron [Joseph Heller authored
>   the famous novel *Catch-22* in 1961.]

I knew that Scotty was due to be rotated, but couldn't believe that it would happen at the same time mine would. Scotty had completed 67 missions, and again we were to continue sharing space on travel orders to succeeding assignments. From our first days in Preflight School at Santa Ana on November 15th, 1942, to January 3rd, 1945, we had been together, with the one exception of Advanced Flight School. Where would we go from here?

Our departure was scheduled for the morning of January 5th, but was put on hold due to a heavy rainstorm. I spent the day making the rounds of friends in the squadron and arranged for the clerk to type up a duplicate schedule of my last mission on December 10th. I posted it on the bulletin board and asked, as was the custom, for everyone to sign it. It was like the signing of the high school yearbook. In all, signatures of 70 men with whom I had served created a treasured memento.

On the morning of January 6th, I made my parting goodbyes to the many friends I had acquired during the 7½ months of the most precarious times of my life. We were ordinary men doing extraordinary deeds and humbly bore the mantle of liberation from tyranny. I was proud to have served with each of them. I rode with Brassfield and Brent to the flight line where we were met by the two-man crew who would fly us to Naples. My friend and crew chief Ezra Baer was there to see me off.

We climbed aboard and were soon in takeoff position. We rumbled down that familiar runway for the last time and were soon airborne and climbing to about 1,000 feet for the short run to Capodichino airdrome in Naples. Standing in the navigator's compartment behind the flight deck, I strained to catch my last look at that beautiful island that I had called home since my arrival on May 17th, 1944. My stay had been much shorter than I had ever expected it would be and would assume its place as one of my "fortunes of war."

Chapter 22

Going Home

N APLES HELD NO INTEREST for me now. I had been there a few times on squadron business and had seen all that I considered worthwhile. Besides, now I was on my way home. Ruth and the refuge of home were the only sights I craved.

The five of us shook hands with our chauffeurs, wished them luck, and then turned toward the administration building. I stood for a moment, scanning the horizon and gazing at Mount Vesuvius in the distance to the south near the Bay of Naples. Smoke and steam still drifted serenely from its crater. Somewhere deep in her bowels churned the fire that would someday again seek freedom and bring horror and devastation to bewildered families crudely housed on her skirts and at her feet, even as they tend their lush vineyards in the rich soil.

It had happened in March 1944 and had wiped out 80 percent of the 340th Bomb Group's B-25s based at its foot. The first recorded eruption in history occurred on August 24th, 79 A.D., destroying the cities of Herculaneum, Pompeii, and Stabaie. Nine destructive eruptions had occurred over the centuries, adding to the total, in excess of 50. Pompeii was my only concession to my present anti-sightseeing resolve.

An Army bus took us to the staging facility for boarding the USS *West Point*, the former SS *America* luxury liner converted for wartime troop transport. Our home for several days of waiting for departure would be a very old and once elegant marble-encrusted spa, the Terme Hotel, equipped to accommodate several hundred returnees.

My first act was to mail a short letter to Ruth, telling her I was on my way, figuring it would reach her before the ship landed in America.

We registered at the desk manned by U.S. Army clerks and were each assigned rooms. My admiration for the resourcefulness of the Army Engineers, or whoever was responsible for securing housing for transient troops, took a big leap. Each room was equipped with marble wash basin and large sunken bathtub, floored over to provide space for an Army cot, and a conventional toilet. A clothes-hanging rack was added to complete the modifications. I visualized the space in its former glory as a retreat for wealthy Italians.

A larger room down the hall had been converted into a central shower where we enjoyed the luxury of hot mineral water. A central mess hall provided excellent meals, which helped ease the time until departure. The old adage that an Army traveled on its stomach still applied, and we were not disappointed, though we wondered why we couldn't get "vittals" like this on Corsica.

I learned that the ship would be loaded with 2,500 officers and 5,000 enlisted men. But where were the other 7,000 plus, and when would they be assembled to board ship all in about a 12-hour time span? That was not my concern, however, and so I set about to relax and enjoy the fruits that this leisure could provide. I met several men whom I had known in Flight School and at Greenville, and I compared notes with them about our combat service. We filled the time writing letters, playing cards, and seeing some movies that were yet to be shown at the 489th.

One day, I was stopped in the lobby by a Brigadier General who asked me if I would like a quick trip back to the States. He was seeking to fill out a volunteer crew to fly a B-25 back across the South Atlantic route and still needed a first pilot. After a furlough, the crew would tour around the United States promoting the purchase of War Bonds. It sounded glamorous and appealing.

My first impulse was to say I had flown enough well-maintained but still war-weary planes over long stretches of water and wasn't about to challenge my luck again. But, instead, I thanked him for asking and declined with the statement that I was grounded and heading back for medical treatment. He turned away and soon buttonholed another pilot, and then another who went off with him to an office, probably to sign on for the escapade.

How strange, I thought, that these high-ranking officers were into the work of raw-recruiting fliers for hazardous duty in such an informal manner. A similar much-earlier encounter came to mind, when I had been approached by the General at Mather Field, California, to volunteer for a P-61 Black Widow night-fighter group headed for the deadly skies to fight against the German veterans over the English Channel. But the method seemed to work. For some, it wasn't easy to turn down a General, and war history showed that both jobs were filled.

While I was in Naples in early January waiting for the departure of the USS *West Point*, I finally discovered the purpose for General Cannon's request of my home address. Ruth had received a very kind and heart-warming personal letter from the General, dated December 17th, 1944, and postmarked December 19th. She had photostatic copies made and submitted one for publication in the Pure Oil Company Newsletter.

Mount Vesuvius, near the Bay of Naples.

HEADQUARTERS
TWELFTH AIR FORCE
APO 650

17 December 1944

Mrs. Alexander C. Stewart
1414 East 65th Place
Chicago, Illinois

Dear Mrs. Stewart:

I am very happy to be able to tell you that your husband, Lieutenant Alexander C. Stewart, has been awarded the highly coveted Distinguished Flying Cross for outstanding achievement in action against the enemy. I know you will be glad to hear this.

Only a few of our men who fly in battle against the enemy have been so honored. The high qualities that your husband has displayed reflect the inspiration that his loved ones exert in his life, and had no small part in making this achievement possible.

Lieutenant Stewart, by his courage and devotion to duty, has set an example which has made his comrades proud to serve with him in this war for high ideals. As the Commander of the Air Force in which he serves, I also take pride in his accomplishments and appreciate the more intimate joy which I know is yours at this moment.

It is a genuine pleasure to have had with me, in the Twelfth Air Force, such an outstanding airman.

Very sincerely,

JOHN K. CANNON
Major General, U S Army

Major General John K. Cannon's letter to Ruth Stewart on the occasion of Alex receiving the Distinguished Flying Cross.

Major General John K. Cannon, Commander, 12th Air Force.
From History and Personnel, 489th, 340th Bomb Group, 1947

Finally, after nine days of killing time, we were given notice on January 15th that we would board the *West Point* the next day, January 16th, 1945, and that we were to pick up our cabin assignments and have them in hand with our shipping orders at the gangplank. Arriving at the pier, I walked about three blocks to the check-in point and soon joined the cabin-finding melée on board. I was glad I had heeded P.B.'s advice to reduce my luggage to one B-4 bag and a musette bag: "You'll be doing a lot of walking and those bags get heavy and mighty awkward in those narrow ship corridors."

I found my assigned cabin on the Upper Deck and was surprised that I would share it with 11 other guys. In a space that probably accommodated two to four people in the civilian mode, there were four tiers of bunks, three beds high. At one end was a bathroom that stretched the full 12-foot width of the cabin, about three feet deep, with one entrance door. At one end was a toilet, at the other end a shower stall. Along the wall was a counter with two wash basins. The corner behind the door to the corridor was a 2x2-foot space for our luggage, to be stacked floor to ceiling. You can imagine the job of getting to your stuff if necessary.

I dug into my B-4 bag, found a change of underwear, socks, and shirt, and some extra handkerchiefs. My bag landed about mid-way in the stack, and I was lucky to get a bottom bunk. The higher you were the warmer it got, and I wondered about the quality of the air with 12 sweating men. But I was surprised to find that the room was well ventilated, and we slept in comfort.

Meals were served in three shifts starting at 6:00 a.m. and we were each allotted two meals per day. Our cabin drew the 6:00 a.m. breakfast and the 3:00 p.m. supper. It was a struggle to get up and dressed and fight the crowd to the dining hall at such an early hour. But, after the first day, I juggled my schedule with someone who didn't eat breakfast and got on the 9:00 shift. We had to show our meal pass for the first day or two, then everyone seemed to get adjusted and passes were ignored.

The ship was manned by the U.S. Navy, and the food was terrific. We were able to leave the dining room with fresh fruit, crackers, and small boxes of cereal to fill the void of the missing meal.

The mighty ship was finally loaded, and blasts from the huge steam horns announced our departure in late afternoon. I joined many others on deck and we were soon moving out of the Bay of Naples, heading into the beautiful Mediterranean waters. It was quite a thrill to be aboard a floating city with thousands of weary but happy men heading for home.

Although I had written to Ruth that I was headed for home, I was anxious to give her current word. I learned that I could send a Radiogram to her from the ship, and went to a desk in the Ship's Store to file the message. What she received was printed on a Western Union Telegram Form, the coding of which meant little to me:

CAU6 INTL=CD SANSORIGINE VIA RCA   1945 JAN 19 AM 8 29

EFM MRS A STEWART=
1808 EAST 72 ST CHGO=

HOPE TO SEE YOU SOON. MY THOUGHTS ARE WITH YOU LOVE AND KISSES=

A STEWART.   1945 Jan 19 PM 12 16

                                           MAIL

CAU6 INTL=CD SANSORIGINE VIA RCA was obviously an international code probably assigned to the ship or perhaps to the Mediterranean Theater of Operations. We had been underway two or three days and were still in the Mediterranean. RCA probably stood for Radio Corporation of America. The two dates indicate a span of about 16 hours from transmission to arrival in Chicago. The word MAIL was handwritten, and I assumed that the message had probably been phoned to Ruth, then confirmed by mail, a wartime process due to the shortage of telegram delivery manpower.

Ezra Baer, my crew chief sent me a birthday greeting and though it was not dated, it must have been sent on or about March 15th, 1945. He was then based with the 340th Bomb Group in Rimini, Italy. He sent it to my mother's home in Chicago, and she must have forwarded it to me. It bore what I felt was the same origin: CD SANSO RIGINE VIA RCA.

The *West Point* was said to be among the fastest liners in the world and was scheduled for an eight-day trip to Boston. Its pace through the Mediterranean did not prove its speedy reputation, as we were close to five days getting to the Straits of Gibraltar before venturing into the vast Atlantic Ocean. Many were on deck as we approached the great Rock and affirmed its famous claim to solidity. Its stalwart majesty towered above as we passed, and I was thrilled at having seen it. I learned that near its base had been an RAF Fighter field of British Spitfires that had performed outstanding service against the enemy.

As we entered the Atlantic, we rendezvoused with a U.S. Navy destroyer that would serve as our escort halfway to Boston. Now the *West Point* could do its stuff, and its throttles were opened to a speed said to be 20 or 22 knots per hour. Three days to Boston looked possible.

At mid-ocean, the possible threat of attack by German submarines was behind us, and with three blasts from its horns, the destroyer peeled off, did a 180-degree turn, and disappeared over the eastern horizon. I felt a little surge of anxiety, wondering if the Germans were wise to our methods and would be lurking in the deep waters that we were now approaching. Sinking a transport loaded with 7,500 men would be quite a prize over which Hitler could gloat.

But the Navy had things well in hand, and the ship took on a zig-zag course that was designed to avoid a torpedo impact. I learned that a moving target with constant change in direction and variance in travel pattern was a difficult challenge for a submarine aiming at its prey. A U-Boat needed five minutes of fixed bead on its target for a successful strike. The *West Point* charged ahead at what seemed to be top speed and never wavered.

Life on the ship became routine, and time was spent on deck in pleasant weather, listening to the dance music of a good-sized soldier orchestra that played at designated times. In this huge assemblage of men were about 20 nurses and Red Cross girls that were billeted as a group in cabins on the Promenade Deck. For dancing, they were the "property" of the higher ranking officers. But the lack of partners was no deterrent to several fleet-of-foot enlisted men who graced the deck boards with their jitterbug expertise. Pairs of men dancing the wild steps together was quite a sight before several of the girls left their waltzing cheek-to-cheek officers and split up the male dancers, adding popular, and at times gymnastic, gyrations to the choreography. The audience of some 2,000 men, standing and sitting on every possible perch, wildly cheered its approval. We were all hungry for these therapeutic touches of American life that had played a part in making the war more bearable.

I had come down with a bad head cold sometime after Gibraltar and sought directions to the Sick Bay for treatment and medication. The infirmary was located way below decks in a balcony section of the huge hold. I descended a long, narrow open stairway and saw the living space of several thousand enlisted men, sleeping, reading, smoking, playing cards, or huddled in conversation. Their bunks were in closely assembled tiers, five or six beds high. The view provided an answer as to how 7,500 men could be accommodated.

The atmosphere lacked adequate ventilation, and I felt for their discomfort though I heard no complaints from those with whom I spoke. One infantryman told me, "This is heaven compared to what I've been in for the last two years. I'm finally going home and I'd swim if I had to."

We were fortunate in making a bee-line from Gibraltar to Boston, thus avoiding the winter storms and icebergs common to the North Atlantic that were encountered by our ships sailing from the British Islands. We had some heavy rains and strong winds, but not much heavy sea action. Quite a few men became seasick, but most of the aviators were not affected. Seldom had they been airsick, and happily I had never been airsick or seasick. All in all, I had been enjoying the voyage until I came down with the cold.

Word passed that we would anchor in Boston after midnight of January 25th, but debarkation would not begin till daylight. A schedule was issued informing our cabin that we would get off at about 5:30 in the afternoon. That meant spending all day on the ship, with America so near and yet so far from our anxious feet. I awoke and went to breakfast, a little startled that we were not moving, then remembered that we were in our Boston berth. There, on January 26th, it was nine degrees below zero.

At 5:00 p.m., we joined the line-up heading for the gangplank, all bundled up in winter garb. We descended to the pier and immediately walked into a long depot-like building that housed railroad tracks and our waiting train. Lugging my B-4 and musette bags, I stepped aboard the first coach with vacant seats, tossed my stuff in the overhead rack, and waited for motion.

There were many Gray Ladies, those angelic Red Cross Volunteers in gray uniforms, on hand to greet us and fill our pockets with cigarettes and candybars and to serve a generous cup of hot coffee and a handful of donuts. Best of all, I was captivated by their very loving and caring manner. Many of them no doubt had sons and even husbands in service. They were not young, and I admired their commitment to the icy conditions to give us such a warm welcome.

Some of us thought there might be a huge welcome home at dockside, but later decided that would happen only when the war was over. We really didn't much care about a big reception, and the Gray Ladies seemed to satisfy our needs with a personalized attention that a massive crowd could never provide.

With the train loaded, we finally moved out to the main line that would take us 30 miles west to Camp Miles Standish, a large reception center for returnees. The train chugged into the camp and stopped near a trackside clearing where we were greeted by some officers and noncoms. We lined up, bags at our side, while an officer voiced a brief word of welcome over the PA system and instructions regarding disposition of luggage, barracks location, dining hall, and assembly hall. We were issued barracks assignments and tagged our bags accordingly before boarding buses for the three-block ride to the assembly hall, a brief word of welcome by the Base Commander, and a preview of the dinner that awaited us. Around 9:00 p.m., we walked a short distance to the huge mess hall and joined one of four cafeteria-style lines where a server took our orders for T-bone steaks and the doneness we desired.

We moved on up the line and selected from a grand array of food that we had forgotten existed. Milk came only in quarts, and many loaded two on their trays. I took one quart and drank it all. I sat at a long picnic-style table with others and was soon served the steak I had ordered, grilled to medium perfection.

Departing the mess hall, I found my barracks and luggage and claimed a cot, went to the latrine, took some aspirin for my cold, then went in search of a telephone. There were several outdoor phone booths spotted around the camp, with men shivering in lines one to two blocks long, waiting their turn. I joined a line and found it moved very slowly. Phone service in 1945 was not automated, and most of the men were probably calling collect rather than feeding untold numbers of coins into a slot. The process involved giving the operator the number to be called, telling her it was a collect call, then her ringing the number and announcing the call to the answering person, getting the okay to reverse the charges, and finally connecting the two. You were allowed three minutes talking time, then a warning that your time was up.

The calls averaged about five minutes each, and I was only able to endure the sub-zero temperatures for about a half hour. My cold was getting the better of me, and I figured I was not going to talk to Ruth that night. I broke from the line, retreated to the barracks, and went to bed with a worthy snort of whiskey warming my innards. I was glad I had saved space in my bag for a fifth of Old Grandad, left over from my rest leave on Malta.

In the morning, I sought a phone in the PX and then outside, but had no luck. The long lines persisted, so I decided to wait for a chance later in the day. None occurred. I got word that my shipping orders were ready and that I would board a train at 5:00 p.m. for Fort Sheridan, Illinois. It was Thursday, January 27th, 1945.

The train departed on time. I claimed a lower berth and hoped for some good sleep and recovery from my still miserable cold. For some inconceivable reason, the train did not make the time I had hoped for or expected. There were many stops and delays and slow travel, stretching the trip for three nights and two days. We pulled into the Fort Sheridan rail siding at 8:00 Sunday morning, January 30th. I was told my orders would be issued at about noon, and I would be free to go home and start my 21-day furlough.

I finally found a telephone in the PX and placed a collect call to Ruth.

"Yes, yes, I'll accept the charges," she told the operator .

"Hello honey, I'm home," I hollered with a trembling voice.

"Alex, where are you?"

"I'm up here at Fort Sheridan. I just got off the train."

"When will you be home?"

"This afternoon, maybe about 4:00."

"Oh, Alex, I can't believe it, I can hardly wait."

Her voice broke. She was crying.

I told her I would take the North Shore electric to the Loop, then get the Illinois Central at Randolph Street or maybe a taxi.

"Ace, I'm so glad your back, I'm so happy, I love you so much."

"Same here Ruthie."

We said our goodbyes and I hung up the receiver.

Exhilaration surged through me as I savored the moment. I had rehearsed my first homecoming speech to her so many times, but that script had now failed me. I heard her beautiful voice, her words of love, her joy and excitement that jumped over the wires.

God's gift to me was alive and well . . . and waiting. There had been no brass bands in Boston or parades, and there were none here at Fort Sheridan that morning. But I saw the image of Ruth's beautiful face, her golden hair and sparkling eyes, through my misting eyes. Ruth was my Gibraltar, the solid rock of my life. No man could ever hope for more.

As the saying went, my stomach thought my throat had been cut. I was hungry after the long night, and there were virtually no snacks on the train. I was ready for breakfast! I had noticed that the servers behind the steam tables in the mess hall didn't look like Army men and was told they were German prisoners that had been brought to America for wartime incarceration. They were all quite well-fed and healthy looking, and I decided they had the better part of the war. They served up a fine breakfast with hotcakes, bacon, and eggs fried to order and several kinds of fruit and cereal, which I enjoyed immensely.

Checking with Headquarters, I was given my travel orders, which detailed my 21-day furlough and my next duty station. I gathered my stuff, caught a shuttle ride to the main gate, and boarded a North Shore electric train that delivered me to Chicago's Loop at its terminal on Wabash Avenue. Descending the long flight of stairs from the El platform, I reached street level and entered an idling Yellow Cab as I told the driver my destination. He turned left onto Randolph Street and headed for the Outer Drive. It was a cold Sunday with little traffic. We crossed the bridge over the Illinois Central Railroad then turned south on the boulevard that fed the Outer Drive bordering Lake Michigan.

Long forgotten but familiar sights caught my attention. The famous Buckingham Fountain, the Grant Park Band Shell, the Field Museum of Natural History, and huge Soldier's Field, the memorial sports stadium project built and named after World War I to honor the veterans of that conflict. Feeling at home was becoming a reality.

We skirted the lake shore where the waves from a heavy surf were icing the sandy beaches and massive breakwater stones. We arrived at the entrance to Jackson Park, passed near the Windermere East Hotel where Ruth's brother, Bud Wasson, had staged our family wedding dinner 16 months earlier, and drove by the Museum of Science and Industry, anchored on the north shore of the Jackson Park Lagoon where as youngsters we had fished for bullheads and where we were prohibited from ice-skating because of drownings due to thin ice — and where brother David, at age 17, had saved the life of the man who had fallen from his rowboat. We finally crossed the bridge over the yacht channel and the cab exited the park, entered Jeffrey Avenue at 67th Street, crossed the IC tracks at 71st Street, and turned right on 72nd. Each street and landmark were engraved in my memory. And in just three more blocks and Ruth and I would be locked in that long-awaited embrace.

Ruth had been watching through the window for my arrival and ran down the stairs to the front entrance hall when she saw me coming up the walk. I threw open the door at the moment she hit the last stair and she flew into my arms. An adequate description of my feelings, our words, our sensations fails me. We stood for long moments just hugging and kissing, mixing our tears of relief and happiness, then laughing from sheer joy. What a finale to our long and treacherous, fear-filled separation.

We climbed the two flights of stairs and were met at the door by Ruth's older sister and mother, Alice and Clara Wasson, and their warm welcome and happy tears.

Ruth had also invited my parents and sisters, who were to come for dinner. I heard the doorbell ring and then the greeting of Mother, Dad, Jean, and Margaret. They were in and seated as I was changing to a clean uniform.

I hurried and was soon scooping them into my arms, hugging and kissing, crying and laughing, and all thanking God for my safe deliverance. It was the moment of a lifetime!

We were just finishing Mrs. Wasson's fine roast-beef dinner when I had a fit of nausea and retreated to the bathroom where I lost everything I had eaten. The luxury of real home-cooking, its flavors and richness, was foreign to my system, now conditioned to the blandness of Army fare. Combined with the excitement and thrill of being home, my stomach rebelled and was for the next few meals, alarmingly belligerent. I had weighed 154 pounds when I entered the Army in 1941. I was a solid 175 pounds when I left for Corsica in May 1944. Now, in January 1945, I was back to 154 pounds. I was ready for more calories, and after a few days did begin gaining weight.

We all enjoyed a long talk that first night home, punctuated with many questions and answers, then soon were politely stifling our yawns. My folks were ready to leave and Ruth and I were both ready to be alone. After my call from Fort Sheridan, she had called the Country Club Cooperative Apartment Hotel and was able to engage the same one-room suite we had occupied on our honeymoon. Her small overnight suitcase was packed for the three-night limit allowed by the hotel's resident manager. After that, we would move to my bedroom in my parents' home, which I had vacated on September 26th, 1941.

Dad let us borrow Ray's old 1935 Dodge four-door, to which he had fallen heir in Ray's absence, and we headed for our second honeymoon at 69th and South Shore Drive. I again carried Ruth across the threshold, hung out the "Do Not Disturb" sign, then closed and chained the door.

Following my 21 days at home, my orders instructed me to report to the Army Air Forces Redistribution Station #3 at Santa Monica, California, no later than midnight on the 24th of February 1945. The days before our departure would be filled with a bouquet of family celebrations. All the relatives made me feel like a hero.

Ruth's brother Bud and wife, "Big Ruth," arranged a great day for us. Bud and I rode downtown on the IC and had lunch at the Boston Oyster House, went to a play at a theater on Michigan Avenue, walked to the Field Building basement for mild exercise, steam-bath, hot shower, and body rub-down in Charles Allman's gymnasium, then upstairs to the long bar for a pair of martinis.

Cooled down, we then walked to the Empire Room of the Palmer House at Wabash Avenue and Monroe Street where we met the two Ruths for a grand evening of dinner and dancing. The popular entertainer-singer, Hildegarde, was the featured act. She was very gracious to her audience and warmly welcomed the many servicemen present. Chicago, renowned for its hospitality, was declared "The Town" for partying GIs.

Another evening was spent with my brother Cameron and his wife Rita, dinner at a fine restaurant, preceded by martinis at the bar. Cam had hoped the celebration and drinks would let me open up on stories of my combat experiences. But Ruth and I had decided we were out for fun and didn't want to mar the occasion with war talk.

We also had a fine dinner evening with Ruth's oldest sister, Viola, and her husband Al

Carlson, and their daughter and son Betty and Wayne. Other aunts, uncles, and cousins were there to add to the festivities.

Ruth's aunt Annie and Uncle Joe Bonneau served us a grand lunch one day. Uncle Joe was known as her "swearing uncle" and did not hesitate to vent his peppered opinions of Adolf Hitler.

And, of course, my family outdid themselves in providing every comfort imaginable. A large dinner was attended by my Uncle Henry Stewart, and his second wife Evangeline and their five-year-old son Gordon Stewart. Another evening was spent with Henry and Nellie Marcy. Henry was Dad's friend and former voice student and had given the American Flyer electric train to David and me when we were kids in 1929.

And Ruth's brother Bud took me as a guest to the monthly meeting of the Chicago Retail Gasoline Dealer's of which he was a local officer. Bud owned two Standard Oil Service Stations and had been quite successful, in spite of wartime restrictions. After dinner and speeches, card tables were set up and Poker games commenced. My Army pay had not yet caught up with me, and I was a little low on funds. Bud gave me $50 and told me to have some fun, win or lose. Two hours later, and after growing and dwindling fortunes, the games ended and I handed $50 back. I was even. I never was much of a card player or gambler and was pleased with my score against these veterans.

While home, we also visited the families of pre-war friends who were still away in the Service and inquired into their whereabouts, securing current addresses and reports of their activities.

Ruth had informed her supervisor at Pure Oil Company that I had returned and that she would be leaving her job to travel with me to my future assignments. She regretted not being able to give them more notice, but they took her departure in stride and thanked her for her loyal service during the difficult time of my absence. We visited her office downtown in the Pure Oil Building and met many of the coworkers she had written about in her letters. They were a grand group of people, and the girls had a great time flirting with me, their way of teasing Ruth. It was obvious to me that Ruth had carved a deep place in their hearts.

My remaining days at home were running out and the wartime pendulum of hellos and goodbyes commenced its inevitable rhythm. Ruth and I were preparing our clothing and other needs for the long train trip to California when on February 19th the *Chicago Tribune* splashed the ominous headlines in large black letters, "MARINES LAND ON IWO JIMA." The report gave details of the invasion by the 3rd, 4th, and 5th Marine Divisions. Brother David was a Pharmacist Mate Third Class in the Navy, on draft by the 23rd Marine Regiment of the 4th Division, serving as a company aid man. His job was to render first-aid to wounded infantrymen in the thick of battle. We knew he was on the Iwo invasion, and we knew he was on front-line duty.

This news thrust a black cloud over our family, and their fears for David's ability to escape serious injury or death dominated their conversation. They turned to me for some possible measure of support or reassurance. Of course, I had no better information than they did, and I could only say that I felt David was a tower of strength, capable of taking care of himself if given half a chance. But privately, my fears matched or perhaps exceeded theirs.

The next day, February 20th, 1945, Ruth and I left for California. Mother chose that day to write a letter to Ray who was still in the Philippines.

Dear Ray:

I received another letter from you with the snap shots and will save them all for you. I have never destroyed a letter or card or snap or article which you have sent home while in service. I am going through all some day and label them. I have all the other boys too.

Well, I must tell you that Alex and Ruth left tonight on the Challenger for Santa Monica, California. They will be at that beautiful hotel which has been turned into a rest home for servicemen. They will be there a month or more according to Alex' condition. He looks wonderful. He shows some nervousness, however but he always was somewhat of a nervous type. Ruth looks wonderful.

Beverly was over this evening for a little while. She always feels a comfort to come over here when she is down. She has many lovely qualities. One is a great unselfishness. She never seems to be cherishing every thing for herself. She sends David everything she can think of that he might like or be able to use.

Continued from the 20th.......Feb.22-'45

Dear Ray:

It is early morning and I have had little sleep. I went to sleep for 4 hours, but David is so much on my mind, due to the war, that I do not sleep long. I usually find that in a great crisis, to be up and vigilant may help in some way. God will know that I am trying. David is in that terrible battle at Iwo. We can tell by "4th Div.23rd Marines." People say put your trust in God and don't worry, but I wish I could be like that. I just feel God needs our help. I know this may be my own philosophy but that is how I feel. I am not working myself up but feel that alertness is necessary at a time like this.

Write to him often and send a little snap of yourself and a word of love, as he may be needing it badly. One does not know a minute ahead what is waiting.

My dearest love to you and my loving heart to watch over you. Love

Mother

As Mother's letter was traveling the long and treacherous journey to the Southwest Pacific, Ruth and I were drawing ever closer to the Redistribution Station #3 located in the

Del Mar Hotel on the beach at Santa Monica.

The *Challenger* glided smoothly into its siding in the Los Angeles depot shortly after noon of February 24th and seemed to heave a sigh of relief as it expelled the air that had brought the mammoth diesel to a stop in its Western Terminus. We had enjoyed the journey, resting in our bedroomette compartment, eating generous meals served by courteous, white-jacketed waiters in the sparkling dining car, and talking mostly with other servicemen in the Club Car while sipping coffee or soft drinks or, for me, an occasional cocktail. The reports on Iwo Jima drew everyone's rapt attention.

This was my first time back to the Santa Monica area since I had brought a B-25 to the North American Aircraft plant for special modification in December 1943. And it was the first time ever for Ruth to visit Santa Monica. The weather was sunny and pleasant as the Army bus tooled the

Pharmacist Mate Third Class David Barton Stewart, age 21, as a Medical Corpsman with the Marines on his last furlough in Chicago, 1944.

streets and boulevards and finally deposited us at the door of this once elegant hotel, now wearing the colors and symbols of the U.S. Army Air Forces. Like many similar facilities, it had been appropriated by the government for use in the processing of returning fliers and in determining the direction of their future assignments. The Del Mar was set up for married men; the singles went to the air base at Santa Ana, where many of us had started our aviation careers in 1942.

After registration, I was given the schedule of appointments that would be met over a

Sergeant Raymond R. Stewart and Pharmacist Mate Third Class David B.
Stewart at their reunion in Hawaii before going into combat, December 1944.

ten-day period. It was not to be a rest hotel, as Mother had said in her letter to Ray, but a clearing house for evaluating the men for continuing service, either in the States or in new foreign service locations. I would be scrutinized and tested by a total of nine officers, each with his own medical or administrative specialty, one per day. Both Ruth and I were impressed with the care and attention exercised in this process, and I was to reflect and comment on this and similar treatment I had observed during my entire Army experience. Ours was a government that cared, and I never saw evidence of any slipshod methods or carelessness that would bring discredit to the person or the service.

In the evening, we sought entertainment and good food at a few of the famous California eateries. On our second night in town we went to dinner with others where Ruth ate roast leg-of-lamb with a light coating of gravy. In the middle of the night, accompanied by my loud snoring, she found herself on her knees in front of the commode, heaving and retching. The attack was determined the next day by an Army doctor to be food poisoning, with the gravy pinpointed as the culprit. Ruth was utterly miserable, and spent two days in bed ingesting medications and resting. The food poisoning was bad enough, she said, but to have me snoring away, oblivious to her discomfort, was almost more than she could bear.

My fourth appointment was pivotal in my evaluation process, a rather exhaustive interview with an Army psychiatrist. The doctor had been a combat flight surgeon in Europe and like many others had considerable training and experience in psychiatry. He was acquainted with the symptoms of extreme combat fatigue in air crews and determined that I was a candidate for treatment in one of several Army Air Forces convalescent facilities.

Nearing the close of the interview the doctor said, "Lieutenant, how would you like to go to the convalescent hospital at Fort George Wright at Spokane, Washington? You and Mrs. Stewart could find quarters in the city and you could commute daily to the base for physical training, occupational therapy — working with your hands — and counsel with a physician assigned to you for evaluation and treatment. Would you like to do that?"

I looked at Ruth, we smiled and nodded agreement. I had not given much thought to my continuing service and was not at all anxious to return to a flying assignment just yet. Many returnees were being parceled out as instructors to various Flight Schools around the country, but I was unable to place myself in that posture. I thought that some day I might be able to transition into a twin-engined attack bomber, the A-26, that had been added to the stable of Army planes — perhaps even train newcomers in it. The A-26 had a performance specification that grabbed the attention of veteran B-25 and B-26 pilots. But at that time and for the foreseeable future, I chose Spokane. Ruth sensed that the doctor had seen in my behavior and attitude a need for rehabilitation that was not apparent to the layman — or to me.

Before we left the hotel for the train, I received a telegram from Scotty saying he was being sent to Fort Wright and that I might try for a similar assignment. I could hardly believe that once more we were going to be stationed together!

After 1,000 miles to Portland, Oregon, and an afternoon change of trains for the remaining 375 miles to Spokane, we were glad for an overnight stay in a Spokane hotel before starting the search, with Scotty's help, for in-town living quarters.

On our second inquiry, we located a nice room with kitchen privileges in a well-built gray-stone home at South 905 Monroe Street. The owner, Mrs. Rooney lived there with her young daughter, Margo, who would stand, fascinated, watching me kiss Ruth goodbye each morning. Mr. Rooney worked in a Bremerton, Washington, shipyard.

Scotty was staying with his grandmother in her apartment, a short distance from our quarters. We had a happy reunion with my old friend, the prelude to many memorable times.

I registered in at the Fort Wright hospital and was assigned to a physician whom I liked very much. For hands-on therapy, I selected the sheet-metal shop where I made a handsome solid-brass bedlamp and a fine stainless-steel serving tray with the initial "S" engraved in the center. This activity would serve my needs until a space became available in the auto shop where I could work on the beat-up 1938 Plymouth I had purchased that was badly in need of an overhaul. Hopefully, it would provide transportation for us until the end of the war.

We had arrived in Spokane on March 6th and were well into a comfortable routine. I was enjoying the work in the shop, had been introduced to riding some fine old retired

Army cavalry horses that had lost their ambition to give novice riders a bad time, and was gaining some needed weight on the excellent meals served in the officers mess. Ruth would ride the city bus out to the Fort most days and join me for supper at a cost of 35 cents. But, for some forgotten reason, she didn't come out on March 20th.

When I came home to our room, Ruth was lying on the bed. I went to her and before I could say anything she burst into sobs. "David is dead. He was killed on Iwo Jima. A letter came today from your mother."

In that instant my world fell apart. The greatest fear I had harbored during my whole time in the Army had become a reality. I was devastated.

When I finally recovered enough to listen, Ruth read Mother's letter to me:

> My dear Alex and Ruth:
>
> My darlings I am writing tonight with a heart full of grief and also great love. Our darling David was killed in the battle of Iwo Jima. I would have sent a telegram but thought it best for you both to receive the message by letter. We received the telegram from the Navy department late of last Friday evening, night before last. I could not write before as I was overcome with great grief, attention to my darling girls, and trying to keep up for Dad's sake.
>
> We have had many friends principally of our neighbors calling, relatives coming and staying quite long and poor little Bevie to comfort. There is little I can say to help you and we will try to write daily letters. We have been helped so much by all these dear ones, and I know you will feel their comfort too through my letters.
>
> Cam and Re have been wonderful. I called them and they came right over as soon as the store closed. They then went over and got Bevie, and her girl friend who was with her at the time. This girl friend has a fiance in Iwo who is in the hospital with a shoulder bone shattered. Bevie's mother and grandmother stayed home next three days (Sat.) and took Mary Ann and her with her to Peoria and returned at a late hour last night. Her mother thought the long ride into the country would help to tire her so she would sleep, which she did. She does not eat however, but has felt better today. I called the church this morning and Bev said it seems the sermon was just for her. It was a most beautiful and marvelous sermon.
>
> After the friends left Cam and Re were here to take us out to dinner. It was a nice dinner and we all talked long of David and they went to the store. Cam and Re are deeply grieved as were Kathleen and Ed and Henry and Evangeline and all our nice friends and neighbors. Ruth, I did not have your mother come over today, as we could not arrange to go and get her, but she will come when she is able as will many others. I let her know early Saturday, and she was touched and overcome.
>
> Dr. Bowman came over at quarter to six, and offered consolation and prayer and we are arranging a memorial service for Easter Sunday at 4:00 PM. The flowers will be there and it is resurrection day and we feel it is

most fitting. It is to be held along with another family who have just lost a son in service. The McArthur family. It will be in the Chapel where you were married.

There is one thing you can be rest assured of David. He was a wonderful Christian before he went into combat. He was everything one could wish for and I read in his last letters the feeling he might not come through and that he wanted everything to be right. He dearly loved his brothers and sisters (including Ruth and Rita) and that we were all very close to him. He says he could never have got, what he had gained by being in the armed forces. I have many treasures for you to read when you can. His letters were marvelous. He wrote a beautiful letter to Miss Powers, his piano teacher, which is one of the richest treasures she possesses.

I said memorial services were to be in the Chapel but I am not sure but the service will be in the sanctuary.

There is one comforting thought I have. He very likely lost his life while trying to save others lives. Another thought is, that I know he was a real true Christian and is now in Heaven.

We are all bearing up as we should and I know you both will also. David's feelings to all was perfect, and he dearly loved all.

Not only we, but the world has lost a great soul. For twenty-one years he seemed to feel deeply and knew lots. I can tell by his last letters that he had great fears for a safe return. I have no idea of the date, as the Navy did not tell us. This information will follow. As near as we can tell it was about February 26th.

I am having a beautiful picture of him done for us and Rita, and if these come out alright will have one for you also. Take all the comfort you can from my letter and rest assured you will hear from me often because I know you are far away and I can give you what others cannot.

Hoping you are both in good health and taking every care of yourselves. I know that is what you will do.

Our love to you both,
Mother and Dad

P.S. I hope you will write to Ray often as he will need your comfort at this zero hour. God bless you and keep you both.

Mom.

My head was in a swirl. Images of David's last moments in battle alternated with our tears and we collapsed in each other's arms . . . over and over again, until our energies were exhausted. Sleep finally prevailed, fitful and broken.

Up before dawn, I told Ruth I would go out to Fort Wright and that she could join me for lunch. I bathed and dressed, rode the bus, and got off near the office of the Base Chaplain. He received me graciously and listened to my brief account of David's loss. My

grief was still uncontrollable, and I made little sense. I was reaching out for something —
comfort perhaps, as much for myself as for Mother and Dad and my sisters.

I had brought Mother's letter and handed it to the Chaplain to read.

"You have a fantastic mother, Alex. See how she has already set aside her grief and her
deep, emotional wounds, seeking to comfort and help the others in their terrible distress.
And she is doing it for you too. It is amazing that she is able to write as she has, and only
48 hours after receiving the telegram."

I sat there in a rather numbed state as he prayed for me and the family, unable to grasp
the full nature of his petitions, but satisfied that God was aware of our tribulations and that
peace would soon be upon us. I thanked him for his kindness and his promise to keep lifting me and the family to God in prayer.

Before going to see my doctor, I stopped by the woodworking shop where Scotty was
busy at the lathe, turning a handsome cigar humidor. Ruth had phoned Scotty and had told
him of David's death before I got home, and he seemed anxious to see me. He turned off
the lathe and we sat for a cup of coffee. Scotty listened to my brief description of
Mother's letter and expressed his sympathy for our loss. He then suggested that we ask our
doctors for a three-day pass so that we could go to his family's family farm at Spangle,
Washington, 18 miles south of Spokane. I thought it was a fine idea.

My doctor was stunned at the news of David's death, talked about him at some length,
then okayed my request for the pass. He saw the delaying potential of the event in my
rehabilitation and told me that we would not be watching the clock until I would be
absolutely ready to return to active duty. In his capacity, he had total control over the
patient's readiness for service.

That evening I wrote to Mother, expressing all the love and sympathy I could muster
and reassured her of the healing process that we were now experiencing. I told her of the
pending visit to Scotty's farm and all the help I had received from the Chaplain and the
doctor. I admired her for her fortitude and her reaching out to all of us with her great love.
I had celebrated my 25th birthday on March 15th, three days before her letter about David
had arrived, and told her of Ruth's fine birthday dinner and cake she had made and which
Scotty had shared with us.

True to her word, Mother wrote again on March 20th.

Dearest Alex and Ruth:

This is only a short time after my last letter but I told you I would be
writing right away.

I am so glad the birthday was a success. That is what we all hoped it
would be, after so many months away, and you could really try your own
cooking Ruth, on your young flier husband.

I know you will enjoy the trip to the farm, though as I have often said,
one soon gets tired of their own cooking.

My dear ones, you have been much in our minds these days. Our girls
are just wonderful people. They help me with the friends who come in and
help with the work, comfort Dad, answer the phone and door bell and
write letters.

Margaret has been home from school this week but is going back tomorrow. Jean is still home tomorrow as she has to work on Saturday this week. I don't know as I will be going back to the office. I may try to get some short hour work, as I want to be home with Dad. He is too lonely for me to be away and just now his sorrow is so great.

We have much to be thankful for. This is our first big trouble, in fact our only trouble in 39 years. We are trying to console ourselves but, dear ones, it is very hard, but as you know we would not want our darling to come home with both legs or arms off or suffer a constant pain or be without eyesight. I really think that he is better off to be laid away than to be a terrible wreck. Not for my sake, but for his. I would want my own back in any case, and be willing to wait upon them and care for them the rest of my life, but life is such a burden to one's self.

Well my little darling will know no more battles or suffering, but oh, how I long for him, and yet why should I wish him back here to face another invasion and then another and maybe more.

There is one thing I know and that is: he was a child of Christ, and wanted no misgivings. He had made his peace and was at home with God. My darling is going to be right here with us, in his beautiful spirit his loving heart will be ours. We are doing all we can to comfort our dear ones too. That is why I write often and tenderly to you, dear hearts. I know you are with me always.

If you can do so, please write to Ray often as he will so love to hear from you, especially in this trouble. Our love and prayers are with you.

I had a long talk to your mother tonight Ruth and she gave me comfort.

Most lovingly,
>Mother and all.

P.S. I am quite sure I will be writing tomorrow but if I do not, will be in another day. I know you too, are away from all. I also wanted to say that I think the work projects are just fine and I know it will be a nice lamp. You will enjoy his hand-craft. Just like the gloves you made, Ruth. I know once I took two aprons and made a house-dress and thought I was quite smart.

Re and Cam are very busy and likely they will write to you very soon.

Our loving hearts reach across the expanse of western plains and mountains to you and across the Pacific to dear Ray and up to Heaven to David.

Love,
>Mother.

Mother's love and compassion for us seemed boundless, and her lifetime ability of focusing on the daily condition in the lives of her family in times of stress was indeed remarkable. She was the first to initiate in others and in herself the surrender of David to God's eternal home. I believe she truly felt that David had fulfilled his calling, and she neither showed nor expressed any bitterness toward the Japanese or to our government.

Jean, the younger of my two sisters, was a consistent letter writer of the family and matched Mother in her loyalty to us. And if any of them would have had difficulty in writing to us, I would have guessed it would be Jean. But her compassion and sensitivity to our emotional welfare was superb. Her letter to Ray, written on March 20th, 1945, was a 12-page masterpiece of comfort, a portion of which is shared here:

Dearest Darling Ray:

By the time this letter reaches you in the Philippines you will have heard through Mother of the death of our beloved David. We wanted so much to write to you immediately, but in our grief stricken state it seemed best to wait a few days.

The invasion of Iwo started just before Alex completed his furlough. Although he tried to assure us that David was a tower of strength and well equipped to take care of himself as well as others, we could see that he was worried and nervous about him in spite of it. Our hearts are heavy when we think of such a sorrowful ending to his wonderful life.

There is one side of it all which is comforting and that is the thought that he was ready to go. A certain tone in his last letters seemed to indicate that he had little hope of returning. We all know that our darling David was never one to look on the dark side of things. He never suffered from complexes or fears of any kind, and when last he spoke of the complete lack of discrimination which exists in mass warfare, we couldn't help but think he had some gloomy forebodings of the combat he was about to enter. We find it so difficult to write to you about this tragedy, Ray, because we know you are not at home where the atmosphere is so much more secure, and you won't be in the company of people who can share your loving thoughts and words of praise for David.

Only last Sunday, when our sadness was greatest, Dad remarked that he didn't know what we would do without the women. He said, "Just look at the way you can go about dusting the parlor and arranging the boy's pictures on top of the piano." I said, "Dad, when I have been in the homes of other people who were holding wakes for their loved ones, I wondered how they could possibly do those commonplace, everyday tasks and when people come in, turn and weep over their loss." Now that time has come in our home and I find that we act just like other people.

Mother, our beloved Mother, whom I never thought could endure such a separation, is holding up better than the rest of us. Probably some of the strength and fortitude which it undoubtedly took to raise a big family is still at her command. Sometimes it seems that it is, by some divine power, imparted to us, and it supports our broken spirits.

During these past few days we have talked endlessly about David and his wonderful life. You would almost think we had kept a diary to hear us recall the details of his work, his music, his school days, his home-life, and last but not least, his great love of people.

When we think of his outstanding musical ability we can't help but think that it was another bond which linked him to all who had the supreme pleasure of hearing him. I remember an evening we once spent at the home of the Hiltons. David played many of his best selections and finished with the Second Hungarian Rhapsody by Liszt. They were astounded and said they had never heard anything like it outside Carnegie Hall in New York. Mrs. Hilton got up and shook his hand and said, "I have met David the man, and now I want to meet David the musician. It is an honor to know him."

When he played at the hotel in New York for Dad's cousins, they insisted that only two people could play the piano, Paderewski and David. In the face of such compliments his sense of humor always rose to the surface, he'd smile and say thank you, in his modest way, and then joke about them thinking he was so wonderful.

To recall his high school graduation speech has also been a great source of joy to us. It was so beautifully written, and in such advanced style and delivered by him like a seasoned orator. There was no question but that peoples' emotions were much disturbed. Dean Smith from Chicago University, when complimenting him afterward, said he wished he could write and deliver an equally remarkable one. (The dean evidently noticed that the audience was not held spell-bound by his speech as they were by David's).

Well Ray, it appears that I could expound at great length on all his talents and still not cover everything. But as no word regarding him would be complete without mentioning that above all things his deepest desire was to become a doctor and save lives, I could not close without saying that if he died in that way, he was brave and happy at the last, despite the awful battle. I feel confident that if he had his choice of a way to depart it would be in a courageous attempt to save the life of a fellow comrade. We all remember with what forgetfulness of self he dove into the Jackson Park Lagoon to save a drowning, crippled man. He was seventeen then (summer of 1940) and thereafter was intent on saving lives.

At his suggestion, prior to the invasion of Iwo, the medical corpsmen all carried the blood plasma in their first aid kits. In other invasions the plasma was administered at the battalion aid stations, but he believed they could save more lives by not waiting to remove men to aid stations, and he won out. He wanted it done where the men fell, and recently we saw a picture in the paper which showed a corpsman giving it to a wounded Marine on Iwo in a foxhole.

His work in the Marines was just a continuation of what he had already started at Billings Hospital. The big doctors all praised his ability to assist them in the surgery and many of the patients didn't want anyone else to look after them in their rooms.

It is hard indeed to give up a person who has lived a full and happy life such as his. We are so glad he was appreciated while he was here because oftentimes outstanding personalities and genii are not recognized until after their deaths. He never had to want for things because his versatility and great love for people magnetized them before they had a chance to know him. He was everybody's friend and a friend he was in return — from the rich and happy to the humble and suffering.

Mother and Dad often remarked that Nature had been good to him, endowing him with more talents than she usually gave to many lives, but he gave all the credit to them. David said that although he had a new responsibility in life, his dear wife, it was his intention after the war to see that his beloved parents wanted for nothing. He thanked them for his wonderful start in life and hoped he would never be a discredit to it, and that it would ever serve as an inspiration for his life ahead.

In closing, Ray, be assured we are holding up very well. We have your pictures on the piano under some beautiful, soft pink and blue feather flowers, and everyone who comes in sees David in his most perfect setting-between his two big brothers. But most of all, we have you three in our hearts, never to be moved, and ever to be a source of great joy to all.

"May the Lord bless you and keep you, the Lord make his face to shine upon you and be gracious unto you, the Lord lift up the light of his countenance upon you, and give you peace."

All our love and deep affection

Your loving sister,
Jean

Dad was not as quick in his acceptance of David's sacrifice. It has been a universal observation that fathers have the hardest time in the giving up of a son and Dad's grief seemed to confirm that attitude. He wrote to us on April 3rd, 1945:

Dear Ruth and Alex,

You will be quick to note, and pardoned if you remark, that this is the first letter I have sent you since the Shadow of Death darkened our door, and turned our home from a happy meeting place for all, into a chamber of desolation and weeping.

Since its founding forty years ago, we can gratefully say that this is the only visitation of intense sorrow that has befallen us, and everything around us seems to share in our bereavement, robbing us of our usual and normal joy.

Mother and I with practiced and sometimes forced fortitude have tried to hold our chins up and keep our eyes dry, but a long moment arrives too often when resistance fails; and our broken hearts force themselves to the front; and refuse to be restrained.

Your sisters have shared, but more often have led in deep and loud expressions of grief, and like children lost in a great whirling city, we weep in each others arms, and involuntarily refuse to be comforted.

As yet, none of us have become reconciled to the unalterable truth that David has forever left us. His pictures are spread with yours, Ray's and others all over the piano, and we are awaiting the fling of his long arms about us, and the warmth of his loving cheek against ours.

But we must await entrance into another world for this realization, and this is all that bears us up.

Our worries are now divided between Ray and you, and will not subside till war is over. I always escaped military service, but never dreamed that war would so darken my closing years, and tear my own flesh and blood from the guardianship I have always rejoiced in.

Your mother is the brave keeper of this castle called home, shines in her loveliness in those darkened spots, speaks comfort to us in rich heavenly tones, and constantly forgets her own precious welfare.

Dear children I must stop, I have hardly been able to see a word I have written.

Affectionately, Dad

Ruth and I were very moved by Dad's letter and were deeply touched by his profound grief. I wondered if he would ever get over such a loss. But my parents' love knew no partiality and the loss of any of us would have produced equal suffering.

Reading my father's letter, a friend observed:

Your father's letter, in its terse, succinct style, affected me deeply — it was a cry from the depths of his soul. Immediately I thought of King David's grief over the death of his son (2 Samuel 18:33): "The king was shaken. He went up to the room over the gateway and wept. As he went, he said: O my son Absalom! My son, my son Absalom! If only I had died instead of you — O Absalom, my son, my son!"

The commentary in my study Bible says, "O my son Absalom! — one of the most moving expressions in all literature of a father's love for a son — in spite of all that Absalom had done." The father's response expressing the profound sense of loss is very like your father's response to losing David.

The family had not had word as to the exact date and time of David's death. David had written of men with whom he was teamed in preparation for the Iwo Jima invasion, one of whom was Edward Mitchell Wallace of Hamlet, North Carolina. Prior to the invasion they had spent many spare hours studying their medical books, seeking information that would enable them to save more lives.

On April 9th, 1945, Edward Mitchell Wallace wrote:

To the Stewart family:

"I am sorry that I could not have lived longer than this, for I wished so much to show the world just what I could be, and to do justice to my family for all they have done for me. I owe them a world of gratitude, and I have never begun to repay them."

So ended the last conversation that my dearly beloved friend, David Barton Stewart, and your son and brother carried on together, for when we next came face to face with each other, there was only one of us, for his soul had departed and had gone to rest — at peace with the world and with a record satisfactory, I know, to all the saints in heaven.

It has been my task to return and let you know just why and for what he died. I hardly feel fit to sit here this night and write to you, for Bart meant so much to me, that I had rather have gone with him.

Back in November of last year, I was in the hospital in Hawaii recuperating from an illness that I had contracted on Saipan. One Sunday afternoon prior to returning to duty, something told me in a strange way that upon my return I would meet someone who would mean everything to me and would take precedence over all my former friends. Several days later I returned to my organization and a new fellow had moved into my tent, we became acquainted right away, and I knew then, that this was the person who was to become a symbol of all that I saw in human life. Yes, Dave and I became great friends, and whenever you saw one of us, there was the other. He came into my company and we stayed together in the field. In December we knew we would be embarking soon for a tough and dangerous mission, and so Dave and I promised one another that whatever came our way, we would be together, and would do everything possible to help the other.

The first of November saw us embarking and going on maneuvers. I went aboard a transport, and Dave's platoon went aboard an LST. We had several liberties together in Honolulu and then started on our mission to Iwo Jima. We both formed great plans as to what we would do, and now we were going to operate in action. When we reached Saipan, I went aboard the LST with the rest of my company and we sailed the rest of the voyage together.

Dave often spoke to me of all you folks at home. Every night we would play chess until late, and then go up on deck and talk. There was something that kept worrying him and he finally told me that he wanted everything to be right between him and all the members of the family.

On the night of February 18th we had run into some very nasty weather, and it was too cold and rainy to sleep topside, so we talked and talked about this and that, and then went below and slept until 4:00 AM. We got up, went to breakfast, and then went on deck and talked until daylight. There were a great many things on Dave's mind and he wanted to get them off, he was worried, and I knew it, he wasn't afraid for there wasn't an ounce of fear in him. Along about daylight, he told me that this was his rendezvous with death, that his time was up. I tried to build up his confidence and so put him off with a laugh, but he was serious, and so I had to revert to a serious attitude before I could make him believe that we all felt that way one time or another. We both had said our prayers, and I know that God had heard us, for Dave didn't ask to live or be spared, but only to do the job that lay before him to the best of his ability.

The word was soon passed for everyone to warm their equipment and go below to their tractors; far ahead of us lay that peaceful and serene little rock, with ships and planes blasting away. We shook hands, said goodbye and wished the other luck. Dave was in tractor #2-4 and I was in tractor #3-4, he was in the first personnel wave and I the second. We debarked from the ship and started toward the beach. Dave's tractor lands at 9:00 and my tractor lands at 9:05. We were covered with machine gun fire all over the beach. Dave's wave had advanced across the first terrace and was sweeping up over the second as we crossed the first. I kept jumping from hole to hole and looking to see if anyone was hit, but no one was hit, and so moved up to the bottom of the second terrace, when I noticed someone with a bandage on his face. I ask him if he is alright, and he replies, "yes." Then one of the fellows from Dave's platoon comes running down the terrace, yelling, "Wallace, run up there quick, Stewart has been hit." I advance across to the top of the terrace, and machine gun fire was raking the whole stretch. I see two men lying in the sand and I knew one was Bart. I almost got hit, and jumped into a hole on the top of the terrace about ten yards from Bart. I start yelling at the top of my voice for him to crawl into my hole, but he doesn't answer. Someone from his platoon had been hit, and he crawled into a small hole. Dave had gone charging right across the open, and was hit but didn't move for a few moments. He was hit in the shoulder, gave the wounded man a shot of morphine, cut away his pants leg and bandaged the wound. All this while lying down flat. Then he rolled over on his side and got a full burst of fire in the chest, stomach and neck. He died instantly. About the fourth time I yelled, he hadn't answered. So I had my pack off, and gave my rifle to one of the machine gunners to hold, fastened my helmet and started across, but someone grabs me saying its suicide to go out there. Then the fellow who Dave went out to get, who was hit in the leg, raises up and says, "its no use, he died instantly, don't try to make it." But we dash across anyway. I see Dave is dead, grab the other fellow by the hands and drag him down into the hole. Before I finished working on him, I got hit in the back and arm with shrapnel, but it wasn't enough to stop me. I knew that Dave was dead, and I couldn't do anything to help him. He was hit at exactly 9:15 AM. I knew that it was impossible for me to shed a tear for I never felt so much like crying in all my life, but there was the job to be done, and I had my elbows buried in work. A couple minutes later everyone gets help — a whole mortar squad wiped out, and the corpsman with the mortar platoon has his leg blown off, and I get him back to the beach.

It was a tough, long and weary fight day and night until the ninth day. Simmitt, who was with the third platoon, and I were hit on that day, February 27th. I was evacuated to the Marshalls, Pearl Harbor and then back here. I got my orders at Pearl Harbor to come back to the States. I am now waiting 30 days leave, and I have planned to come to Chicago to see all of you.

I had hoped to write a letter which might be something of a source of comfort to you, for I realize that grief must hang heavy on your shoulders, and I know how much Dave meant to you. I often wonder why it was I that was spared and not Dave. He could have had so much more to live for than I. I know that his absence has changed me and I only hope that someday I might be able to step up and do the job that was his mission to perform. Dave loved his fellow man. "Greater love hath no man than that he lay down his life for his fellow man." Lay down his life is exactly what he did, and his art has been recognized, and he shall be awarded posthumously some high medal of honor.

I must go now, but I hope to be able to talk to all of you soon. I remain

Your friend always,
Edward Mitchell Wallace

Mother had copied the letter in long hand and sent it to us so that we would have the full story of David's last hours. Edward Wallace had been mentioned in some of David's last letters home and there was no question that they valued each other's friendship and were committed to the horrendous task of saving the lives of fallen Marines while under the most vicious fire.

Although it was comforting to have the account of David's action in his first and only combat and to know that his death was instant and not one following a period of long suffering, his loss was very difficult to bear. Because of our closeness in age as brothers we had been almost inseparable as children and as adolescents. But separated by war, we found ourselves on diverse tracks and lost much of that personal relationship that we both had thrived upon and cherished.

Edward Wallace's quotation of John 16:13 wherein Jesus said, "Greater love hath no man than this, that a man lay down his life for his friends" brought to mind that passage from the Sermon on the Mount in Matthew 5:48 where Jesus advised, "Be ye therefore perfect, even as your Father which is in heaven is perfect."

In all of our Christian experience we could never characterize ourselves as perfect or achieving perfection in our earthly realm. But now, in the laying down of his life, in his complete and total act of selflessness, I felt David had attained that heavenly perfection.

The three-day pass that Scotty and I had secured preceded a weekend and stretched into five days at the Rohwer farm. The nearby sleepy village of Spangle bore the distinction of being the gateway to the Palouse Country, a vast fertile region that had been settled by German immigrants and still populated by their industrious, hard-working family heirs. The sight of endless fields of growing wheat epitomized "the amber waves of grain" phrase that we had sung in "America the Beautiful."

The Rohwer family's principal crops were wheat and peas, the kind used for split-pea soup, and I imagined that we possibly had sampled some of this very farm's production in one or more of the many Army mess halls in which we had dined.

Scotty's parents, Jacob and Pauline, were gracious hosts and made Ruth and me feel like members of the family. Scotty's younger brother Earl was the wartime stay-at-home son, excused from service to help run the farm. Like Scotty, Earl was a graduate of Washington State University where he had studied agriculture and was able to apply to the farm his knowledge of many of the modern methods he had acquired.

Mrs. Rohwer's farm production included the raising of chickens and eggs, and she was quick to remind Scotty that she was badly in need of a brooder. This city boy didn't know, but was soon to learn, that a brooder was an enclosed shelter where hens sat on eggs to hatch baby chicks. With a simple plan in hand, Scotty and I rode in the old pickup truck to a nearby town and bought lumber, chicken wire, and shingles for the project.

We spent two or three days sawing and hammering, and, in the process, literally beating out of our systems the frustrations and the misfortunes of war that had lurked below the surface. I had moments when visions of David loomed before me, and the flood-gates would open and I would have to set the tools aside and look out across the fields to replace the devilish scene of Iwo Jima with the peaceful view of God's creation. I knew it would take some time for me to regain rational perspective and accept the council of the Chaplain and my doctor that the period of mourning would have to run its course.

Scotty introduced us to their farm animals, and for the first time in my life I squeezed the teats of a few cows. I was told that my milking prowess would approach perfection when I could make an inch or so of foam on the top of the milk in the pail. I never reached that level of performance, having spent most of my energy learning to balance on a one-legged stool while holding a bucket at the proper angle between my knees. I knew how to massage the throttles on a B-25, but it took some learning and practice to get the proper rhythm and the rolling finger motion on old bossy's appendages.

The Rohwers also had a few horses, and I was introduced to Rex, a gray and black rascal that Mr. Rohwer referred to as a Cayuse — literally "a horse," so called by Western cowboys, glamorizing the name borrowed from a tribe of Oregon Indians. Rex was rather small, and I thought to ride him would be just "duck soup." Scotty had cautioned me that Rex could be rather rude, but encouraged me to take a turn around the small corral. I did so without mishap, but was glad to release Rex to friendlier hands. Ruth rode Rex quite well, at a snail's pace, and I determined that he was just nuts about girls.

Mrs. Rohwer set a marvelous table of delicious meals and satisfied every craving that we had been deprived of on Corsica. Two meats, bacon and sausage, and the freshest eggs for breakfast were complimented with pancakes, homemade jams and jellies, and quantities of stimulating black coffee. And two meats again at lunch (referred to as "dinner" on the farm), and finally two or three meats for supper, with all the fresh garden produce one could manage — everything topped off with tantalizing pies and cakes. Scotty may not have gained weight, but I sure did.

Ruth and I slept in a double bed in the large open area of the unfinished second floor, while Scotty and Earl shared an adjacent room that adequately contained their snoring and insulated them from mine.

We each had our first experience at sleeping in a feather-bed, our bodies creating deep canyons in goose-down while the canyon walls closed in around and on top, mocking the nighttime chill from March winds careening over golden hills and assaulting the ancient but sturdy farm house. After a day of honing marginal skills with hammer and saw and drying wind-primed noses on mackinaw sleeves, we yielded to the call of the geese and slept like little children. Our time with the Rohwers was wonderfully healing, if short-lived, and the reality of my rehabilitation would soon be beckoning.

Back at Fort Wright, my reservation for a stall in the auto shop was finally filled, and I backed my war-weary 1938 Plymouth into a clean, well-equipped garage-type building and commenced with the repairs that I had decided were of immediate importance. My goal was to make the coupe as roadworthy as possible, with no preconceived idea of longevity.

First on the agenda was to remove the engine, the radiator, and all other appendages that would need fine tuning. Scotty watched with interest and then wondered what he could do to help. I chose for him a time-consuming job that I didn't particularly relish, the rebuilding of the carburetor. He set about with the rebuild kit, pages of instructions, and my shallow threat that if the engine wouldn't start it would be his fault. He completed his job long before the carburetor was needed and placed it in a box inside the car.

I completely stripped the engine, removing all pistons, valves, bearings, crank and cam shafts, and other essentials, and installed either new replacements or reconstituted parts. I had the worn-to-egg-shape cylinders rebored to a 15,000th oversize, the scarred crank shaft throws shaved to 10,000th undersize, and the main bearing journals turned to 25,000th undersize. New bearing inserts were unavailable so I had the parts house re-babbitt and bore my old ones to fit the newly turned surfaces.

I installed a new battery, spark plugs, distributor, and wiring, and relined the brakes and overhauled the wheel and master cylinders. A few leaks were repaired in the radiator, and new hoses took care of the cooling system. The stick-shift transmission and the clutch were the only components that didn't require overhaul or replacement. I did buy an inexpensive seat cover, which calmed the prickly attitude of the old, rough upholstery. Of the five tires, two appeared to be serviceable and one could pass for a spare. The others were replaced with two new skins, after an argument with the Ration Board.

The day of the "shake-down cruise" finally arrived, and all the patients and instructors from the auto shop gathered in the yard, betting for or against the car's ability to start. Because of the tightness of the new engine parts, I feared that the starter would not turn the engine over without some preliminary run-in. An instructor hooked me up behind a truck and towed me around the yard a few times while I held the transmission in high gear, allowing the oil to coat the cylinders and bearings. I felt confident that everything would work okay.

I called for all final bets to be placed, and I believe I had covered about $20 of some skeptics' money. The final moment came.

I turned the key to ON, stepped on the starter, and after a longer turnover time than I cared for, that old engine with its odd collection of bastard parts roared into life. It chugged and coughed, but it ran . . . for perhaps a minute or two. It was obvious that a few adjustments were needed, especially to the carburetor, but I couldn't fault Scotty. He had done his job well, and he did bet *with* me, not against me. I felt the same exhilaration that I had known back in November 1941 at Camp Wallace, Texas, when I had built and driven an odd assembly of truck parts.

Money changed hands and both winners and losers congratulated me. Even some of the winners didn't think the car would start, but they wouldn't bet against my determination.

Ruth and I now, hopefully, had our transportation secured for the trip to my next duty assignment, but had no indication from the doctor as to when that would occur. I continued with the occupational therapy and eventually regained my confidence and the desire to return to flying status, though I didn't care to get into the instructor mode.

Scotty and I each got another three-day pass and planned a fishing trip with Earl and their neighbor friend, Dick Denny. We rented two cabins at Twin Lakes, Washington, one for the three bachelors and the other for Ruth and me. Whether we caught fish or not, we were well stocked with food from the farm, including a package of frozen steaks from the Rohwer locker at the Spangle Locker Plant.

But we did catch a worthy mixture of trout — rainbows, lake, and brook — and had one especially fine fish fry. Ruth was initiated into cooking for four young men with ravenous appetites. One huge breakfast of pancakes, fried eggs, and sausage was finally topped off with a round of T-bone steaks!

It was a beautiful excursion for us and contributed to my renewed well-being. Counsel with the doctor indicated that I soon would be ready to return to active duty. For some time, Ruth and I had attended the Saturday night dances at the Officers Club and there met the permanent duty officers in charge of reassigning patients to active-duty service.

The officer in charge of assignments in the Central Flying Command had the only B-25 facility that interested me, the Enid Army Air Field at Enid, Oklahoma. My old high school friend from Chicago, Larry McBrearty, had been stationed there for almost three years, and Ruth and I decided we should try for the assignment. Enid was an Advanced Flight Training School, and B-25s were being introduced to upper classmen cadet students in the second half of their Advanced training. Though I wasn't anxious to be an instructor, I felt this was a better situation than one that might channel me into another overseas combat assignment.

I expressed my preference for Enid to Assignments Officer Hugh Crawford, and in due time appropriate orders were issued, dated May 18th, 1945. In addition to travel time, I requested and was granted a ten-day delay en route, setting my arrival time in Enid for June 9th. This provided a total of 22 days from May 19th. I had explained to my doctor that I felt the need to spend some time with my family, as I had not seen them since before the word of David's death had been received. I had enough leave accumulated, and felt this would be a good way to use some of it.

Ruth and I packed for the trip in the afternoon of May 18th before driving to Scotty's farm home for a goodbye dinner. This would be the first assignment that separated us, excluding that freakish one where we were sent to different Advanced Flight Schools, since our meeting at Santa Ana on October 15th, 1942. It was a hard goodbye to folks who had opened their home and their hearts to us and saw us through what was one of the most trying times of our lives.

We had an early morning start from Mrs. Rooney's home and a hug and a kiss from little Margo. The Plymouth was loaded with essentials, and we headed toward Coeur D'Alene, Idaho, then on down to our first scheduled stop at Bozeman, Montana. Four-hundred-plus miles later, with the sun streaking toward the Western horizon, we had a flat tire where a roadside sign announced "Bozeman 5 Miles." But the spare was still holding air and the promise of getting us to the central business district of this front door to Yellowstone National Park.

The best and probably the only hotel in town had a room, on the third floor. Judging from the sparse activity, we wondered why the desk clerk assigned us to the top floor, then decided that the maid service was a twice-per-week ritual and the lower floors were awaiting their semi-weekly clean-up.

We found a small, attractive cafe on the southwest corner of a street intersecting the main drag and ate one of the largest and perhaps the tastiest T-bone steak of our lives. The owner at the cash register gave me the location of the local Ration Board, which we spotted for easy access in the morning. I wondered at the size of the animal whose loin produced steaks that filled and even overlapped a full-sized dinner plate. "Real big" was the only assessment the owner could render.

With travel orders in hand, we visited the Ration Board and were issued, without hassle, a coupon for the purchase of two new tires to fit the Plymouth. A nearby service garage mounted the tires, checked the air pressure in the others, and used the best old tire for a spare.

The rest of our journey passed without mishap. Our route took us to Chicago by way of Billings, Fargo, Minneapolis, and Madison. Because I was traveling for the convenience of the government, I was supplied with adequate gasoline ration coupons at Spokane, and with the authority of my travel orders, I could secure additional coupons from local Ration Boards if the need arose. I could register no fault with the car's performance and decided my overhaul of the engine was pretty good.

At home, in Chicago, everyone was happy to see us and many commented on the apparent success of my convalescence and treatment at Fort Wright.

I had been concerned about any lingering sadness and grief of Mother and Dad and sisters Jean and Margaret from David's death, but it appeared that they all had passed the hardest period of mourning and had been able to restore normality to their lives. They were able to talk freely about David and had accepted his service and sacrifice as heroic misfortunes of war. On that score, they were doing much better than I had done.

The family naturally was still concerned about Ray and me, for although the war in Europe was drawing to a close, the Pacific conflict was still raging and none of us knew what the future might hold for us. But I felt my length of service and combat contribution would be adequate to keep me Stateside and help in the combat training of the new pilots emerging from the training schools.

Ray, however, was certainly in a vulnerable situation. As a Sergeant in the Medical Corps of the 96th Infantry Division, he had led a nine-man team in the emergency care and treatment of wounded in Company B of the 321st Battalion Aid Station as they were evacuated from front-line service. And he had participated in the invasion of Okinawa and the Philippines, where he was still under the threat of Japanese fire.

Whenever Ruth and I had visited our families in Chicago on our travels, Mother had produced recent letters from David and from Ray for us to read, which were usually more detailed than their missives written directly to us. It had been my experience that letter writing could become quite a chore with several repetitions of material, and I understood the reason for brevity.

Ray had written a letter to Dad from Okinawa on May 5th, 1945, which I found to be quite poignant, and a little unusual for Ray, who was now 30 years old:

Dear Dad,

I have just finished a letter to you and Mother. Every now and then I like to write a somewhat chatty letter to you and address it to your studio. I know that when you arrive there daily you may have a little lonely feeling until your first pupil arrives.

I've received your three or four letters which you have sent me in the last month or so and am always glad to get them. You always remind me of some of the happy days gone by. I often think of the days we painted the house together, or fixed the chimney and when we installed the new heating system.

I suppose I have neglected to praise you directly for your handy work, your ideals, your love and your loyalty to your family. Although I never admitted these things to you I was always conscious of them and I often told my friends and outsiders.

You and I, as well as the rest of the boys have had our ins and outs but I guess that is something that goes on in every family.

I think about you all the time Dad, and I know you have just gone through the most sorrowful period of your life.

I'm glad that Mother is home now so you two can have a lot of time together. I told Mom I wanted her to go downtown with you often and have lunch and dinner together. You folks can't always get the food you want at the grocery store and besides Mom might not like to do much cooking.

I'll be writing to you again in a day or two. Remember that I like to receive your letters. God Bless you, Dad.

Love . . . Ray

The progress of the war, the securing of bases such as Iwo Jima for the emergency land-ing of damaged B-29s shot up on their raids of Nipponese targets, and the planned and pending threat of the invasion of Japan itself, all chewed at the gut. Even now, it was being predicted that an invasion of the Japanese mainland would render a million or more Amer-ican casualties. There was no way that I could reassure my parents that Ray would be all right. Their recovery from the shock of David's loss had to be an automatic veneer em-ployed for the benefit of the feelings of others. They would not consciously impose a continuing grief on anyone. Mother especially was a champion in this regard. She had at her command a fantastic means of turning her attention to the needs of her listeners, her soft, endearing voice backed by her sweet and genuine smile. . . . Don't tell *me* about heros!

There were heros on the battlefields, in foxholes, on ships at sea, in bombers and fight-ers battling in the skies, in filthy, wretched prisons, and those entombed forever in sunken ships. And there were the heros at home, still rendering up their sons and husbands and fathers to a cause that was begging for an ending. They did it, and they smiled, for your sake and mine.

Dad had written to many old friends, some who had emigrated to America near the time that he had, and others who remained in Great Britain, telling them of David's death. Their replies, letters of sympathy, were very moving and they strove to offer to the family visions of the nobility of his sacrifice.

In his letter to Dad, Reverend John Green, Pastor *Emeritus* of the Congregational Church of Rockaway Beach, New York, wrote in part:

Dear Friend Alex,   May 28, 1945

The heart rending news of your son David's death for a few days com-pletely upset me. Now that I have a firmer grip on my feelings I can trust myself to write to you, to his mother and to each member of your family.

Truly Dell and I mingle our tears with those of his parents and his broth-ers and sisters, but at the same time we are not forgetful to be proud of David and to rejoice in him.

No possible ending of his earthly life could have been more glorious, more rewarding for all his parents and teachers have done for him, than this. He went forth an American boy, your boy, to fight for and maintain the Four Freedoms. It is our right to be proud of him.

Alex and Margaret, you have not lost your son David. God gives him back to you in the sainted spirit of one who held not even life a prize more sacred than a hero's crown.

Both Father and Mother have done one of the noblest services a citizen can render to the country in giving of your own to the cause of Liberty. To set men free in every nation — to give equal rights to life and happiness — to create a world brotherhood — these are the holy purposes for which your soldier boy — David — fought and died. Never did men engage in a holier cause. The very principal transfigures the soul of every soldier. Harry Lauder, that singer of Scotch songs, added one of his own compositions as he faced what you dear parents are going through today:

> "The days are long, the nights are drear,
> The anguish breaks my heart,
> But, Oh, I'm proud my one and only
> Laddie did his part.
> For God knows best; His will be done;
> His grace does me employ;
> I do believe I'll meet again
> My one and only boy."

Alex! Margaret! fail not in remembering:

> "We cannot always trace the way,
> Where Thou Almighty One dost move!
> But we can always, always say
> 'God is Love.'
> "There are no errors
> In the Eternal plan.
> All things work together
> For the final good of man!"

Dell joins me in sending our love to each of you and to the children whom we have seen and those we were not privileged to see when you visited us two years past.

Lovingly yours,
Dell and John

And then came the sentiments of W. E. Hambley, now a resident of North Wales. He wrote in part:

My dear Alec,

I have just read your letter and am deeply grieved to read that your dear boy has paid the "great sacrifice" with his life. Oh, the broken homes and hearts that this dreadful war has caused! Husbands, Fathers, Sons and Sisters, all have given their precious lives in the battle for freedom, truth and righteousness, and they might have lost their lives in a less nobler and heroic way. It is a noble and praiseworthy death to die.

Many families have lost up to five of their precious sons in the huge havoc! We all realize their loss, which is heartbreaking, and yet the way in which they are bearing their sorrow and gulping down their grief, no words can describe such heroism. They gave their dear ones willingly and loyally. If they returned safe and sound, well and good, and God be praised, but when they failed to return, and the sad news came to them, their quiet submissiveness and resignation, no words can possibly describe. It is in poignant experiences of this kind that one's weakness or strength come to the surface.

One woman I heard of who had lost one of her sons in the R.A.F. was expressing to a friend how terribly upset she was, when her friend in no unsympathetic words asked her, "And did you really expect him back safe and sound after all he had to face and go through?". . . She had not thought of it in that way. As I said, dear Alec, in my previous letter, The R.A.F. is the most hazardous and perilous of all the services and the wonder is that any of them ever come back, and yet they do!! Most of these young fellows and many of them still in their teens — How they can face shot and shell and "Keep their head" up there is beyond our understanding.

> "O may those Saints who from their labors rest,
> Fight as the Saints, who nobly fought of old,
> and win with them, the victor's crown of gold."

Now goodbye dear Alec. My love and sincerest sympathy to you and your sweet wife, and to all your dear ones. . . .

Your old friend.

W. E. Hambley

It became obvious to me that the folks on the home front were coping very well with David's loss and that they had resumed their daily lives in good order. As Mother had said, "Life goes on and we have each other to care for." They also had a host of loving friends who keep them fortified in their daily realm. And they were not the only parents to lose a son. As Mother noted, it was maybe too much to expect that with three of us in service we would all emerge unscathed.

Our time for departure for Enid was at hand. With a round of final dinners and parties tucked into our memories, we headed out for the 800-mile drive to north-central Oklahoma. Our route was mapped by way of St. Louis, Springfield, Joplin, Tulsa, and the final lap to Enid. And with the exception of an annoying problem with the ignition system and an early stop in Joplin to locate and fix a loose copper shim in the distributor that now and again shorted out the power supply — and a wrong highway direction provided by my lady navigator that cost us about 20 non-productive miles — our trip was uneventful.

Chapter 23

Enid, Oklahoma — Chicago

C RUISING INTO ENID IN THE afternoon of June 8th, 1945, we quickly located the apartment of our pre-war friends, Larry and Lorraine McBrearty. When they heard that we were coming to Enid, they wrote immediately that we must plan on staying with them until we located our own housing. It had been 3½ years since we had seen them. They had been married some time during the first year of Larry's Army service and now had their first child, beautiful little Diane. Larry had been stationed at Enid for over two years and held the rank of Technical Sergeant, working in the personnel office. He felt secure in this long-term assignment, and there was no indication that he would see any overseas duty. The war in Europe had ended, and the progress in the Pacific seemed to be well enough along that there would be no need for him there. Length of service and family status were known to preclude foreign assignments.

Our first evening together was as festive as wartime restrictions would allow. Lorraine was a beautiful, gracious hostess, and she and Ruth combined their culinary skills to produce a fine chicken dinner. Wartime poultry came in the whole, undressed form and required the removal of all the innards before cutting into fryable portions. How they took turns plunging their hands into the dark recesses of the bird while closing their eyes to the sight of the slick, resistant emerging entrails is a description best left unsaid. It also should be noted that the shape of some of the final edible parts were difficult to identify. But the girls were proud, and Larry and I were too smart and too well fed to offer any disparaging observations.

Conversation focused on the type of duty that I might pursue at Enid. I asked Larry if there was some "cushy" kind of job that I might go after, such as Safety Officer or Test Pilot of B-25s after engine overhauls or engine changes. He couldn't speculate, but suggested I see him in his office after I had checked in at Headquarters in the morning, and he would help me review my service record.

I signed in at Base Headquarters of Enid Army Air Field at 9:00 a.m. and was assigned to Squadron B, 2518th AAF Base Unit. I then found Larry's office and laid out before him my entire 201 file and flying record. Points were allocated to many phases of service and included months of domestic and foreign assignments, attainment of rank, and, best of all, the five points for each of the six combat campaigns in which I had participated and the eight Air Medals and the one Distinguished Flying Cross I had been awarded. Listed on a form, they totaled 128 points.

"Stew, you have enough points to get out of the Army. They're letting out guys with less points than you have."

The war in Europe was over and the Military had all the men already under arms in my category that would be needed to finish the Pacific War. Most of the air action was at that time against the Japanese homeland, and that was being handled with B-29 Super Fortresses. The heavy bomber pilots with short tours of duty returning from Europe would fill any gaps they might have. Plenty of fighter pilots also would be coming back.

If I was interested in getting out, Larry would be able to set it up for me right there and then.

I called Ruth and told her what Larry had said, and asked her how she felt about it. She urged me to go ahead. Larry immediately called Sergeant Jimmy O'Donnell at Headquarters and gave him all the information needed to set the wheels in motion. I was to report to Jimmy the next morning to sign some papers.

When I met with Jimmy, he pointed to a blackboard on his office wall listing the names of several officers and enlisted men. My name was #1 to be released from active duty. Jimmy said it would take three or four weeks for my orders to come through and that I would not be required to perform any duties in the interim.

To get in my four hours per month of flying time to qualify for flight pay, I flew co-pilot for Bus Taylor — an old friend from Corsica with whom I had flown several missions — on a trip to Big Spring, Texas, for a weekend reunion with some other returnees from Corsica. That trip took care of four of my needed eight hours. I had not manned the controls of a B-25 during the six months since leaving Corsica and was anxious to have one more flight before my return to civilian life. I relieved Bus at the controls a few times on the way to Big Spring, and he let me do the takeoff from Big Spring on Sunday and the landing at Enid, both from the copilot's seat.

"Damn, Alex, you did that better than most guys did from the left seat. Why weren't you a flight leader?"

"Didn't want to show you guys up, Bus."

In addition, my six month's rest hadn't hurt a bit!

The squadron Commander had arranged for me to fly in the back seat of an AT-6 North American 600 hp single-engine Advanced trainer. I had flown it for gunnery training in Advanced Flight School at Yuma, Arizona, two years previous. After a one-hour period where I never touched the controls, I went for a sight-seeing ride while the pilot practiced various maneuvers. The next day I talked him into checking me out again in the AT-6, to which he agreed.

After one hour of dual instruction and one hour of dual transition, he okayed me for solo. The next day, I checked out the same plane and flew my final two required hours and made a total of seven landings. I signed the Form One individual plane log, recording my solo flight-time and that I observed no mechanical or visible defects in the aircraft. I had completed the eight hours needed to secure the flying pay for the two months that would accrue from the time I had been returned to flying status at Fort Wright until I was released from the Army. The flight-time requirement during my stay at the hospital was automatically waived due to my status as a patient, so my pay was not penalized. As a married First Lieutenant with flight pay, longevity pay, and other allowances, I was receiving close to $400 per month. I doubted that I would do as well as a civilian.

I took one last look at the flight line and suddenly realized that I might never pilot a plane again. I felt a tug of nostalgia at all the thrills and excitement I had experienced and how I had extended my service from that of a peacetime "buck-private" in a dead-end branch of the service to a skilled and highly qualified pilot in the greatest air force in the world. And it all happened in a little less than four years.

We had been at Enid for about two weeks when Larry and Lorraine received some startling news. Larry had entered the Army in September 1941, a week or two before I did, and had been stationed at two or three camps in the States for all that time. Now he was being assigned to a personnel outfit bound for service on the island of Guam in the South Pacific. He couldn't believe it and neither could we. His shipping notice didn't allow much time, but somehow he was able to close out his apartment and get his wife and daughter headed for Chicago before he boarded transportation for the West Coast.

As it turned out, he got a long boat ride across the Pacific. The war ended, and he had a long return trip. He later referred to it as a six-month cruise.

Ruth and I had stayed with the McBreartys for those three nights before we found and rented a clean four-room cottage at 1915 West Randolph Street. The little cottage, however, did have two drawbacks. Seated at the kitchen table and eating our first evening meal, we noticed tiny black specks appearing in the butter. Looking closely, we decided they were alive. We scraped them off, only to have a new horde appear. After supper, we asked our neighbor what those could possibly be.

"Wheat lice! They come every season with the wheat harvest and they're so small they come right through the screens."

They won't hurt you, but they weren't very appetizing.

In the middle of one of the first nights in our cottage, we were startled instantly wide awake by a freight train blasting its steam whistle. It sounded like it was coming right through our bedroom. We both jumped out of bed as the huge light on the engine glared into our eyes and again blasted its whistle. We ran into the kitchen and looked out to see the engine slowly tugging a long line of gondola-type freight cars laden with newly harvested wheat.

The next day we learned that a rail siding cut across the corner of our back yard during the wheat harvest.

"But what about the whistle blowing at 2:00 a.m.?" I asked. There was nothing but our little side street intersecting the train tracks and no traffic at that hour — why was the whistle blowing?

Ruth and I learned to cope with both problems. We ate our evening meals at the Officers Club and actually got used to the whistle.

My orders for transfer to Fort Sheridan, Illinois, finally came through, and we packed up for the long trip home. We had our last dinner at the Officers Club the evening before our departure, slept our last night under the threat of the relentless railroad whistle, and headed toward my final U.S. Army destination.

Somewhere in Missouri I checked the air pressure in the tires and noticed that the treads on the two rear tires were wearing down quite rapidly and were only a little better than smooth. I decided that the old car had suffered a pretty bad accident at some time in its wartime life and the frame had been bent. The rear wheels had been dog-legging down the road for 4,000 miles, literally grinding down the tread thickness. This was the first signal to me that we should replace the car as soon as possible after reaching Chicago.

We had crossed the great Mississippi River at St. Louis and were almost within shouting distance of the Windy City when I heard strange noises knocking in the engine. Stopped for gas, I listened to the sounds of connecting rod and main bearings playing a drumbeat tune on their journals and decided that with luck we could make it to Mother's house. We covered the last 50 miles at about 35 mph and immediately backed the car into one of Dad's vacant garages. Repairs had to be made before we could even try to dispose of the old girl.

Our family reunion was a joyous occasion and all were amazed that I was being released from active Army duty before the war in the Pacific had ended. I had only to go to Fort Sheridan for the processing procedure, get a final physical examination and review of all military records, and pick up my final pay and release orders. I rode the North Shore electric to and from the Fort and arrived back at Mother's in late afternoon of July 7th, 1945. Eleven days of remaining leave time — terminal leave — was added to my discharge date, making my official date of release July 18th, 1945. After three years, nine months, and twenty-two days, I was once again a civilian.

Mother and Dad had taken the train to Lake Geneva, Wisconsin, for a week of vacation and rest. Jean was home, recovering from an illness, and Margaret was on the summer vacation from her teaching position at Yale Elementary School. Ruth and I were invited by Mother to stay with them until we were situated in our regained civilian mode. And, of course, the first item on my agenda was to restore the car to salable condition.

The first morning home I removed the large oil pan located under the crankcase and found the accumulation of handfuls of babbitt, the soft, metal alloy that coated the surfaces of both the connecting rod and main bearings. The re-babbitted bearings that I had purchased in Spokane proved to be a poor substitute for original factory-made parts and had failed to withstand the forces of engine operation. The impacted surfaces looked like worms had been eating away and creating tiny road maps. I was fortunate in locating factory-made replacement bearing inserts at Warshawski's, an old-time parts house on South State Street, for $12.50. I had the car in running order the next day.

The following afternoon, I drove to "automobile row" at 72nd Street and Stony Island Avenue and offered the car for sale to the first dealer I encountered. I accepted his cash offer of $250, the same amount I had paid for it. I was glad to be rid of it, though it had served us well and I had made money with it from the Army travel allowances it had generated. It also had provided me with much-needed occupational therapy at Spokane, as well as exercising my mechanical knowledge and skills.

Adjusting to civilian life with the country still at war in the Pacific presented me with problems I had not fully anticipated. By law, my former employer was required to reinstate me in my old job or one of equal rank, but I had no interest in dispatching servicemen to repair defective refrigerators. Two young women now did the job, much reduced in volume, that had been handled pre-war by six men and were each paid $175 monthly. However, opportunities for returning military pilots in flying jobs were nonexistent and would remain so until some time after the end of the conflict. And airline travel was still generally restricted to civilians engaged in war industries, to military priorities, and to governmental and emergency needs.

Ruth's brother Bud by virtue of his ownership of two Standard Oil Company service stations, had strong connections with the company executives and secured an interview opportunity for me with their general sales manager. There were no openings in Chicago, but I was offered a job as reseller salesman in their Milwaukee, Wisconsin, branch. Ruth and I decided that I should accept the position, as it was the only promising opportunity at hand. And Milwaukee was still close enough to Chicago for us to make frequent visits to see our families. A company-owned car was included, solving our transportation needs. We realized I needed to start somewhere, and this would fill that need. My starting date with Standard was set for July 15th, 1945.

The war raged on in the Pacific, and Ray's safety and welfare continued to be of real concern. He had been in the invasion of Okinawa and now was mired in the battle of the Philippines. His status as a medical technician in a company aid station, directing the first-aid efforts of about ten men was hazardous duty, and his unit was being subjected to enemy shelling and air attacks.

Mother had left her job as a clerk in the War Bond office after the death of David in order that she might be with Dad and tend to his needs. Margaret continued with her teaching at Yale Elementary school, although she was presently off for summer vacation. Jean's work at Scott-Foresman textbook publishers had been her mainstay for many years and she was destined to carry on there for many more.

Brother Cameron, now 35, and Rita still lived at 85th Street and Constance Avenue with their two children, Sharron and Susan. Cam had purchased a delicatessen-type store at

85th and Stony Island Avenue in early 1944 and had prospered due to his buying connections with certain hard-to-get foods, cigarettes, and especially soap flakes for clothes washing. These were all attractive items for the many customers who stood three deep at the counter waiting to make their purchases. Although Cam had been required to register for the Service early in the war, his family status no doubt had ruled against him as a likely prospect for the military, which probably was a good thing as Cam possessed a rather rebellious nature and usually would not take orders from anyone. But he was physically tough, and a very hard worker with an ingratiating personality. He was smart, creative, resourceful, and talented.

In the time preceding our departure for Milwaukee, I had to convert my wardrobe to civilian garb. I purchased the basics at Bud's favorite clothier, Raymond Levine, at the southern suburb of Roseland. Ruth worked over her things and added some odds and ends, all of which we packed in two footlockers and two suitcases. Some wedding presents that had been stored awaited our return and now caused problems with the closing of luggage lids.

With Cameron helping with bag and baggage and delivering us to the depot, we boarded the Chicago North Shore and Milwaukee railroad for the 100-mile trip to what was commonly referred to as "beer town." Arriving in early afternoon, a taxi delivered us and our worldly possessions to the Schroeder Hotel where we claimed our reservation and hopefully a stay not to exceed three days.

The shortage of affordable housing due to demands of the long wartime needs, especially in industrial centers like Milwaukee and cities and towns close to military establishments, loomed as our primary problem. The daily newspapers were devoid of any advertisements that could satisfy our needs or our budget. We soon learned that inside knowledge of a suitable vacancy would be our housing salvation.

We had learned before leaving Chicago that pre-war friends Eileen and Les Diveley of Fort Wayne, Indiana, were being transferred by Les's employer, Cutler-Hammer Company, to the plant in Milwaukee where Les was to serve as a chemical engineer in the finishing department. The Diveley's arrival coincided with ours, and they, too, were staying at the Schroeder Hotel. Cutler-Hammer had provided them with two housing opportunities — a 1½-room furnished efficiency apartment in the Underwood Hotel at 7416 Harwood Avenue in the western suburb of Wauwatosa, or a five-room first-floor unfurnished apartment in a duplex on the north side. The latter suited their needs, and they expected their furniture to arrive in a few days from Fort Wayne. They arranged for us to rent the small high-rise apartment, although the $75 monthly rental was really more than we could afford. After two nights in the Schroeder, we moved to Wauwatosa and settled in our adequate but sparse apartment, determined to stay only until we could find something less expensive.

The *Milwaukee Journal*, the leading newspaper of the city, sold early editions of he Sunday paper on Saturday night, and we found the sales room swamped with desperate home hunters snapping up the "for rent" sections. On our second Saturday night visit to the *Journal*, we found an ad for a two-room furnished apartment at 38th and Clark Street with the instruction to apply at the Dipsy Doodle Ice Cream Parlor after 10:00 a.m. on Sunday. It was the only promising ad from a total listing of 14 rental units.

Ruth and I decided to drive out to the Dipsy Doodle immediately and not wait for Sunday. "The least we can do is have some ice cream," I suggested, "and maybe we can get a preview of the apartment and circumvent the Sunday requirement."

We entered the Dipsy Doodle, sat at the counter, and were served by the middle-aged owner. There was no one else was in the store. As we ate, I talked to him about his ad in the *Journal*. I explained that I was just released from the Army after almost four years of service, was now working for Standard Oil, that we were living in an apartment that we could not afford, and that we needed to make a change.

He explained that the apartment was actually a ground-floor enclosed back porch behind the ice cream parlor and had a rather long narrow living room, furnished with a fold-out studio couch that made up as a double bed, a sofa, an upholstered chair, floor lamp, and a small square dining table and two kitchen chairs. At one end was a tiny bathroom with a shower-equipped tub and a tiny kitchen with a small sink, gas stove, a few cabinets, and an old fashioned ice box. Included with the rental of $37.50 per month was a one-car garage. The entrance to the apartment was through the back yard off 38th Street next to the garage. The entire apartment measured about 10 feet by 24 feet. When the studio couch was opened out for sleeping, there was less than one foot of walking clearance between it and the sofa. We later observed that we had a wall-to-wall bed.

Ruth and I had finished our ice cream and I told the owner that we were definitely interested and that we would return in the morning to see it. But I noticed that he had looked us over quite carefully and had asked some rather probing questions. I had a feeling that he might be ready to make a deal with us right then and not wait for Sunday, and I was right.

He locked the store, turned down the lights, and led us through the back room to the entrance to the apartment. It wasn't fancy — the furniture was rather old but very clean and well cared for, the appointments and decorations simple but in good taste. All we had to furnish was our linens and cooking and eating utensils.

I huddled with Ruth and together we decided to take it. At $37.50 per month, our rental outlay would be half that of the Underwood. I also reminded Ruth that Standard Oil would reimburse me $5 per month for company-car garage rental, which made the deal that much sweeter. We shook hands with the owner and I wrote him a check for the first month's rent.

We gave notice to the Underwood the following Monday and moved a few days later. We had not lived out the full month's rental there and were unable to get any refund for the unused time, though we tried. Housing was so critical that we felt fortunate in being able to get the Dipsy Doodle apartment. Rentals had been frozen by government edict at the beginning of the war, and there would be no relief for landlords until war's end. It was a serious offense for landlords to charge above the frozen pre-war rates, as well as for renters to pay cash excesses "under the table" in order to get the place.

On August 6th, a few days after moving into the Dipsy Doodle back-porch appendage — the official address being 3827 West Clark Street — word flashed around the world that the first atomic bomb had been dropped on Hiroshima, Japan. Milwaukee and the rest of the nation was electrified by the news, and we all expected an immediate surrender. But the Japanese resistance persisted, and a second atomic bomb was dropped on Nagasaki on August 9th. The next day Japan opened peace negotiations and, finally, on August 15th, accepted the terms of the Potsdam Declaration, which detailed the stringent conditions of surrender. The official peace treaty was signed aboard the battleship USS *Missouri* on September 2nd, 1945.

There were joyous celebrations by citizens in every city, town, and hamlet across the country and by American troops in far-flung lands around the world. At long last, the shooting war was over and the struggle for occupation of Japan would begin, just as it had in Germany a few months previous. Prior to the dropping of the atomic bombs, American forces were being amassed for the invasion of the Japanese mainland, with the prediction of more than one million casualties. We were all relieved that the war ended before such spilling of blood.

On September 8th, 1945, Ray wrote to the folks from his location on Mindora Island in the Philippines:

> Every available plane and ship is being used to transport men and supplies to the occupation forces on Japan. I don't know if our 96th Division will do any occupation service. General MacArthur says he will use eighteen divisions for the occupation of Japan and Korea plus special units from the Army, Navy and Air Force. They are bringing three divisions from the States which have seen little or no combat. There are also divisions over here that have seen very little combat. They might get their required number without using the 96th and others that have seen much action. It is said that Japan will be entirely disarmed by October 10th. The First Cavalry Division is in Tokyo now as are several others. If we had not moved off Okinawa before the war ended, I bet we would be on Japan now.
>
> There is no way of knowing when I will be coming home. It could be as long as six months, a long time to sit around doing nothing. As I see it, the troop requirements for the occupation come first. I heard they are using aircraft carriers to transport troops to Japan and will probably use them for fellows homeward bound. Although they are slower moving, I would prefer coming home on an LST as they have, by far, the best food. As usual, Mom, I still place good food as my number one priority.

Our personal celebration was rather subdued as we reflected on the intensity and tragedy of the many conflicts that finally led to victory. Thoughts of David, now buried in the Fourth Marine Division Cemetery on Iwo Jima, clouded my vision and I struggled to focus on something besides the infamy of the Japanese. We were happy for Ray and for the hundreds of thousands of men who were deployed around the world and for their families who must all certainly be chorusing a huge sigh of relief.

When we reviewed the carnage that had been forced on the world by these mass-murdering despots, we felt a certain hollowness to the victory. Like vermin, their defeat commanded a huge price, paid with the sacrifice by peace-loving people of life and limb and their hard-earned resources. And little did the average person realize the extent of the costs, financial, and emotional or the nature of our commitment and our role in the rebuilding process of the conquered nations.

My work as a reseller salesman with Standard Oil progressed quite well, though efforts were compromised by the continuing shortage of vital products. Gasoline rationing had ceased and most petroleum products were in ample supply. But we felt the pinch in the rationing of tires, batteries, and certain accessories. My territory included about 20 retail service stations, plus a few garages and car agencies. An allocation of 80 to 100 tires was spread extremely thin, and the larger volume dealers let it be known that they expected more than a token share. Standard could not possibly supply all their needs, which forced the dealers to buy all kinds of competitive brands and other competitive products, thus creating habits that we found hard to break. But with the decrease in war demands in the coming months, the shortage situation eased and it wasn't long before we salesmen were twisting dealer arms to place larger orders.

Ruth and I liked Milwaukee and made many friends in the neighborhood and at the Washington Park Presbyterian Church, where we became members soon after our arrival. We were especially fond of the minister, Dr. Thomas Lyter, who was quick to form a young couples' group called The Mariners, which was attractive to many returning servicemen and their brides. The rationing of fresh meat still prevailed, and some of the covered-dish suppers were often unbalanced — one memorable meal included seven bowls of escalloped potatoes, one jello mold, and one small meat loaf! Our activity usually included a special Bible study and work on some sort of mission project.

From the time the war ended in the Pacific in August 1945 until October, Ray was assigned to limited duty working in the dispensary of Company C of the 321st Medical Battalion on Mindora Island in the Philippines. The Army was using most of the available men, supplies, and shipping for the occupation of Japan while those scheduled to go home were biding their time until shipping became available. The 96th Division had had a long and hard combat service and was not going to be used in the Occupation.

On December 7th, 1945, Ray boarded a Liberty ship bound for Leyte Island and his assignment to the 28th Replacement Depot. He wrote letters home every day or two, keeping the folks posted as to when he would be heading for the U.S. Duty consisted of about 30 minutes of daily physical workout and drill. Many of the men were assigned to KP duty, but Ray was fortunate in not having to serve. He said he had not had KP for 2½ years, and he didn't care to finish his Army service in the kitchen.

Shipping day finally arrived on December 18th when he boarded the USS *Barnstable* for an 18-day trip to San Francisco and the thrill of passing under the Golden Gate Bridge. He had chosen Camp Stoneman at Los Angeles for his point of separation from the service and rode with several hundred other men on a ferry boat to LA. Assigned to a barracks for a couple days of processing and physical examinations, he was finally declared a civilian and was set free of the Army on January 13th, 1946, after 39 months of service.

He phoned Mother and Dad from San Francisco and gave them his schedule. That one long train trip to Chicago was his last hurdle before being reunited with the family.

In December 1945, Ruth became pregnant and we were delighted. We wanted and had planned for the first addition to our family, and her condition was confirmed by Dr. Olson, father of the movie actress Nancy Olson. He estimated the birth would occur in late August 1946.

This did present a problem that we hadn't adequately anticipated. The back-porch apartment of the Dipsy Doodle was not the most desirable place for a baby to start life, but we decided that somehow we would work things out if nothing else became available. Ruth was also concerned that the limited refrigeration of the old icebox was not suitable for storage of the baby's formula. In the latter stage of her pregnancy, Ruth made friends with many of the neighbors, as she took to walking for needed exercise. She rang many doorbells, explained our need for larger quarters, and asked if they knew of any forthcoming vacancies. She was persistent in her quest and did not get discouraged.

One day she talked to a Mrs. Schmidt on 39th Street who told her of a duplex building that she and her husband owned on 36th; the elderly lady occupant was hospitalized with a very serious illness and was not expected to live. "If she dies, you folks can have her second floor apartment."

That presented us with somewhat of a dilemma. We wanted the apartment, but we certainly couldn't hope the lady would die. Of course, we realized we had no control over the situation and that we would just let it take care of itself. In the meantime, I contacted my pre-war employer in Chicago, R. Cooper, Jr. Inc., the General Electric Distributor for home appliances. Bernice Greenwald told me that they had just received their first shipment of post-war refrigerators and that she would be glad to hold one for me for later shipment when we firmed up on a new address. It would be a six-cubic-foot unit for about $100 plus Railway Express freight charges.

About two weeks later, Mrs. Schmidt called to report that we could have the apartment. Then the daughter of the deceased called to say that she wanted to keep several items of her mother's furniture but that she would sell to us any of the remaining items we might want. We selected all the rugs, an old fashioned oak dining room set, a rocker, a small desk, a kitchen table and two chairs, a gas stove, and a few other odds and ends, all for $66.

We soon arranged to move from the Dipsy Doodle. I called Bernice and had the refrigerator shipped to arrive the day we moved into 1957 North 36th Street. We bought a new sofa and matching easy chair, a mahogany kneehole desk and chair, and a handsome lamp for the desk. Ruth's mother gave us an old but nice double bed and matching dresser stored in her basement locker, which I dragged in a borrowed trailer from Chicago. We were finally set up and ready for the baby's arrival.

Our daughter was born at Milwaukee Maternity Hospital on August 27th, tipping the scales at 8 pounds, 14½ ounces. And we named her Nancy Claire Stewart. We decided that she was the "toast of Milwaukee" and the most beautiful production of the post-war baby boom.

The new apartment was comfortable and served our needs. The rental rate was still frozen by the government at $47.50 per month, including garage and for which I was reimbursed $5 per month by Standard Oil. But there was one drawback: the apartment had its own coal-fired heating system, for which I had to purchase coal and keep the fire going during the cold winter months. I soon perfected a chain-operated damper control system that Ruth could operate from a thermostat to provide warmth while I was at work, though I managed to route myself home for lunch most of the time to stoke the furnace. I banked the fire at night, and we always awoke to a warm house on cold mornings.

Milwaukee was a clean city, and most of its inhabitants kept very clean households. I swept or vacuumed the front and back stairways every Saturday, and twice each year I vacuumed, then wet-mopped, our half of the large floored attic where we stored out-of-season clothing and luggage.

When Nancy was nine months old, Ruth's brother Bud and "Big Ruth" came to Milwaukee in mid-week to serve as her God-Parents and witness her baptism by Dr. Lyter. The brief ceremony was held in our living room on May 22nd, 1947, after which Ruth served a fine roast-beef dinner.

But the good times on 36th Street were not to last. We endured the ice and severe snow of the 1947-1948 winter and were enjoying the spring of '48 when we received an eviction notice. The Schmidts had sold their duplex on North 39th Street and now needed our apartment for themselves. Housing was still suffering from wartime shortages. We were very disappointed but had no recourse.

I composed an ad for insertion in the classified section of the Milwaukee Journal:

> War Veteran — Standard Oil Sales Rep, wife and child desperately need
> two bedroom apartment or flat. Willing to tend furnace and care for lawns
> and snow. Please phone 2-1234.

The one and only response came from Ruth Awe, who lived with her aged, widowed father at 1306 South 46th Street. In spite of his advanced years, Mr. Awe still did manual work in a scrap-iron yard. His daughter hoped to get him some relief from the household chores and was thus attracted to my ad.

We vacated 36th Street on schedule and moved to the south side. I believe we were actually in West Allis, Wisconsin, and no longer in Milwaukee. I do remember that it was south of National Avenue.

Mr. Awe was a rather cantankerous individual, and I soon learned that he wasn't too happy with me tending the coal stoker in the furnace. When it snowed, he always had the walks and steps cleared before I got home from work. Then he would gripe and complain that I wasn't holding up my end of the bargain. I did my best, and his daughter laughed sympathetically and agreed that "he didn't like some young upstart veteran fooling around the place." This had been his territory for 40 years, and he meant to keep it.

Sometime in mid-1946, about 1½ years after brother David had been killed on Iwo Jima, his young widow Beverly remarried and moved to the San Francisco area. She had apparently relinquished all responsibility for David's remains, or perhaps this was an automatic procedure when the widow of a war casualty remarried. Whatever the circumstances, Mother had notified the government, requesting the return of David's remains from the Fourth Marine Cemetery on Iwo Jima for reburial in Chicago. Many months or even a few years were to pass before this would take place.

On November 26th, 1948, Dad and Mother received a 1½ page Western Union telegram from the government advising that the remains of the late PHM3C David B. Stewart were en route to the United States and would be available

> for transport to Thos. E. Corcoran Funeral Dir., 1411 East 67th Street, Chicago Ill. (F/B: Beverly, Illinois) as soon as practicable after arrival at San Francisco.

About six weeks later, another telegram informed them of the arrival of the remains on the West Coast and that the funeral director had been directed to secure them upon their arrival by train in Chicago. A military escort would accompany the casket to its final resting place, designated by Mother and Dad as Mount Hope Cemetery in the Beverly Hills region on Chicago's far southwest side.

A memorial service was to be conducted by Dr. Harold Bowman, pastor of the First Presbyterian Church, and the funeral director was to notify the obituary sections of the Chicago newspapers. The *Chicago Tribune* identified the obituary of each serviceman with the imprint of an American flag, which was helpful in spotting those particular announcements. David's funeral service was announced and set for January 18th, 1949, almost four years after his death on that treacherous volcanic island.

Though we had all made our adjustments to civilian life and the sting of war and our psychological wounds and grievous loss were coated with a veneer of acceptance, there was a vacancy in our lives. I once asked Mother if she might do better by having David's remains stay in the Fourth Marine Division Cemetery on Iwo Jima. Many friends feared that his return would just reopen all the wounds that were healing and would be an emotional burden that she did not have to bear.

But Mother had long since pondered and then resolved these thoughts in her personal and quiet reflections, telling us she had known ever since David died that his "great spirit" had left his earthly body and entered God's eternal home. But now, she stated, maybe like a "mother hen," she wanted all other family nestled under her wing. The United States and Illinois, she insisted, was David's birthplace, and the great country for which he fought, and its people for which he gave his life, and it should be in its soil that he be interred. Only then, Mother stated, would she know that for her the war was finally over and the final curtain had been drawn on this dark scene in our lives.

I was amazed at her eloquence and her resolve. At age 65, and having endured all of the difficulties and hardships of birthing and raising a large family while worrying over, encouraging, and championing all of their enterprises, their whims, dangers, hardships, and failures — and being that unwavering source of love and inspiration to a loving and loyal mate — even now her total life's commitment to her family and her patriotism to her country proved faultless.

Many friends and even some strangers gathered for the memorial service in the funeral chapel. It was the time of celebration for the life of my brother, given so nobly in the pursuit of saving the lives of his fellow Marines. Standing with the family at the flag-draped casket, I was approached by a young man of David's age, casually dressed and leaning on a cane.

"Are you a brother of the deceased," he asked with quivering voice, tears in his eyes.

"Yes, David was three years younger," I answered.

He looked at David's photograph and said, "He saved my life, just a few seconds before he was killed."

I could hardly believe what I was hearing. Here was the last person to see my brother alive, a man who carried the scars that would daily for the rest of his life, remind him of David's lifesaving repairs and his total, unflinching devotion to the duty he vowed to uphold. And then, in the blink of an eye, David was committed to eternity.

David had written that "there is no discrimination in mass warfare," and with all of his talents, destined for greatness as a prodigious musician, as a brilliant student of medicine, as an inspiring leader, orator, and visionary of his young peers, his reconstituted destiny was now capsulized in stanching the flow of life from the shattered leg of a helpless Marine in a shallow depression of volcanic sand on a seemingly worthless Pacific island.

With the press of visitors offering sympathy and condolences, I lost track of David's limping beneficiary. And when I looked later, wanting to talk more with him, he was gone. I searched the visitor's book for his name, but he had not signed it, and in the following days, I would have forgotten it. He had paid his respects, voiced his love, shed tears of gratitude, then vanished.

The comforting memorial service ended and many mourners lined up in their cars for the procession to Mount Hope. The family rode in the funeral cars behind the hearse, the flag over the casket visible to casual citizens standing along the curbs, many men poised with hats in hand, even in the January chill. The war had ended almost 3½ years before, but the people still remembered and honored those many men who had made the supreme sacrifice, now being returned for homeland burial.

Dad and Mother, Jean, Margaret, Cameron and Rita, Ray, Ruth and myself in our cars were all tearless but solemn, deep in our private thoughts. We had long-since cried, though sometimes, caught up in a moment of remembrance, wetness lurked again. We had known the ravages of war on each of our lives. I sometimes wondered how life would have been had there not been a war. Now, David's return seemed to be the final chapter in this strangest of books.

Dad had said to me at home before the funeral service that it was hard to believe David was back in Woodlawn. He must have been visualizing for the moment that handsome, vibrant, loving son striding up the front walk and engulfing him in his strong embrace. In all his grief, Dad's love for family, for God, and for country had never faltered; his patriotism never wavered. He rode in the procession in what appeared to be calm, silent disbelief.

For the time being, Mother's attention was on all of us and spoke of our current special needs and concerns. Her voice was calm and sweet, embroidered with an animated lilt as she spoke in what Dad had often referred to as her "heavenly tones." Encouragement, confidence, and hope were the standard ingredients in her life's recipe, and she was now providing generous portions.

The procession entered the main gate of Mount Hope, then bore to the left on the main drive and stopped near the gravesite. I instructed Mother and the others to remain in the warm car while Ray, Cameron, and I assisted others as pallbearers. We placed the casket on the lowering belts, and then I returned to the car and assisted Mother in walking on the winter-hardened turf to her place beside the grave. Dad stood with us as family and friends gathered around, speaking to one another with whispered voices, our breaths visible in the crisp air. The young Army Corporal escort took his place at the foot of the casket.

Mother watched and carefully listened to Dr. Bowman as he voiced the brief service, committing David to his final resting place. As he added "Amen" to the closing prayer, Mother looked up, then placed her hand on his and thanked him for his kind services. She then turned her attention to the military escort, the Army Corporal who had accompanied the casket from its shipping point in San Francisco to Chicago.

The soldier removed the American flag from the casket and folded it in the triangular-shaped prescribed manner. With the flag tucked in the crook of his left arm, he stepped around and faced Mother. In rigid stance, he rendered a crisp salute as he recited the touching words of gratitude from the United States government:

> Mrs. Stewart, this flag is presented to you on behalf of our grateful nation as a token of its appreciation for the honorable and faithful service rendered by your beloved son, David Barton Stewart.

With these final words, he presented the flag to Mother.

All the family and other mourners stood silently, some apprehensively. I wondered how Mother would react. Would this be the moment when all of the pent-up grief and emotion that she might have suppressed during the intervening years crash in one final convulsive release?

Her indomitable spirit was in control. Her love was never confined to just family and friends, but reached out to encircle everyone with whom she came in contact. And now, facing this young stranger, the once feisty little girl, birthed in a poverty-ridden shack in the Missouri River bottoms of Kansas City, stood before the casket of her young heroic son and, at least for me, donned the exquisite mantel of the true hero, the motherhood source of all heroes.

Accepting the flag, she clasped it to her breast while still holding the soldier's hand. She raised her sparkling eyes from the flag to the youthful sincerity lighting his countenance. She smiled, as she had always smiled for her own children, sweetly and honestly. Her voice was gentle and clear, her words gracious and tender:

"Thank you young man. You must be very tired from your long journey."

Index

by Lori L. Daniel

Nona Hengen, of Spangle, Washington, is an illustrator of books, magazine articles, and greeting card art. She holds a Master's degree in History and a Ph.D. in Education, but painting and writing have been her lifelong avocations. An award-winning artist, her work has been marketed widely throughout the U.S. and Canada. Her cover design, "An Historic Vote," appeared on the 1998 State of Washington voter's pamphlet, depicting Sacajawea, Meriwether Lewis, and York, William Clark's black slave, casting ballots 100 years before Indians and women voted and 60 years before slaves were freed and could vote.

Hengen was an elementary school teacher before becoming a lecturer in Education at Indiana University, Bloomington. In 1962, she was a Fulbright Scholar in Germany. In 1980, she resigned from her position as Associate Professor of Education at Indiana University to pursue her painting career.

Hengen is also the author of 13 books, including *Gateway to the Palouse*, in its 5th edition, as well as numerous magazine articles.